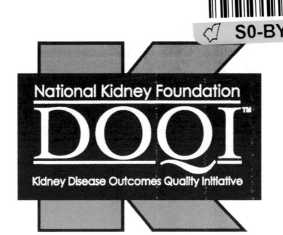

Clinical Practice Guidelines For Chronic Kidney Disease: Evaluation, Classification and Stratification

K/DOQI™ Disclaimer

These guidelines are based upon the best information available at the time of publication. They are designed to provide information and assist decision making. They are not intended to define a standard of care, and should not be construed as doing so. Neither should they be interpreted as prescribing an exclusive course of management.

Variations in practice will inevitably and appropriately occur when clinicians take into account the needs of individual patients, available resources, and limitations unique to an institution or type of practice. Every healthcare professional making use of these guidelines is responsible for evaluating the appropriateness of applying them in the setting of any particular clinical situation.

The recommendations for research contained within this document are general and not meant to imply a specific protocol.

GENERAL ACKNOWLEDGEMENTS

The NKF gratefully acknowledges the support of Amgen, Inc., Founding and Principal Sponsor of K/DOQI.

We also thank Bayer Diagnostics and Ortho Biotech Products, L.P., K/DOQI Implementation Partners.

NKF-DOQI and K/DOQI are trademarks of the National Kidney Foundation, Inc.

In citing this document, please refer to the original source as follows:

National Kidney Foundation. *K/DOQI Clinical Practice Guidelines for Chronic Kidney Disease: Evaluation, Classification and Stratification.* Am J Kidney Dis 39:S1-S266, 2002 (suppl 1)

These Guidelines, as well as all other K/DOQI guidelines, can be accessed on the Internet at: *www.kdoqi.org*

National Kidney Foundation, Inc.
30 E. 33rd Street
New York, NY 10016
212-889-2210

Chronic Kidney Disease

Work Group and Evidence Review Team Membership

Andrew S. Levey, MD, *Chair*
New England Medical Center
Boston, MA

Josef Coresh, MD, PhD, *Vice Chair*
Johns Hopkins Medical Institutions
Baltimore, MD

Adult Work Group Members

Kline Bolton, MD, FACP
University of Virginia Hospital
Charlotesville, VA

Bruce Culleton, MD
Foothills Hospital, University of
Calgary
Calgary, Alberta
Canada

Kathy Schiro Harvey, MS, RD, CSR
Puget Sound Kidney Center
Mountlake Terrace, WA

T. Alp Ikizler, MD
Vanderbilt University Medical Center
Nashville, TN

Cynda Ann Johnson, MD, MBA
University of Iowa
Iowa City, IA

Annamaria Kausz, MD, MS
New England Medical Center
Boston, MA

Paul L. Kimmel, MD
National Institutes of Diabetes and
Digestive and Kidney Diseases
Bethesda, MD

John Kusek, PhD
National Institutes of Diabetes and
Digestive and Kidney Diseases
Bethesda, MD

Adeera Levin, MD, FRCP
St. Paul's Hospital
Vancouver, British Columbia
Canada

Kenneth L. Minaker, MD
Massachusetts General Hospital
Boston, MA

Robert Nelson, MD, PhD
National Institutes of Diabetes and
Digestive and Kidney Diseases
Phoenix, AZ

Helmut Rennke, MD
Brigham & Women's Hospital
Boston, MA

Michael Steffes, MD, PhD
University of Minnesota
Minneapolis, MN

Beth Witten, MSW, ACSW, LSCSW
Witten and Associates, LLC
Overland Park, KS

Pediatric Work Group Members

Ronald J. Hogg, MD, *Chair*
Medical City Hospital
Dallas, TX

Susan Furth, MD, PhD
Johns Hopkins University
Baltimore, MD

Kevin V. Lemley, MD, PhD
Stanford University School of Medicine
Stanford, CT

Ronald J. Portman, MD
University of Texas Health Sciences
Center—Houston
Houston, TX

George Schwartz, MD
University of Rochester School of Medicine
Rochester, NY

Evidence Review Team

Joseph Lau, MD, *Director*
New England Medical Center
Boston, MA

Ethan Balk, MD, MPH, *Assistant Director*
New England Medical Center
Boston, MA

Ronald D. Perrone, MD
Tauqeer Karim, MD
Lara Rayan, MD
Inas Al-Massry, MD

Priscilla Chew, MPH
Brad C. Astor, PhD, MPH
Deirdre DeVine, MLitt

K/DOQI Support Group

Garabed Eknoyan, MD, *Co-Chair*
Baylor College of Medicine
Houston, TX

Nathan Levin, MD, FACP, *Co-Chair*
Renal Research Institute
New York, NY

Sally Burrows-Hudson, RN
William Keane, MD
Alan Kliger, MD
Derrick Latos, MD, FACP

Donna Mapes, DNSc, RN
Edith Oberley, MA
Kerry Willis, PhD

K/DOQI
CLINICAL PRACTICE GUIDELINES
FOR CHRONIC KIDNEY DISEASE: EVALUATION
CLASSIFICATION AND STRATIFICATION

Table of Contents

Tables

K/DOQI National Kidney Foundation

Figures

Grading Rationale Statements

Grade	Level of Evidence
S	Analysis of individual patient data from a single large, generalizable study of high methodological quality (for example, NHANES III)
C	Compilation of original articles (evidence tables)
R	Review of reviews and selected original articles
O	Opinion

AASK	African American Study of Kidney Disease and Hypertension
ABPM	Ambulatory blood pressure monitoring
ACE-inhibitor	Angiotensin converting enzyme inhibitor
ADA	American Diabetes Association
AFT	Autonomic function testing
Alb	Albumin
ASCVD	Atherosclerotic cardiovascular disease
ASN	American Society of Nephrology
AST	American Society of Transplantation
ASTP	American Society of Transplant Physicians
AV	Arterio-venous
BAP	Bone alkaline phosphatase
BDI	Beck Depression Inventory
BEE	Basal energy expenditure
BMI	Body mass index
BP	Blood pressure
BPI	Blood pressure index
BSA	Body surface area
BUN	Blood urea nitrogen
CAD	Coronary artery disease
CCD	Clinical cardiovascular disease
C_{Cr}	Creatinine clearance
CDI	Cognitive Depression Index
CES-D	Center for Epidemiological Studies-Depression
CG equation	Cockcroft-Gault equation

CHD	Coronary heart disease
CHF	Congestive heart failure
C_{in}	Inulin clearance
CKD	Chronic kidney disease
COOP	Dartmouth COOP Clinical Improvement System
COX 2	Cyclo-oxygenase type 2
CPG	Clinical practice guideline
CPM	Clinical performance measure
CQI	Continuous quality improvement programs
Cr	Creatinine
CRF	Chronic renal failure
CT	Computed tomography
C_{TSCr}	Clearance of creatinine due to tubular secretion
C_{Urea}	Urea clearance
CVD	Cardiovascular disease
D	Day(s)
DBP	Diastolic blood pressure
DCCT	Diabetes Control and Complications Trial
DEI	Dietary energy intake
DEXA	Dual energy x-ray absorptiometry (bone densitometry)
DM	Diabetes mellitus
DM I	Type 1 diabetes mellitus
DM II	Type 2 diabetes mellitus
DMMS	Dialysis Morbidity and Mortality Study
DMSA	Dimercaptosuccinic acid
DOQI	Dialysis Outcomes Quality Initiative
DPI	Dietary protein intake
DTPA	Diethylene triamine pentaacetic acid
DUKE	Duke Health Profile
DUSOI	Duke Severity of Illness
E_{Cr}	Extra-renal creatinine elimination rate
EDTA	Ethylene diamine tetraacetic acid
EDX	Electrodiagnosis
EEG	Electroencephalogram
EMG	Electromyography
ESRD	End-stage renal disease
Exp	Exponent
FSGS	Focal segmental glomerulosclerosis
G_{Cr}	Creatinine generation rate
GFR	Glomerular filtration rate
GN	Glomerulonephritis
HBP	High blood pressure

HCFA	Health Care Financing Administration (currently Centers for Medicare and Medicaid Services, CMS)
HD	Hemodialysis
HDFP	Hypertension Detection and Follow-Up Program
HDL	High density lipoprotein
Hgb	Hemoglobin
HI	Health Index
HIV	Human immunodeficiency virus
HLA	Human leukocyte antigen
HOPE	Heart Outcomes Prevention Evaluation
HOT	Hypertension Optimal Trial
Hr	Hour(s)
HR	Heart rate
HTN	Hypertension
ICD-9	International Classification of Diseases, 9th revision
ICTP	Type I collagen cross linked telopeptides
IDDM	Insulin dependent diabetes mellitus
IDNT	Irbesartan in Diabetic Nephropathy Trial
IEQ	Illness Effects Questionnaire
IHD	Ischemic heart disease
IN	Interstitial nephritis
IOM	Institute of Medicine
IPTH	Intact parathyroid hormone
IRMA	Intraretinal microvascular abnormalities
IVP	Intravenous pyelography
JNC-VI	Sixth report of the Joint National Committee for the Prevention, Detection, Evaluation, and Treatment of High Blood Pressure
K/DOQI	Kidney Disease Outcomes Quality Initiative
KDQOL	Kidney Disease Quality of Life
KPS	Karnofsky Performance Scale
Krt/V_{urea}	Renal urea clearance divided by volume of distribution
Kt/V_{urea}	Urea clearance divided by volume of distribution
LDL	Low density lipoprotein
LMW	Low molecular weight
LV	Left ventricle
LVH	Left ventricular hypertrophy
MAG3	Mercaptoacetyltriglycine
MAP	Mean arterial pressure
Max	Maximum
MCD	Medullary cystic disease
MCS	SF-36 Mental Component Summary
MDRD Study	Modification of Diet in Renal Disease Study

MI	Myocardial infarction
Min	Minute(s)
Min	Minimum
MNT	Medical nutrition therapy
Mo	Month(s)
MR	Magnetic resonance
MRI	Magnetic resonance imaging
MSP	Multidimensional Scale of Perceived Social Support
N	Number of subjects in subgroup
N	Number of subjects in sample or population
NA	Not applicable
NAE	Normal urinary albumin excretion
NAG	N-acetyl-β-D-glucosaminidase
NCEP	National Cholesterol Education Program
NCHS	National Center for Health Statistics
NCV	Nerve conduction velocity
ND	No data
NHANES III	Third National Health and Nutrition Examination Survey
NIDDM	Non-insulin dependent diabetes mellitus
NIH	National Institutes of Health
NK	Natural killer
NKF	National Kidney Foundation
No.	Number
NPNA	Normalized protein nitrogen appearance
NS	Non-significant
NSAID	Non-steroidal anti-inflammatory drug
PARADE	Proteinuria, Albuminuria, Risk Assessment, Detection, and Elimination
P_{Cr}	Plasma or serum creatinine concentration
PCS	SF-36 Physical Component Summary
PD	Peritoneal dialysis
PEM	Protein-energy malnutrition
PICP	Procollagen type I carboxy-terminal propeptides
P_{in}	Plasma inulin
PKD	Polycystic kidney disease
PN	Pyelonephritis
PNA	Protein equivalent of total nitrogen appearance
PTH	Parathyroid hormone
PVD	Peripheral vascular disease
QST	Quantitative sensory testing
QWB	Quality of Well-being Scale

RBC	Red blood cell
RBP	Retinol binding protein
RDA	Recommended dietary allowance
RENAAL	Reduction of Endpoints in Non-Insulin Dependent Diabetes Mellitus with the Angiotensin II Antagonist Losartan
RHIE	Rand Health Insurance Experiment
RPA	Renal Physicians Association
RR	Relative risk
SAS-SR	Social Adjustment Scale Self-Report
SBP	Systolic blood pressure
SBW	Standard body weight
SCL 90R	Symptom Checklist-90R
S_{Cr}	Serum creatinine concentration
SD	Standard deviation
SDS-PAGE	Sodium dodecyl sulfate-polyacrylamide gel electrophoresis
SE	Standard error
SF-36	RAND Medical Outcomes Study 36-Item Health Survey
SGA	Subjective global assessment
SIP	Sickness Impact Profile
SLE	Systemic lupus erythematosus
SLS	Satisfaction with Life Scale
SMBG	Self-monitoring of blood glucose
Sn	Sensitivity
Sp	Specificity
STAI	State Trait Anxiety Inventory
SUN	Serum urea nitrogen
TOD	Target organ damage
TS_{Cr}	Tubular creatinine secretion rate
UAC	Urine albumin concentration
$U_{Alb/Cr}$	Urine albumin-to-creatinine ratio
U_{Cr}	Urine creatinine concentration
U_{in}	Urine inulin concentration
UKPDS	United Kingdom Prospective Diabetes Study
UNA	Urea nitrogen appearance
US	United States
USRDS	United States Renal Data System
UUN	Urine urea nitrogen
V	Urine flow rate
V_{Urea}	Volume of distribution of urea
WBC	White blood cell

WHO	World Health Organization
Wk	Week(s)
Yr	Year(s)
β-2-MG	β-2-Microglobulin
Δ	Difference/change

Foreword

From its rudimentary beginnings in the 1960s, through its widespread and increasing availability to the present, dialysis has provided lifesaving replacement therapy for millions of individuals with end-stage renal disease (ESRD). Parallel advances in understanding the course of progressive kidney disease and its complications have resulted in the development of interventions that can slow the progression and ameliorate the complications of chronic kidney disease. Thus, while dialysis has made it possible to prolong the lives of patients with ESRD, today it is also possible to retard the course of progression of kidney disease, to treat accompanying comorbidity earlier, and to improve the outcomes and quality of life of all individuals afflicted with kidney disease, well before replacement therapy becomes necessary. Yet, the application of these advances remains inconsistent, resulting in variations in clinical practice and, sadly, in avoidable differences in patient outcomes.

In keeping with its longstanding commitment to improving the quality of care delivered to all patients with kidney disease and the firm conviction that substantial improvements in the quality and outcomes of their care are achievable, the National Kidney Foundation (NKF) launched in 1995 the Dialysis Outcomes Quality Initiative (DOQI), supported by an educational grant from Amgen, Inc., to develop clinical practice guidelines for dialysis patients and health care providers. Since their publication in 1997, the DOQI guidelines have had a significant and measurable impact on the care and outcomes of dialysis patients. The frequency with which they continue to be cited in the literature and serve as the focus of national and international symposia is but a partial measure of their impact. The DOQI guidelines have also been translated into more than a dozen languages; selected components of the guidelines have been adopted in various countries across the world; and they have provided the basis for clinical performance measures developed and put into effect by the Health Care Financing Administration (recently renamed the Center for Medicare and Medicaid Services) in the United States.

In the course of development of DOQI it became evident that in order to further improve dialysis outcomes, it is necessary to improve the health status of those who reach ESRD and that therein exists an even greater opportunity to improve outcomes for all individuals with kidney disease, from earliest kidney damage through the various stages of progression to kidney failure, when replacement therapy becomes necessary. It was on this basis that in the Fall of 1999, the Board of Directors of the NKF approved a proposal to move the clinical practice guideline initiative into a new phase, in which its scope would be enlarged to encompass the entire spectrum of kidney disease, when early intervention and appropriate measures can prevent the loss of kidney function in some, slow the progression of the disease in many others, and ameliorate organ dysfunction and comorbid conditions in those who progress to kidney failure and ESRD. This enlarged scope increases the potential impact of improving outcomes of care from the hundreds of thousands on dialysis to the millions of individuals with kidney disease who may never require dialysis. To reflect these expanded goals, the reference to "dialysis" in DOQI was changed to "disease," and the new initiative was termed Kidney Disease Outcomes Quality Initiative (K/DOQI™).

The objectives of K/DOQI are ambitious and the challenges are considerable. As a first and essential step it was decided to adhere to the guiding principles that were instrumental in the success of DOQI. The first of these principles was that the development of guidelines would be scientifically rigorous and based on a critical appraisal of the available evidence. The second principle was that the participants involved in developing the guidelines would be multidisciplinary. This was especially crucial because the broader nature of the new guidelines will require their adoption across several specialties and disciplines. The third principle was that the Work Groups charged with developing the guidelines would be the final authority on their content, subject to the requirements that they be evidence-based whenever possible, and that the rationale and evidentiary basis of each guideline would be explicit. By vesting decision-making authority in highly regarded experts from multiple disciplines, the likelihood of developing clinically applicable and sound guidelines is increased. Finally, the guideline development process would be open to general review, in order to allow the chain of reasoning underlying each guideline to undergo peer review and debate prior to publishing. It was believed that such a broad-based review process would promote a wide consensus and support of the guidelines among health care professionals, providers, managers, organizations, and recipients.

To provide a unifying focus to K/DOQI it was decided that its centerpiece would be a set of clinical practice guidelines on the evaluation, classification, and stratification of chronic kidney disease (CKD). This initial set of guidelines will provide a standardized terminology for the evaluation and classification of kidney disease; the proper monitoring of kidney function from initial injury to end stage; a logical approach to stratification of kidney disease by risk factors and comorbid conditions; and consequently a basis for continuous care and therapy throughout the course of chronic kidney disease. Eventually, K/DOQI will include interventional guidelines. Some of these are currently under development, based on the staging and classification developed by these initial CKD guidelines.

We are proud to present this first set and centerpiece of K/DOQI guidelines. The Work Group appointed to develop the guidelines screened over 18,000 potentially relevant articles; over 1,100 were subjected to preliminary review and over 350 were then selected for formal structured review of content and methodology. While considerable effort has gone into the development of the guidelines during the past 24 months, and great attention has been paid to detail and scientific rigor, it is only their incorporation into clinical practice that will assure their applicability and practical utility.

We ask for your support in the implementation of these guidelines. It is hoped that implementation plans developed by the Advisory Board will assure the same acceptance of K/DOQI by the broader spectrum of professionals who provide primary care for kidney disease as that which DOQI received from those who provide dialysis care.

On behalf of the NKF, we would like to acknowledge the immense effort and contributions of those who have made these guidelines possible. In particular, we wish to acknowledge the following: the members of the Work Group and Evidence Review Team charged with developing the guidelines, without whose tireless effort and commitment this first set of K/DOQI guidelines would not have been possible; the members of the Support Group, whose input at monthly conference calls was instrumental in resolving the problems encountered over the 24 months it has taken to reach this stage; the members of the K/DOQI Advisory Board, whose insights and guidance were essential in broadening the applicability of the guidelines; Amgen, Inc., which had the vision and foresight to appreciate the merits of this initiative and provide the funds necessary for its development; and the NKF staff assigned to K/DOQI, who worked so diligently in attending to the innumerable details that needed attention at every stage of guideline development and in meeting our near impossible deadlines.

A special debt of gratitude goes to Andrew S. Levey, MD, Chair of the Work Group, for his leadership, intellectual rigor, innumerable hours of dedication, and invaluable expertise in synthesizing the guidelines; and to Joseph Lau, MD, Director of the Evidence Review Team, for providing crucial methodological rigor and staff support in developing the evidentiary basis of the guidelines.

In a voluntary and multidisciplinary undertaking of such magnitude, numerous others have made valuable contributions to these guidelines but cannot be individually acknowledged here. To each and every one of them we extend our sincerest appreciation.

Garabed Eknoyan, MD
K/DOQI Co-Chair

Nathan W. Levin, MD
K/DOQI Co-Chair

INTRODUCTION: CHRONIC KIDNEY DISEASE AS A PUBLIC HEALTH PROBLEM

Chronic kidney disease is a worldwide public health problem. In the United States, there is a rising incidence and prevalence of kidney failure, with poor outcomes and high cost. There is an even higher prevalence of earlier stages of chronic kidney disease.

Increasing evidence, accrued in the past decades, indicates that the adverse outcomes of chronic kidney disease, such as kidney failure, cardiovascular disease, and premature death, can be prevented or delayed. Earlier stages of chronic kidney disease can be detected through laboratory testing. Treatment of earlier stages of chronic kidney disease is effective in slowing the progression toward kidney failure. Initiation of treatment for cardiovascular risk factors at earlier stages of chronic kidney disease should be effective in reducing cardiovascular disease events both before and after the onset of kidney failure.

Unfortunately, chronic kidney disease is "under-diagnosed" and "under-treated" in the United States, resulting in lost opportunities for prevention. One reason is the lack of agreement on a definition and classification of stages in the progression of chronic kidney disease. A clinically applicable classification would be based on laboratory evaluation of the severity of kidney disease, association of level of kidney function with complications, and stratification of risks for loss of kidney function and development of cardiovascular disease.

CHARGE TO THE K/DOQI WORK GROUP ON CHRONIC KIDNEY DISEASE

In 2000, the National Kidney Foundation (NKF) Kidney Disease Outcome Quality Initiative (K/DOQI) Advisory Board approved development of clinical practice guidelines to define chronic kidney disease and to classify stages in the progression of chronic kidney disease. The Work Group charged with developing the guidelines consisted of experts in nephrology, pediatric nephrology, epidemiology, laboratory medicine, nutrition, social work, gerontology, and family medicine. An Evidence Review Team, consisting of nephrologists and methodologists, was responsible for assembling the evidence. The goals adopted by the Work Group are listed in Table 1.

Defining chronic kidney disease and classifying the stages of severity would provide a common language for communication among providers, patients and their families, investigators, and policy-makers and a framework for developing a public health approach to affect care and improve outcomes of chronic kidney disease. A uniform terminology would permit:

1. More reliable estimates of the prevalence of earlier stages of disease and of the population at increased risk for development of chronic kidney disease
2. Recommendations for laboratory testing to detect earlier stages and progression to later stages

Table 1. Goals of the CKD Work Group

Definition of chronic kidney disease and classification of the stages of chronic kidney disease, irrespective of underlying cause

Evaluation of laboratory measurements for the clinical assessment of kidney disease

Association of the level of kidney function with complications of chronic kidney disease

Stratification of the risk for loss of kidney function and development of cardiovascular disease

3. Associations of stages with clinical manifestations of disease
4. Evaluation of factors associated with a high risk of progression from one stage to the next or of development of other adverse outcomes
5. Evaluation of treatments to slow progression or prevent other adverse outcomes.

Clinical practice guidelines, clinical performance measures, and continuous quality improvement efforts could then be directed to stages of chronic kidney disease.

The Work Group did not specifically address evaluation and treatment for chronic kidney disease. However, this guideline contains brief reference to diagnosis and clinical interventions and can serve as a "road map," linking other clinical practice guidelines and pointing out where other guidelines need to be developed. Eventually, K/DOQI will include interventional guidelines. The first three of these, on bone disease, dyslipidemia, and blood pressure management are currently under development. Other guidelines on cardiovascular disease in dialysis patients and kidney biopsy will be initiated in the Winter of 2001.

This report contains a summary of background information available at the time the Work Group began its deliberations, the 15 guidelines and the accompanying rationale, suggestions for clinical performance measures, a clinical approach to chronic kidney disease using these guidelines, and appendices to describe methods for the review of evidence. The guidelines are based on a systematic review of the literature and the consensus of the Work Group. The guidelines have been reviewed by the K/DOQI Advisory Board, a large number of professional organizations and societies, selected experts, and interested members of the public and have been approved by the Board of Directors of the NKF.

FRAMEWORK

The Work Group defined "chronic kidney disease" to include conditions that affect the kidney, with the potential to cause either progressive loss of kidney function or complications resulting from decreased kidney function. Chronic kidney disease was thus defined as the presence of kidney damage or decreased level of kidney function for three months or more, irrespective of diagnosis.

The target population includes individuals with chronic kidney disease or at increased risk of developing chronic kidney disease. The majority of topics focus on adults (age ≥18 years). Many of the same principles apply to children as well. In particular, the classification of stages of disease and principles of diagnostic testing are similar. A sub-committee of the Work Group examined issues related to children and participated in development of the first six guidelines of the present document. However, there are sufficient differences between adults and children in the association of GFR with signs and symptoms of uremia and in stratification of risk for adverse outcomes that these latter issues are addressed only for adults. A separate set of guidelines for children will have to be developed by a later Work Group.

The target audience includes a wide range of individuals: those who have or are at increased risk of developing chronic kidney disease (the target population) and their families; health care professionals caring for the target population; manufacturers of instruments and diagnostic laboratories performing measurements of kidney function; agencies and institutions planning, providing or paying for the health care needs of the target population; and investigators studying chronic kidney disease.

There will be only brief reference to clinical interventions, sufficient to provide a basis for other clinical practice guidelines relevant to the evaluation and management of chronic kidney disease. Subsequent K/DOQI clinical practice guidelines will be based on the framework developed here.

DEFINITION OF CHRONIC KIDNEY DISEASE

The Work Group developed the following operational definition of chronic kidney disease (Table 2).

Table 2. Definition of Chronic Kidney Disease

Criteria
1. Kidney damage for ≥3 months, as defined by structural or functional abnormalities of the kidney, with or without decreased GFR, manifest by *either*:   • Pathological abnormalities; or   • Markers of kidney damage, including abnormalities in the composition of the blood or urine, or abnormalities in imaging tests
2. GFR <60 mL/min/1.73 m^2 for ≥3 months, with or without kidney damage

Abbreviation: GFR, glomerular filtration rate

Table 3. Chronic Kidney Disease: A Clinical Action Plan

Stage	Description	GFR (mL/min/1.73 m²)	Action*
	At increased risk	≥90 (with CKD risk factors)	Screening, CKD risk reduction
1	Kidney damage with normal or ↑ GFR	≥90	Diagnosis and treatment, Treatment of comorbid conditions, Slowing progression, CVD risk reduction
2	Kidney damage with mild ↓ GFR	60–89	Estimating progression
3	Moderate ↓ GFR	30–59	Evaluating and treating complications
4	Severe ↓ GFR	15–29	Preparation for kidney replacement therapy
5	Kidney failure	<15 (or dialysis)	Replacement (if uremia present)

Shaded area identifies patients who have chronic kidney disease; unshaded area designates individuals who are at increased risk for developing chronic kidney disease. Chronic kidney disease is defined as either kidney damage or GFR <60 mL/min/1.73 m² for ≥3 months. Kidney damage is defined as pathologic abnormalities or markers of damage, including abnormalities in blood or urine tests or imaging studies.

* Includes actions from preceding stages.

Abbreviations: GFR, glomerular filtration rate; CKD, chronic kidney disease; CVD, cardiovascular disease

Classification of Chronic Kidney Disease

Table 3 shows the classification of stages of chronic kidney disease, including the population at increased risk of developing chronic kidney disease, and actions to prevent the development of chronic kidney disease and to improve outcomes in each stage.

Why "Kidney"?

The word "kidney" is of Middle English origin and is immediately understood by patients, their families, providers, health care professionals, and the lay public of native English speakers. On the other hand, "renal" and "nephrology," derived from Latin and Greek roots, respectively, commonly require interpretation and explanation. The Work Group and the NKF are committed to communicating in language that can be widely understood, hence the preferential use of "kidney" throughout these guidelines. The term "End-Stage Renal Disease" (ESRD) has been retained because of its administrative usage in the United States referring to patients treated by dialysis or transplantation, irrespective of their level of kidney function.

Why Develop a New Classification?

Currently, there is no uniform classification of the stages of chronic kidney disease. A review of textbooks and journal articles clearly demonstrates ambiguity and overlap in the meaning of current terms. The Work Group concluded that uniform definitions of terms and stages would improve communication between patients and providers, enhance public education, and promote dissemination of research results. In addition, it was believed that uniform definitions would enhance conduct of clinical research.

Why Base a New Classification System on Severity of Disease?

Adverse outcomes of kidney disease are based on the level of kidney function and risk of loss of function in the future. Chronic kidney disease tends to worsen over time.

Therefore, the risk of adverse outcomes increases over time with disease severity. Many disciplines in medicine, including related specialties of hypertension, cardiovascular disease, diabetes, and transplantation, have adopted classification systems based on severity to guide clinical interventions, research, and professional and public education. Such a model is essential for any public health approach to disease.

Why Classify Severity as the Level of GFR?

The level of glomerular filtration rate (GFR) is widely accepted as the best overall measure of kidney function in health and disease. Providers and patients are familiar with the concept that "the kidney is like a filter." GFR is the best measure of the kidneys' ability to filter blood. In addition, expressing the level of kidney function on a continuous scale allows development of patient and public education programs that encourage individuals to "Know your number!"

The term "GFR" is not intuitively evident to anyone. Rather, it is a learned term, which allows the ultimate expression of the complex functions of the kidney in one single numerical expression. Conversely, numbers are an intuitive concept and easily understandable by everyone. It is fortunate then that once the term "GFR" is learned, the expression "Know your number!" becomes intuitive and easily understood.

Why Include an "Action Plan"?

Action is necessary to improve outcomes, which is the ultimate goal of the NKF. No clinical practice guideline, irrespective of the rigor of its development, can accomplish its intended improvement in outcome without an implementation plan. This has been the charge of the Advisory Board. The process has been set in motion in parallel with that of development of the guidelines.

PREVALENCE OF CHRONIC KIDNEY DISEASE IN THE UNITED STATES

Using the definition and stages of chronic kidney disease, the Work Group was able to provide rough estimates of the prevalence of each stage in adults from the Third National Health and Nutrition Examination Survey (NHANES III) (Table 4). Methods for estimating

Table 4. Stages and Prevalence of Chronic Kidney Disease (Age ≥ 20)

Stage	Description	GFR (mL/min/1.73 m^2)	Prevalence* N (1000s)	%
1	Kidney damage with normal or ↑ GFR	≥90	5,900	3.3
2	Kidney damage with mild ↓ GFR	60–89	5,300	3.0
3	Moderate ↓ GFR	30–59	7,600	4.3
4	Severe ↓ GFR	15–29	400	0.2
5	Kidney failure	<15 (or dialysis)	300	0.1

* Data for Stages 1–4 from NHANES III (1988–1994)[1]. Population of 177 million adults age ≥20 years. Data for Stage 5 from USRDS (1998)[2] include approximately 230,000 patients treated by dialysis, and assume 70,000 additional patients not on dialysis. GFR estimated from serum creatinine using MDRD Study equation based on age, gender, race and calibration for serum creatinine. For Stages 1 and 2, kidney damage estimated by spot albumin-to-creatinine ratio >17 mg/g in men or >25 mg/g in women on two measurements.

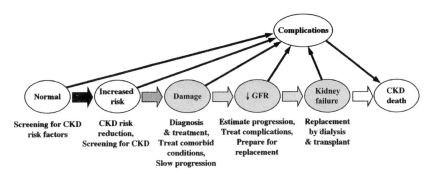

Fig 1. Evidence model for stages in the initiation and progression of chronic kidney disease, and therapeutic interventions. Shaded ellipses represent stages of chronic kidney disease; unshaded ellipses represent potential antecedents or consequences of CKD. Thick arrows between ellipses represent factors associated with initiation and progression of disease that can be affected or detected by interventions: susceptibility factors (black); initiation factors (dark gray); progression factors (light gray); and end-stage factors (white). Interventions for each stage are given beneath the stage. Individuals who appear normal should be screened fo CKD risk factors. Individuals known to be at increased risk for CKD should be screened for CKD. Modified and reprinted with permission.[3]

prevalence are detailed in Part 10, Appendix 2. The prevalence of chronic kidney disease in children is too low to provide accurate estimates of prevalence of each stage based on data from NHANES III.

FUTURE DIRECTIONS

The framework that has been adopted can be used to develop an evidence model of the course of chronic kidney disease (Fig 1). It is anticipated that clinical practice guidelines for interventions to reduce adverse outcomes in patients with chronic kidney disease can be based on this model.

This line of logic allows for the ultimate construction of a list of modifiable risk factors at each stage of chronic kidney disease, as shown in Table 5.

REVIEW OF EVIDENCE

The guidelines developed by the Work Group are based on a systematic review of the literature using an approach based on the procedure outlined by the Agency for Healthcare Research and Quality (formerly the Agency for Health Care Policy and Research) with modifications appropriate to the goals. An Evidence Review Team was appointed by the NKF to collaborate with the Work Group to conduct a systematic review of the literature on which to base the guidelines. A detailed explanation of these methods is provided in Part 10, Appendices 1 and 2; Table 6 provides a brief listing of the steps involved in this approach.

Table 5. Potentially Modifiable Risk Factors for Development and Progression of Chronic Kidney Disease According to Stage

Risk Factors

Stage	Description	Lack of Awareness	Proteinuria	Hypertension	Dyslipidemia	Hyperglycemia	Anemia	Nutritional Factors	Thrombogenic Factors	Oxidative Stress	Elevated Homocysteine	Menopause	Smoking	Infection/Inflammation	Other Uremic Toxins	Depression/Poor Mental Health	Poor Physical Functioning	Vocational Disability	Poor Social Functioning
	At increased risk																		
1	Kidney damage with normal or ↑ GFR																		
2	Kidney damage with mild ↓ GFR																		
3	Moderate ↓ GFR																		
4	Severe ↓ GFR																		
5	Kidney Failure																		

Table 6. Approach to the Evidence Review

Develop and refine topics;

Determine approach to topics:
Established concepts—summary of published reviews and selected original articles;

New concepts—systematic review of original articles and analysis of primary data, if available.

Retrieval of evidence (literature review);

Analysis of primary data from the Third National Health and Nutrition Examination Survey (NHANES III) and other sources;

Evaluation of evidence (types and quality);

Synthesis of evidence (tables);

Translation of evidence into clinical practice guidelines;

Identification of guidelines suitable for translation into clinical performance measures;

Public review and revisions;

Approval by Board of Directors of the NKF.

Example of Format for Evidence Tables

Author, Year	No. of Subjects	Applicability	GFR Range* (mL/min/1.73 m^2) 0 30 60 90 120	Results	Quality
Smith, 1999	1,000	♦♦♦	━━┼━━	⬇	●
Jones, 1995	500	♦♦	$S_{Cr} = 3.4$ mg/dL	⬆	◐
Rodriguez, 1995	250	♦♦	━━━	⬆	◐
Johnson, 1995	500	♦♦♦	━┼━	⬌	○
Klein, 1995	1,500	♦♦	$S_{Cr} \approx 0.9$–4.0 mg/dL	3.3 g/dL	◐
Roberts, 1995	500	♦	❘	3.7 g/dL	◐
Doe, 2000	500	♦♦	$S_{Cr} = 2.9 \pm 0.6$ mg/dL	3.2 g/dL	○

Shading is used to distinguish studies that do not report on the association between GFR and the table's outcome measure (e.g., serum albumin levels); unshaded studies use arrows to represent the strength and direction of the reported association.

* Where GFR data were not available, S_{Cr} values (in mg/dL) are given.

♦♦♦ Sample is representative of the target population, or results are definitely applicable to general chronic kidney disease population irrespective of study sample.

♦♦ Sample is representative of a relevant sub-group of the target population. For example, sample is only representative of people with a narrow range of GFR, or only a specific relevant subgroup, such as elderly individuals or patients with diabetic kidney disease. In addition, studies of association of level of kidney function with complications that report serum creatinine levels rather than estimated GFR are assigned to this category.

♦ Sample is representative of a narrow subgroup of patients only, and not well generalizable to other subgroups. For example, the study includes only patients with a rare disease. However, studies of such narrow subgroups may be extremely valuable for demonstrating "exceptions to the rule."

A uniform format for summarizing the strength of evidence has been developed using four dimensions: study size, applicability, results, and methodological quality. An example of an evidence table is shown in the above table. Within each table, studies are ordered first by methodological quality (best to worst), then by applicability (most to least), and then by study size (largest to smallest). Detailed evidence tables are on file at the National Kidney Foundation.

Applicability

Applicability (also known as generalizability or external validity) addresses the issue of whether the study population is sufficiently broad so that the results can be generalized to the population of interest at large. The study population is typically defined by the inclusion and exclusion criteria. The target population was defined to include patients with chronic kidney disease and those at increased risk of chronic kidney disease, except where noted. A designation for applicability was assigned to each article, according to a three-level scale. In making this assessment, sociodemographic characteristics were considered, as were the stated causes of chronic kidney disease and prior treatments.

GFR Range

For all studies, the range of GFR (or creatinine clearance [C_{Cr}]) is represented graphically when available (see table above). The mean or median GFR is represented by a vertical line, with a horizontal bar showing a range that includes approximately 95% of study participants. Studies without a vertical or horizontal line did not provide data on the mean/median or range, respectively. When GFR or C_{Cr} measurements are not available, serum creatinine levels are listed as text.

Results

Results are represented by prevalence levels, proportions (percents) for categorical variables, mean levels for continuous variables, and associations between study measures. Symbols indicate the type and significance of associations between study measures:

⇧	Positive association (measurement increases or decreases in the same direction as GFR)
⇔	No association (measurement does *not* vary with level of GFR)
⇩	Negative association (measurement changes in inverse direction as GFR)
↑ or ↓	Statistically significant association (p <0.05)

The specific meanings of these symbols are explained in the footnotes of tables where they appear. Some informative studies reported only single point estimates of study measures (eg, mean data) rather than associations. Where data on associations were limited, evidence tables provide these point estimates. Studies that provide data on associations and studies that provide only point estimates are listed and ranked separately, with shading used to distinguish them (as in the table, Example of Format for Evidence Tables).

Quality

Methodological quality (or internal validity) refers to the design, conduct, and reporting of the clinical study. Because studies with a variety of types of design were evaluated, a three-level classification of study quality was devised:

● Least bias; results are valid. A study that mostly adheres to the commonly held concepts of high quality, including the following: a formal study; clear description of the population and setting; clear description of an appropriate reference standard; proper measurement techniques; appropriate statistical and analytic methods; no reporting errors; and no obvious bias.

◉ Susceptible to some bias, but not sufficient to invalidate the results. A study that does not meet all the criteria in category above. It has some deficiencies but none likely to cause major bias. Includes retrospective studies and case series.

○ Significant bias that may invalidate the results. A study with serious errors in design or reporting. These studies may have large amounts of missing information or discrepancies in reporting. Includes prospective and retrospective studies and case series.

Strength of Evidence

Each rationale statement has been graded according the level of evidence on which it is based.

Grading Rationale Statements

Grade	Level of Evidence
S	Analysis of individual patient data from a single large, generalizable study of high methodological quality (for example, NHANES III)
C	Compilation of original articles (evidence tables)
R	Review of reviews and selected original articles
O	Opinion

GUIDELINE STATEMENTS

Guideline statements are grouped into four parts, corresponding to the four goals of the CKD Work Group. Guideline statements are reproduced in the Executive Summary. The reader is referred to specific pages for rationale, evidence tables and references.

DEFINITION AND CLASSIFICATION OF STAGES OF CHRONIC KIDNEY DISEASE (PART 4, p. 43)

Chronic kidney disease is a major public health problem. Improving outcomes for people with chronic kidney disease requires a coordinated worldwide approach to prevention of adverse outcomes through defining the disease and its outcomes, estimating disease prevalence, identifying earlier stages of disease and antecedent risk factors, and detection and treatment for populations at increased risk for adverse outcomes. The goal of Part 4 is to create an operational definition and classification of stages of chronic kidney disease and provide estimates of disease prevalence by stage, to develop a broad overview of a "clinical action plan" for evaluation and management of each stage of chronic kidney disease, and to define individuals at increased risk for developing chronic kidney disease. Studies of disease prevalence were evaluated as described in Appendix 1, Table 147. Data from NHANES III were used to develop estimates of disease prevalence in adults as described in Appendix 2.

GUIDELINE 1. Definition and Stages of Chronic Kidney Disease (p. 43)

Adverse outcomes of chronic kidney disease can often be prevented or delayed through early detection and treatment. Earlier stages of chronic kidney disease can be detected through routine laboratory measurements.

- The presence of chronic kidney disease should be established, based on presence of kidney damage and level of kidney function (glomerular filtration rate [GFR]), irrespective of diagnosis.
- Among patients with chronic kidney disease, the stage of disease should be assigned

---

Stages of Chronic Kidney Disease

Stage	Description	GFR (mL/min/1.73 m²)
1	Kidney damage with normal or ↑ GFR	≥90
2	Kidney damage with mild ↓ GFR	60–89
3	Moderate ↓ GFR	30–59
4	Severe ↓ GFR	15–29
5	Kidney failure	<15 or dialysis

Chronic kidney disease is defined as either kidney damage or GFR <60 mL/min/1.73 m² for ≥3 months. Kidney damage is defined as pathologic abnormalities or markers of damage, including abnormalities in blood or urine tests or imaging studies.

based on the level of kidney function, irrespective of diagnosis, according to the K/DOQI CKD classification:

GUIDELINE 2. Evaluation and Treatment (p. 66)

The evaluation and treatment of patients with chronic kidney disease requires understanding of separate but related concepts of diagnosis, comorbid conditions, severity of disease, complications of disease, and risks for loss of kidney function and cardiovascular disease.

- Patients with chronic kidney disease should be evaluated to determine:
  - Diagnosis (type of kidney disease);
  - Comorbid conditions;
  - Severity, assessed by level of kidney function;
  - Complications, related to level of kidney function;
  - Risk for loss of kidney function;
  - Risk for cardiovascular disease.
- Treatment of chronic kidney disease should include:
  - Specific therapy, based on diagnosis;
  - Evaluation and management of comorbid conditions;
  - Slowing the loss of kidney function;
  - Prevention and treatment of cardiovascular disease;
  - Prevention and treatment of complications of decreased kidney function;
  - Preparation for kidney failure and kidney replacement therapy;
  - Replacement of kidney function by dialysis and transplantation, if signs and symptoms of uremia are present.
- A clinical action plan should be developed for each patient, based on the stage of disease as defined by the K/DOQI CKD classification (see table on page 13).

Stages of Chronic Kidney Disease: A Clinical Action Plan

Stage	Description	GFR (mL/min/1.73 m^2)	Action*
1	Kidney damage with normal or ↑ GFR	≥90	Diagnosis and treatment, Treatment of comorbid conditions, Slowing progression, CVD risk reduction
2	Kidney damage with mild ↓ GFR	60–89	Estimating progression
3	Moderate ↓ GFR	30–59	Evaluating and treating complications
4	Severe ↓ GFR	15–29	Preparation for kidney replacement therapy
5	Kidney failure	<15 (or dialysis)	Replacement (if uremia present)

Chronic kidney disease is defined as either kidney damage or GFR <60 mL/min/1.73 m^2 for ≥3 months. Kidney damage is defined as pathologic abnormalities or markers of damage, including abnormalities in blood or urine tests or imaging studies.

* Includes actions from preceding stages.

Abbreviations: CVD, cardiovascular disease

- Review of medications should be performed at all visits for the following:
  - Dosage adjustment based on level of kidney function;
  - Detection of potentially adverse effects on kidney function or complications of chronic kidney disease;
  - Detection of drug interactions; and
  - Therapeutic drug monitoring, if possible.
- Self-management behaviors should be incorporated into the treatment plan at all stages of chronic kidney disease.
- Patients with chronic kidney disease should be referred to a specialist for consultation and co-management if the clinical action plan cannot be prepared, the prescribed evaluation of the patient cannot be carried out, or the recommended treatment cannot be carried out. In general, patients with GFR <30 mL/min/1.73 m^2 should be referred to a nephrologist.

GUIDELINE 3. Individuals at Increased Risk of Chronic Kidney Disease (p. 75)

- Some individuals without kidney damage and with normal or elevated GFR are at increased risk for development of chronic kidney disease.
  - All individuals should be assessed, as part of routine health encounters, to determine whether they are at increased risk of developing chronic kidney disease, based on clinical and sociodemographic factors.
  - Individuals at increased risk of developing chronic kidney disease should undergo testing for markers of kidney damage and to estimate the level of GFR.
  - Individuals found to have chronic kidney disease should be evaluated and treated as specified in Guideline 2.
  - Individuals at increased risk, but found not to have chronic kidney disease, should be advised to follow a program of risk factor reduction, if appropriate, and undergo repeat periodic evaluation.

EVALUATION OF LABORATORY MEASUREMENTS FOR CLINICAL ASSESSMENT OF KIDNEY DISEASE (PART 5, p. 81)

The definition and staging of chronic kidney disease depends on the assessment of GFR, proteinuria, and other markers of kidney disease. The goals of Part 5 are to evaluate the accuracy of prediction equations to estimate the level of GFR from serum creatinine, the accuracy of ratios of protein-to-creatinine concentration in untimed ("spot") urine samples to assess protein excretion rate, and the utility of markers of kidney damage other than proteinuria. As described in Appendix 1, Table 151, the Work Group evaluated studies according to accepted methods for evaluation of diagnostic tests. To provide a more comprehensive review, the Work Group attempted to integrate the systematic review of specific questions with existing guidelines and recommendations.

GUIDELINE 4. Estimation of GFR (p. 81)

Estimates of GFR are the best overall indices of the level of kidney function.

- The level of GFR should be estimated from prediction equations that take into account the serum creatinine concentration and some or all of the following variables: age, gender, race and body size. The following equations provide useful estimates of GFR:
  - In adults, the MDRD Study and Cockcroft-Gault equations;
  - In children, the Schwartz and Couna han-Barratt equations.
- The serum creatinine concentration alone should not be used to assess the level of kidney function.
- Clinical laboratories should report an estimate of GFR using a prediction equation, in addition to reporting the serum creatinine measurement.
- Autoanalyzer manufacturers and clinical laboratories should calibrate serum creatinine assays using an international standard.
- Measurement of creatinine clearance using timed (for example, 24-hour) urine collections does not improve the estimate of GFR over that provided by prediction equations. A 24-hour urine sample provides useful information for:
  - Estimation of GFR in individuals with exceptional dietary intake (vegetarian diet, creatine supplements) or muscle mass (amputation, malnutrition, muscle wasting);
  - Assessment of diet and nutritional status;
  - Need to start dialysis.

GUIDELINE 5. Assessment of Proteinuria (p. 100)

Normal individuals usually excrete very small amounts of protein in the urine. Persistently increased protein excretion is usually a marker of kidney damage. The excretion of specific types of protein, such as albumin or low molecular weight globulins, depends on the type of kidney disease that is present. Increased excretion of albumin is a sensitive marker for chronic kidney disease due to diabetes, glomerular disease, and hypertension. Increased excretion of low molecular weight globulins is a sensitive marker for some types of tubulointerstitial disease. In this guideline, the term "proteinuria" refers to increased urinary excretion of albumin, other specific proteins, or total protein; "albuminuria" refers specifically to increased urinary excretion of albumin. "Microalbuminuria" refers to albumin excretion above the normal range but below the level of detection by tests for total protein. Guidelines for detection and monitoring of proteinuria in adults and children differ because of differences in the prevalence and type of chronic kidney disease.

Guidelines for Adults and Children:
- Under most circumstances, untimed ("spot") urine samples should be used to detect and monitor proteinuria in children and adults.
- It is usually not necessary to obtain a timed urine collection (overnight or 24-hour) for these evaluations in either children or adults.
- First morning specimens are preferred, but random specimens are acceptable if first morning specimens are not available.
- In most cases, screening with urine dipsticks is acceptable for detecting proteinuria:
  - Standard urine dipsticks are acceptable for detecting increased total urine protein.
  - Albumin-specific dipsticks are acceptable for detecting albuminuria.
- Patients with a positive dipstick test (1+ or greater) should undergo confirmation of proteinuria by a quantitative measurement (protein-to-creatinine ratio or albumin-to-creatinine ratio) within 3 months.
- Patients with two or more positive quantitative tests temporally spaced by 1 to 2 weeks should be diagnosed as having persistent proteinuria and undergo further evaluation and management for chronic kidney disease as stated in Guideline 2.
- Monitoring proteinuria in patients with chronic kidney disease should be performed using quantitative measurements.

Specific Guidelines for Adults:
- When screening adults at increased risk for chronic kidney disease, albumin should be measured in a spot urine sample using either:
  - Albumin-specific dipstick;
  - Albumin-to-creatinine ratio.
- When monitoring proteinuria in adults with chronic kidney disease, the protein-to-creatinine ratio in spot urine samples should be measured using:
  - Albumin-to-creatinine ratio;
  - Total protein-to-creatinine ratio is acceptable if albumin-to-creatinine ratio is high (>500 to 1,000 mg/g).

Specific Guidelines for Children Without Diabetes:
- When screening children for chronic kidney disease, total urine protein should be measured in a spot urine sample using either:
  - Standard urine dipstick;
  - Total protein-to-creatinine ratio.
- Orthostatic proteinuria must be excluded by repeat measurement on a first morning specimen if the initial finding of proteinuria was obtained on a random specimen.
- When monitoring proteinuria in children with chronic kidney disease, the total protein-to-creatinine ratio should be measured in spot urine specimens.

Specific Guidelines for Children With Diabetes:
- Screening and monitoring of post-pubertal children with diabetes of 5 or more years of duration should follow the guidelines for adults.
- Screening and monitoring other children with diabetes should follow the guidelines for children without diabetes.

GUIDELINE 6. Markers of Chronic Kidney Disease Other Than Proteinuria (p. 112)

Markers of kidney damage in addition to proteinuria include abnormalities in the urine sediment and abnormalities on imaging studies. Constellations of markers define clinical presentations for some types of chronic kidney disease. New markers are needed to detect kidney damage that occurs prior to a reduction in GFR in other types of chronic kidney diseases.

- Urine sediment examination or dipstick for red blood cells and white blood cells should be performed in patients with chronic kidney disease and in individuals at increased risk of developing chronic kidney disease.
- Imaging studies of the kidneys should be performed in patients with chronic kidney disease and in selected individuals at increased risk of developing chronic kidney disease.
- Although several novel urinary markers (such as tubular or low-molecular weight proteins and specific mononuclear cells) show promise of future utility, they should not be used for clinical decision-making at present.

ASSOCIATION OF LEVEL OF GFR WITH COMPLICATIONS IN ADULTS (PART 6, p. 123)

Many of the complications of chronic kidney disease can be prevented or delayed by early detection and treatment. The goal of Part 6 is to review the association of the level of GFR with complications of chronic kidney disease to determine the stage of chronic

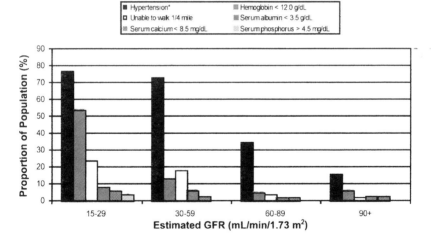

*≥140/90 or antihypertensive medication   p-trend <0.001 for each abnormality

Estimated prevalence of selected complications, by category of estimated GFR, among participants age ≥20 years in NHANES III, 1988 through 1994. These estimates are not adjusted for age, the mean of which is 33 years higher at an estimated GFR of 15 to 29 mL/min/1.73 m^2 than that at an estimated GFR ≥90 mL/min/1.73 m^2.

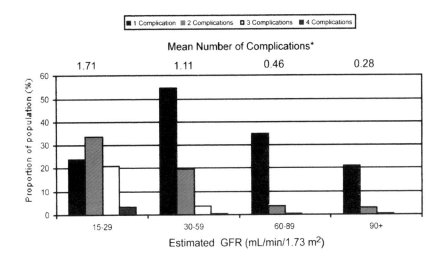

*p-trend <0.001

Estimated distribution of the number of complications shown in figure by category of estimated GFR among participants age ≥20 years in NHANES III, 1988 through 1994. These estimates are not adjusted for age, the mean of which is 33 years higher at an estimated GFR of 15 to 29 mL/min/1.73 m^2 than that at an estimated GFR of ≥90 mL/min/1.73 m^2.

kidney disease when complications appear. As described in Appendix 1, Table 152, the Work Group searched for cross-sectional studies that related manifestations of complications and the level of kidney function. Data from NHANES III were also analyzed, as described in Appendix 2.

Because of different manifestations of complications of chronic kidney disease in children, especially in growth and development, the Work Group limited the scope of the review of evidence to adults. A separate Work Group will need to address this issue in children.

The Work Group did not attempt to review the evidence on the evaluation and management of complications of chronic kidney disease. This is the subject of past and forthcoming clinical practice guidelines by the National Kidney Foundation and other groups, which are referenced in the text.

Representative findings are shown by stage of chronic kidney disease in the figures above and below, showing a higher prevalence of each complication at lower GFR, and a larger mean number of complications per person and higher prevalence of multiple complications at lower GFR. These and other findings support the classification of stages of chronic kidney disease and are discussed in detail in Guidelines 7 through 12.

GUIDELINE 7. Association of Level of GFR With Hypertension (p. 124)

High blood pressure is both a cause and a complication of chronic kidney disease. As a complication, high blood pressure may develop early during the course of chronic kidney disease and is associated with adverse outcomes — in particular, faster loss of kidney function and development of cardiovascular disease.

- Blood pressure should be closely monitored in all patients with chronic kidney disease.
- Treatment of high blood pressure in chronic kidney disease should include specification of target blood pressure levels, nonpharmacologic therapy, and specific antihypertensive agents for the prevention of progression of kidney disease (Guideline 13) and development of cardiovascular disease (Guideline 15).

GUIDELINE 8. Association of Level of GFR With Anemia (p. 136)

Anemia usually develops during the course of chronic kidney disease and may be associated with adverse outcomes.

- Patients with GFR <60 mL/min/1.73 m^2 should be evaluated for anemia. The evaluation should include measurement of hemoglobin level.
- Anemia in chronic kidney disease should be evaluated and treated (see K/DOQI Clinical Practice Guidelines for Anemia of Chronic Kidney Disease, Guidelines 1–4).

GUIDELINE 9. Association of Level of GFR With Nutritional Status (p. 145)

Protein energy malnutrition develops during the course of chronic kidney disease and is associated with adverse outcomes. Low protein and calorie intake is an important cause of malnutrition in chronic kidney disease.

- Patients with GFR <60 mL/min/1.73 m^2 should undergo assessment of dietary protein and energy intake and nutritional status (see K/DOQI Clinical Practice Guidelines for Nutrition in Chronic Renal Failure, Guidelines 23 and 26).
- Patients with decreased dietary intake or malnutrition should undergo dietary modification, counseling and education, or specialized nutrition therapy (see K/DOQI Clinical Practice Guidelines for Nutrition in Chronic Renal Failure, Guidelines 24 and 25).

GUIDELINE 10. Bone Disease and Disorders of Calcium and Phosphorus Metabolism (p. 163)

Bone disease and disorders of calcium and phosphorus metabolism develop during the course of chronic kidney disease and are associated with adverse outcomes.

- Patients with GFR <60 mL/min/1.73 m^2 should be evaluated for bone disease and disorders of calcium and phosphorus metabolism.
- Patients with bone disease and disorders of bone metabolism should be evaluated and treated (see forthcoming K/DOQI Clinical Practice Guidelines on Bone Metabolism and Disease in Chronic Kidney Disease).

GUIDELINE 11. Neuropathy (p. 180)

Neuropathy develops during the course of chronic kidney disease and may become symptomatic.

- Patients with chronic kidney disease should be periodically assessed for central and peripheral neurologic involvement by eliciting symptoms and signs during routine office visits or exams.

- Specialized laboratory testing for neuropathy in patients with chronic kidney disease is indicated only in the presence of symptoms.

GUIDELINE 12. **Association of Level of GFR With Indices of Functioning and Well-Being (p. 186)**

Impairments in domains of functioning and well-being develop during the course of chronic kidney disease and are associated with adverse outcomes. Impaired functioning and well-being may be related to sociodemographic factors, conditions causing chronic kidney disease, complications of kidney disease, or possibly directly due to reduced GFR.

- Patients with GFR <60 mL/min/1.73 m^2 should undergo regular assessment for impairment of functioning and well-being:
  - To establish a baseline and monitor changes in functioning and well-being over time;
  - To assess the effect of interventions on functioning and well-being.

STRATIFICATION OF RISK FOR PROGRESSION OF KIDNEY DISEASE AND DEVELOPMENT OF CARDIOVASCULAR DISEASE (PART 7, p. 197)

The major outcomes of chronic kidney disease are loss of kidney function, leading to complications and kidney failure, and development of cardiovascular disease. The goals of Part 7 are to define risk factors for progression of chronic kidney disease and to determine whether chronic kidney disease is a risk factor for cardiovascular disease. Because of the well-known association of cardiovascular disease and diabetes, the Work Group considered patients with chronic kidney disease due to diabetes separately from patients with chronic kidney disease due to other causes. As described in Appendix 1, Table 153, the Work Group searched primarily for longitudinal studies that related risk factors to loss of kidney function (Guideline 13) and that related proteinuria and decreased GFR to cardiovascular disease (Guidelines 14 and 15). It was beyond the scope of the Work Group to undertake a systematic review of studies of treatment. However, existing guidelines and recommendations were reviewed, as were selected studies, to provide further evidence of efficacy of treatment.

GUIDELINE 13. **Factors Associated With Loss of Kidney Function in Chronic Kidney Disease (p. 197)**

The level of kidney function tends to decline progressively over time in most patients with chronic kidney diseases.

- The rate of GFR decline should be assessed in patients with chronic kidney disease to:
  - Predict the interval until the onset of kidney failure;
  - Assess the effect of interventions to slow the GFR decline.
- Among patients with chronic kidney disease, the rate of GFR decline should be estimated by:
  - Computing the GFR decline from past and ongoing measurements of serum creatinine;
  - Ascertaining risk factors for faster versus slower GFR decline, including type (diagnosis) of kidney disease and nonmodifiable and modifiable factors.

- Interventions to slow the progression of kidney disease should be considered in all patients with chronic kidney disease.
  - Interventions that have been proven to be effective include:
    - (1) Strict glucose control in diabetes;
    - (2) Strict blood pressure control;
    - (3) Angiotensin-converting enzyme inhibition or angiotensin-2 receptor blockade.
  - Interventions that have been studied, but the results of which are inconclusive, include:
    - (1) Dietary protein restriction;
    - (2) Lipid-lowering therapy;
    - (3) Partial correction of anemia.
- Attempts should be made to prevent and correct acute decline in GFR. Frequent causes of acute decline in GFR include:
  - Volume depletion;
  - Intravenous radiographic contrast;
  - Selected antimicrobial agents (for example, aminoglycosides and amphotericin B);
  - Nonsteroidal anti-inflammatory agents; including cyclo-oxygenase type 2 inhibitors;
  - Angiotensin-converting enzyme inhibition and angiotensin-2 receptor blockers;
  - Cyclosporine and tacrolimus;
  - Obstruction of the urinary tract.
- Measurements of serum creatinine for estimation of GFR should be obtained at least yearly in patients with chronic kidney disease and more often in patients with:
  - GFR <60 mL/min/1.73 m^2;
  - Fast GFR decline in the past (≥4 mL/min/1.73 m^2 per year);
  - Risk factors for faster progression;
  - Ongoing treatment to slow progression;
  - Exposure to risk factors for acute GFR decline.

GUIDELINE 14. Association of Chronic Kidney Disease With Diabetic Complications (p. 230)

The risk of cardiovascular disease, retinopathy, and other diabetic complications is higher in patients with diabetic kidney disease than in diabetic patients without kidney disease.

- Prevention, detection, evaluation, and treatment of diabetic complications in patients with chronic kidney disease should follow published guidelines and position statements.
- Guidelines regarding angiotensin-converting enzyme inhibitors or angiotensin-receptor blockers and strict blood pressure control are particularly important since these agents may prevent or delay some of the adverse outcomes of both kidney and cardiovascular disease.
- Application of published guidelines to diabetic patients with chronic kidney disease should take into account their "higher-risk" status for diabetic complications.

GUIDELINE 15. Association of Chronic Kidney Disease With Cardiovascular Disease (p. 238)

Patients with chronic kidney disease, irrespective of diagnosis, are at increased risk of cardiovascular disease (CVD), including coronary heart disease, cerebrovascular disease, peripheral vascular disease, and heart failure. Both "traditional" and "chronic kidney disease-related (nontraditional)" CVD risk factors may contribute to this increased risk.

- All patients with chronic kidney disease should be considered in the "highest risk" group for cardiovascular disease, irrespective of levels of traditional CVD risk factors.
- All patients with chronic kidney disease should undergo assessment of CVD risk factors, including:
  - Measurement of "traditional" CVD risk factors in all patients;
  - Individual decision-making regarding measurement of selected "CKD-related" CVD risk factors in some patients.
- Recommendations for CVD risk factor reduction should take into account the "highest-risk" status of patients with chronic kidney disease.

Part 2. Background

NKF KIDNEY DISEASE OUTCOMES QUALITY INITIATIVE (K/DOQI)

Since their publication in the Fall of 1997, the National Kidney Foundation (NKF) Dialysis Outcome Quality Initiative (DOQI) Guidelines have become an integral part of nephrology practice throughout this country and in many parts of the world. It is widely acknowledged that the DOQI Guidelines have had an impact in improving quality of care and outcomes of patients treated by dialysis. In the Fall of 1999, the NKF decided to focus its attention on the millions of people with earlier stages of chronic kidney disease, who through early diagnosis and treatment, could possibly avoid the progression of their disease to development of kidney failure and other adverse outcomes. The goal of this new initiative, the Kidney Disease Outcomes Quality Initiative (K/DOQI), is to improve the quality of care and outcomes of all individuals with kidney disease by developing clinical practice guidelines for the management of patients in earlier stages of kidney disease. This guideline, *Chronic Kidney Disease: Evaluation, Classification and Stratification*, will serve as the foundation for future guidelines by standardizing the definition and classification of stages of chronic kidney disease, laboratory evaluation of kidney disease, association of the level of kidney function with complications, and stratification of risk for adverse outcomes of kidney disease. Future guidelines will focus on diagnosis and treatment of complications of earlier stages of kidney disease, ameliorating its complications, retarding the progression of the disease, reducing the morbidity and mortality of cardiovascular disease, and reducing the morbidity and mortality of kidney failure. The ultimate objectives are to improve the quality of care and outcomes of all individuals with kidney disease and to reduce the risk of developing kidney disease.

THE PROBLEM

Chronic kidney disease is a worldwide public health problem. In the United States, there is a rising incidence and prevalence of kidney failure, with poor outcomes and high cost. The incidence and prevalence of end-stage renal disease (ESRD) have doubled in the past 10 years and are expected to continue to rise steadily in the future (Fig 2). Data from the 2000 Annual Data Report of the US Renal Data System (USRDS) documents the incidence of ESRD in 1998 of more than 85,000, or 308 per million individuals per year at risk. The point prevalence of ESRD on December 31, 1998 was more than 320,000, or 1,160 per million population, of whom 72% were treated by dialysis and 28% had functioning kidney transplants.

Despite advances in dialysis and transplantation, the prognosis of kidney failure remains bleak. The USRDS reports more than 63,000 deaths of patients with ESRD in 1998, and an annual mortality rate of dialysis patients in excess of 20%. Expected remaining lifetimes of patients treated by dialysis were far shorter than the age-matched general population, varying (depending on gender and race) from 7.1 to 11.5 years for patients aged 40 to 44 years, and from 2.7 to 3.9 years for patients aged 60 to 64 years. Morbidity

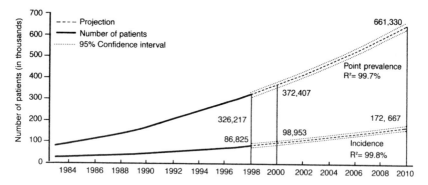

Fig 2. Incidence and prevalence of end-stage renal disease in the United States. Incident patients refers to new cases during the year. Point prevalent patients refers to patients alive on December 31st of the year. Solid vertical lines represent complete data for 1998 and expected data for 2000. Projections for future years are based on extrapolation of regression equations. R^2 for regression equations is given. Data from USRDS 2000 Annual Data Report.[4]

of kidney failure is also high. The mean number of comorbid conditions in dialysis patients is approximately 4 per patient, the mean number of hospital days per year is approximately 15, and self-reported quality of life is far lower than the general population. Total Medicare and non-Medicare costs for ESRD treatment in 1998 were $12.0 billion and $4.7 billion, respectively. There is an even higher prevalence of earlier stages of chronic kidney disease. Mortality, morbidity, hospitalizations, quality of life, and costs for caring for patients with earlier stages of chronic kidney disease have not been systematically studied.

Historically, the evaluation and management of chronic kidney disease has focused on diagnosis and treatment of specific kidney diseases, and dialysis or transplantation for kidney failure. Increasing evidence, accrued in the past decades, indicates that the adverse outcomes of chronic kidney disease can be prevented or delayed through interventions during earlier stages of chronic kidney disease, irrespective of the cause. Unfortunately, chronic kidney disease is "under-diagnosed" and "under-treated" in the United States. This leads to lost opportunities for prevention of complications and worse outcomes for patients with chronic kidney disease.

STRATEGIES FOR EARLY DETECTION AND INTERVENTION

Earlier stages of kidney disease can be detected through laboratory testing. Measurement of serum creatinine and estimation of GFR can identify patients with reduced kidney function. Measurement of urinary albumin excretion can identify some, but not all, patients with kidney damage. Screening asymptomatic individuals at increased risk could allow earlier detection of chronic kidney disease.

Currently, the US Preventive Health Services Task Force does not recommend urinalysis or measurement of serum creatinine in otherwise healthy adults. Until recently, recommendations for screening for chronic kidney disease in adults were largely focused on patients with hypertension. A recent analysis of the NHANES III database indicated that only 70% of individuals in the United States with elevated serum creatinine had hypertension.[5] More recent guidelines by the NKF–Proteinuria, Albuminuria, Risk Assessment, Detection, and Elimination (PARADE)[6,7] and the American Diabetes Association[8] recommend periodic evaluation of all individuals at increased risk for kidney disease and those with diabetes for albuminuria. Appropriate measurement and interpretation of urine albumin and serum creatinine in all individuals with hypertension and diabetes could identify a large number of patients with earlier stages of chronic kidney disease. However, it is likely that evaluation programs targeting only individuals with hypertension and diabetes will miss a large number of individuals with other causes of chronic kidney disease. Testing criteria could be expanded beyond just diabetes or hypertension, as recommended in the NKF-PARADE position paper.

Therapeutic interventions at earlier stages of chronic kidney disease are effective in slowing the progression of chronic kidney disease. The major therapeutic strategies that have been tested include strict blood glucose control in diabetes, strict blood pressure control, angiotensin-converting enzyme (ACE) inhibitors and angiotensin-receptor blockers, and dietary protein restriction. The study of kidney diseases in the transplant population has long focused on prevention and treatment of allograft rejection. Thus far, no large-scale clinical trials of kidney transplant recipients have evaluated therapies that are effective in slowing progression of diseases in native kidneys. However, within the past few years, observational studies have demonstrated that non-immunological factors, such as proteinuria and higher blood pressure, appear to be risk factors in diseases of transplanted as well as native kidneys.

Conceivably, treatment of CVD risk factors in earlier stages of chronic kidney disease could reduce adverse outcomes of cardiovascular disease before and after development of kidney failure. However, few patients with chronic kidney disease have been included in population-based epidemiological studies of cardiovascular disease or long-term, randomized clinical trials. Therefore, the NKF Task Force on Cardiovascular Disease developed an evidence model for cardiovascular disease in chronic kidney disease (Fig 3) and developed criteria for extrapolation of evidence on the efficacy of risk-factor reduction therapies from the general population to patients with chronic kidney disease. In general, the Task Force concluded that most interventions that are effective in the general population should also be applied to patients with chronic kidney disease. The NKF has initiated two other K/DOQI Work Groups that are developing clinical practice guidelines for the evaluation and management of specific cardiovascular disease risk factors in defined target populations with chronic kidney disease. These will be available in the near future. In addition, other professional organizations are focusing on other risk factors or other target populations.

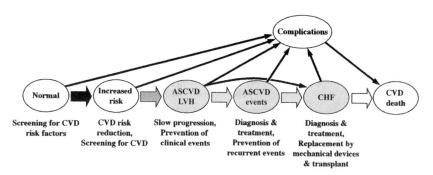

Fig 3. Evidence model for stages in the initiation and progression of cardiovascular disease, and therapeutic interventions. Shaded ellipses represent stages of cardiovascular disease; unshaded ellipses represent potential antecedents or consequences of CVD. Thick arrows between ellipses represent factors associated with initiation and progression of disease that can be affected or detected by interventions: susceptibility factors (black); initiation factors (dark gray); progression factors (light gray); and end-stage factors (white). Interventions for each stage are given beneath the stage. Individuals who appear normal should be screened for CVD risk factors. Individuals known to be at increased risk for CVD should be screened for CVD. Modified and reprinted with permission.[9]

OVERVIEW OF CURRENT STATUS OF TREATMENT FOR CHRONIC KIDNEY DISEASE

It is difficult to evaluate the current status of treatment for chronic kidney disease. A systematic search yielded few guidelines for diagnosis and management of earlier stages of chronic kidney disease (Table 7). While the USRDS is charged with compiling and reporting data on incidence, prevalence, outcomes, and cost of dialysis and transplantation, patients with earlier stages of chronic kidney disease are not systematically tracked by any public health agency in the United States. In addition, standards of care have not been defined in a universally accepted format. Therefore, there is no ongoing effort to ascertain adherence to standards for care or outcomes for patients with earlier stages of chronic kidney disease. The National Institute for Diabetes, Digestive and Kidney Disease is beginning a prospective cohort study of patients with decreased GFR to determine factors that are associated with adverse outcomes of chronic kidney disease. However, even in the absence of such studies, there is substantial evidence of "under-diagnosis" and "under-treatment."

Analysis of data from NHANES III on the adequacy of drug treatment of hypertension in patients with elevated serum creatinine revealed that only 75% of patients with hypertension and elevated serum creatinine had received treatment.[5] However, only 11% had their blood pressure reduced to <130/85 mmHg, the level recommended by the Sixth Report of the Joint National Committee on the Prevention, Detection, Evaluation and Treatment of High Blood Pressure (JNC VI), and the NKF to slow the progression of

Table 7. Published Guidelines and Recommendation for Chronic Kidney Disease

Year	Topic	Stage of CKD	Format	Organization
1993	Optimal Hemodialysis Prescription	Kidney Failure	CPG	RPA
1994	Reducing Morbidity and Mortality in Dialysis Patients	Kidney Failure	Workshop Report	NIH
1994[a]	Standards of Care for Diabetes Mellitus	Kidney Damage, ↓ GFR	Position Paper	ADA
1995	Prevention of Progression	↓ GFR	Workshop Report	NIH
1995	Treatment of Patients with Renal Failure	Kidney Disease	Consensus	Royal College of Physicians
1995	Kidney Transplant Recipient Evaluation	Kidney Failure	CPG	ASTP
1995	Screening and Management of Microalbuminuria in Diabetes	Kidney Damage	Consensus Conference	NKF
1996[a]	Diabetic Nephropathy	Kidney Damage, ↓ GFR	Position Paper	ADA
1997[b]	Hemodialysis Adequacy	Kidney Failure	CPG	NKF DOQI
1997[b]	Peritoneal Dialysis Adequacy	Kidney Failure	CPG	NKF DOQI
1997[b]	Anemia	Kidney Failure	CPG	NKF DOQI
1997[b]	Hemodialysis Vascular Access	Kidney Failure	CPG	NKF DOQI
1998	Criteria for Renal Transplantation	Kidney Failure	Consensus Conference	AST
1998	Cardiovascular Disease	Kidney Failure, ↓ GFR	Special Report	NKF
1998	Conservative Management of Chronic and Progressive Renal Failure	↓ GFR	CPG	New Zealand Nephrologist Consensus Group
1999	Proteinuria (PARADE)	Kidney Damage	Position Paper	NKF
1999	Anemia	Kidney Failure, ↓ GFR	CPG	Working Party for European Best Practice Guidelines
1999	Initiation of Dialysis	Kidney Failure	CPG	Canadian Society of Nephrology
1999	Anemia	Kidney Failure, ↓ GFR	CPG	Canadian Society of Nephrology
1999	Vascular Access	Kidney Failure	CPG	Canadian Society of Nephrology
1999	Delivery of Hemodialysis	Kidney Failure	CPG	Canadian Society of Nephrology
1999	Adequacy and Nutrition in Peritoneal Dialysis	Kidney Failure	CPG	Canadian Society of Nephrology
1999	Recommendations for Management and Referral	↓ GFR	CPG	Canadian Society of Nephrology
2000	Nutrition	Kidney Failure	CPG	NKF-K/DOQI
2000	Initiation and Withdrawal of Dialysis	Kidney Failure	CPG	RPA/ASN
2000	Kidney Transplant Recipient Monitoring	↓ GFR	CPG	AST
2001	Hypertension	Kidney Damage, ↓ GFR	Position Paper	NKF

[a] Updated in 2001; [b] Updated in 2000

Abbreviations: ADA, American Diabetes Association; AST, American Society of Transplantation; ASTP, American Society of Transplant Physicians; CPG, clinical practice guideline; DOQI, Dialysis Outcomes Quality Initiative; K/DOQI, Kidney Disease Outcomes Quality Initiative; NIH, National Institutes of Health; NKF, National Kidney Foundation; RPA, Renal Physicians Association

chronic kidney disease. Only 27% had their blood pressure reduced to <140/90 mm Hg, the level recommended by JNC-VI to prevent cardiovascular disease in individuals without pre-existing target organ damage.

In another study, hospital records from Medicare beneficiaries in Georgia were analyzed for adequacy of diagnosis and ACE inhibitor treatment of diabetic and hypertensive kidney disease.[10] Among patients with diabetes, urine protein was measured in only 63%. Among those with proteinuria, ACE-inhibitors were prescribed in only 33% and the finding was recorded in the discharge summary in only 8%. Serum creatinine was measured in 97% of diabetic patients. Among those with elevated serum creatinine, ACE-inhibitors were prescribed in only 32% and the finding was reported in the discharge summary in only 10%. Among nondiabetic patients with hypertension, tests for urine protein were performed in only 59%. Among those with proteinuria, ACE-inhibitors were prescribed in only 13% and the finding was recorded in the discharge summary in only 13%. Serum creatinine was measured in 91% of nondiabetic hypertensive patients. Among those with elevated serum creatinine, ACE-inhibitors were prescribed in only 26% and the finding was recorded in the discharge summary in only 11%. Thus, neither elderly diabetic nor hypertensive patients, who are at increased risk for chronic kidney disease, were adequately evaluated or treated with proven agents.

Data from the second phase of USRDS Dialysis Morbidity and Mortality Study (DMMS Wave 2) was analyzed for adequacy of preparation for initiation of dialysis.[11] Among patients beginning hemodialysis, 52% of patients had severe anemia (hematocrit <28%), 54% did not have a permanent vascular access (temporary catheter for 60 days of initiation of dialysis), 39% were referred to a nephrologist late (less than 3 months prior to initiation of dialysis), and 24% initiated dialysis at very low levels of kidney function (estimated GFR <5 mL/min/1.73 m^2). Among patients beginning peritoneal dialysis, 42% had severe anemia, 27% were referred to a nephrologist late, and 19% initiated dialysis with very low levels of kidney function.

These are but a few examples from a literature replete with evidence of inadequate diagnosis and treatment of earlier stages of chronic kidney disease, even though appropriate interventions have been shown to improve outcomes. Overall, these findings suggest that diagnosis and treatment in the community fall far short of the few recommended guidelines that have been developed.

PART 3. CHRONIC KIDNEY DISEASE AS A PUBLIC HEALTH PROBLEM

The purpose of this section is to review the general state of knowledge at the start of the Work Group. This review will provide a detailed framework for the questions the Work Group chose to ask (Table 8).

PUBLIC HEALTH APPROACH TO CHRONIC KIDNEY DISEASE

Solutions to public health problems require strategies for prevention of adverse outcomes of disease. Prevention requires a clear understanding of prevalence and outcomes of disease, earlier stages of disease, antecedent risk factors, and appropriate treatments for populations at risk. There is a spectrum of risk for adverse outcomes, ranging from "very high risk" in those with the disease, to "high risk" in those with risk factors for developing the disease, to "low risk" for those without the disease or its risk factors. The population as a whole includes many more individuals at low risk than at high risk. Public health measures addressing chronic diseases include strategies to prevent adverse outcomes in individuals at very high risk and high risk, as well as widespread adoption of life-style modifications to reduce the average risk profile of the population.

With regard to risk stratification for adverse outcomes from chronic kidney disease, patients with chronic kidney disease would be included in the "very high risk" group. Individuals without chronic kidney disease, but with risk factors for chronic kidney disease ("CKD risk factors"), would constitute the "high risk" group. Individuals without chronic kidney disease or CKD risk factors would constitute the "low risk" group.

Most chronic kidney diseases tend to progress and worsen over time. The risk of adverse outcomes in chronic kidney disease can be further stratified by the severity of disease and rate of progression. Therefore, for most patients, the risk of adverse outcomes tends to increase over time.

The major task of the Work Group was to develop "A Clinical Action Plan"—an approach to chronic kidney disease that relates stages of severity of chronic kidney disease to strategies for prevention and treatment of adverse outcomes.

To accomplish this task it was first necessary to outline the conceptual approach, including operational definitions of chronic kidney disease and the stages of severity of chronic kidney disease; determination of the prevalence of chronic kidney disease; issues in the evaluation and management of various types of chronic kidney disease; definition of individuals at increased risk of chronic kidney disease; definition of outcomes of chronic kidney disease; association of complications of chronic kidney disease with decreased kidney function; modalities of kidney replacement therapy; and an approach to chronic kidney disease using the guidelines.

STAGES OF SEVERITY OF CHRONIC KIDNEY DISEASE

The USRDS provides reliable nationwide data regarding the incidence, prevalence, treatment patterns, outcomes, and cost of the end-stage renal disease, the most severe stage of chronic kidney disease. There are no uniform definitions of earlier stages of kidney

Table 8. Questions and Methods

	Questions	Part, Section; Guideline	Method of Evidence Review; Types of Studies
1	*Chronic Kidney Disease: A Clinical Action Plan*	Part 1, Executive Summary	Overall synthesis
2	*Operational definition of chronic kidney disease and stages of chronic kidney disease*	Part 4, Classification; Guideline 1	Overall synthesis
3	*What is the prevalence of stages of chronic kidney disease in the United States?*	Part 4, Classification; Guideline 1	Analysis of primary data; NHANES III
4	*What is the prevalence of dipstick-positive proteinuria in children, and what is the normal range for proteinuria in children?*	Part 4, Classification; Guideline 1	Review of primary articles: Cross-sectional studies Analysis of primary data; NHANES III
5	*What is the prevalence of elevated albumin-to-creatinine ratio in adults, and in subgroups defined by age and by level of GFR?*	Part 4, Classification; Guideline 1	Analysis of primary data; NHANES III
6	*What are normal values of GFR during growth and aging?*	Part 4, Classification; Guideline 1	Review of textbooks, reviews and primary articles; Cross-sectional and longitudinal studies
7	*What is the prevalence of decreased GFR in the general population and in subgroups of the population defined by age?*	Part 4, Classification; Guideline 1	Analysis of primary data; NHANES III
8	*What is the level of GFR corresponding to the onset of kidney failure?*	Part 4, Classification; Guideline 1	Review of primary articles; Cross-sectional studies
9	*What are the major types (diagnosis) of chronic kidney disease?*	Part 4, Classification; Guideline 2	Review of textbooks and reviews
10	*What are the actions necessary for evaluation and management of chronic kidney disease, irrespective of diagnosis?*	Part 4, Classification; Guideline 2	Review of textbooks and reviews
11	*What are the risk factors for chronic kidney disease, and what is the prevalence of individuals at increased risk?*	Part 4, Classification; Guideline 3	Review of textbooks, reviews, and primary articles; Cross-sectional studies.
12	*Are estimates of GFR based on prediction equations incorporating serum creatinine and other factors more accurate than estimates of GFR based on serum creatinine alone or measurement of creatinine clearance?*	Part 5, Evaluation; Guideline 4	Review of primary articles; Studies of diagnostic testing
13	*Are spot urine albumin-to-creatinine ratio and the spot total urine protein-to-creatinine ratio accurate measures of urine albumin and total protein excretion rates, respectively?*	Part 5, Evaluation; Guideline 5	Review of primary articles; Studies of diagnostic testing
14	*What is the relationship between markers of kidney damage, types of chronic kidney disease, and clinical presentations?*	Part 5, Evaluation; Guideline 6	Review of textbooks and reviews
15	*Are other urinary markers of kidney damage applicable for clinical practice?*	Part 5, Evaluation; Guideline 6	Review of primary articles; Studies of diagnostic testing
16 –21	*What is the level of GFR at the onset of high blood pressure, anemia, malnutrition, bone disease, neuropathy, and impaired overall functioning and well-being?*	Part 7, Association; Guidelines 8–12	Review of primary articles; Cross-sectional studies Analysis of primary data; NHANES III and other studies
22	*What risk factors are associated with more rapid loss of kidney function?*	Part 7, Stratification; Guideline 13	Review of primary articles; Cohort studies
23	*Among patients with diabetes, what is the association of relationship of presence and severity of kidney disease to the risk of diabetic complications?*	Part 7, Stratification; Guideline 14	Review of reviews; Cross-sectional studies Review of primary articles; Cohort studies
24	*Is chronic kidney disease a risk factor for the development of cardiovascular disease?*	Part 7, Stratification; Guideline 15	Review of reviews; Cross-sectional studies Review of primary articles; Cohort studies
25	*Can the classifications of severity, diagnosis (types), and clinical presentations of chronic kidney disease be integrated to simplify the diagnostic and therapeutic approach?*	Part 9, Approach to CKD	Overall synthesis

disease, nor is there reliable information on the prevalence, treatment patterns, outcomes, and cost of these earlier stages, nor information on how many people choose to forego dialysis and transplantation despite kidney failure. Risk factors for the development of chronic kidney disease have not been well described, and there is no reliable estimate of the size of the population at risk. This section introduces the rationale for developing a definition of chronic kidney disease and classification of stages of severity; risk factors for adverse outcomes of chronic kidney disease; the relationship between disease severity and rate of progression as risks for adverse outcomes; the definitions and stages defined by the Work Group; and laboratory tests for the detection of each stage.

Rationale for Developing a Definition of Chronic Kidney Disease and Classification of Stages of Severity

Defining chronic kidney disease and classifying the stages of severity would provide a common language for communication among providers, patients and their families, investigators, and policy-makers, and a framework for developing a public health approach to affect care and improve outcomes of chronic kidney disease. A uniform terminology would permit:

1. More reliable estimates of the prevalence of earlier stages of disease and of the population at increased risk for development of chronic kidney disease;
2. Recommendations for laboratory testing to detect earlier stages and progression to later stages;
3. Associations of stages with clinical manifestations of disease;
4. Evaluation of factors associated with a high risk of progression from one stage to the next or of development of other adverse outcomes;
5. Evaluation of treatments to slow progression or prevent other adverse outcomes.

Clinical practice guidelines, clinical performance measures, and continuous quality improvement efforts could then be directed to stages of chronic kidney disease.

Defining chronic kidney disease and stages of severity requires "categorization" of continuous measures of markers of kidney damage and level of kidney function. Identifying the stage of chronic kidney disease in an individual is not a substitute for diagnosis of the type of kidney disease or the accurate assessment of the level of kidney function in that individual. However, recognition of the stage of chronic kidney disease would facilitate application of guidelines, performance measures, and quality improvement efforts.

In other fields of medicine, classifications of stages of severity of illness have been adopted with apparent success, such as the New York Heart Association classification of heart disease. Within nephrology and related disciplines, classifications of disease severity have been developed that are based on "categorization" of continuous measures of disease severity. For example, the Joint National Committee for the Prevention, Detection, Evaluation and Treatment of High Blood Pressure has defined stages of hypertension based on blood pressure level. The National Cholesterol Education Program has defined stages of hypercholesterolemia based on serum cholesterol level. Diabetic kidney disease is classified according to the magnitude of albuminuria. Criteria for enrollment into the Medicare ESRD Program and "listing" for cadaveric kidney transplantation are based, in part, on the level of serum creatinine. These classifications have facilitated epidemiological studies, clinical trials, and application of clinical practice guidelines.

Risk Factors for Adverse Outcomes of Chronic Kidney Disease

A risk factor is defined as an attribute that is associated with increased risk of an outcome. In principle, there are four kinds of risk factors for adverse outcomes of chronic kidney

Table 9. Types of Risk Factors for Adverse Outcomes of Chronic Kidney Disease

Type	Definition
Susceptibility factors	Increased susceptibility to kidney damage
Initiation factors	Directly initiate kidney damage
Progression factors	Cause worsening kidney damage and faster decline in kidney function after initiation of kidney damage
End-stage factors	Cause complications in patients with kidney failure

disease which were defined by the Work Group as "CKD risk factors" (Table 9). This guideline concerns itself primarily with identifying susceptibility and initiation factors to define individuals at high risk of developing chronic kidney disease, and with progression factors, to define individuals at high risk of worsening kidney damage and subsequent loss of kidney function.

Relationship Between Disease Severity and Rate of Progression as Risks for Adverse Outcomes

In principle, one may distinguish between the severity of disease and the risk for adverse outcomes of disease. The severity of disease can be determined from measurements of level of organ function, complications in other organ systems, morbidity (symptoms and clinical findings), and impairment in overall function and well-being. In general, the risk for adverse outcomes is related to the severity of disease. In addition, the risk for adverse outcomes is also dependent on the rate of progression to a more severe stage or the rate of regression to a less severe stage.

For the case of chronic kidney disease, these concepts can be illustrated by Fig 4.

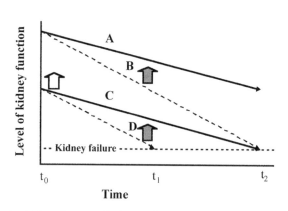

Fig 4. Kidney function decline in chronic kidney disease. See text.

The vertical axis shows the level of kidney function. The horizontal axis shows time over an interval of several years. The horizontal dotted line corresponds to the level of kidney function at the onset of kidney failure. The declines in kidney function in 4 individual patients (A through D) are illustrated as diagonal lines. At the discovery of chronic kidney disease (t_0), patients A and B share identical levels of kidney function, as do patients C and D, but the level of function is lower in patients C and D than for patients A and B. Patients A and C have identical rates of decline in kidney function, as do patients B and D, but the rate of decline is faster in patients B and D than in patients A and C. Patient D, with the lower initial level of kidney function and the faster rate of decline in kidney function, reaches kidney failure first (t_1). Patient B, with the higher initial level of kidney function but faster rate of decline, and patient C, with the lower initial level of kidney function and slower rate of decline, reach kidney failure at the same time (t_2). Patient A, with the higher initial level of kidney function and the slower rate of decline in kidney function, has not reached kidney failure by the end of follow-up (t_2). Figure 4 illustrates that the risk of developing kidney failure depends both on the level of kidney function at the discovery of chronic kidney disease and the rate of decline in kidney function. The object of therapy for chronic kidney disease would be to detect kidney disease at a higher level of kidney function (open arrow) and to reduce the rate of decline in kidney function thereafter (filled arrows), thereby reducing adverse outcomes of chronic kidney disease.

Operational Definition of Chronic Kidney Disease and Stages

One of the first tasks of the Work Group was to define chronic kidney disease, irrespective of the specific pathological features of the disease. For this definition, the Work Group used a combination of the presence of kidney damage and level of kidney function.

Definition and Detection of Kidney Damage

Chronic kidney damage is defined as structural abnormalities of the kidney that can lead to decreased kidney function. The level of glomerular filtration rate (GFR) is accepted as the best measure of overall kidney function in health and disease. Pathologic studies show that substantial kidney damage can be sustained without decreased GFR. Micro-puncture studies in animal models of chronic kidney disease show that the maintenance of normal GFR despite kidney damage is due to an adaptive increase in glomerular capil-lary blood flow and pressure in response to decreased ultrafiltration coefficient and reduced number of nephrons.

Markers of kidney damage vary depending on the type of kidney disease and may include abnormalities in the composition of the blood or urine or abnormalities in imaging tests, with or without decreased GFR. For example, albuminuria is widely accepted as a marker of glomerular damage, and the excretion of even small amounts of albumin (microalbuminuria) is the earliest manifestation of diabetic kidney disease. In large amounts, albumin excretion can readily be detected by tests of total urine protein, whereas detection of minimal amounts requires specific, sensitive assays.

One of the major obstacles to detection of kidney damage using measurements of urine albumin or total protein is the necessity for collection of a timed urine sample.

Recently, many investigators have provided evidence that the ratio of concentrations of albumin-to-creatinine or total protein-to-creatinine in a spot urine sample accurately reflects the excretion rates of albumin or total protein in timed urine samples. One of the questions posed by the Work Group was: *Do spot urine albumin-to-creatinine ratio and total protein-to-creatinine ratio provide accurate measures of urine albumin and protein excretion rates, respectively?*

In addition to its importance as a marker of kidney damage, albuminuria is also an important prognostic factor for the progression of kidney disease and development of cardiovascular disease. The NKF issued a position paper in 1999 on the evaluation and management of adults with albuminuria. The initiative, known as "Proteinuria, Albuminuria, Risk Assessment, Detection, and Elimination (PARADE)," emphasizes findings related to proteinuria as a risk factor for cardiovascular disease, proteinuria as a mediator and marker of progressive kidney disease, and persistent massive proteinuria as the inciting factor that leads to the nephrotic syndrome.[6] An accompanying report on the evaluation and management of proteinuria and nephrotic syndrome in children was issued in 2000.[7] The CKD Work Group has used the recommendations of PARADE in developing its recommendations for laboratory testing and evaluation of proteinuria and albuminuria.

Other examples of markers of damage in chronic kidney disease include abnormalities in the urine sediment and abnormalities on imaging studies of the kidney. One of the questions posed by the Work Group was: *Are other urinary markers of kidney damage applicable for clinical practice?*

High blood pressure was not defined as a marker of kidney damage because high blood pressure has other causes. The relationship between high blood pressure and kidney disease is complex, as high blood pressure is both a cause and a consequence of kidney disease. Throughout the guideline, the Work Group has provided information on high blood pressure, including the prevalence of high blood pressure at stages of chronic kidney disease, and the role of high blood pressure as a risk factor for loss of kidney function.

Definition and Detection of Decreased GFR and Relationship With Age

As a rule, kidney failure due to chronic kidney disease is preceded by a stage of variable length during which GFR is decreased. GFR is affected by a number of factors in addition to kidney disease, and not all individuals with decreased GFR have chronic kidney disease. Mild reduction in GFR was defined as chronic kidney disease only in the presence of kidney damage (Stage 2). However, because of the risk of complications, moderate (Stage 3) to severe (Stage 4) reduction in GFR and kidney failure (Stage 5) were defined as chronic kidney disease, irrespective of the presence of kidney damage. Other than kidney disease, the most important factor affecting GFR is age. GFR rises during infancy and declines during aging. Therefore, mild reduction in GFR may be "normal" at the extremes of age and, in the absence of kidney damage, is not considered to be chronic kidney disease. A clinical action plan based on the level of GFR requires knowledge of age-associated normal values. One of the questions posed by the Work Group was: *What are normal values of GFR during growth and aging?*

Unfortunately, measurement of GFR is inconvenient, and in most studies, as in clinical practice, the level of kidney function is estimated from the serum creatinine concentration. This is difficult because a variety of factors other than GFR, including age, gender, race, and body size, affect the serum creatinine concentration. To circumvent these limitations, most clinical texts recommend measuring creatinine clearance to estimate the level of GFR. However, as indicated previously, collection of a timed urine specimen can be difficult. One of the questions posed by the Work Group was: *Are estimates of GFR based on prediction equations incorporating serum creatinine as well as these other factors more accurate than estimates of GFR based on serum creatinine alone or measurement of creatinine clearance?*

Definition and Detection of Kidney Failure

Most texts define kidney failure as severe reduction in kidney function that is not compatible with life, because its attendant complications become increasing risks for mortality. Individuals at this stage have been said to have "end-stage renal disease" (ESRD) because they require dialysis or transplantation to sustain life. Since 1972, the Medicare ESRD Program has borne 80% of the costs of dialysis and transplantation for approximately 93% of patients in the United States, allowing near universal access to treatment for kidney failure. Indeed, treatment with dialysis or transplantation has become almost synonymous with the diagnosis of chronic kidney failure. Such a definition of kidney failure has obvious operational and administrative advantages. However, it lacks precision. First, patients who have kidney failure may survive for variable periods of time without treatment by dialysis or transplantation. Second, some signs and symptoms of kidney failure appear at higher levels of kidney function that are compatible with long survival. Third, some have advocated "early initiation of dialysis" or "pre-emptive" kidney transplantation prior to the onset of kidney failure. Fourth, many patients living with dialysis or a kidney transplant find the phrase "end-stage" threatening and misleading. Thus, it would be preferable to define kidney failure as a combination of signs and symptoms of uremia and a specific level of kidney function. One of the questions posed by the Work Group was: *Is it possible to identify the level of kidney function corresponding to the stage of kidney failure?*

PREVALENCE OF CHRONIC KIDNEY DISEASE

As described earlier, the USRDS tracks the prevalence of kidney failure in the United States. One of the questions posed by the Work Group was: *What is the prevalence of earlier stages of chronic kidney disease, based on the definitions and methods for measurement discussed above?*

Prevalence of Kidney Damage

Guidelines by the American Academy of Pediatricians recommend screening school-age children for proteinuria using the urine dipstick. Therefore, a large number of studies have been conducted to estimate the prevalence of proteinuria in children. One of the questions posed by the Work Group was: *What is the prevalence of dipstick-positive proteinuria in children?* On the other hand, fewer studies have determined the normal range of proteinuria in children. Another question asked by the Work Group was: *What is the normal value for proteinuria in children?*

In contrast, current guidelines by the US Preventive Health Services Task Force do not suggest routine screening of adults for proteinuria. Data from two community-based screening programs, the Framingham Study[12] and the Okinawa Study,[13] demonstrate an approximately 10% prevalence of dipstick-positive proteinuria in adults. The prevalence was higher in older than younger individuals and higher in women than men. However, there are serious limitations to these studies. First, the urine dipstick is not sensitive to small amounts of albumin, and thus these studies would not have detected most patients with microalbuminuria. Second, neither timed urine collections nor protein-to-creatinine ratios were measured, and thus the dipstick test result was affected by the state of diuresis in addition to the magnitude of proteinuria. Furthermore, at least some of the individuals in these studies with proteinuria also had reduced kidney function. Thus, they provide only a rough guide to the likely prevalence of individuals with kidney damage due to chronic kidney disease. Another question posed by the Work Group was: *What is the prevalence of elevated urine albumin-to-creatinine ratio in adults; and in subgroups defined by age and level of GFR?*

Prevalence of Decreased GFR

A 1998 report from the third cycle of the National Health and Nutrition Examination Survey (NHANES III), conducted from 1988 to 1994, estimated that 6.2 million individuals over age 12 years had reduced kidney function, defined as a serum creatinine concentration ≥ 1.5 mg/dL[1] (Fig 5). This represents an almost 30-fold higher prevalence of reduced kidney function compared to the prevalence of ESRD during the same interval. This same report estimated that there were 2.5 million individuals with serum creatinine ≥ 1.7 mg/dL and 800,000 individuals with serum creatinine ≥ 2.0 mg/dL. Because of differences

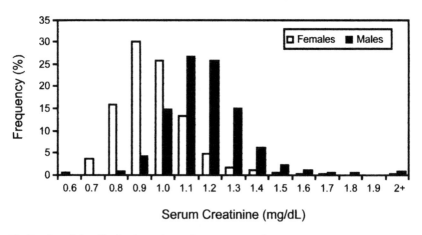

Fig 5.   Creatinine distribution: US population age ≥ 20 by sex, NHANES III, 1988–1994, N = 15,600.

in creatinine generation, the prevalence of elevated serum creatinine varied by age, gender, and ethnicity, with a higher prevalence in older compared to younger individuals, in men compared to women, and in non-Hispanic blacks compared to non-Hispanic whites or Mexican-Americans. As discussed later in this report, these apparently minor elevations in serum creatinine may well reflect substantial decreases in GFR, especially in the elderly. This suggests that the number of individuals with reduced kidney function, defined as reduced GFR, may be much higher than these estimates based on increased serum creatinine levels. One of the questions posed by the Work Group was: *What is the prevalence of decreased GFR in the general population and in subgroups defined by age?*

EVALUATION AND MANAGEMENT OF CHRONIC KIDNEY DISEASE

Diagnosis of chronic kidney disease is based primarily on etiologic and pathologic classification. Refinements in serologic tests and introduction of percutaneous biopsy technique have led to increasingly sophisticated classifications. Unfortunately, nomenclature has not been standardized, which hampers the development of strategies for prevention and treatment.[14] It is anticipated that a future Work Group will address the role of kidney biopsy. *One of the tasks of the Work Group was to recommend a classification of the types of kidney disease for application of these guidelines.*

Another task was to describe the actions necessary for evaluation and management of chronic kidney disease, irrespective of diagnosis. The Work Group recommended that these tasks be grouped as follows: treatment of comorbid conditions, prevention or slowing the loss of kidney function, prevention and treatment of cardiovascular disease, prevention and treatment of complications of decreased kidney function, preparation for kidney failure, and replacement of kidney function (if necessary and desired) by dialysis and kidney transplantation.

INDIVIDUALS AT INCREASED RISK FOR CHRONIC KIDNEY DISEASE

Data from the USRDS indicates the incidence of ESRD is disproportionately high among older individuals, certain ethnic minorities, and individuals with hypertension, diabetes, and autoimmune diseases. This suggests that demographic and clinical factors may be risk factors for the development or progression of chronic kidney disease. In addition, individuals with a family history of kidney disease appear to be at higher risk of developing kidney disease. This appears to be true for most types of kidney diseases, suggesting the presence of genes coding for susceptibility factors for the development or progression of kidney disease in general, as well as genes coding for specific kidney diseases, such as autosomal dominant polycystic kidney disease or Alport's syndrome. Finally, patients who have recovered from an episode of acute kidney failure, whether due to acute tubular necrosis or other parenchymal diseases, may also be at risk of developing chronic kidney disease.

The prevalence of individuals at increased risk for development of chronic kidney disease has not been studied systematically. *One of the tasks of the Work Group was to assemble a list of potential CKD risk factors and the prevalence of individuals with these risk factors.*

OUTCOMES OF CHRONIC KIDNEY DISEASE

The Work Group considered two major outcomes of chronic kidney disease: loss of kidney function leading to kidney failure and development of cardiovascular disease. Of course, kidney failure is the most visible outcome of chronic kidney disease, and loss of kidney function is associated with complications in virtually every organ system. Cardiovascular disease was considered separately because: (1) cardiovascular disease events are more common than kidney failure in patients with chronic kidney disease; (2) cardiovascular disease in patients with chronic kidney disease is treatable and potentially preventable; and (3) chronic kidney disease appears to be a risk factor for cardiovascular disease.

Loss of Kidney Function

A number of studies have examined factors associated with more rapid loss of kidney function in chronic kidney disease. Some diseases are associated with a faster loss of kidney function than others, while some patient factors are known to predict a faster loss of function, irrespective of the underlying disease. Identification of risk factors for progression can provide insight into the mechanisms of progressive loss of kidney function as well as identification of patients at higher risk for adverse outcomes. One of the questions posed by the Work Group was: *What are the risk factors associated with a more rapid loss of kidney function?*

Cardiovascular Disease

The 1998 Report of the NKF Task Force on Cardiovascular Disease in Chronic Renal Disease drew attention to cardiovascular disease as an outcome of chronic kidney disease.[9] The Task Force recommended that patients with chronic kidney disease be considered in the "highest risk group" for subsequent cardiovascular disease (CVD) events. The excess risk of cardiovascular disease is due, in part, to a higher prevalence of conditions that are recognized as risk factors for cardiovascular disease in the general population ("traditional" CVD risk factors) and to hemodynamic and metabolic factors characteristic of chronic kidney disease ("CKD-related" CVD risk factors).

In addition, the Task Force emphasized the high mortality from cardiovascular disease. Cardiovascular disease is the leading cause of death in patients with kidney failure. After adjusting for age, gender, race, and diagnosis of diabetes, mortality from cardiovascular disease is far higher in patients with kidney failure compared to the general population. Among patients treated by dialysis, the risk ranges from 500-fold higher in individuals aged 25–35 to 5-fold higher in individuals aged >85 years (Fig 6). Excess mortality also appeared higher in kidney transplant recipients, despite the preferential selection of patients without cardiovascular disease for transplantation.

One of the questions posed by the Work Group was: *Is chronic kidney disease a*

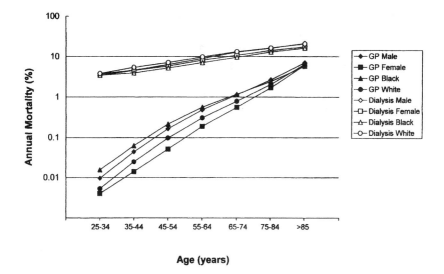

Fig 6. Cardiovascular mortality in the general population (NCHS) and in ESRD treated by dialysis (USRDS). CVD mortality defined by death due to arrhythmias, cardiomyopathy, cardiac arrest, myocardial infarction, atherosclerotic heart disease, and pulmonary edema in the general population (data from NCHS multiple cause mortality data files, ICD-9 codes 402, 404, 410–414, and 425–429, 1993) compared to ESRD treated by dialysis (data from USRDS special data request HCFA form 2746, field numbers 23, 26–29, and 31, 1994–1996). Reprinted with permission.[9]

risk factor for the development of cardiovascular disease? Because of the well-known association of cardiovascular disease and diabetes, it seemed reasonable that the analysis should distinguish patients with diabetes from other causes of chronic kidney disease. Among patients with diabetes, the Work Group summarized information related to the association of chronic kidney disease and diabetic complications. Among patients with other causes of kidney disease, the Work Group summarized information related to the association of chronic kidney disease and cardiovascular disease.

COMPLICATIONS OF DECREASED GFR

Decreased GFR is associated with complications in virtually all organ systems. These complications are manifested first by high blood pressure and abnormalities in laboratory tests and then by symptoms and abnormalities in physical examination. In general, the severity of complications worsens as level of GFR declines, although the actual levels of GFR where the complications first appear and then worsen vary depending on the complication. Among the most important complications are high blood pressure, anemia, malnutrition, bone disease, neuropathy, and decreased overall functioning and well-being. At very low levels of GFR, these complications are common and collectively known as "uremia" or the "uremic syndrome." The pathogenesis of these complications varies among organ systems and is often complex. In many cases, early treatment can prevent or ameliorate complications.

Since signs and symptoms of kidney failure appear and increase in severity as GFR declines, it should be possible to identify levels of GFR that are associated with the appearance of particular signs and symptoms. One of the questions posed by the Work Group was: *What is the level of GFR at the onset of high blood pressure, anemia, malnutrition, bone disease, neuropathy, and decreased overall functioning and well-being?*

KIDNEY REPLACEMENT THERAPY: DIALYSIS AND TRANSPLANTATION

Dialysis and transplantation are effective, although not optimal, therapies for kidney failure. The aging of the population and the rising prevalence of diseases causing chronic kidney disease, such as hypertension and diabetes, suggest that kidney failure will be a growing public health problem in the future and that dialysis and transplantation will become more widely used in the United States and around the world. These therapies require intensive resources; therefore, measures to increase the efficiency of these treatments will be necessary. It will be necessary to improve the preparation of patients for kidney replacement therapy, as well as to improve the efficacy of dialysis and transplantation.

Preparation for Kidney Replacement Therapy

Much of the morbidity of kidney failure is due to complications that arise during the stage of decreased GFR. Many studies have shown a relationship between severity of complications before kidney replacement therapy and outcomes.[15] Possibly, improved treatment during the stage of decreased GFR would lead to improved outcomes of kidney replacement therapy.

In addition, the onset of kidney failure is usually associated with severe psychosocial stress. Stress derives from the fear of complications, from treatment, from limitations of functioning and well being, and from reduced life expectancy. A team approach to the management of patients is usually required, including physicians, nurses, dietitians, social workers, pharmacists, and physical, occupational, and vocational rehabilitation professionals as well as patients' families. Patient education must begin far in advance in order to prepare patients to cope with their illness and the demands of their treatment as well as possible. Clinical practice guidelines are being developed by the Renal Physicians Association to address preparation for kidney replacement therapy.

Dialysis and Transplantation

The past decade has seen dramatic improvements in dialysis and transplantation. Advances in basic science and technology are needed to pave the way for continuing improvement. Each advance will require careful clinical study to assess its efficacy, effectiveness, and efficiency. As discussed earlier, NKF-DOQI clinical practice guidelines were restricted primarily to the care of patients with kidney failure treated by dialysis. The original DOQI guidelines have now been updated and published under the K/DOQI banner.[16] New guidelines are under development by the NKF and other organizations to address other aspects of dialysis care and the care of patients treated by kidney transplantation.

APPROACH TO CHRONIC KIDNEY DISEASE USING THESE GUIDELINES

Finally, the Work Group attempted to integrate the classifications of stages, types (diagnosis), and clinical presentations of chronic kidney disease presented in this guideline. The results provide a simplified approach to common clinical problems in chronic kidney disease, including screening, differential diagnosis, utility of proteinuria in diagnosis and treatment, estimating and slowing progression, cardiovascular disease risk assessment and reduction, clinical evaluation of adults with decreased GFR, and decreased GFR and chronic kidney disease in the elderly.

PART 4. DEFINITION AND CLASSIFICATION OF STAGES OF CHRONIC KIDNEY DISEASE

Chronic kidney disease is a major public health problem. Improving outcomes for people with chronic kidney disease requires a coordinated worldwide approach to prevention of adverse outcomes through defining the disease and its outcomes, estimating disease prevalence, identifying earlier stages of disease and antecedent risk factors, and detection and treatment for populations at increased risk for adverse outcomes. The goal of Part 4 is to create an operational definition and classification of stages of chronic kidney disease and provide estimates of disease prevalence by stage, to develop a broad overview of a "clinical action plan" for evaluation and management of each stage of chronic kidney disease, and to define individuals at increased risk for developing chronic kidney disease. Studies of disease prevalence were evaluated as described in Appendix 1, Table 150. Data from NHANES III were used to develop estimates of disease prevalence in adults as described in Appendix 2.

GUIDELINE 1. DEFINITION AND STAGES OF CHRONIC KIDNEY DISEASE

Adverse outcomes of chronic kidney disease can often be prevented or delayed through early detection and treatment. Earlier stages of chronic kidney disease can be detected through routine laboratory measurements.

- The presence of chronic kidney disease should be established, based on presence of kidney damage and level of kidney function (glomerular filtration rate [GFR]), irrespective of diagnosis.
- Among patients with chronic kidney disease, the stage of disease should be assigned based on the level of kidney function, irrespective of diagnosis, according to the K/DOQI CKD classification (Table 10).

BACKGROUND

Chronic kidney disease is a major public health problem. Adverse outcomes of chronic kidney disease can be prevented through early detection and treatment. Earlier stages of chronic kidney disease can be detected through routine laboratory measurements.

The USRDS provides reliable nationwide data regarding the incidence, prevalence, treatment patterns, outcomes, and cost of kidney failure treated by dialysis and transplantation, the most severe stage of chronic kidney disease. This guideline provides a definition of chronic kidney disease as well as definitions and estimates of prevalence of earlier stages of kidney disease.

Chronic kidney disease is defined according to the presence or absence of kidney damage and level of kidney function—irrespective of the type of kidney disease (diagnosis). Among individuals with chronic kidney disease, the stages are defined based on the level of kidney function. Identifying the presence and stage of chronic kidney disease in an individual is not a substitute for accurate assessment of the cause of kidney disease,

Table 10. Stages of Chronic Kidney Disease

Stage	Description	GFR (mL/min/1.73 m²)
1	Kidney damage with normal or ↑ GFR	≥90
2	Kidney damage with mild ↓ GFR	60–89
3	Moderate ↓ GFR	30–59
4	Severe ↓ GFR	15–29
5	Kidney failure	<15 (or dialysis)

Chronic kidney disease is defined as either kidney damage or GFR <60 mL/min/1.73 m² for ≥3 months. Kidney damage is defined as pathologic abnormalities or markers of damage, including abnormalities in blood or urine tests or imaging studies.

extent of kidney damage, level of kidney function, comorbid conditions, complications of decreased kidney function, or risks for loss of kidney function or cardiovascular disease in that patient. Defining stages of chronic kidney disease requires "categorization" of continuous measures of kidney function, and the "cut-off levels" between stages are inherently arbitrary. Nonetheless, staging of chronic kidney disease will facilitate application of clinical practice guidelines, clinical performance measures and quality improvement efforts to the evaluation, and management of chronic kidney disease.

RATIONALE

Definition and Classification

Definition of chronic kidney disease (O). Chronic kidney disease has been defined according to the criteria listed in Table 11.

Table 11. Definition of Chronic Kidney Disease

Criteria
1. Kidney damage for ≥3 months, as defined by structural or functional abnormalities of the kidney, with or without decreased GFR, manifest by *either*: • Pathological abnormalities; or • Markers of kidney damage, including abnormalities in the composition of the blood or urine, or abnormalities in imaging tests
2. GFR <60 mL/min/1.73 m² for ≥3 months, with or without kidney damage

Methods to estimate GFR are discussed in Guideline 4. Markers of kidney damage are discussed in Guidelines 5–6.

Table 12. Definition and Stages of Chronic Kidney Disease

GFR (mL/min/1.73 m²)	With Kidney Damage*		Without Kidney Damage*	
	With HBP**	Without HBP**	With HBP**	Without HBP**
≥90	1	1	"High blood pressure"	"Normal"
60–89	2	2	"High blood pressure with ↓ GFR"	"↓ GFR"ᵃ
30–59	3	3	3	3
15–29	4	4	4	4
<15 (or dialysis)	5	5	5	5

Shaded area represents chronic kidney disease; numbers designate stage of chronic kidney disease.

* Kidney damage is defined as pathologic abnormalities or markers of damage, including abnormalities in blood or urine tests or imaging studies.
** High blood pressure is defined as ≥140/90 in adults and >90th percentile for height and gender in children.

ᵃ May be normal in infants and in the elderly.

Stages of chronic kidney disease (R, O). Among individuals with chronic kidney disease, the stage is defined by the level of GFR, with higher stages representing lower GFR levels. Table 12 illustrates the classification of individuals based on the presence or absence of markers of kidney disease and level of GFR, according to definition and staging of chronic kidney disease proposed by this guideline. In addition, it includes columns for the presence or absence of high blood pressure, because of the complex relationship of high blood pressure and chronic kidney disease.

All individuals with GFR <60 mL/min/1.73 m² for ≥3 months are classified as having chronic kidney disease, irrespective of the presence or absence of kidney damage. The rationale for including these individuals is that reduction in kidney function to this level or lower represents loss of half or more of the adult level of normal kidney function, which may be associated with a number of complications (Part 6).

All individuals with kidney damage are classified as having chronic kidney disease, irrespective of the level of GFR. The rationale for including individuals with GFR ≥60 mL/min/1.73 m² is that GFR may be sustained at normal or increased levels despite substantial kidney damage and that patients with kidney damage are at increased risk of the two major outcomes of chronic kidney disease: loss of kidney function and development of cardiovascular disease (Part 7).

The methods to estimate GFR and assess markers of kidney damage are not completely sensitive or specific in detecting decreased GFR and kidney damage, respectively. Thus, misclassification is possible, and clinicians should carefully consider all aspects of the patient's clinical presentation in interpreting test results and determining evaluation and management. For the definition of chronic kidney disease, the Work Group selected cutoff levels for GFR and markers of kidney damage that maximize specificity, acknowledging potential loss of sensitivity. Clinicians should be especially careful in the evaluation of individuals with borderline abnormal results for markers of kidney disease, mild decrease in GFR (60 to 89 mL/min/1.73 m²), high blood pressure, and of other individuals at increased risk of chronic kidney disease. Risk factors for chronic kidney disease are discussed in Guideline 3.

Decreased GFR without kidney damage (R, O). Individuals with GFR 60 to 89 mL/min/1.73 m² without kidney damage are classified as "decreased GFR." Decreased GFR without recognized markers of kidney damage is very frequent in infants and older adults, and is usually considered to be "normal for age." The age-related decline in GFR in adults is accompanied by pathological findings of global glomerular sclerosis and cortical atrophy. The consequences of declining GFR with age have not been carefully studied. It is interesting to speculate whether the increasing incidence of end-stage renal disease in the elderly could be due, in part, to age-associated decline in GFR.

Other causes of chronically decreased GFR without kidney damage in adults include vegetarian diets, unilateral nephrectomy, extracellular fluid volume depletion, and systemic illnesses associated with reduced kidney perfusion, such as heart failure and cirrhosis. It is not certain whether individuals with chronically decreased GFR in the range of 60 to 89 mL/min/1.73 m² without kidney damage are at increased risk for adverse outcomes, such as toxicity from drugs excreted by the kidney or acute kidney failure. After much discussion and input from expert reviewers, the Work Group concluded that there is insufficient evidence to label individuals with GFR 60 to 89 mL/min/1.73 m², but without markers of kidney damage, as having chronic kidney disease. In clinical practice, it may be difficult to determine whether individuals with decreased GFR have chronic

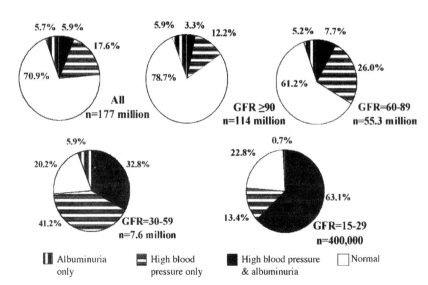

Fig 7. Prevalence of albuminuria and high blood pressure (%) in US adults age ≥20 years, NHANES III, 1988–1994. Based on one-time assessment of albuminuria, blood pressure, and estimated GFR.

Table 13. Prevalence of GFR Categories: NHANES III 1988–1994 US Adults Age ≥20

GFR (mL/min/1.73 m²)	N*	Prevalence (95% CI)	Millions of Individuals (95% CI)
≥90	10,183	64% (63–66)	114 (106–122)
60–89	4,404	31% (30–33)	55.3 (50–61)
30–59	961	4.3 % (3.8–4.7)	7.6 (6.5–8.6)
15–29	52	0.2% (0.1–0.3)	0.4 (0.2–0.5)

GFR estimated from serum creatinine using MDRD Study equation based on age, gender, race and calibration for serum creatinine.

* N is based on number of individuals in each listed GFR range in NHANES III, 1988–1994. Prevalence and number of individuals estimated by extrapolation to population of US adults age ≥20 (N = 177 million). Based on one-time assessment of estimated GFR.

kidney disease. Recommendations for a clinical approach to elderly individuals with decreased GFR is given in Part 9.

High blood pressure in chronic kidney disease and in individuals with decreased GFR without kidney disease (R). High blood pressure is not included in the definition of chronic kidney disease or its stages. However, high blood pressure is a common cause and consequence of chronic kidney disease, and as reviewed later, patients with chronic kidney disease and high blood pressure are at higher risk of loss of kidney function and development of cardiovascular disease. High blood pressure is also common in older individuals without chronic kidney disease and is associated with accelerated GFR decline with age and more marked pathological abnormalities in the kidneys. Individuals with high blood pressure should be carefully evaluated for the presence of chronic kidney disease, especially those with decreased GFR.

Prevalence of chronic kidney disease and level of kidney function in the general population (S). The prevalence of chronic kidney disease, based on the definition above, was estimated using data from NHANES III and USRDS (Fig 7 and Tables 13 and 14). For the analysis of NHANES III data, GFR was estimated from serum creatinine

Table 14. Prevalence of Stages of Chronic Kidney Disease and Levels of Kidney Function in the US

	Stages of CKD			Levels of Kidney Function		
	N (1000's)*	(%)		GFR (mL/min/1.73 m²)	N (1000's)*	(%)
1	10,500[a] 5,900	5.9[a] 3.3		≥90	114,000	64.3
2	7,100[a] 5,300	4.0[a] 3.0		60–89	55,300	31.2
3	7,600	4.3		30–59	7,600	4.3
4	400	0.2		15–29	400	0.2
5	300	0.2		<15 (or dialysis)	300	0.2

* Data for Stages 1–4 from NHANES III (1988–1994). Population of 177 million with age ≥20 years. Data for Stage 5 from USRDS (1998),[2] includes approximately 230,000 patients treated by dialysis, and assumes 70,000 additional patients not on dialysis. Percentages total >100% because NHANES III may not have included patients on dialysis. GFR estimated from serum creatinine using MDRD Study equation based on age, gender, race and calibration for serum creatinine.

[a] For Stages 1 and 2, kidney damage was assessed by spot albumin-to-creatinine ratio >17 mg/g (men) or >25 mg/g (women) on one occasion (larger prevalence estimate) or on two measurements (smaller prevalence estimate). Albuminuria was persistent in 54% of individuals with GFR ≥90 mL/min/1.73 m² (n = 102) and 73% of individuals with GFR 60–89 mL/min/1.73 m² (n = 44).

concentration using a prediction equation derived from the Modification of Diet in Renal Disease (MDRD) Study,[17,18] elevated urine albumin-to-creatinine ratio was taken as a marker of chronic kidney disease, and high blood pressure was defined as blood pressure $\geq 140/90$ mm Hg or taking medications for high blood pressure. These parameters were ascertained on a single occasion. A subgroup of NHANES III participants underwent repeat measurement of albuminuria. Elevated albumin-to-creatinine excretion was persistent in 61% of the subjects with albuminuria (n = 163). Therefore, these estimates of prevalence should be considered as rough approximations of the true prevalence. The rationales for these assumptions and cut-off levels are discussed in more detail below.

KIDNEY DAMAGE
Definition (O)
Kidney damage is defined as structural or functional abnormalities of the kidney, initially without decreased GFR, which over time can lead to decreased GFR. As described earlier, markers of kidney damage include abnormalities in the composition of the blood or urine or abnormalities in imaging tests. This section will emphasize proteinuria as a marker of kidney damage because it has been studied most thoroughly, including in NHANES III.

Proteinuria as a marker of kidney damage (R). Proteinuria is an early and sensitive marker of kidney damage in many types of chronic kidney disease. Albumin (molecular weight [MW] = 68,000 daltons) is the most abundant urine protein in most types of chronic kidney disease. Low molecular weight (LMW) globulins are the most abundant urine proteins in some types of chronic kidney disease. In this and later guidelines, the term proteinuria includes albuminuria, increased urinary excretion of other specific proteins, and increased excretion of total urine protein. On the other hand, the term albuminuria has been used only when referring to increased urinary albumin excretion. Older laboratory methods, such as the urine dipstick or acid precipitation, detect most urine proteins. Microalbuminuria refers to excretion of small but abnormal amounts of albumin, which requires recently developed, more sensitive laboratory methods that are now widely available.

Normal protein excretion (S, R). Normal mean value for urine albumin excretion in adults is approximately 10 mg/d. Albumin excretion is increased by physiological variables, such as upright posture, exercise, pregnancy, and fever. Normal mean value for urine total protein is approximately 50 mg/d. Major constituents of normal urine protein are albumin, LMW proteins filtered from the blood, and proteins derived from the urinary tract.

In practice, it is difficult to collect a timed urine specimen. As described in Guideline 5, the urinary excretion rate for albumin and total protein can be estimated from the ratio of albumin or total protein to creatinine concentration in an untimed ("spot") urine specimen. Because protein excretion varies throughout the day, the normal ratio varies throughout the day. The ratio in a first morning specimen correlates most closely with overnight protein excretion rate, whereas the ratio in mid-morning specimens correlates

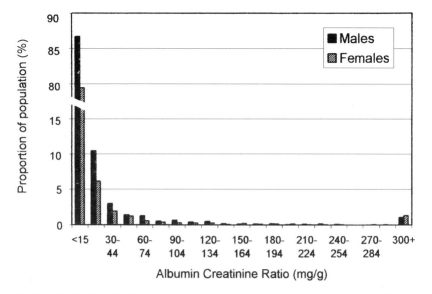

Fig 8. Distribution of albumin-to-creatinine ratio in US men and women, NHANES III (1988–1994), age ≥20. N = 14,836.

most closely with 24-hour protein excretion rate. Creatinine excretion is higher in normal men than women; therefore, the values in the general population (Fig 8) and cut-off values for abnormalities in urine albumin-to-creatinine ratio are lower for men than women (Table 15).

Definition of proteinuria and albuminuria in adults (R). Table 15 shows definitions for proteinuria and albuminuria, including gender specific cut-off values for microalbuminuria and albuminuria. Cut-points for definition of abnormal urine total protein and

Table 15. Definitions of Proteinuria and Albuminuria

	Urine Collection Method	Normal	Microalbuminuria	Albuminuria or Clinical Proteinuria
Total Protein	24-Hour Excretion (varies with method)	<300 mg/day	NA	>300 mg/day
	Spot Urine Dipstick	<30 mg/dL	NA	>30 mg/dL
	Spot Urine Protein-to-Creatinine Ratio (varies with method)	<200 mg/g	NA	>200 mg/g
Albumin	24-Hour Excretion	<30 mg/day	30–300 mg/day	>300 mg/day
	Spot Urine Albumin-Specific Dipstick	<3 mg/dL	>3 mg/dL	NA
	Spot Urine Albumin-to-Creatinine Ratio (varies by gender[a])	<17 mg/g (men) <25 mg/g (women)	17–250 mg/g (men) 25–355 mg/g (women)	>250 mg/g (men) >355 mg/g (women)

[a] Gender-specific cut-off values are from a single study.[19] Use of the same cut-off value for men and women leads to higher values of prevalence for women than men. Current recommendations from the American Diabetes Association define cut-off values for spot urine albumin-to-creatinine ratio for microalbuminuria and albuminuria as 30 and 300 mg/g, respectively, without regard to gender.[8]

albumin are set to maximize specificity (avoid false positives), thus, the upper limit of "normal" typically extends far above the normal mean value, resulting in low sensitivity (many false negatives).

Normal albumin excretion in children (C). Normal values for albumin excretion in children are not well established. Although increased urine albumin excretion reflects glomerular injury better than other urinary proteins in both adults and children, many pediatric nephrologists continue to monitor levels of total protein rather than albumin in patients with proteinuria. Hence, reports of normal albumin rates in children are

Table 16. Albumin Excretion Rate: Normal Range in Children

Author, Year	No. of Subjects*	Applic-ability**	Urine Collection Method	Albumin Excretion Rate (mg/24 hr)		Albumin Excretion Rate (µg/min)		Quality
				Mean	Range	Mean	Range	
Davies,[21] 1984	183 boys	↑↑	Split 24 hr	6.6[a] (Day: 8.2[a] Night: 4.0[a])	ND	4.6[a] (Day: 5.6[a] Night: 2.8[a])	ND	●
	191 girls			8.3[a] (Day: 11.1[a] Night: 4.3[a])		5.8[a] (Day: 7.7[a] Night: 3.0[a])		
Bangstad,[22] 1993	76: <13 y	↑↑↑	Overnight	5.3	0.3–34	3.7	0.2–23	○
	67: ≥13 y			8.4	1.6–50	5.8	1.1–35	
Cowell,[23] 1986	120	↑↑↑	24 hr	6.0	1–38	4.2	0.7–26.4	○
Salardi,[24] 1990	71	↑↑↑	24 hr	2.55	0.3–17.3	1.8	0.2–17.0	○
Marshall,[25] 1986	64	↑↑↑	Overnight	3.5[c]	0.6–13	2.4[c]	0.4–9.0	○
Ellis,[26] 1977	50	↑↑↑	24 hr	5.5	0–13.3	3.8	0–9.2	○
Mathiesen,[27] 1986	36	↑↑↑	Overnight	ND	1.5–20 (<15 in 97%)	ND	1–14 (<10 in 97%)	○
Brøchner-Mortensen,[28] 1979	28	↑↑↑	3 hr (supine)	ND	ND	8.3[b]	≈2–32[a,b]	○
Mortensen,[29] 1990	47 boys 4–12 y	↑↑	Overnight	1.9	ND	1.3	ND	○
	58 boys 13–19 y			3.9		2.7		
	30 girls 4–12 y			2.0		1.4		
	74 girls 13–19 y			3.3		2.3		
Dahlquist,[30] 1987	21	↑↑	24 hr	ND	ND	6	2–18.5	○
Erman,[31] 1990	32	↑	8 hr, overnight	5.7	1.8–16.5	3.9	1.3–11.5	○
Holl,[32] 1999	94	↑↑	Overnight	ND	0.3–17.3[a]	ND	0.2–12[a]	○
Huttunen,[33] 1981	68	↑↑	Short timed	7.0[c,d]	0.4–193[c]	4.9[c,d]	0.3–134[d]	○
Chiumello,[34] 1989	42	↑↑	Overnight	ND	ND	<10	ND	○
Laborde,[35] 1990	16	↑↑	3 hr	3.6	0.9–17.6	2.5	0.6–12.2	○
Mullis,[36] 1988	16	↑↑	12 hr overnight	3.5[a] 5.2[a]	0–6.6[a] 0–9.5[a]	2.4[a] 3.6[a]	0–4.6[a] 0–5.7[a]	○

* In all studies, each subject had one urine measurement.

** For this table, the generalizability scale was adjusted to reflect the broader target population (all healthy boys and girls) as follows:

↑↑↑ Sample is representative of a wide spectrum of healthy children, including both sexes and a range of ages.

↑↑ Sample is representative of a relevant subgroup of healthy children, such as a narrow range of ages, a homogenous ethnicity, or a single sex.

↑ Sample is representative of a narrow subgroup of healthy children not well generalizable to all healthy children (e.g., boys of a limited age range).

[a] per 1.73 m² BSA
[b] Estimate from graph
[c] Median
[d] Per m² body surface area

Abbreviations: hr, hour; y, year

relatively few in number, and most have been published in the past 15 years. However, a literature search of articles describing albumin excretion in children revealed one study in 1970. This original paper[20] considered the best measurement of glomerular integrity to be albumin clearance factored by creatinine clearance. It concluded that the ratio of the concentration of albumin to creatinine in spot urine samples is the most accurate method for estimating albumin clearance and provides a better marker of glomerular permeability to albumin than the 24-hour albumin excretion rate. The results were expressed as mg albumin per mg creatinine, but subsequent papers have used a variety of methods to express albumin excretion, making comparisons between studies very difficult. Tables 16 and 17 give mean values and ranges for albumin excretion rate and

Table 17. Urine Albumin-to-Creatinine Ratio: Normal Range in Children

Author, Year	No. of Subjects*	Applic-ability**	Urine Collection Method	Albumin/Creatinine Ratio (mg/g) Mean	Range	Quality
Davies,[21] 1984	183 boys 191 girls	♀♀	Split 24 hr	6.1 8.9	$1.7–21.8^{d}$ 2.0–39.9	●
Elises,[37] 1988	377	♀♀♀	AM spot	6.6	0.6–26.5	○
Ginevri,[38] 1993	368	♀♀♀	2nd AM spot	21.5	105.0^{b}	○
Houser,[39] 1986	108: 2 mo–4 y 171: 4–62 y	♀♀♀	Random spot	17.1 12.9	4.2–62 3.0–37.8	○
Hjorth,[40] 2000	14: < 1 mo 35: 1–12 mo 66: 1–5 y 61: 6–10 y 71: 11–15 y	♀♀♀	Random spot	ND	155^{c} 33.6^{c} 29.2^{c} 23.9^{c} 18.6^{c}	○
Schultz,[41] 1999	208^{d}	♀♀♀	Overnight	8.1	1.8–38.2	○
Bangstad,[22] 1993	76: < 13 y 67: ≥ 13 y	♀♀♀	Overnight	8.8 9.7	1.7–46 1.7–119	○
Gibb,[42] 1989	73^{e}	♀♀♀	AM spot	2.9	0.4–18.6	○
Marshall,[25] 1986	64	♀♀♀	Overnight	8.4^{f}	$3.8–32.7^{g}$	○
Barratt,[29] 1970	58	♀♀♀	AM spot	ND	$≈ 10–300^{h}$	○
Schultz,[43] 2000	96 boys 113 girls	♀♀	AM spot	7.1 8.0	3.5–23.9 3.5–30.0	○
Yap,[44] 1991	28: neonate 29: 1–3 mo 28: 4–6 mo 26: 7–23 mo 28: 2–4 y	♀♀	Random/ AM spot	46.3 44.3 35.9 15.6 11.8	$4.8–132.2^{g}$ ND ND ND $4.9–29.1^{g}$	○
Jefferson,[45] 1985	21	♀♀	Random spot	11	4–32	○
Cesarini,[46] 1996	17	♀♀	Pre- and post-exercise spot	Pre-exercise: 14.8 Post-exercise: 6.6	ND	○
Erman,[31] 1990	10: 5–10 y 22: 10–20 y	♀	8 hr overnight	11.5 6.0	4–28 2.2–11.6	○
Mullis,[36] 1988	16	♀♀	AM spot	8.8	0.3–20	○

* Except where noted, each subject had one urine measurement.
** See footnote to Table 15 for explanation of applicability scale for this table.

^{a} Geometric mean ×/÷ (tolerance factor)^{2}
^{b} 97th percentile
^{c} 90th percentile
^{d} 602 urine measurements

^{e} 171 urine measurements
^{f} Median
^{g} 95% confidence interval
^{h} Estimated from graph

Abbreviations: hr, hour; AM, morning; y, year; mo, month

Table 18. Prevalence of Albuminuria in Adults: NHANES III

Albumin/ Creatinine Ratio	N	US Adult Prevalence (SE)
Normal	12,478	88.4% (0.4)
Microalbuminuria	2,040	10.6% (0.4)
Albuminuria	318	1.1% (0.1)
Totals	14,836	100%

This table shows prevalence of albuminuria detected in a single spot urine test.

Abbreviation: SE, standard error

albumin-to-creatinine ratio in children (neonates through age 20 years), and also emphasize some of the ways in which published reports have differed. Overall, the values appear similar to the values observed for adults.

Prevalence of proteinuria in adults (S). Table 18 shows the prevalence of albuminuria estimated from the albumin-to-creatinine ratio in a single spot urine collection in 14,836 adults studied in NHANES III. Based on these results, it is estimated that approximately 20.2 million adults (11.7%) have abnormal urine albumin excretion.

Albuminuria was persistent on repeat evaluation in only 61% of individuals; hence, these prevalence estimates based on a single spot urine are likely overestimates, especially for microalbuminuria. (Appendix 2 discusses the reproducibility of data on albuminuria and microalbuminuria.)

Among adults, the prevalence of albuminuria varies by age (Table 19) and presence (Table 20) or absence (Table 21) of diabetes. The prevalence is approximately 30% in adults with age ≥70 years: 26.6% with microalbuminuria and 3.7% with albuminuria. At all ages, the prevalence is higher among individuals with diabetes. Among individuals with a history of diabetes, the prevalence of microalbuminuria and albuminuria is 43.2% and 8.4%, respectively, at age ≥70 years. Among individuals without a history of diabetes the prevalence of microalbuminuria and albuminuria is 24.2% and 3.0%, respectively, at age ≥70 years.

Table 19. Prevalence of Albuminuria by Age Group: NHANES III

Albumin/ Creatinine Ratio	Prevalence (SE) by Age Group (Years)			
	20–39	40–59	60–69	≥70
Normal	93.1% (0.6)	89.9% (0.7)	81.8% (1.4)	69.8% (1.3)
Microalbuminuria	6.6% (0.6)	9.1% (0.6)	16.2% (1.2)	26.6% (1.2)
Albuminuria	0.4% (0.1)	1.0% (0.2)	2.0% (0.4)	3.7% (0.5)

This table shows prevalence of albuminuria detected in a single spot urine test.

Abbreviation: SE, standard error

Table 20. Prevalence of Albuminuria Among Individuals with a History of Diabetes: NHANES III

Albumin/ Creatinine Ratio	Prevalence (SE) by Age Group (Years)			
	20–39	40–59	60–69	≥70
Normal	66.9% (10.5)	64.1% (3.8)	54.3% (4.2)	48.4% (3.6)
Microalbuminuria	28.0% (10.0)	30.0% (4.0)	39.1% (4.3)	43.2% (3.5)
Albuminuria	5.1% (3.0)	6.0% (2.0)	6.6% (1.9)	8.4% (2.3)

This table shows prevalence of albuminuria detected in a single spot urine test.

Abbreviation: SE, standard error

Prevalence of proteinuria in children (C). Prevalence of proteinuria is lower in children. A compilation of studies shows that 1% to 10% of children may have proteinuria on initial screening using the urine dipstick, but that <1% have persistent proteinuria, as defined by positive results on repeated testing (Table 22). Similarly, the prevalence of increased urine albumin excretion on initial screening varies from 1% to 10% (Table 23).

Prevalence of Stage 1 and Stage 2 chronic kidney disease (S). The proportion of adults with GFR ≥90 and 60–89 mL/min/1.73 m^2 with albuminuria is shown in Fig 7. Among US adults with a GFR ≥90 mL/min/1.73 m^2, 9.2% had an elevated albumin-to-creatinine ratio (including 3.3% without hypertension and 5.9% with hypertension). As shown in Table 14, this group corresponds to approximately 5.9% of all US adults, or 10.5 million people in the years 1988 to 1994. On repeat examination, 54% (n = 102) of a subsample with albuminuria had a persistently positive result. Therefore, the prevalence of *persistent* albuminuria would be 3.3% of US adults with GFR ≥90 mL/ min/1.73 m^2, or 5.9 million. This is the estimated prevalence of Stage 1 chronic kidney disease.

Among adults with GFR 60 to 89 mL/min/1.73 m^2, the prevalence of albuminuria was 12.9%, corresponding to 4.0% of all US adults, or 7.1 million people. On repeat examination, 73% of a subsample with albuminuria (n = 44) had a persistently positive test. Therefore, the prevalence of persistent albuminuria would be 3.0% of US adults with GFR 60–84 mL/min/1.73 m^2, or 5.3 million. This is the estimated prevalence of Stage 2 chronic kidney disease.

Note that persistent albuminuria is not the only marker of kidney damage. NHANES III did not ascertain other markers of kidney damage, such as abnormalities of the urine sediment and abnormal imaging tests; thus, any estimate based on NHANES III data is likely to underestimate the true prevalence of chronic kidney damage.

Table 21. Prevalence of Albuminuria Among Individuals without a History of Diabetes: NHANES III

Albumin/ Creatinine Ratio	Prevalence (SE) by Age Group (Years)			
	20–39	40–59	60–69	≥70
Normal	93.3% (0.6)	91.4% (0.7)	85.4% (1.5)	72.8% (1.4)
Microalbuminuria	6.3% (0.6)	7.9% (0.6)	13.2% (1.3)	24.2% (1.3)
Albuminuria	0.3% (0.1)	0.7% (0.2)	1.4% (0.3)	3.0% (0.5)

This table shows prevalence of albuminuria detected in a single spot urine test.

Abbreviation: SE, standard error

Table 22. Proteinuria: Prevalence in Nondiabetic Children

Author, Year	No. of Subjects	Applic-ability*	Method of Urine Collection	Proteinuria Definition	Prevalence of Proteinuria (%) 1 Test	2 Tests	≥3 Tests	Quality
Murakami,[47] 1991	7,349,928	↑↑↑	AM	≥15 mg/dL	1.2	0.17		●
Lin,[48] 2000	4,311,516	↑↑↑	AM	≥30 mg/dL	3.11	0.35		●
Vehaskari,[49] 1982	8,954	↑↑↑	Random/AM^a	≥1+	3.5^b	2.5	0.1	●
Wagner,[50] 1968	4,897	↑↑↑	Random	≥1+ / ≥1+	5.4 / 1.7	1.1		●
Randolph,[51] 1967	3,628	↑↑↑	Random/AM	1+ / 2+	6.3 / 2.1		0^c / 0^c	●
Johnson,[52] 1974	3,626	↑↑	Random	≥1+	1.5	0.8	0.6	●
Wolman,[53] 1945	11,822	↑	Random/AM	30 mg/dL	2.6		0.07	●
Kunin,[54] 1964	3,429	↑↑↑	ND	ND	1.4–2.9	0.3	0.1	○
Meadow,[55] 1969	2,125	↑↑↑	Mostly AM	≥1+	"Often"	0.8	0.2	○
Mitchell,[56] 1990	732	↑↑↑	Random	≥1+	4			○
Harnill,[57] 1911	124	↑↑↑	Random	Trace	7			○
Dodge,[58] 1976	12,252	↑↑	Random	≥0 mg/dL	11.8	6.3	2.1–3.2	○
Hogg,[59] 1998	9,355	↑↑	AM	≥1+	0.25	0.08		○
Silverberg,[60] 1974	27,722	↑↑	Random	≥2 +/≥1+		0.5	0.16	○
Silverberg,[61] 1973	23,427	↑↑	Random	≥2 +/≥1+		1.6	0.5	○
Bashford,[62] 1926	1,000	↑	Random/AM^d	ND^e	5.8	0.4		○

* See footnote Table 15 for explanation of applicability scale for this table.

^a Both random and AM studies were done in all subjects.
^b Proteinuria in at least 1 of 4 specimens in 10.7%; 3.5% if only 1 specimen had been tested.
^c 4 or more tests
^d First test was random; "final" test was AM if random was positive.
^e Article refers to trace as positive protein test in other subjects described in the same paper.

Abbreviation: AM, morning

Table 23. Albuminuria: Prevalence in Nondiabetic Children

Author, Year	No. of Subjects	Applic-ability*	Method of Urine Collection	Proteinuria Definition	Prevalence of Albuminuria (%) 1 Test	Quality
Mueller,[63] 1999	4,088	↑↑↑	Random	$U_{Alb/Cr}$ > 30 mg/g / $U_{Alb/Cr}$ > 200 mg/g	12 / 2.4	○
Pugia,[64] 1999	6,187	↑↑↑	AM	$U_{Alb/Cr}$ > 30 mg/g / $U_{Alb/Cr}$ > 150 mg/g	2.6 / 0	○
Hoy,[65] 1998	405	↑↑	Random	$U_{Alb/Cr}$ > 12 mg/g / $U_{Alb/Cr}$ > 30 mg/g	24 / 7	○
Bernard,[66] 1997 (Study 1)	220	↑↑	ND	UAC > 200 mg/L	6	○
Bernard,[66] 1997 (Study 2)	150	↑↑	ND	UAC > 23.6 mg/L / UAC > 200 mg/L	11.3 / 1.3	○

* See footnote Table 15 for explanation of applicability scale for this table.

Abbreviations: $U_{Alb/Cr}$, urinary albumin-to-creatinine ratio; AM, morning; UAC, urine albumin concentration

Table 24. Normal GFR in Children and Young Adults

Age (Sex)	Mean GFR ± SD (mL/min/1.73 m²)
1 week (males and females)	40.6 ±14.8
2–8 weeks (males and females)	65.8 ±24.8
>8 weeks (males and females)	95.7 ±21.7
2–12 years (males and females)	133.0 ±27.0
13–21 years (males)	140.0 ±30.0
13–21 years (females)	126.0 ±22.0

*Data based on three studies.[69-71]

Abbreviation: SD, standard deviation

Decreased GFR

GFR as an index of kidney function (R). The level of GFR is accepted as the best measure of overall kidney function in health and disease. In principle, the level of GFR is the product of the number of nephrons and the single nephron GFR. Therefore, GFR can be affected by chronic kidney disease, which reduces the number of nephrons, or by hemodynamic factors that affect single nephron GFR. In chronic kidney disease, as in normal individuals, GFR is modulated by hemodynamic factors.

Normal range and variability of GFR (S, R). The normal level of GFR varies according to age, gender, and body size. It is conventional to adjust GFR to "standard" body size (surface area of 1.73 m²). Among normal adults, the inter-individual coefficient of variation (standard deviation divided by the mean) of GFR (adjusted for body surface area) within the normal population is approximately 15% to 20%.[67] The normal mean (standard devation) GFR in young adults is approximately 120 to 130 (20 to 25) mL/min/1.73 m². Children reach adult values for mean GFR by approximately age 2 years (Table 24).[68,69]

Figure 9 and Table 25 show the range of GFR in adults according to age, derived from normal men using inulin clearance.[72] Normal values in women are assumed to be 8% lower at all ages.[67,73] After approximately age 20 to 30 years, the normal mean value for GFR declines with age in both men and women, with a mean decrease of approximately 1 mL/min/1.73 m² per year. Thus, by age 70, the normal mean value is approximately 70 mL/min/1.73 m². At all ages, the range of normal GFR is wide.

Data from NHANES III are shown in Figs 9 and 10; these include men and women in the general population, including those with chronic kidney disease. In part, the

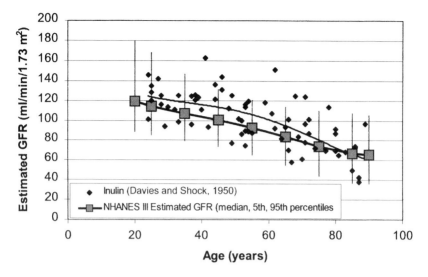

Fig 9. GFR versus age. Estimated GFR percentiles for the US population using NHANES III serum creatinine, age, sex, and race data (see Part 10, Appendix 2) by age compared to a regression of inulin clearance measurement of GFR on age among 70 healthy male participants. (Data abstracted from Davies and Shock.[72])

inclusion of women and individuals with chronic kidney disease may account for the slightly lower mean values observed in the NHANES III compared to the data from normal men in Fig 9.

Factors other than age also affect GFR. As shown in Table 24, GFR is slightly lower in young women than in young men. This difference appears to persist at older ages. Pregnancy has a major effect on GFR, with GFR reaching values of 140% of normal during the end of the second trimester.

Additional factors that may affect GFR to a lesser degree include: transient increases

Table 25. Normal GFR in Adults Extrapolated from Data in 72 Healthy Men

Age (y)	Men* GFR (mL/min/1.73 m²)				Women** GFR (mL/min/1.73 m²)			
	Mean	SD	−2 SD	+ 2SD	Mean	SD	−SD	+2SD
20–29	128	26	77	179	118	24	71	165
30–39	116	23	70	162	107	21	64	149
40–49	105	21	63	147	97	19	58	135
50–59	93	19	56	130	86	17	51	120
60–69	81	16	49	113	75	15	45	104
70–79	70	14	42	98	64	13	39	90
80–89	58	12	35	81	53	11	32	75

* Values for GFR in normal men by age.[72] Mean GFR for age categories in men based on linear regression.[74] Regression equation is GFR = −1.163 (Age) + 157.0. GFR range assumes a standard deviation of GFR divided by the mean (SD/M, also known as the coefficient of variation) of 20%.

** Assumes that values for women are 8% lower at all ages.[67,73]

Abbreviations: y, years; SD, standard deviation(s)

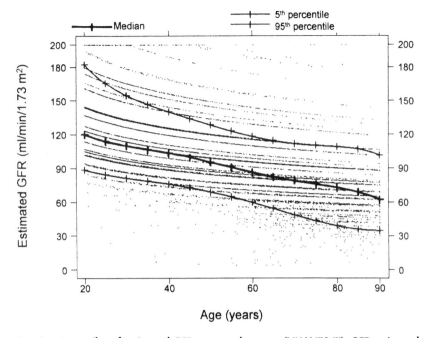

Fig 10. Percentiles of estimated GFR regressed on age (NHANES III). GFR estimated from serum creatinine using MDRD Study equation based on age, gender, and race (see Part 10, Appendix 3). Age ≥20, N = 15,600.

Table 26. Prevalence of GFR Categories in Adults

GFR mL/min/1.73 m²	Age Group (y) 20–39	40–59	60–69	≥70
≥90	86.0%	55.7%	38.5%	25.5%
60–89	13.7%	42.7%	53.8%	48.5%
30–59	—ᵃ	1.8%	7.1%	24.6%
15–29	—ᵃ	—ᵃ	—ᵃ	1.3%
N (millions):	82	55	20	20

GFR estimated from serum creatinine using MDRD Study equation based on age, gender, race and calibration for serum creatinine. Data from NHANES III (1988–1994). N = 15,000. Based on one-time assessment of estimated GFR.

ᵃ Fewer than 20 cases; data not considered reliable.

in GFR after a high protein meal, a lower GFR in individuals following a habitually low protein diet, and antihypertensive agents (effect on GFR varies by class of agent), especially in patients with chronic kidney disease.

Definition of decreased GFR (R, O). The Work Group defined decreased GFR as <90 mL/min/1.73 m^2. The interpretation of decreased GFR varies depending on age, duration, and the presence or absence of markers of kidney damage.

The lower limit of normal GFR varies with age. For example, as shown in Table 25, GFR <90 mL/min/1.73 m^2 would be abnormal in a young adult. On the other hand, a GFR of 60–89 mL/min/1.73 m^2 could be normal from approximately 8 weeks to 1 year of age and in older individuals. It is possible that GFR 30 to 59 mL/min/1.73 m^2 could also be normal in individuals at the extremes of age, in vegetarians, after unilateral nephrectomy or in an older individual. It is likely that a GFR <30 mL/min/1.73 m^2 is abnormal at all ages other than neonates. For these reasons, the Work Group based the definition of chronic kidney disease solely on the level of GFR only in individuals with GFR <60 mL/min/1.73 m^2, whereas individuals with GFR 60 to 89 mL/min/1.73 m^2 were considered to have chronic kidney disease only if they also had a marker of kidney damage (see Table 12, p. 45).

Decreased GFR may be acute or chronic. An acute decrease in GFR does not necessarily indicate the presence of kidney damage. For example, it is well known that a brief period of mildly decreased blood flow to the kidneys or transient partial obstruction of the urinary tract may cause decreased GFR without kidney damage. However, a sustained decrease in blood flow or prolonged obstruction is often associated with kidney damage. Chronically decreased GFR is more often associated with kidney damage. The Work Group arbitrarily chose a cut-off value of greater than 3 months for the definition of chronic kidney disease.

As discussed earlier, individuals with decreased GFR should be evaluated for markers of kidney damage to determine whether they have chronic kidney disease and to determine the cause of reduced kidney function. Even if there is no evidence of kidney damage, individuals with chronically decreased GFR may be at increased risk for adverse outcomes (for example, toxicity from drugs excreted by the kidney, and acute kidney failure in a wide variety of circumstances).

Association of level of GFR with complications (S, R, C, O). Decreased GFR is associated with a wide range of complications in other organ systems, manifested by high blood pressure, laboratory abnormalities, and symptoms. Severity of complications worsens as level of GFR declines (Part 6, Guidelines 7 through 12). The Work Group defined categories of decreased GFR as mild (Stage 2, 60 to 89 mL/min/1.73 m^2), moderate (Stage 3, 30 to 59 mL/min/1.73 m^2), and severe (Stage 4, 15 to 29 mL/min/1.73 m^2). Although these definitions are arbitrary, evidence compiled in later guidelines supports these broad categories and cut-off levels.

Prevalence of decreased GFR by age (S). The prevalence of decreased GFR is higher in the elderly (Table 26). Approximately 14.9 million individuals ≥70 years

(74.5%) of age have decreased GFR. As already stated, not all individuals with decreased GFR have kidney disease. The prevalence of persistent albuminuria by GFR level and age group have not been determined, preventing an accurate estimate of the prevalence of chronic kidney disease among the elderly.

The prevalence of decreased GFR is lower in children. The Schwartz formula was used to estimate GFR in children aged 12 to 19 years in the NHANES III database. The lowest 1% of children had GFR below approximately 100 mL/min/1.73 m^2. Reliable estimates of prevalence of categories of decreased GFR (mild, moderate, or severe) in children are not available from NHANES III.

Kidney Failure

Definition of kidney failure (R, O). Kidney failure is defined as either (1) a level of GFR to <15 mL/min/1.73 m^2, which is accompanied in most cases by signs and symptoms of uremia, or (2) a need for initiation of kidney replacement therapy (dialysis or transplantation) for treatment for complications of decreased GFR, which would otherwise increase the risk of mortality and morbidity. Some patients may need dialysis or transplantation at GFR ≥15 mL/min/1.73 m^2 because of symptoms of uremia. The Work Group acknowledges that the level of GFR selected for this definition is arbitrary and may need to be modified based on advances in kidney replacement therapy.

End-stage renal disease (R). End-stage renal disease (ESRD) is an administrative term in the United States, based on the conditions for payment for health care by the Medicare ESRD Program, specifically the level of GFR and the occurrence of signs and symptoms of kidney failure necessitating initiation of treatment by replacement therapy. ESRD includes patients treated by dialysis or transplantation, irrespective of the level of GFR.

The K/DOQI definition of kidney failure differs in two important ways from the definition of ESRD. First, not all individuals with GFR <15 mL/min/1.73 m^2 or with signs and symptoms of kidney failure are treated by dialysis and transplantation. Nonetheless, such individuals should be considered as having kidney failure. Second, among treated patients, kidney transplant recipients have a higher mean level of GFR (usually 30 to 60 mL/min/1.73 m^2) and better average health outcomes than dialysis patients. Kidney transplant recipients should not be included in the definition of kidney failure, unless they have GFR <15 mL/min/1.73 m^2 or have resumed dialysis.

The Work Group anticipated that most kidney transplant recipients would be considered to have chronic kidney disease according to the proposed classification. First, GFR is lower in patients with a solitary kidney and is even lower in kidney transplant recipients because of toxicity from immunosuppressive agents used to prevent and treat rejection, such as cyclosporine and tacrolimus. Second, biopsy studies demonstrate pathologic damage due to acute and chronic rejection in virtually all transplant recipients, even if serum creatinine is normal. However, because markers of kidney damage are not sensitive to tubulointerstitial or vascular damage, it is likely that some kidney transplant patients will have GFR ≥60 mL/min/1.73 m^2 without markers of kidney damage. Such patients would not be classified as having chronic kidney disease by the proposed classification. The Work Group would consider them to be at increased risk of chronic kidney disease. Thus, all patients with a kidney transplant would be considered either to have chronic kidney disease or to be at increased risk of chronic kidney disease.

Relationship of GFR to other measures of kidney function in kidney failure (S). A number of measurements, including GFR, have been used to quantify the level of kidney function among patients with kidney failure. The K/DOQI Nutrition in Chronic Renal Failure Guidelines[75] and Peritoneal Dialysis Adequacy Guidelines Update 2000[16] recommend the decision to initiate dialysis in adults be based on a combination of measurements of kidney function, as well as nutritional status. These guidelines are reproduced here:

Peritoneal Dialysis Adequacy Guideline 1: When to Initiate Dialysis—Kt/V_{urea} Criterion (Opinion)
"Unless certain conditions are met, patients should be advised to initiate some form of dialysis when the weekly renal Kt/V_{urea} (Krt/V_{urea}) falls below 2.0. The conditions that may indicate dialysis is not yet necessary even though the weekly Krt/V_{urea} is less than 2.0 are:

1. Stable or increased edema-free body weight. Supportive objective parameters for adequate nutrition include a lean body mass >63%, subjective global assessment score indicative of adequate nutrition, and a serum albumin concentration in excess of the lower limit for the lab, and stable or rising; and;

2. Nutritional indications for the initiation of renal replacement therapy are detailed in Guideline 27 of the K/DOQI Clinical Practice Guidelines on Nutrition in Chronic Renal Failure, part of which is reproduced as Guideline 2 of the PD Adequacy Guideline.

3. Complete absence of clinical signs or symptoms attributable to uremia.

A weekly Krt/V_{urea} of 2.0 approximates a kidney urea clearance of 7 mL/min and a kidney creatinine clearance that varies between 9 to 14 mL/min/1.73 m^2. Urea clearance should be normalized to total body water (V) and creatinine clearance should be expressed per 1.73 m^2 of body surface area. The GFR, which is estimated by the arithmetic mean of the urea and creatinine clearance, will be approximately 10.5 mL/min/1.73 m^2 when the Krt/V_{urea} is about 2.0."

Peritoneal Dialysis Adequacy Guideline 2 and Nutrition in Chronic Renal Failure Guideline 27: Indications for Renal Replacement Therapy (Opinion)
"In patients with chronic kidney failure (e.g., GFR <15–20 mL/min) who are not undergoing maintenance dialysis, if protein-energy malnutrition (PEM) develops or persists despite vigorous attempts to optimize protein and energy intake and there is no apparent cause for malnutrition other than low nutrient intake, initiation of maintenance dialysis or a renal transplant is recommended."

The CKD Work Group searched for studies of measures of kidney function, dietary

Table 27. Description of MDRD Study Participants Who Developed Kidney Failure: Kidney Function

Measurement	Mean	SD	Range
Serum creatinine (mg/dL)	6.9	1.9	3.3–11.5
BUN (mg/dL)	62	18	28–118
Kt/V$_{urea}$	1.7	0.6	0.8–3.2
GFR (^{125}I-iothalamate clearance)*	9.1	3.0	4.1–18.2
GFR (MDRD Study equation)*	9.6	3.3	4.9–18.3
C$_{Cr}$ (measured)*	10.8	4.5	3.9–25.7
C$_{Cr}$ (Cockcroft-Gault equation)*	12.6	4.2	6.2–25.3
(C$_{Cr}$ + C$_{urea}$)/2*	8.4	3.1	3.3–18.8

Data from Levey, 1998.[76]

* Units for clearance measurements: mL/min/1.73 m^2

Abbreviation: SD, standard deviation

intake, and nutritional status at the onset of kidney replacement therapy. The largest and most comprehensive study is the one reported in abstract by the MDRD Study Group.[76] This study included 88 patients who were referred to their physicians by the MDRD Study investigators for initiation of dialysis because of symptoms or findings of uremia prior to the end of the study. Prescribed protein intake during the study was 0.6 g/kg/d, either as food or from food and a mixture of essential amino acids and ketoacids. The median interval from final GFR to initiation of dialysis in the study group was 89 days. Because these patients were participating in a clinical trial, the mean level of kidney function and nutritional status may be higher than in patients beginning dialysis in the general population. Tables 27 and 28 show measures of kidney function and nutritional status in these patients with kidney failure just prior to initiation of dialysis. The comparison of measured GFR to other kidney function measurements is shown in Table 29. These data show that estimated GFR provides only a rough approximation of other measures of kidney function. This provides additional justification for performing other measures of kidney function to assess the need for kidney replacement therapy, as recommended in the K/DOQI Peritoneal Dialysis Guidelines.[16] It was the opinion of the Work Group that these measurements should be obtained in patients with estimated GFR <15 mL/min/1.73 m^2, since, as described below, few patients begin dialysis at higher levels of GFR.

Level of GFR at initiation of replacement therapy (S, C). Clinicians initiate replacement therapy based on the level of kidney function, presence of signs and symptoms of uremia, the availability of therapy, and patient or surrogate preferences. There is variability among individuals in the relationship of level of kidney function to signs

Table 28. Description of MDRD Study Participants Who Developed Kidney Failure: Dietary Intake and Nutritional Status

Measurement	Men Mean	Men SD	Women Mean	Women SD
Energy Intake (kcal/kg/d)	22.0	6.2	20.1	5.9
Protein Intake (g/kg/d)	0.61	0.19	0.59	0.20
Weight (kg)*	80.7	10.9	65.5	12.0
BSA (m²)*	1.97	0.15	1.69	0.14
BMI (kg/m²)	26.1	2.8	25.2	4.9
V_{urea} (L)*	43.5	4.4	31.3	3.1
Albumin (g/dL)	4.0	0.4	3.9	0.4
Transferrin (mg/dL)	241	39	240	38
Arm muscle area (cm²)*	40	11	28	11
Body fat (%)*	25	5.4	32	7.1
Urine creatinine (mg/kg/d)*	15.1	3.2	13.1	3.3

Data from Levey, 1998.[76]

* p <0.01 for comparison of men vs. women

Abbreviation: SD, standard deviation

Table 29. Comparison of Kidney Function Measurements in MDRD Study Participants Who Developed Kidney Failure

Measurement	Correlation (R^2)	Mean Δ*	Median Δ*
$1/S_{Cr}$	0.65	—	—
BUN	0.25	—	—
Kt/V_{urea}	0.51	—	—
GFR (MDRD Study Eq.)*	0.71	0.54	1.32
C_{Cr} (measured)*	0.72	1.74	1.57
C_{Cr} (Cockcroft-Gault Eq.)*	0.68	3.56	3.54
$(C_{Cr} + C_{urea})/2$*	0.72	−0.71	0.96

Units for clearance measurements: mL/min/1.73 m²; Correlations with measured GFR (^{125}I-iothalamate clearance). Data from Levey, 1998.[76]

* Δ is the difference between measured and estimated GFR.

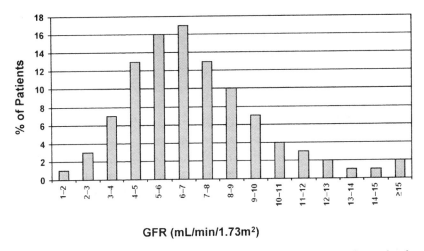

Fig 11. Level of GFR at initiation of replacement therapy (USRDS). Data from Obrador et al.[77]

and symptoms of uremia. Notably, there is variability within and among health care systems in the availability of therapy.

The level of GFR at the beginning of dialysis has been estimated in more than 90,000 patients in the United States between 1995 and 1997, using data collected on the Medical Evidence Report (HCFA Form 2728) and the MDRD Study prediction equation (Fig 11).[77] The mean (SD) level of serum creatinine was 8.5 (3.8) mg/dL. The mean (SD) level of GFR at initiation of treatment was 7.1 (3.1) mL/min/1.73 m². The proportion of patients initiating dialysis with a predicted GFR of 10 to 15, 5 to 10, and <5 mL/min/1.73 m² was 11%, 63%, and 24%, respectively; 98% of patients began dialysis with predicted GFR ≤15 mL/min/1.73 m².

Tables 30, 31, and 32 summarize other studies of the level of kidney function at initiation of dialysis. Overall, the results of these studies are consistent with the data from the MDRD Study (Table 27) and the large study shown in Fig 11.

Factors associated with level of kidney function at initiation of dialysis (R). Timing of initiation of replacement therapy varies by modality, clinical characteristics, and sociodemographic characteristics. Patients who receive a pre-emptive transplant or who are started on peritoneal dialysis begin replacement therapy at higher mean levels of GFR than patients starting hemodialysis. Dialysis is initiated at higher mean levels of

Table 30. GFR at Start of Hemodialysis

Author, Year	No. of Subjects	Applicability	Mean Kidney Function Measure	Quality
Arora,[78] 1999	135	👫	GFR = 7.8 mL/min/1.73 m²	◐

Table 31. Creatinine Clearance at Start of Hemodialysis

Author, Year	No. of Subjects	Applicability	Mean Kidney Function Measure	Quality
Jungers,[79] 1993	218	✝✝✝	C_o = 6.9 mL/min	O
Sesso,[80] 1997	113	✝✝✝	C_o = 6.1 mL/min	O

GFR among patients who are older, or who have diabetes, cardiovascular disease, and other comorbid conditions.

Prevalence of kidney failure (S). The incidence and the prevalence of reported ESRD have doubled in the past 10 years in the United States (Fig 2). Data from the 2000 Annual Data Report of the USRDS documents the incidence of ESRD in 1998 of more than 85,000, or 308 per million individuals per year at risk. The point prevalence of ESRD on December 31, 1998 was more than 320,000, or 1,160 per million population, of whom 72% were treated by dialysis (230,000 patients, or 835 per million population) and 28% had functioning kidney transplants (90,000 patients, or 325 per 100,000). The number of individuals with GFR <15 mL/min/1.73 m² not on dialysis has not been estimated reliably.

The prevalence of kidney failure treated by dialysis varies by age. On December 31, 1998, there were approximately 75,000 adults over 70 years of age (97 per million) with kidney failure treated by dialysis, compared to approximately 1,800 children (2.1 per million).

LIMITATIONS

There are a number of limitations to the proposed definition and classification of chronic kidney disease. The Work Group believes that these limitations should be identified, but does not think that they invalidate the proposal. Instead, these limitations should serve to stimulate further research to refine the definition and classification.

First, as described later in Guideline 6, the known markers of kidney damage are not sensitive, especially for tubulointersitial and vascular disease and for diseases in the kidney transplant. Thus, the prevalence of chronic kidney disease may be substantially higher than the Work Group has estimated, and recognition of patients with chronic kidney disease may be limited due to misclassification. Second, as described in Guideline 4, the MDRD Study prediction equation has not been validated extensively at levels of GFR ≥90 mL/min/1.73 m²; thus, it is difficult to estimate the level of GFR above 90 mL/min/1.73 m², and it may be difficult to distinguish between Stage 1 and Stage 2 of chronic

Table 32. Serum Creatinine at Start of Hemodialysis

Author, Year	No. of Subjects	Applicability	Mean Kidney Function Measure	Quality
Fink,[81] 1999	5,388	✝✝✝	S_o = 9.16 mg/dL	O
Jungers,[79] 1993	218	✝✝✝	S_o = 11.1 mg/dL	O
Sesso,[80] 1997	113	✝✝✝	S_o = 9.9 mg/dL	O
Iofel,[82] 1998	220	✝✝	S_o = 10.9 mg/dL	O
Ifudu,[83] 1996	139	✝✝	S_o = 12.6 ± 5.2 mg/dL	O

kidney disease. Third, as described earlier, the cause of age-related decline in GFR and high blood pressure is not known. Possibly, it may be due to chronic kidney disease. If so, it would be more appropriate to classify individuals with GFR 60 to 89 mL/min/1.73 m² without apparent markers of kidney damage as having chronic kidney disease rather than "decreased GFR." Fourth, the GFR cut-off values for Stages 3 to 5 have been selected based on limited data with respect to the relationship between complications and level of GFR. Further studies may permit refinement of these cut-off values. Fifth, the association of level of GFR with complications of chronic kidney disease does not prove a causal relationship between the two. Nonetheless, in many cases there is adequate evidence of a causal relationship, and even if there is not, the associations accurately describe the burden of illness associated with the severity of chronic kidney disease. Sixth, prevalence estimates for stages of chronic kidney disease and the associations of level of GFR with complications are based largely on an analysis of data from NHANES III that has not yet been peer-reviewed. However, the Work Group believes that Appendix 2 provides sufficient detail to evaluate the methods.

CLINICAL APPLICATIONS

There are a large number of clinical applications of the proposed definition and stages of chronic kidney disease. An overall approach to evaluation and treatment of patients with chronic kidney disease is given in Guideline 2, and recommendations for individuals at increased risk of chronic kidney disease are given in Guideline 3. Clinical applications are also given at the conclusion of each subsequent guideline. Finally, additional recommendations for evaluation, diagnosis, and treatment of chronic kidney disease are given in Part 9.

IMPLEMENTATION ISSUES

Implementation of a new approach to the patient, classification of severity, and assessment of risk for chronic kidney disease will require appropriate professional, patient, and public education effort, as well as administrative and regulatory changes.

Professional, Patient, and Public Education

Components of the implementation plan, which determined the success of K/DOQI, are under development and will be applied to these guidelines. They include: widespread dissemination and easy access to the guidelines; educational interactive programs aimed at health professionals, patients, providers, administrators, manufacturers, and policy makers; information tools and systems to facilitate adherence; development of clinical performance measures; incorporation of guidelines into continuous quality improvement programs; development of quality assessment instruments; and update and review of the pertinent literature on an ongoing basis.

Administrative and Regulatory Changes

Revision of Medicare forms and HCFA billing codes will be necessary. For example, classification of kidney disease by the International Classification of Disease (9th Edition) (ICD-9) is based on duration (acute versus chronic), diagnosis, clinical presentation, markers of damage, and kidney function impairment. The K/DOQI classification proposes that both diagnosis and stage (severity) should be included in the classification of chronic kidney disease. This would facilitate using administrative databases for epidemiological and outcomes surveys.

RESEARCH RECOMMENDATIONS

The Workgroup acknowledges that the proposed definition and classification chronic kidney disease and stages is arbitrary and can be refined by further research.

The normal range for GFR was defined using a relatively small number of individuals. It would be useful to conduct a large cross-sectional study of GFR in general population, across the full range of age, gender, race, ethnicity, protein intake, with adjustment for other factors, including high blood pressure, diabetes, and other conditions that affect GFR. This study would permit validation of prediction equations based on serum creatinine or other filtration markers within the normal range of GFR.

The outcomes of individuals with various stages of chronic kidney disease are not defined. A cohort study of patients with chronic kidney disease would enable definition of the relationship between factors and outcomes of stages of chronic kidney disease. This would be particularly useful in defining the relationships among stages of chronic kidney disease, progression of chronic kidney disease, initiation and progression of cardiovascular disease, health service utilization, and barriers to care.

Age-related rise in blood pressure and decline in GFR may be responsible for a large number of individuals in Stage 3 (GFR 30 to 59 mL/min/1.73 m^2). There are even more individuals with high blood pressure and decreased GFR (GFR 60 to 89 mL/min/1.73 m^2), who have not been classified as having chronic kidney disease. It would be useful to conduct cross-sectional and cohort studies of elderly individuals with normal and abnormal blood pressure and GFR to assess the effect of high blood pressure and decreased GFR in this population.

GUIDELINE 2. EVALUATION AND TREATMENT

The evaluation and treatment of patients with chronic kidney disease requires understanding of separate but related concepts of diagnosis, comorbid conditions, severity of disease, complications of disease, and risks for loss of kidney function and cardiovascular disease.

- Patients with chronic kidney disease should be evaluated to determine:
  - Diagnosis (type of kidney disease);
  - Comorbid conditions;
  - Severity, assessed by level of kidney function;
  - Complications, related to level of kidney function;
  - Risk for loss of kidney function;
  - Risk for cardiovascular disease.
- Treatment of chronic kidney disease should include:
  - Specific therapy, based on diagnosis;

Table 33. Stages of Chronic Kidney Disease: A Clinical Action Plan

Stage	Description	GFR (mL/min/1.73 m²)	Action*
1	Kidney damage with normal or ↑ GFR	≥90	Diagnosis and treatment, Treatment of comorbid conditions, Slowing progression, CVD risk reduction
2	Kidney damage with mild ↓ GFR	60–89	Estimating progression
3	Moderate ↓ GFR	30–59	Evaluating and treating complications
4	Severe ↓ GFR	15–29	Preparation for kidney replacement therapy
5	Kidney failure	<15 (or dialysis)	Replacement (if uremia present)

Chronic kidney disease is defined as either kidney damage or GFR <60 mL/min/1.73 m² for ≥3 months. Kidney damage is defined as pathologic abnormalities or markers of damage, including abnormalities in blood or urine tests or imaging studies.

* Includes actions from preceding stages.

Abbreviations: CVD, cardiovascular disease

- Evaluation and management of comorbid conditions;
- Slowing the loss of kidney function;
- Prevention and treatment of cardiovascular disease;
- Prevention and treatment of complications of decreased kidney function;
- Preparation for kidney failure and kidney replacement therapy;
- Replacement of kidney function by dialysis and transplantation, if signs and symptoms of uremia are present.
- A clinical action plan should be developed for each patient, based on the stage of disease as defined by the K/DOQI CKD classification (see Table 33).
- Review of medications should be performed at all visits for the following:
  - Dosage adjustment based on level of kidney function;
  - Detection of potentially adverse effects on kidney function or complications of chronic kidney disease;
  - Detection of drug interactions;
  - Therapeutic drug monitoring, if possible.
- Self-management behaviors should be incorporated into the treatment plan at all stages of chronic kidney disease.
- Patients with chronic kidney disease should be referred to a specialist for consultation and co-management if the clinical action plan cannot be prepared, the prescribed evaluation of the patient cannot be carried out, or the recommended treatment cannot be carried out. In general, patients with GFR <30 mL/min/1.73 m² should be referred to a nephrologist.

BACKGROUND

Historically, the evaluation and management of chronic kidney disease has focused on diagnosis and treatment of specific kidney diseases and dialysis or transplantation for kidney failure. An action plan for patients with chronic kidney disease also requires interventions during the earlier stages of kidney disease, irrespective of the cause of kidney disease. This includes evaluation and management of comorbid conditions, slowing progression of kidney disease, cardiovascular disease risk reduction, preventing and treating complications of chronic kidney disease, and preparation for kidney replacement therapy.

RATIONALE

Diagnosis (R, O). Classification of the type of kidney disease is based on pathology and etiology. A simplified classification, and the distribution of types of kidney disease leading to ESRD are given in Table 34. The definitive diagnosis of the type of kidney disease is based on biopsy or imaging studies. Biopsy and invasive imaging procedures are associated with a risk, albeit usually small, of serious complications. Therefore, these procedures are often avoided unless a definitive diagnosis would change either the treatment or prognosis. In most patients, well-defined clinical presentations and causal factors provide a sufficient basis to assign a diagnosis of chronic kidney disease. An approach to diagnosis, based on concepts elaborated on in this report, is given in Part 9.

Diabetic kidney disease is a type of glomerular disease, but it is singled out here because it is the largest single cause of kidney failure. Both type 1 and type 2 diabetes cause chronic kidney disease. Because of the higher prevalence of type 2 diabetes, it is the more common cause of diabetic kidney disease. The clinical features, natural history and treatment for diabetic kidney disease are well known because it has been the subject of numerous epidemiological studies and clinical trials. Diabetic kidney disease usually follows a characteristic clinical course after the onset of diabetes, first manifested by microalbuminuria, then clinical proteinuria, hypertension, and declining GFR. Clinical trials have established a number of effective treatments to slow the development and progression of diabetic kidney disease, including strict glycemic control, angiotensin-converting enzyme inhibitors and angiotensin receptor blockers, blood pressure control, and perhaps dietary protein restriction.

A variety of diseases, including other glomerular diseases, vascular diseases, tubulointerstitial diseases, and cystic diseases, are often grouped together under the label "nondiabetic kidney diseases" for the purpose of epidemiological studies and clinical trials. Amongst these, hypertensive nephrosclerosis and glomerular diseases are the second and third most common causes of kidney failure. The various diseases in this group differ widely based on history, clinical presentation, risk for progression, and response to treatment. Differentiation among the diseases can be difficult, often requiring kidney biopsy or invasive imaging studies. An approach to diagnosis, based on the history, and a review of clinical presentations of chronic kidney disease, are given in Part 9. Specific therapies are available to reverse abnormalities in structure and function for some types of chronic kidney disease: for example, immunosuppressive medications for autoimmune glomerular diseases, antibiotics for urinary tract infections, removal of urinary stones, relief of obstruction, and cessation of toxic drugs. A thorough search for "reversible causes" of decreased kidney function should be carried out in each patient with chronic kidney disease.

Kidney disease in the transplant is probably the fourth largest cause of kidney failure.

Pathology	Etiology (Examples*)	Prevalence Among Patients with ESRD**
Diabetic Glomerulosclerosis	Diabetes Mellitus Type 1 Type 2	33%
Glomerular Diseases (Primary or Secondary)		19%
Proliferative glomerulonephritis	Systemic lupus erythematosis,	
Mesangial proliferative glomerulonephritis	vasculitis, bacterial endocarditis,	
Membranoproliferative glomerulonephritis	chronic hepatitis B or C, HIV	
Focal proliferative glomerulonephritis	infection	
Diffuse proliferative glomerulonephritis		
Crescentic glomerulonephritis		
Noninflammatory glomerular diseases		
Minimal change disease	Hodgkin's disease	
Focal glomerular sclerosis	HIV infection, heroin toxicity	
Membranous nephropathy	Drug toxicity, solid tumors	
Fibrillary glomerular diseases	Amyloidosis, light chain disease	
Hereditary nephritis (Alport's)		
Vascular Diseases		21%
Diseases of large-size vessels	Renal artery stenosis	
Diseases of medium-size vessels Nephrosclerosis	Hypertension	
Diseases of small vessels Microangiopathy	Sickle cell disease, hemolytic uremic syndrome (including cyclosporine or tacrolimus toxicity)	
Tubulointerstitial Diseases		4%
Tubulointerstitial nephritis		
Pyelonephritis	Infection, stones	
Analgesic nephropathy	NSAID	
Allergic interstitial nephritis	Antibiotics	
Granulomatous interstitial nephritis	Sarcoidosis	
Autoimmune interstitial nephritis	Uveitis	
Noninflammatory tubulointerstitial diseases		
Reflux nephropathy	Vesico-ureteral reflux	
Obstructive nephropathy	Malignancy, prostatism, stones	
Myeloma kidney	Multiple myeloma	
Cystic Diseases		6%
Polycystic kidney disease	Autosomal dominant or recessive	
Tuberous sclerosis		
Von Hippel Lindau		
Medullary cystic disease		
Diseases in the Transplant		—[a]
Chronic rejection		
Drug toxicity	Cyclosporine or tacrolimus	
Recurrent disease	Glomerular diseases	
Transplant glomerulopathy		

* Examples of some causes for specific pathologic types
** Approximate, based on USRDS Annual Data Report 1998[2] (on the Internet, see
  www.usrds.org/2kpdf/oo_precis.pdf#p1). Prevalence varies with age.

[a] Not recorded as a cause of ESRD in USRDS.

Abbreviations: HIV, human immunodeficiency virus; NSAID, non-steroidal anti-inflammatory drug

Table 35. Classification and Management of Comorbid Conditions in Chronic Kidney Disease

Type of Comorbid Condition	Examples	Management Goals
Diseases causing CKD	Diabetes High blood pressure Obstruction of the urinary tract	Improve CKD, Improve functioning and well-being, Integration of care with management of CKD
Diseases unrelated to CKD	Chronic obstructive pulmonary disease, Gastroesophageal reflux disease, Degenerative joint disease, Alzheimer's disease, Malignancies	Improve functioning and well-being, Integration of care with management of CKD

Cardiovascular disease (CVD)	Atherosclerotic CVD
	  Coronary heart disease
	  Cerebrovascular disease
	  Peripheral vascular disease
	Left ventricular hypertrophy
	Heart failure
		Evaluation and management of traditional and CKD-related CVD risk factors,
		Possibly improve CKD,
		Improve functioning and well-being,
		Integration of care with management of CKD

Both immunologic and non-immunologic factors appear to play an important role. The most common causes are chronic rejection, toxicity due to cyclosporine or tacrolimus, recurrent disease, and transplant glomerulopathy. In addition, differential diagnosis includes all the diseases that can occur in the native kidney. For a variety of reasons, especially the ease and safety of kidney biopsy, there is generally a much lower threshold for performing invasive procedures to establish a definitive diagnosis in kidney transplant recipients.

Comorbid conditions (R, O). Patients with chronic kidney disease have a large number of comorbid conditions. Comorbidity is defined as conditions other than the primary disease (in this case, chronic kidney disease). Complications of chronic kidney disease, such as hypertension, anemia, malnutrition, bone disease and neuropathy, are not considered as comorbid conditions. It is useful to consider three types of comorbid conditions (Table 35).

Diseases which cause chronic kidney disease. Evaluation and management of these diseases is important for patients' well being and may improve the course of chronic kidney disease. This is particularly important for patients with diabetes and high blood pressure, the leading causes of chronic kidney disease and cardiovascular disease in the United States.

Unrelated diseases, which may lead to impairments of functioning and well-being but do not affect the course of chronic kidney disease. Evaluation and management is important for patients' health and well-being.

Cardiovascular disease. Cardiovascular disease is singled out from among the possible comorbid conditions to emphasize its complex relationship with chronic kidney disease, and its importance as a preventable cause of morbidity and mortality in patients with chronic kidney disease.

In all cases, management of comorbid conditions must be integrated into the overall care of patients with chronic kidney disease. Examples include adjustment of drug dosages, interpretation of symptoms, and minimizing treatment complications, including acute decline in kidney function. In patients with normal or mildly decreased GFR (CKD Stages 1-2), integration of care for chronic kidney disease and these comorbid conditions may be relatively simple. However, in patients with moderate to severe reduction in GFR (CKD Stages 3-4) and in patients with kidney failure (CKD Stage 5), integration of care is complex and requires careful coordination among all providers.

Risk of loss of GFR (R, O). Risk of kidney failure depends on the level of GFR (severity) at detection of kidney disease and the rate of loss of GFR thereafter. Level of GFR can be improved by specific treatment in some chronic kidney diseases, but not in most others.

Rate of loss of GFR (progression of kidney disease) is affected by diagnosis and by modifiable and nonmodifiable patient factors. These factors can be assessed even before the decline in GFR, thereby allowing implementation of interventions to slow progression while GFR is still normal. Some therapies to prevent or slow the loss of GFR are specific for the diagnosis, while others are non-specific. Factors associated with progression of kidney disease are discussed in Guideline 13.

It is difficult to estimate the rate of progression until there has been a decline in GFR. In diseases characterized by a quantifiable marker of damage—for example, albuminuria in diabetic kidney disease—progression, stability, or regression can be estimated by change in the marker. For most diseases, however, quantitative relationships between changes in markers and progression have not been established.

Severity of disease and complications (R, O). Decreased GFR is associated with a wide range of complications due to disorders in other organ systems, which are manifested by hypertension, laboratory abnormalities, and symptoms. Complications due to disorders in other organ systems are associated with worse outcomes. Early detection and treatment of complications can improve outcomes. The prevalence of complications of chronic kidney disease is mainly related to the level of GFR. Interpretation of signs and symptoms in patients with chronic kidney disease should be guided by the level of GFR.

Kidney functions other than GFR may be altered by chronic kidney disease. These include maintenance of the filtration barrier for plasma proteins (abnormalities include albuminuria and proteinuria), reabsorption or secretion of water or specific solutes (abnormalities include tubular syndromes), and various endocrine functions (erythropoietin deficiency causes anemia, parathyroid hormone excess causes bone disease, and vitamin D deficiency causes bone disease). For most chronic kidney diseases, severity in other abnormalities of function parallels the severity of decreased GFR. Prevention and treatment of complications of chronic kidney disease includes specific therapies related to the pathogenesis of complications—for example, erythropoietin for anemia and vitamin D for bone disease.

Stage	Description	GFR (mL/min/1.73 m²)	Complications HBP or Lab Abnormality	Symptoms
1	Kidney damage with normal or ↑ GFR	≥90	_a	_a
2	Kidney damage with mild ↓ GFR	60–89	±	–
3	Moderate ↓ GFR	30–59	+	±
4	Severe ↓ GFR	15–29	++	+
5	Kidney failure	<15 (or dialysis)	+++	++

Kidney damage is defined as pathologic abnormalities or markers of damage, including abnormalities in blood or urine tests or imaging studies.

[a] Manifestations of kidney damage may occur during this stage even though GFR is not decreased, as described in Guideline 6 (e.g., nephrotic syndrome, nephritic syndrome, urinary tract symptoms, tubular syndromes).

Abbreviations and Symbols: GFR, glomerular filtration rate; HBP, high blood pressure;
–, none; ±, possible; +, mild; ++, moderate; +++, severe

Table 36 shows the association of levels of GFR with complications of chronic kidney disease. Patients with GFR 60 to 89 mL/min/1.73 m² usually have hypertension and may have laboratory abnormalities indicative of dysfunction in other organ systems, but usually no symptoms. Patients with GFR 30 to 59 mL/min/1.73 m² have laboratory abnormalities in several other organ systems, but few symptoms. Patients with GFR 15 to 29 mL/min/1.73 m² usually have laboratory abnormalities in many organ systems and have mild symptoms. Patients with GFR <15 mL/min/1.73 m² usually have many symptoms and laboratory abnormalities in several organ systems, collectively known as the "uremic syndrome." The association of complications of chronic kidney disease with the level of GFR is discussed in Part 6, Guidelines 7 through 12.

Risk of cardiovascular disease (R, O). Cardiovascular disease may be a cause and complication of chronic kidney disease. Irrespective of diagnosis, the increased risk of cardiovascular disease in individuals with chronic kidney disease can be attributed to: (1) a higher prevalence of "traditional" CVD risk factors; and (2) risk factors related to the hemodynamic and metabolic complications of chronic kidney disease ("CKD-related" or "nontraditional" CVD risk factors). Treatment and prevention of cardiovascular disease in chronic kidney disease includes risk factor reduction as well as specific therapies for cardiovascular disease and should begin as early as possible. CVD risk factors may become more prevalent or more severe as GFR declines; therefore, as GFR declines, treatment must intensify. Cardiovascular disease in chronic kidney disease is discussed in Guideline 15.

Kidney replacement therapy for uremia (R, O). Signs and symptoms of severe decrease in GFR, collectively, are known as "uremia" or the "uremic syndrome." Replacement therapy (dialysis and transplantation) is effective in improving the most serious features of uremia, irrespective of the type of chronic kidney disease. Patients require education and advance preparation to cope with the stresses of kidney failure, to choose a modality of kidney replacement therapy, and to undergo evaluation for that modality. It is recommended that preparation for kidney replacement therapy begin when GFR declines below 30 mL/min/1.73 m². All patients should probably be instructed to preserve suitable veins for possible future vascular access construction. The indications for initiation of kidney replacement therapy are based on the level of kidney function and presence of signs and symptoms of uremia. Most individuals begin dialysis or receive a kidney transplant when GFR is less than 15 mL/min/1.73 m².

Drug prescribing in chronic kidney disease (R). Patients with chronic kidney disease are prescribed a large number of medications. In addition, patients may take other medications, such as over-the-counter medications, "non-traditional" medications, vitamins and supplements, herbs, and drugs of abuse. A thorough review of the medication list and all other medications should be conducted at each visit. Drug dosage should be adjusted for the level of estimated GFR. Drugs with potentially adverse effects on kidney function or complications of decreased kidney function should be discontinued if possible. Drug-drug interactions should be considered. Because of possible alterations in volume of distribution, protein binding, drug elimination, and drug-drug interactions in chronic kidney disease, therapeutic drug monitoring should be performed, if possible. A large amount of information is available to providers in texts, manuals, and databases for handheld computers. Interpretation may be facilitated by the similarity between the classification of levels of kidney function proposed in this guideline and the recommendations for pharmacokinetic studies of drugs in patients with decreased kidney function made by the Food and Drug Administration[84] (on the Internet, *http://www.fda.gov/cder/guidance/1449fnl.pdf*).

Barriers to adherence in chronic kidney disease (R, O). Healthy people make choices that could ultimately shorten their lives, such as smoking, drinking or eating too much, not exercising, missing prescribed medications, and failing to get an annual physical. Those with chronic health conditions requiring lifestyle changes and clinician-initiated visits are more likely to be noncompliant.[85] Patients with chronic kidney disease live day-to-day with such a chronic condition. Other factors linked with noncompliance are shown in Table 37.[85-98]

Table 37. Factors Linked with Noncompliance in Chronic Diseases

Misunderstanding instructions[85]	Forgetfulness[94,95]
High stress[86]	Perception of negative side effects[90,94,95]
Depression[86-88]	Perception of less benefit from treatment[87]
Coping by avoidance[86]	Lessening of symptoms[94]
Belief that powerful others control health outcome[86,87,89]	Perception that illness affects work and life[96]
Unemployment[87,90]	Less confidence in care providers[87];
Lower income[86]	Less time with physicians[91]
Less social support[87]	Drug abuse history[97]
Less family support[85,87]	Male gender and medication compliance[87]
Many chronic illnesses[91,92]	Female gender and diet compliance[87]
Need for many medications[87,93]	Black race[87,97,98]
Limited medication access[87]	

Because the terminology "noncompliance" or "nonadherence" often leads to prejudice and negative stereotyping, it is recommended that "self-management behaviors" be substituted.[99] The Work Group recommends assessment of barriers to adherence in all patients with chronic kidney disease and incorporation of self-management behaviors into the treatment plan at all stages.

Referral to specialists (O). Frequently the primary care provider will make the diagnosis of chronic kidney disease. Referral to a nephrologist or other specialist for consultation or co-management should be made after diagnosis under the following circumstances: a clinical action plan cannot be prepared based on the stage of the disease, the prescribed evaluation of the patient cannot be carried out, or the recommended treatment cannot be carried out. These activities may not be possible either because the appropriate tools are not available or because the primary care physician does not have the time or information needed to do so. In general, patients with GFR <30 mL/min/ 1.73 m^2 (CKD Stages 4-5) should be referred to a nephrologist.

LIMITATIONS

This guideline provides a conceptual framework to the evaluation and management of chronic kidney disease, but does not provide sufficient details to guide health care providers in the management of individual patients with chronic kidney disease or the design of public policy to improve outcomes for the target population. Subsequent guidelines will elaborate on the concepts in this guideline, but it is beyond the scope of these guidelines to provide specific instructions for evaluation and management. This will be the topic of forthcoming K/DOQI guidelines and guidelines by other organizations. The ultimate goal is to develop specific guidelines for each action at each stage of disease.

CLINICAL APPLICATIONS

Almost all aspects of the evaluation and management of chronic kidney disease in textbooks of nephrology could be re-written to incorporate the stages of chronic kidney disease proposed in this guideline. Part 9 provides an approach to selected topics using this classification.

IMPLEMENTATION ISSUES

Development of a clinical action plan for all patients with chronic kidney disease is an enormous undertaking that will require coordinate effort of many government and nongovernmental organizations. The National Institute of Diabetes, Digestive and Kidney Disease (NIDDK) has established a National Kidney Disease Education Program. The NKF is committed to developing an implementation plan for the K/DOQI CKD guidelines and to working with the NIDDK and other organizations to develop a national program.

RESEARCH RECOMMENDATIONS

Much research is needed to define diagnostic and therapeutic strategies to reduce adverse outcomes of chronic kidney disease at each stage of disease. It will also be important to assess the effect of implementing these guidelines on the outcomes of chronic kidney disease.

GUIDELINE 3. INDIVIDUALS AT INCREASED RISK OF CHRONIC KIDNEY DISEASE

Some individuals without kidney damage and with normal or elevated GFR are at increased risk for development of chronic kidney disease.

- All individuals should be assessed, as part of routine health encounters, to determine whether they are at increased risk of developing chronic kidney disease, based on clinical and sociodemographic factors.
- Individuals at increased risk of developing chronic kidney disease should undergo testing for markers of kidney damage, and to estimate the level of GFR.
- Individuals found to have chronic kidney disease should be evaluated and treated as specified in Guideline 2.
- Individuals at increased risk, but found not to have chronic kidney disease, should be advised to follow a program of risk factor reduction, if appropriate, and undergo repeat periodic evaluation.

BACKGROUND

Epidemiological studies show an increased risk for chronic kidney disease, especially kidney failure, among individuals with certain clinical and sociodemographic characteristics. This suggests that there are risk factors for chronic kidney disease. In principle, prevention of adverse outcomes of chronic kidney disease could be facilitated by evaluating individuals with risk factors, to enable earlier detection, and by risk factor reduction in individuals without chronic kidney disease, to prevent or slow the development of chronic kidney disease.

RATIONALE
Definition of Risk Factors (R)

A risk factor is defined as an attribute that is associated with increased risk of an outcome. In principle, the relationship between the risk factor and the outcome may be either *causal* or *non-causal*. Causal risk factors are determinants of the outcome, and successful intervention to reduce exposure to them would improve outcomes. Non-causal risk factors may be associated with the outcome through confounding or reverse causation. Interventions to reduce exposure to non-causal risk factors would not necessarily improve outcomes.

Classification of risk factors (R). A useful classification of risk factors has been used in cardiovascular disease epidemiology[100] and is shown in Table 38.

Risk factors for chronic kidney disease (R, O). In principle, risk factors for development of chronic kidney disease would include susceptibility factors and initiation

Table 38. Classification of Risk Factors

Classification	Definition of Risk Factor
Category I	Factors for which interventions have been *proven* to lower risk
Category II	Factors for which interventions are *likely* to lower risk
Category III	Factors for which modification *may* lower risk
Category IV	Factors for which modification is not possible

factors. In addition, because it can be difficult to detect the onset of chronic kidney disease, some risk factors for faster progression may appear to be to susceptibility or initiation factors (Table 39). Note that progression factors may be associated with progression either because initial damage cannot be resolved or because damage is ongoing.

In addition, numerous factors have been shown to be associated with worse outcomes in patients with kidney failure, (such as inadequate dialysis dose, temporary vascular access, anemia, and low serum albumin concentration). These "end-stage" factors have been discussed in previous K/DOQI guidelines and are not relevant for this discussion.

Textbooks and reviews list a large number of potential risk factors for chronic kidney disease. The difficulty of detecting the early stages of chronic kidney disease makes it difficult to determine whether the risk factors so far identified relate more to susceptibility, initiation, or progression. Table 40 contains a partial list of clinical and sociodemographic factors that have been implicated as susceptibility or initiation factors. Progression factors are discussed in more detail in Guideline 13.

Table 41 shows relationships between types of chronic kidney disease and CKD risk factors. For some of these factors (for example, diabetes), interventions (like strict glycemic control) have been *proven* to lower the risk of developing chronic kidney disease (Category I, Table 38). For other factors (for example, hypertension), interventions (like antihypertensive therapy) are *likely* to lower the risk of chronic kidney disease (Category II, Table 38). For other factors (for example, autoimmune diseases), modifica-

Table 39. Types and Examples of Risk Factors for Chronic Kidney Disease

	Definition	Examples
Susceptibility factors	Increase susceptibility to kidney damage	Older age, family history
Initiation factors	Directly initiate kidney damage	Diabetes, high blood pressure, autoimmune diseases, systemic infections, urinary tract infections, urinary stones, lower urinary tract obstruction, drug toxicity
Progression factors	Cause worsening kidney damage and faster decline in kidney function after initiation of kidney damage	Higher level of proteinuria, higher blood pressure level, poor glycemic control in diabetes, smoking

Table 40. Potential Risk Factors for Susceptibility to and Initiation of Chronic Kidney Disease

Clinical Factors	Sociodemographic Factors
Diabetes	Older age
Hypertension	US ethnic minority status: African American, American Indian, Hispanic, Asian or Pacific Islander
Autoimmune diseases	
Systemic infections	
Urinary tract infections	Exposure to certain chemical and environmental conditions
Urinary stones	
Lower urinary tract obstruction	Low income/education
Neoplasia	
Family history of chronic kidney diseases	
Recovery from acute kidney failure	
Reduction in kidney mass	
Exposure to certain drugs	
Low birth weight	

tion of immune responses *might* lower the risk chronic kidney disease (Category III, Table 38). A number of these factors (for example, family history, age, race and ethnicity) are not modifiable (Category IV, Table 38).

Prevalence of individuals with risk factors for chronic kidney disease (R). The prevalence of individuals at increased risk for development of chronic kidney disease has not been studied systematically. However, some idea of the magnitude of the problem can be obtained by reviewing data from recent publications (Table 42).

LIMITATIONS

This guideline provides a conceptual framework to the definition, detection, and evaluation of individuals at increased risk of chronic kidney disease, but does not provide sufficient details to guide health care providers in screening individuals or developing

Table 41. Relationship Between Types of Kidney Disease and Risk Factors for Initiation and Susceptibility to Chronic Kidney Disease

Type of Kidney Disease	CKD Risk Factors
Diabetes (Type 1 & Type 2)	Diabetes mellitus, HBP, family history, US ethnic minority
Glomerular Diseases	Autoimmune diseases, systemic infections, neoplasia, drug or chemical exposure, family history
Vascular Diseases	HBP, family history, US ethnic minority
Tubulointerstitial Diseases	Urinary tract infections, stones, obstruction, toxic drugs
Cystic Diseases	Family history
Disease in the Kidney Transplant	Prior acute rejection, greater HLA mismatches, cyclosporine or tacrolimus, glomerular disease in native kidneys

Abbreviations: HBP, high blood pressure; HLA, human leukocyte antigen

Table 42. Prevalence of Individuals at Increased Risk for Chronic Kidney Disease

Risk Factor	Prevalence Estimated %	Estimated N
Diabetes mellitus[101]	Diagnosed: 5.1% of adults age ≥20	10.2 million
	Undiagnosed: 2.7% of adults age ≥20	5.4 million
Hypertension[102]	24.0% of adults age ≥18	43.1 million
Systemic lupus erythematosus[103]	~0.05% definite or suspected	~239,000
Functioning kidney graft[104]	~0.03%	88,311 as of 12/31/98
African American[105]	12.3%	34.7 million
Hispanic or Latino (of any race)[105]	12.5%	35.3 million
American Indian and Alaska Native[105]	0.9%	2.5 million
Age 60–70[106]	7.3%	20.3 million
Age ≥70[106]	9.2%	25.5 million
Acute kidney failure[107,108]	~0.14%	~363,000 non-federal hospital stays in 1997
Daily NSAID use[109,110]	~5.2% with rheumatoid arthritis or osteoarthritis (assumed daily use)	~13 million assumed daily use
	~30% yearly use	~75 million yearly use

Abbreviation: NSAID, non-steroidal anti-inflammatory drug

screening programs. It is beyond the scope of these guidelines to provide specific instructions for screening.

CLINICAL APPLICATIONS

Universal screening for chronic kidney disease is recommended for children in the United States, but not for adults. However, the list of individuals at increased risk for chronic kidney disease includes a large fraction of the adult population (Table 42). Thus, it is important to carefully consider the definition of individuals at increased risk and methods for testing them. Suggestions (based on opinion) for evaluation of individuals at increased risk for chronic kidney disease are provided in Part 9.

IMPLEMENTATION ISSUES AND RESEARCH RECOMMENDATIONS

Implementation of these guidelines will require education of all health care providers about risk factors for chronic kidney disease and methods of testing. The Sixth Report of the Joint National Committee for the Prevention, Evaluation, Detection and Treatment of High Blood Pressure (JNC-VI) and the American Diabetes Association have issued recommendations for the evaluation of patients with high blood pressure and diabetes, respectively, for chronic kidney disease. However, as indicated in Table 42, a large number of individuals without high blood pressure and diabetes may also be at increased risk. Thus, it will be important to test a larger population than currently targeted, which would increase the cost of health care.

The increased health care costs that would follow implementation of a screening program for chronic kidney disease may well require a more solid base of evidence than is currently available. The Work Group recommends development of a clinical practice guideline focused on this issue in order to develop specific recommendations for evaluating adults for chronic kidney disease. In the past, universal screening was not recommended because of the low prevalence of chronic kidney disease and the lack of treatments to improve outcomes. Data provided in these guidelines suggests that the prevalence of earlier stages of chronic kidney disease is higher than previously known and that earlier detection and treatment to prevent or delay the loss of kidney function and development of cardiovascular disease in chronic kidney disease. If sufficient information is not available to assess the value of testing individuals at increased risk, or of universal screening, the Work Group suggests that research on evaluation programs should be conducted.

PART 5. EVALUATION OF LABORATORY MEASUREMENTS FOR CLINICAL ASSESSMENT OF KIDNEY DISEASE

The definition and staging of chronic kidney disease depends on the assessment of GFR, proteinuria, and other markers of kidney disease. The goals of Part 5 are to evaluate the accuracy of prediction equations to estimate the level of GFR from serum creatinine concentration, the accuracy of ratios of protein-to-creatinine in untimed ("spot") urine samples to assess protein excretion rate, and the utility of markers of kidney damage other than proteinuria. As described in Appendix 1, Table 151, the Work Group evaluated studies according to accepted methods for evaluation of diagnostic tests. To provide a more comprehensive review, the Work Group attempted to integrate the systematic review of specific questions with existing guidelines and recommendations.

GUIDELINE 4. ESTIMATION OF GFR

Estimates of GFR are the best overall indices of the level of kidney function.

- The level of GFR should be estimated from prediction equations that take into account the serum creatinine concentration and some or all of the following variables: age, gender, race, and body size. The following equations provide useful estimates of GFR:
  - In adults, the MDRD Study and Cockcroft-Gault equations
  - In children, the Schwartz and Counahan-Barratt equations.
- The serum creatinine concentration alone should not be used to assess the level of kidney function.
- Clinical laboratories should report an estimate of GFR using a prediction equation, in addition to reporting the serum creatinine measurement.
- Autoanalyzer manufacturers and clinical laboratories should calibrate serum creatinine assays using an international standard.
- Measurement of creatinine clearance using timed (for example, 24-hour) urine collections does not improve the estimate of GFR over that provided by prediction equations. A 24-hour urine sample provides useful information for:
  - Estimation of GFR in individuals with exceptional dietary intake (vegetarian diet, creatine supplements) or muscle mass (amputation, malnutrition, muscle wasting);
  - Assessment of diet and nutritional status;
  - Need to start dialysis.

BACKGROUND

Glomerular filtration rate (GFR) provides an excellent measure of the filtering capacity of the kidneys. A low or decreasing GFR is a good index of chronic kidney disease. Since the total kidney GFR is equal to the sum of the filtration rates in each of the functioning nephrons, the total GFR can be used as an index of functioning renal mass.[111] A decrease in GFR precedes kidney failure in all forms of progressive kidney disease. Monitoring

---

changes in GFR can delineate progression of kidney disease. The level of GFR is a strong predictor of the time to onset of kidney failure as well as the risk of complications of chronic kidney disease. Additionally, estimation of GFR in clinical practice allows proper dosing of drugs excreted by glomerular filtration to avoid potential drug toxicity.

Glomerular filtration rate cannot be measured directly. If a substance in stable concentration in the plasma is physiologically inert, freely filtered at the glomerulus, and neither secreted, reabsorbed, synthesized, nor metabolized by the kidney, the amount of that substance filtered at the glomerulus is equal to the amount excreted in the urine. The fructose polysaccharide inulin has each of the above properties and has long been considered an ideal substance to estimate GFR. The amount of inulin filtered at the glomerulus equals the GFR multiplied by the plasma inulin concentration: $GFR \times P_{in}$. The amount of excreted inulin equals the urine inulin concentration (U_{in}) multiplied by the urine flow rate (V, volume excreted per unit time).

Since filtered inulin = excreted inulin:

$$(1)\ GFR \times P_{in} = U_{in} \times V$$

$$(2)\ GFR = \frac{U_{in} \times V}{P_{in}}$$

The term ($U_{in} \times V$)/P_{in} is defined as the clearance of inulin and is an accurate estimate of GFR. The inulin clearance, in mL/min, refers to that volume of plasma per unit time that is cleared of inulin by renal excretion.

RATIONALE

Criterion Standard

Inulin clearance is widely regarded as the gold standard for measuring glomerular filtration rate. Inulin clearance measurements in healthy, hydrated young adults (adjusted to a standard body surface area of 1.73 m^2) have mean values of 127 mL/min/1.73 m^2 in men and 118 mL/min/1.73 m^2 in women with a standard deviation of approximately 20 mL/min/1.73 m^2.[67] Among adults, numerous studies suggest that glomerular filtration rate is lower at older ages. After age 20 to 30 years, GFR decreases by approximately 1.0 mL/min/1.73 m^2 per year with substantial inter-individual variation even among "healthy" individuals.[112,113] Whether this average decline with aging is optimal in terms of predicting the risk of complications of decreased kidney function and mortality is unknown.

Glomerular filtration rate in the infant differs quantitatively from that in older children and adults. During infancy and through the first 12 to 18 months of life, GFR increases with maturation[69-71] (see Table 23, Guideline 1). Inulin clearance is also the gold standard to measure GFR in children, but is particularly difficult in the neonate because of the lower GFR of neonates and their relatively larger extracellular fluid compartment. These factors extend the study time necessary for techniques relying on equilibration of the marker substance and monitoring of its plasma disappearance rate. Additionally, accurate assessment of the urine flow rate requires bladder catheterization in infants and young children.

Rationale for Alternative Measures

The classic method of inulin clearance requires an intravenous infusion and timed urine collections over a period of several hours making it costly and cumbersome. As a result a number of alternative measures for estimating GFR have been devised. The urinary clearance of exogenous radioactive markers (^{125}I-iothalamate and ^{99m}Tc-DTPA) provide excellent measures of GFR[114] but are not readily available. Plasma clearance of exogenous substances including iohexol and ^{51}Cr-EDTA has been used as well but require estimates of body size, which decreases their precision. Capillary electrophoresis allows for measurement of non-radiolabeled iothalamate in blood and urine with promising results.[115] Serum cystatin C has been used to estimate GFR but data are conflicting as to whether it provides a sufficient improvement to warrant widespread clinical use.[116] The most widely used measures of GFR in clinical practice are based on the 24-hour creatinine clearance or serum creatinine concentration. As discussed below, each of these measurements is associated with serious limitations.

Equations to predict GFR and creatinine clearance from serum creatinine have been tested in a large number of studies whose results are reviewed. Use of relevant equations in children and adults has been shown to give more valid estimates of GFR than serum creatinine alone. Additionally, for the health care provider, it may be easier to recognize clinically important changes in kidney function when dealing with large numbers estimating a physiologically relevant parameter (GFR) rather than small numbers (serum creatinine) which are inversely related to the relevant parameter.

Accuracy of an Equation in Estimating GFR Combines Its Bias and Precision

In choosing a prediction equation to estimate GFR, one should consider both the bias and precision of the equation-generated estimates. Bias expresses the systematic deviation from the gold standard measure of GFR. A prediction equation that consistently overestimates or underestimates the gold standard measure of GFR yields a biased estimate.

An equally important measure of the usefulness of a prediction equation is a measure of its precision. Precision expresses the variability (or dispersion) of prediction equation estimates around the gold standard GFR measure.

Accuracy combines precision and bias. A useful measure of accuracy is a description of percentiles of the distribution of the differences between estimated and measured GFR. In other words, if 99% of the time a prediction equation yields an estimate within 10% of the measured GFR, it would be a very accurate and useful clinical tool. Achieving a high level of accuracy requires both low bias and high precision. Description of the percent of estimates falling within 30% and 50% above or below the measured GFR is a useful measure of accuracy.

Importance of Sample Size

Many of the studies reviewed were small. Since estimates of accuracy from smaller studies can be unreliable, studies presented have at least 100 adults or 50 children. Several large validation studies evaluating the newly developed MDRD Study equation were conducted recently and were only available in abstract form. In order to capture these valuable data the authors were contacted and asked to analyze their data and provide estimates of accuracy for this review. Additional details regarding the evaluation of prediction equations to estimate GFR are reviewed in Part 10, Appendix 3.

Strength of Evidence

Serum creatinine alone is not an accurate index of the level of GFR (R). The use of the serum level of creatinine as an index of GFR rests on three important assumptions: (1) creatinine is an ideal filtration marker whose clearance approximates GFR; (2) creatinine excretion rate is constant among individuals and over time; and (3) measurement of serum creatinine is accurate and reproducible across clinical laboratories. Although the serum creatinine concentration can provide a rough index of the level of GFR, none of these assumptions is strictly true, and numerous factors can lead to errors in estimation of the level of GFR from the serum creatinine concentration alone.

Creatinine excretion by the kidney. Creatinine is freely filtered by the glomerulus, but is also secreted by the proximal tubule. Hence, the amount of creatinine excreted in the urine is the composite of both the filtered and secreted creatinine and can be represented by the following equation:

$$(3)\ U_{Cr} \times V = GFR \times P_{Cr} + TS_{Cr}$$

where TS_{Cr} is the rate of tubular creatinine secretion. Dividing by P_{Cr}:

$$(4)\ C_{Cr} = GFR + C_{TSCr}$$

where C_{TSCr} is the clearance of creatinine due to tubular secretion. Thus, creatinine clearance systematically overestimates GFR. This overestimation is approximately 10% to 40% in normal individuals, but is greater and more unpredictable in patients with chronic kidney disease (Fig 12A). Factors other than the level of GFR can also influence creatinine secretion. Creatinine secretion is inhibited by some common medications, for example, cimetidine and trimethoprim.

In addition, measurement of creatinine clearance is not easy. Urinary clearance measurements require timed urine collections, which are difficult to obtain and often involve errors in collection. Furthermore, day-to-day variation in creatinine excretion exists, making estimation of GFR, even from a valid 24-hour urine collection, imprecise.

Creatinine metabolism. The urinary creatinine excretion represents the difference between creatinine generation in the body (G_{Cr}) and extra-renal creatinine elimination (E_{Cr}):

$$(5)\ U_{Cr} \times V = G_{Cr} - E_{Cr}$$

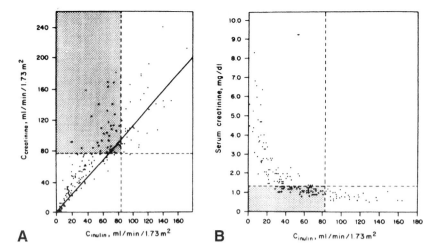

Fig 12. Relationship of creatinine clearance and serum creatinine with GFR (inulin clearance) in patients with glomerular disease. Vertical dashed lines correspond to the lower limit of normal for inulin clearance in the authors' laboratory (82 mL/min/1.73 m²). The horizontal dashed line in the left panel (A) corresponds to the lower limit for creatinine clearance (77 mL/min/1.73 m²); and the horizontal dashed line in the right panel (B) corresponds to the upper limit for the serum creatinine concentration (1.4 mg/dL) in the authors' laboratory. The shaded areas included values for patients in whom GFR is reduced, but creatinine clearance and serum creatinine concentration remain normal. Data from Shemesh et al.[117] Reprinted with permission.[118]

Substituting into equation 3 and re-arranging for P_{Cr} yields the following:

$$(6) \quad P_{Cr} = \frac{G_{Cr} - TS_{Cr} - E_{Cr}}{GFR}$$

It can therefore be inferred that the relationship between serum creatinine and GFR is affected by the generation and extra-renal excretion of creatinine, as well as the filtration and secretion of creatinine by the kidney.

Creatinine is mainly derived from the metabolism of creatine in muscle, and its generation is proportional to the total muscle mass. As a result, mean creatinine generation is higher in men than in women, in younger than in older individuals, and in blacks than in whites. This leads to differences in serum creatinine concentration according to age, gender, and race, even after adjusting for GFR. Muscle wasting is also associated with reduced creatinine generation resulting in lower serum creatinine concentration than expected for the level of GFR in malnourished patients with chronic kidney disease. Creatinine generation is also affected by meat intake to a certain extent, because the process of cooking meat converts a variable portion of creatine to creatinine. Therefore, serum creatinine is lower than expected for the level of GFR in patients following a low protein diet.

Though extra-renal creatinine excretion is minimal in people with normal kidney function, it is increased in patients with chronic kidney disease due to the degradation of creatinine by bacterial overgrowth in the small bowel. As much as two-thirds of total daily creatinine excretion can occur by extra-renal creatinine elimination in patients with severely reduced kidney function.

As a consequence of all these factors, urinary creatinine excretion is lower in chronic kidney disease, leading to systematic overestimation of GFR from serum creatinine. Figure 12B shows that serum creatinine can remain less than 2.0 mg/dL despite reduction in GFR to as low as 15 to 20 mL/min/1.73 m^2. Thus, an elevated serum creatinine is an insensitive index of decreased GFR. Only 60% of patients with decreased GFR had increased serum creatinine. Stated otherwise, 40% of individuals with decreased GFR had a serum creatinine level within the normal range for the laboratory.

Creatinine measurement. In young adults, the normal level for serum creatinine concentration is approximately 1.0 mg/dL. The traditional assay for measurement of creatinine is the alkaline picrate method, which detects non-creatinine chromogens in serum (approximately 0.2 mg/dL), as well as creatinine. Urine does not contain non-creatinine chromogens, nor are these compounds retained in chronic kidney disease. Thus, historically, measured creatinine clearance has systematically underestimated true creatinine clearance. By coincidence, the difference between measured and true creatinine clearance is similar in magnitude to the clearance of creatinine due to tubular secretion. Hence, measured creatinine clearance has historically approximated the level of GFR.

Modern autoanalyzers use serum creatinine assays with less interference by non-creatinine chromogens (for example, kinetic alkaline picrate or enzymatic methods, such as the imidohydrolase method). Consequently, normal levels of serum creatinine are now lower, resulting in higher values for measured creatinine clearance and overestimation of GFR. In order to minimize this overestimation of GFR, autoanalyzer manufacturers and clinical laboratories may calibrate the instruments to report higher serum creatinine values. This calibration is not standardized, leading to variation within and across laboratories. Variation is proportionately greater at low serum creatinine values than at high values.

In addition to non-creatinine chromogens, other substances may also interfere with serum creatinine assays. These substances include ketones and some medications, which may lead to spurious elevation in serum creatinine concentration and underestimation of GFR.

In summary, serum creatinine is affected by the level of GFR and by factors independent of GFR, including age, gender, race, body size, diet, certain drugs, and laboratory analytical methods (Table 43). Therefore, serum creatinine is not an accurate index of the level of kidney function, and the level of serum creatinine alone should not be used to assess the stage of chronic kidney disease.

Table 43. Factors Affecting Serum Creatinine Concentration

	Effect on Serum Creatinine	Mechanism/Comment
Kidney disease	Increase	Decreased glomerular filtration rate; however, increase is blunted by increased tubular secretion of creatinine and by reduced creatinine generation
Reduced muscle mass	Decrease	Reduced creatinine generation; common in children, women, older and malnourished patients
Ingestion of cooked meat	Increase	Transient increase in creatinine generation; however, the increase may be blunted by transient increase in GFR
Malnutrition	Decrease	Reduced creatinine generation due to reduced muscle mass and reduced meat intake
Trimethoprim, cimetidine	Increase	Inhibition of tubular creatinine secretion
Flucytosine, some cephalosporins	Increase	Positive interference with the iminohydrolase and picric acid assays for creatinine, respectively
Ketoacidosis	Increase	Positive interference with picric acid assay for creatinine

Adapted with permission.[119]

Equations estimating GFR based on serum creatinine are more accurate and precise than estimates of GFR from measurement of serum creatinine alone (R, C). Many studies have documented that creatinine production varies substantially across sex, age, and ethnicity.[113] Equations have the advantage of providing an estimate of GFR which empirically combines all of these average effects while allowing for the marked differences in creatinine production between individuals. Figures 13 and 14 show that equation-based estimates perform better than serum creatinine alone.

A number of equations have been developed to predict GFR directly in adult patients (Table 44) and children (Table 45). In addition to equations which directly predict GFR, the most frequently used equation for estimating GFR in adults is the Cockcroft-Gault equation which was developed for estimating creatinine clearance but has been tested

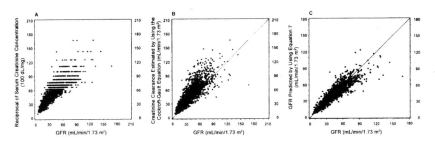

Fig 13. Estimates of GFR versus measured GFR among MDRD Study baseline cohort. GFR measured as urinary clearance of ^{125}I-iothalamate and adjusted for body surface area in 1,628 patients. Estimates include (A) $100/S_{Cr}$ ($R^2 = 80.4\%$), (B) Cockcroft-Gault equation standardized for body surface area ($R^2 = 84.2\%$), and (C) MDRD Study equation 7 ($R^2 = 90.3\%$). R^2 values indicate the percentage of variance of log GFR accounted for in the validation sample (n = 558) by equations derived from the development sample (n = 1,070). Reprinted with permission.[17]

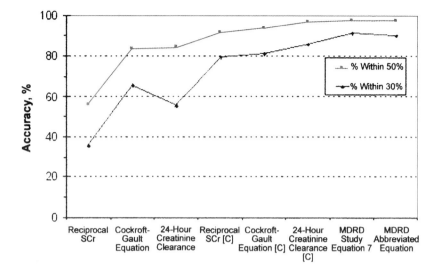

Fig 14. Accuracy of different estimates of GFR in adults, expressed as the percent of estimates within 30% and 50% of the measured GFR in the MDRD Study validation sample (n = 558). Estimates denoted with [C] include a calibration correction of 0.69 for 100/serum creatinine, 0.84 for Cockcroft-Gault equation, and 0.81 for 24-hour creatinine clearance to show performance after bias is eliminated using a multiplicative correction factor. Analysis of MDRD Study[17] data prepared by Tom Greene, PhD.

widely in its prediction of GFR.[120,121] Another equation developed in 1971 for estimation of creatinine clearance by Jelliffe has been used extensively.[122]

Several formulas for estimating GFR in children have been developed as well. The most widely studied of these are the Schwartz[71,123-126] and Counahan-Barratt formulae.[127-129] Both provide an estimate of GFR based on a constant multiplied by the child's height divided by serum creatinine.

Many studies evaluate GFR prediction equations but several methodological aspects limit the ability to compare results across studies (C). A systematic review of the literature reveals that the number of references evaluating GFR prediction methods is vast (>100 references). Studies evaluating GFR prediction equations are listed in Table 46 (Cockcroft-Gault equation) and Table 47 (MDRD Study equation). The presentation of validity data here is limited to four equations: the most widely used equations for estimating GFR in the adult (Cockcroft-Gault) and children (Schwartz and Counahan-Barratt) as well as the newly developed MDRD Study equations.

Techniques to measure creatinine, reference standards for GFR and the statistics used to estimate accuracy, bias, and precision vary widely in published reports. The most frequently used statistic is the correlation coefficient, which has little applicability and cannot be pooled across studies. While most reports specify the methods used to measure

Table 44. Equations Developed to Predict GFR in Adults Based on Serum Creatinine

Equation Author, Year (No. of Subjects)	Equation	Studies Reviewed (Abstracts)[*]
Cockcroft-Gault Equation Cockcroft,[121] 1976 (N = 236)	$C_{Cr}(\text{ml/min}) = \dfrac{(140-Age)\times Weight}{72\times S_{Cr}} \times (0.85 \text{ if female})$	58 (5)[a]
MDRD, Serum Variables Levey,[17] 1999 (N = 1,070, 558 in validation set)	$GFR(\text{ml/min/1.73 m}^2) = 170\times(S_{Cr})^{-0.999}\times(Age)^{-0.176}\times(SUN)^{-0.170}\times(Alb)^{+0.318}$ $\times(0.762 \text{ if female})\times(1.180 \text{ if black})$	1 (6)
Jelliffe Equation, 1973 Jelliffe,[130] 1973 (No data)	$C_{Cr}(\text{ml/min}) = \dfrac{98-0.8\times(Age-20)}{S_{Cr}}\times(0.90 \text{ if female})$	15 (1)
Mawer Equation Mawer,[131] 1972 (N = 16)	Men: $C_{Cr}(\text{ml/min}) = \dfrac{Weight\times[29.3-(0.203\times Age)]\times[1-(0.03\times S_{Cr})]}{(14.4\times S_{Cr})}\times\dfrac{Weight}{70}$ Women: $C_{Cr}(\text{ml/min}) = \dfrac{Weight\times[25.3-(0.175\times Age)]\times[1-(0.03\times S_{Cr})]}{(14.4\times S_{Cr})}\times\dfrac{Weight}{70}$	13 (1)
Hull Equation Hull,[132] 1981 (N = 103, 144 measurements)	$C_{Cr}(\text{ml/min}) = \left(\dfrac{145-Age}{S_{Cr}}-3\right)\times\dfrac{Weight}{70}\times(0.85 \text{ if female})$	12
Jelliffe Equation, 1971 Jelliffe,[122] 1971 (No data)[b]	Men: $C_{Cr}(\text{ml/min}) = \dfrac{100}{S_{Cr}}-12$ Women: $C_{Cr}(\text{ml/min}) = \dfrac{80}{S_{Cr}}-7$	7
Reciprocal Serum Creatinine Equation	$C_{Cr}(\text{ml/min}) = \dfrac{100}{S_{Cr}}$	7 (1)
Gates Equation Gates,[133] 1985 (N = 90, 100 measurements)	Men: $C_{Cr}(\text{ml/min}) = (89.4\times S_{Cr}^{-1.2})+\left(55-Age)\times(0.447\times S_{Cr}^{-1.1})\right)$ Women: $C_{Cr}(\text{ml/min}) = (60\times S_{Cr}^{-1.1})+\left((56-Age)\times(0.3\times S_{Cr}^{-1.1})\right)$	6
Bjornsson Equation Bjornsson,[134] 1983 (N = 50, validation set)	Men: $C_{Cr}(\text{ml/min}) = \dfrac{27-(0.173\times Age)\times Weight\times 0.07}{S_{Cr}}$ Women: $C_{Cr}(\text{ml/min}) = \dfrac{25-(0.175\times Age)\times Weight\times 0.07}{S_{Cr}}$	6
Articles with equations reviewed in ≤3 studies:	Agarwal,[135] Davis-Chandler,[136] Edwards,[137] Hallynck,[138] Levey,[17,18] Mogensen,[139] Nankivell,[140] Robinson,[141] Rowe,[142] Salazar-Corcoran,[143] Sanaka,[144] Siersbaek-Nielsen,[145] Toto,[146] Tourgaard,[147] Walser,[181] Yukawa[148]	26 (3)
	Total number of articles examined:	**64**

Includes equations whose initial development was to predict creatinine clearance subsequently validated as predictors of GFR.

* Total number of studies reviewed for each equation, including abstracts, in parentheses. Individual studies that examined multiple equations are included in the count for each equation.

[a] Includes studies that corrected or did not correct for both gender and body surface area.

[b] Equation presented without a demonstration set.

Abbreviations and units: C_{Cr}, creatinine clearance; S_{Cr}, serum creatinine in mg/dL; Age, in years; Weight in kg; SUN, serum urea nitrogen in mg/dL; Alb, serum albumin in g/dL

Table 45. Equations Developed to Predict GFR in Children Based on Serum Creatinine

Equation Author, Year (No. of Subjects)	Equation	Studies Reviewed*
Schwartz Formula Schwartz,[124] 1976 (N = 186)	$C_{Cr}(\text{ml/min}) = \dfrac{0.55 \times Length}{S_{Cr}}$	32
Counahan-Barratt Equation Counahan,[127] 1976 (N = 108)	$GFR\,(\text{ml/min/1.73 m}^2) = \dfrac{0.43 \times Length}{S_{Cr}}$	9
Shull Equation Shull,[149] 1987 (N = 89, 101 in validation set)	$C_{Cr}(\text{ml/min/1.73 m}^2) = \dfrac{\left[(0.035 \times Age) + 0.236\right] \times 100}{S_{Cr}}$	5
Traub Equation Traub,[150] 1980 (N = 122 , 158 measurements)	$C_{Cr}(\text{ml/min/1.73 m}^2) = \dfrac{0.48 \times Length}{S_{Cr}}$	4
Ghazali-Barratt Equation Ghazali,[151] 1974 (No data)[a]	$C_{Cr}(\text{ml/min/1.73 m}^2) = \dfrac{0.12 \times \left[15.4 + (0.46 \times Age)\right] \times Weight}{S_{Cr} \times BSA}$	4
Articles with equations reviewed in ≤3 studies:	Cockcroft,[121] Coultard,[70] Evans,[152] Hernandez de Acevedo,[153] Jelliffe,[154] Traub,[150] Paap,[155] Parkin[156] Rudd,[157] Schwartz,[71] van den Anker[158]	26
	Total number of articles examined:	42

Table includes equations initially developed to predict creatinine clearance but subsequently validated as predictors of GFR.

* Total number of studies reviewed for each equation, including abstracts, in parentheses. Individual studies that examined multiple equations are included in the count for each equation.

[a] Equation presented without a demonstration set.

Abbreviations and units: Length, body length in cm; C_{Cr}, creatinine clearance; S_{Cr}, serum creatinine in mg/dL; Age, in years; Weight in kg; BSA, body surface area in m²

serum creatinine, only rarely is it known how closely the serum creatinine assay reflects the true creatinine level. This severely limits the ability to compare or combine reported results. (For details, see Part 10, Appendix 3.)

Among adults, the MDRD Study equation provides a clinically useful estimate of GFR (up to approximately 90 mL/min/1.73 m²) (S). The MDRD Study equation (Table 47) has the advantages of having been derived based on:

- GFR measured directly by urinary clearance of ^{125}I-Iothalamate;
- A large sample of >500 individuals with a wide range of kidney diseases;
- Inclusion of both European-American and African-American participants;
- Validated in a large (n > 500) separate group of individuals as part of its development.

This equation provides estimates of GFR standardized for body surface area. The abbreviated version is easy to implement since it requires only serum creatinine, age, sex, and race. The calculations can be made using available web-based and downloadable medical calculators. The abbreviated MDRD Study equation has two equivalent forms (Table 48).

The results of studies reporting equations for estimating a standard measure of GFR

Table 46. Estimating GFR in Adults Using the Cockcroft-Gault Equation: Accuracy and Bias

Author, Year Equation/Sample	No. of Subjects* (Measurements)	Applic-ability	GFR Range (mL/min/1.73 m²) 0 30 60 90 120	Accuracy** 30%	50%	Bias† (%)	Quality
Lewis,[162] 2001[a]	1,775	✝✝		80	94	1	●
Levey,[17] 1999 BSA corrected CG[a]	1,070/558[c]	✝✝✝		65	83	23	●
Bias corrected CG[a,b]				81	94	4[b]	
Rolin,[159] 1984 Uncorrected CG	394 (500)	✝✝✝		73[d]	91	10	●
BSA corrected CG[a]				81[d]	96	3	
Toto,[135] 1997[a]	193	✝✝		78	98	−14	●
Lemann,[160] 1990 Diabetics	136	✝✝		77	92	1	●
Healthy & stone formers	110			96	100	−8	○
Charleson,[151] 1980	100	✝✝✝		66	84	—	○
Waller,[163] 1991	171	✝✝		81	94	0	○
DeSanto,[154] 1991 CKD	124	✝✝		70	85	—	○
	62			48	70	−5	
Healthy	62			92	100	0	
Gault,[120] 1992	100 (197)	✝✝		75	92	5	○
Bedros,[165] 1998 Bias corrected CG[b]	321 (708)	✝✝		68 76	84 93	13 0[b]	○
Goerdt,[166] 1997	127 (142)	✝✝		66	85	25[e]	○

The Cockcroft-Gault equation is: $C_{Cr} \, (\text{ml/min}) = \dfrac{(140 - Age) \times Weight}{72 \times S_{Cr}} \times (0.85 \, \text{if female})$

Markers for measuring GFR include ^{125}I-iothalamate (Levey[17], Rolin[159], Toto[135], Lemann (diabetics)[160], Lewis[162]), Inulin (Lemann (healthy)[160], De Santo[164]), ^{99m}Tc-DTPA (Waller[163], Gault[120]), ^{51}Cr EDTA (Charleson[161]), Iohexol (Goerdt[166]).

* When multiple measurements were made for each subject, the total number of measurements appears in parentheses.
** Accuracy defined as the percent of GFR estimates within 30% or 50% of measured GFR.
† See Part 10, Appendix 3 for definition of bias.

[a] Cockcroft-Gault equation standardized for 1.73 m² body surface area
[b] Bias correction utilized a multiplier which corrected the overall bias of the development set to 0. The bias noted is calculated from the validation (test) set when available.
[c] 1,070 subjects in model development set; 558 subjects in validation set.
[d] Percent of estimates within 35% of the true value.
[e] Bias is rough estimation from the graph.

Abbreviations: CKD, chronic kidney disease; CG, Cockcroft-Gault Equation, BSA, body surface area

with at least 100 adult participants and a plot of predicted versus measured GFR are summarized in Table 46 (Cockroft-Gault equation) and Table 47 (MDRD Study equation). The bias in estimating GFR using the Cockcroft-Gault equation varied markedly across studies (from −14% to +25%). The accuracy measures indicated the majority (median of 75%) of estimated GFRs were within 30% of the measured GFR, an accuracy considered sufficient for good clinical decision-making. The Cockcroft-Gault equation does not include body size. Some studies have standardized the results for body surface area. Other

Table 47. Estimating GFR in Adults
Using the MDRD Study Equation: Accuracy and Bias

Author, Year Equation	No. of Subjects* (Measurements)	Applic- ability	GFR Range (mL/min/1.73 m²) 0 30 60 90 120	Accuracy** 30%	50%	Bias† (%)	Quality
Levey,[17] 1999 Levey,[18] 2000	1,070/558[e]	↑↑↑					●
Equation 1[a]				91	98	3	
Equation 2[b]				92	98	3	
Equation 3[c]				91	98	3	
Equation 4[d]				91	98	3	
Lewis,[162] 2001	1,775	↑↑					◐
Equation 1[a]				88	97	1	
Equation 2[b]				88	98	−1	
Equation 3[c]				88	98	−1	
Equation 4[d]				88	98	−3	
Bedros,[165] 1998	321 (708)	↑↑					○
Equation 4[d]				84	97	−1	

* When multiple measurements were made for each subject, the total number of measurements appears in parentheses.
** Accuracy defined as the percent of GFR estimates within 30% or 50% of measured GFR.
† See Part 10, Appendix 3 for definition of bias.

[a] Equation 1:
$$GFR = 170 \times (S_{Cr})^{-0.999} \times (Age)^{-0.176} \times (BUN)^{-0.170} \times (Alb)^{+0.318}$$
$$\times (0.762 \text{ if female}) \times (1.180 \text{ if African-American})$$
("Equation 7" in Levey,[17] 1999)

[b] Equation 2:
$$GFR = 198 \times (S_{Cr})^{-0.858} \times (Age)^{-0.167} \times (BUN)^{-0.293} \times (UUN)^{+0.249}$$
$$\times (0.822 \text{ if female}) \times (1.178 \text{ if African-American})$$
("Equation 6" in Levey,[17] 1999)

[c] Equation 3:
$$GFR = 270 \times (S_{Cr})^{-1.007} \times (Age)^{-0.180} \times (BUN)^{-0.169}$$
$$\times (0.755 \text{ if female}) \times (1.178 \text{ if African-American})$$
("five-variable" equation in Levey,[18] 2000)

[d] Equation 4:
$$GFR = 186 \times (S_{Cr})^{-1.154} \times (Age)^{-0.203}$$
$$\times (0.742 \text{ if female}) \times (1.210 \text{ if African-American})$$
("four-variable" (abbreviated) equation in Levey,[18] 2000)

[e] 1,070 subjects in model development set; 558 subjects in validation set.

Abbreviations and units: GFR, glomerular filtration rate in mg/mL/1.73 m²; S_Cr, serum creatinine in mg/dL; age, in years; weight in kg; BUN, blood urea nitrogen in mg/dL; Alb, serum albumin in g/dL; UUN, urine urea nitrogen

studies have suggested using lean body mass rather than total weight, especially for obese individuals.

Table 47 shows similar data for several forms of the MDRD Study equation. Within the validation sample of the MDRD Study, the equation developed on an independent sample of 1,070 participants performed better than the Cockcroft-Gault equation (Fig 14). Over 90% of the estimates were within 30% of the measured GFR, with only 2% having an error of greater than 50%. The four different variants of the MDRD Study equation performed similarly using these criteria for accuracy in all of the available data. Thus, the abbreviated MDRD Study equation provides a rigorously developed equation

Table 48. Abbreviated MDRD Study Equation

Estimated GFR (ml/min/1.73m²)
$$= 186 \times (S_{Cr})^{-1.154} \times (Age)^{-0.203} \times (0.742 \text{ if female}) \times (1.210 \text{ if African-American})$$
$$= \exp(5.228 - 1.154 \times \ln(S_{Cr}) - 0.203 \times \ln(Age) - (0.299 \text{ if female}) + (0.192 \text{ if African-American}))$$

For explanation, see text and references 17,18.

| | MDRD Study equation | | | | Cockcroft-Gault Equation | |
| | European-American | | African-American | | | |
Age (Years)	Men	Women	Men	Women	Men	Women
30	1.47	1.13	1.73	1.34	1.83	1.56
40	1.39	1.08	1.65	1.27	1.67	1.42
50	1.34	1.03	1.58	1.22	1.50	1.28
60	1.30	1.00	1.53	1.18	1.33	1.13
70	1.26	0.97	1.49	1.15	1.17	0.99
80	1.23	0.95	1.46	1.12	1.00	0.85

Calculations in this table assume a weight of 72 kg and body surface area (BSA) of 1.73 m^2. Units for serum creatinine are mg/dL (multiply by 88.4 μmol/L = 1 mg/dL).

Abbreviated MDRD Study equation: $GFR = 186 \times (S_{Cr})^{-1.154} \times (Age)^{-0.203} \times (0.742 \ \text{if female}) \times (1.210 \ \text{if black})$

Cockcroft-Gault equation: $C_{Cr} = \dfrac{(140 - Age) \times Weight}{72 \times S_{Cr}} \times (0.85 \ \text{if female})$

Abbreviations and units: GFR, glomerular filtration rate in mg/mL/1.73 m^2; S_{Cr}, serum creatinine in mg/dL; age, in years; weight in kg; C_{Cr}, creatinine clearance

for estimating GFR, which may allow for improved prediction of GFR. (See Part 10, Appendix 3.)

Table 49 shows serum creatinine values which can be used to identify individuals with an estimated GFR of 60 mL/min/1.73 m^2 or less for adults of different ages, genders and ethnicities. All of the values are well below 2.0 mg/dL, which corresponds to an estimated GFR in the range of 25–51 mL/min/1.73 m^2, depending on age, gender, and ethnicity. This equation may be superior to previous equations but the data at this point are quite limited. (See Part 10, Appendix 3.) While this equation is difficult to memorize, it is available on the Internet (www.kdoqi.org) and can be readily programmed or imported into calculators and laboratory systems.

Among children, the Schwartz and Counahan-Barratt formulae provide clinically useful estimates of GFR (C). Several formulae for estimating GFR in children have been developed. Two of these, the Schwartz formula, and the Counahan-Barratt formulas utilize the proportionality between GFR and height/serum creatinine[71,123-129] (Table 44). The difference between the constants cited in the Counahan-Barratt and the Schwartz formula has been attributed to the use of different assays to measure creatinine. The Counahan-Barratt formula was developed using a measure of "true" creatinine and GFR by ^{51}Cr-EDTA plasma clearance, while the original Schwartz formula was developed using inulin clearance and creatinine measured by a modified Jaffe reaction, which may have overestimated true creatinine. Tables 49 and 50 show the results of studies reporting a standard GFR measure, at least 50 pediatric participants, and presenting a plot of predicted versus measured GFR, allowing assessment of the accuracy of the prediction equation in estimating GFR as outlined above.

While a systematic review of the literature yielded over 40 references examining prediction equations to estimate GFR, only a handful used a gold standard measure of

Table 50. Estimating GFR in Children
Using the Schwartz Equation: Accuracy and Bias

Author, Year	No. of Subjects* (Measurements)	Applic-ability	GFR Range (mL/min/1.73 m²) 0 30 60 90 120	Accuracy** 30%	50%	Bias† (%)	Quality
Filler,[167] 1999[a]	381	↑↑↑		—[b]	—[b]	—[b]	●
Schwartz,[124] 1976[c]	77	↑↑↑		75%	92%	ND	●
Seikaly,[168] 1996[d]	133 (176)	↑↑↑		53%	74%	GFR >50: 10% GFR <50: 90%	◐
Hellerstein,[169] 1998[c]	53	↑↑↑		ND	ND	1.5%	◐
Guignard,[170] 1980[c]	72	↑↑		78%	89%	ND	◐
Stake,[171] 1992[e]	205	↑↑		78%	94%	ND	◐
Seikaly,[172] 1998[d]	64 (100)	↑		55%	64%	GFR >90: −7.9% GFR 51–90: −1.7% GFR 31–50: 32.3% GFR <30: 67%	◐
Springate,[173] 1992[f]	87	↑↑		91%	97%	10%	○
Waz,[174] 1993[f]	70	↑↑		56%	73%	20%	○

The Schwartz Equation is: $GFR = \dfrac{0.55 \times Height(\text{cm})}{S_{Cr}(\text{mg/dL})}$ or $\dfrac{43 \times Height(\text{cm})}{S_{Cr}(\mu\text{mol/L})}$

* When multiple measurements were made for each subject, the total number of measurements appears in parentheses.

** Accuracy defined as the percent of GFR estimates within 30% or 50% of measured GFR.

† See Part 10, Appendix 3 for definition of bias.

[a] Reference standard GFR measured by ^{51}Cr-EDTA

[b] The Schwartz formula had a sensitivity of 84% and a specificity of 91% in identifying patients with GFR ≥90 mL/min/1.73 m².

[c] Reference standard GFR measured by inulin

[d] Reference standard GFR measured by iothalamate

[e] Reference standard GFR measured by iohexol

[f] Reference standard GFR measured by Tc-DTPA

GFR and included more than 50 children (Tables 50 and 51). For the Schwartz formula, most studies reported mean differences between estimated and measured GFR. These ranged from −0.4 to 10 mL/min/1.73 m² with SD ranging from 2 to 20 mL/min/1.73 m². The data suggest that the bias of the estimate of the Schwartz formula increases with decreasing GFR.[168,172]

Studies describing the accuracy of the estimate show that approximately 75% of Schwartz formula estimates of GFR are within 30% of the measured GFR by inulin clearance.[124,170,171,176-180] Comparable studies of the Counahan-Barratt formula show 70% to 86% of Counahan-Barratt estimates fall within 30% of GFR measured by ^{51}Cr-EDTA.

Although imprecise, the Schwartz and Counahan-Barratt formulae for estimating GFR in children are convenient and practical. Both use height in the estimate, as height is proportional to muscle mass. The constants used in the equations differ, likely related to the different assays to measure creatinine. For a 5-year-old child who is at median (50th percentile) height for age, the serum creatinine corresponding to a GFR of 60 mL/min/1.73 m² is 1.0 mg/dL using the Schwartz formula and 0.8 mg/dL using the Counahan-

Table 51. Estimating GFR in Children
Using the Counahan-Barratt or Modified Counahan-Barratt Equations: Accuracy and Bias

Author, Year	No. of Subjects* (Measurements)	Applic- ability	GFR Range (mL/min/1.73 m²) 0 30 60 90 120	Accuracy** 30%	50%	Bias† (%)	Quality
Bokenkamp,[175] 1998[a]	83/101	↑↑↑		86%	94%	Absolute bias: −4.6 mL/min/1.73 m²	●
Counahan,[127] 1976[b]	108/83	↑↑		70%	87%	Absolute bias: 1 mL/min/1.73 m²	●
Morris,[128] 1982[b]	94/69	↑↑		83%	93%	ND	●

The Counahan-Barratt Equation is: $GFR = \dfrac{0.43 \times Height(cm)}{S_{Cr}(mg/dL)}$ or $\dfrac{38 \times Height(cm)}{S_{Cr}(\mu mol/L)}$

The Modified Counahan-Barratt Equation is: $GFR = \dfrac{40 \times Height(cm)}{S_{Cr}(\mu mol/L)}$

* When multiple measurements were made for each subject, the total number of measurements appears in parentheses.
** Accuracy defined as the percent of GFR estimates within 30% or 50% of measured GFR.
† See Part 10, Appendix 3 for definition of bias.

[a] Schwartz formula had sensitivity 84% and specificity 91% in identifying patients with GFR > 90 mL/min/1.73 m².
[b] Reference standard GFR measured by ^{51}Cr-EDTA

Barratt formula. This example illustrates that use of both formulas can allow for estimation of kidney function, and even serum creatinine levels <1.0 mg/dL can be associated with substantially impaired kidney function in small children and adults who have low muscle mass or malnutrition.

Creatinine clearance over-estimates GFR; therefore, equations that accurately estimate creatinine clearance overestimate GFR when true creatinine is measured (R, S). The Cockcroft-Gault equation was developed to predict creatinine clearance rather than GFR. The equation was developed in a sample of men and a correction factor for women was proposed.[121] The equation's accuracy in predicting creatinine clearance from 24-hour urine has been evaluated in many publications (Table 46). Evaluation of these data is limited by the use of different assays and variable calibration within creatinine assays across laboratories and over time. Analogous statements apply to studies of the Schwartz formula in children.

The largest study that evaluated the Cockcroft-Gault equation in a single laboratory was the MDRD Study. The serum creatinine assay in this study was calibrated to approximate true creatinine. As a result, the Cockcroft-Gault equation over-estimated GFR by 23%.

Many of the studies evaluating the Schwartz formula in children have substituted creatinine clearance for GFR in assessing it bias and precision in different populations. The bias of Schwartz formula estimates compared to creatinine clearances is relatively small; however, the Schwartz formula has been shown to overestimate inulin clearance, particularly in children with low GFR.[168,169,172] Although formulas that estimate creatinine clearance overestimate GFR, they provide an estimate that is accurate enough for most clinical purposes and represent a better alternative to assessing kidney function than serum creatinine alone.

Measuring 24-hour creatinine clearance to assess GFR is not more reliable than estimating GFR from a prediction equation (R). A 24-hour urine collection is useful for measurement of total excretion of nitrogen, electrolytes, and other substances. However, the use of 24-hour urine collection for the estimation of GFR has consistently been shown to be no more, and often less, reliable than serum creatinine based equations. A 1998 review[181] found five of six studies that found serum creatinine based estimates of GFR to have a lower error than measured creatinine clearance in patients with kidney disease. In addition to collection errors, this is attributed to diurnal variation in GFR and day-to-day variation in creatinine excretion.

In children, several studies have compared the accuracy of prediction equations in estimating GFR with 24 hour or timed creatinine clearance studies.[127,182-186] None of these studies demonstrated substantial improvement in estimating creatinine clearance using a 24-hour or timed urine collection over the use of either the Schwartz or Counahan-Barratt prediction equations. One relatively small study[169] demonstrated a mean difference of 7.0 ± 17.8 mL/min/1.73 m^2 between 24-hour creatinine clearance compared to GFR as measured by inulin clearance. Another documented 30% of 24-hour creatinine clearance studies yielded estimates of GFR more than 30% above or below GFR measured with iothalamate clearance.[184]

Important exceptions may be the estimation of GFR in individuals with variation in dietary intake (vegetarian diet, creatine supplements) or muscle mass (amputation, malnutrition, muscle wasting), since these factors are not specifically taken into account in prediction equations. In these situations, collection of a 24-hour urine sample for measurement of creatinine clearance, or measurement of clearance of an exogenous filtration marker, may provide better estimates of GFR than prediction equations.

Clinical laboratories should provide an estimate of GFR with the results of serum creatinine concentration (O). Laboratories that measure serum creatinine concentration should calculate GFR using an equation. Among adults, the MDRD Study equation may perform better than the Cockroft-Gault equation but the data are very limited. Among children, the Schwartz formula provides a clinically useful estimate of GFR. All four formulas reviewed provide a marked improvement over serum creatinine alone. Calculations by the laboratory, requiring only minimal clinical information, will facilitate the clinical interpretation of kidney function. The utilization of equations, some of which are complex, is much more efficient in the context of a centralized laboratory computer system than performed by individual physicians. Clinical laboratories will need to work with physicians and hospital or health center information system adminstrators to determine a number of practical issues: which prediction equation(s) to use; how to obtain the additional information required for the prediction equation; when to report estimated GFR (only when requested, or each time serum creatinine is measured); what additional information to include on the report (eg, normal values for age and gender,

GFR levels for K/DOQI CKD Stages). The laboratories should mind the importance of calibrating their serum creatinine to the same level as the laboratory in which the equation was developed. In this regard, development of international standards for calibration of serum creatinine assays will be important in allowing for the accurate diagnosis of Stage 2 chronic kidney disease.

Estimation of GFR or creatinine clearance from serum creatinine is critically dependent on calibration of the serum creatinine assay (R). There is substantial variation across laboratories in the calibration of serum creatinine, with systematic differences as large as 0.2 to 0.4 mg/dL not being uncommon. Such differences reflect a very large percentage of the serum creatinine in patients with a serum creatinine of 2.0 mg/dL or less. A 1987 review[187] detailed 8 different existing methods to measure creatinine concentration. For patients with low muscle mass and serum creatinine ≈1.0 mg/dL, the more commonly used Jaffe and modified Jaffe reaction methods systematically overestimated creatinine by 20% to 80% compared to high performance liquid chromatography and dilution mass spectrometry measures which should approximate "true" creatinine. An analysis of College of American Pathologists survey data indicates that systematic differences in calibration of serum creatinine assays accounts for 85% of the difference between laboratories in serum creatinine. Much of the variation was within a method not just between methods. The laboratories surveyed averaged >13% bias in measurement of creatinine, larger than any other analyte examined, as well as substantial variation between laboratories in the bias. In comparison, reproducibility of the serum creatinine measures within a laboratory was much better (average coefficient of variation 8%).[188] Standardization of the assay across laboratories is critical to the ability to diagnose and stage chronic kidney disease. Laboratories should inform clinicians which creatinine assay is used in their laboratory and how it compares to measures of "true" creatinine.

One reason for variation in the calibration of serum creatinine may have been a desire to provide a calculated 24-hour creatinine clearance that is closer to GFR. It is preferable to report estimates of appropriately calibrated true creatinine. The over-estimate of GFR by creatinine clearance can then be corrected explicitly using a correction factor. In the MDRD Study, this correction required multiplying the creatinine clearance by 0.81.[17]

A 24-hour urine sample should be collected to aid in the assessment of nutritional status and the need for kidney replacement therapy (O). The statements about the limited utility of 24-hour urine samples in estimating GFR do not apply to other uses of this urine collection. A 24 hour urine collection can be used to assess urea clearance, weekly Kt/V_{urea}, creatinine clearance, and dietary intake of protein, sodium, potassium, and phosphorus. For details on calculations of urea clearance, weekly Kt/V_{urea}, and dietary protein intake from 24 hour urine, see Part 10, Appendix 3. Guideline 1 reviews recommendations from DOQI guidelines regarding initiation of kidney replacement therapy. Guideline 9 reviews K/DOQI guidelines on assessment of nutritional status.

In principle, accurate measurement of creatinine excretion in a timed urine collection at a single point in time could be used to improve the estimate of 24-hour excretion rates of various solutes from the ratio of solute-to-creatinine concentrations in untimed ("spot") urine samples at later times. Alternatively, estimation of creatinine excretion from factors related to physiologic variables related to creatinine generation and extra-renal elimination (such as age, gender, race, body size, and GFR) could also be used to facilitate estimation of solute excretion rates from the ratio of solute-to-creatinine concentration in spot urine samples. Thus far, the accuracy of prediction equations for creatinine excretion have not been widely studied. Both methods may be limited, how-ever, by variation in solute excretion rates during the day (as occurs with urea nitrogen in individuals with normal kidney function).

LIMITATIONS

Steady State and Average Body Composition

Use of serum creatinine to estimate GFR relies on the individual being in steady state and the ability to estimate the average rate of production of creatinine. Therefore, esti-mates will be unreliable if the level of GFR is changing (such as acute kidney failure), if muscle mass is unusually high or low (such as athletes or malnourished individuals, respectively), or if dietary creatine intake is unusually high or low (such as individuals consuming creatine supplements or vegetarians, respectively). Methods proposed for estimating GFR in acute kidney failure[189] were outside the scope of this review. Selected patients may require clearance procedures to measure (rather than estimate) the level of GFR (Table 52).

Mild Decrease in GFR

Using prediction equations to estimate GFR is much less precise at the higher range of GFR, such as CKD Stages 1-2. Early glomerular injury may lead to compensatory hypertro-phy and hyperfiltration in less affected nephrons, thereby maintaining or increasing GFR. At the upper range of kidney function, the role of the kidney in determining serum creatinine is of comparable magnitude to variation in other factors such as the metabolism of creatine in skeletal muscle and ingested meat in the diet. The degree of creatinine secretion can vary with time, by as much as 10% even within healthy individuals.[111] Additionally, with a mild decrease in kidney function, only a slight increase in the serum creatinine may be seen because of an increase in tubular secretion. Therefore, other markers of early kidney damage are needed to identify early decline in kidney function.

Table 52. Clinical Situations in Which Clearance Measures May be Necessary to Estimate GFR

Extremes of age and body size
Severe malnutrition or obesity
Disease of skeletal muscle
Paraplegia or quadriplegia
Vegetarian diet
Rapidly changing kidney function
Prior to dosing drugs with significant toxicity that are excreted by the kidneys

Progression of Kidney Disease

Measurement of progression of kidney disease is substantially more difficult than diagnosis of the presence of kidney disease since progression of many forms of kidney disease is slow. Estimates of GFR based on serum creatinine will allow for reliable detection of substantial progression (>25% to 50% decline). However, substantial changes in secretion, generation, and extra-renal metabolism of creatinine can occur and will lead to false measures of lower degrees of progression. It is particularly difficult to use serum creatinine alone to assess progression of kidney disease in children, in whom growth and maturation lead to substantial changes in muscle mass.

CLINICAL APPLICATIONS

Serum creatinine-based estimates of GFR using prediction formulas in adults and children provide a basis for classification of chronic kidney disease and detection of substantial progression. For teenagers and young adults, use of both formulas (Schwartz and MDRD Study) may give the clinician a dependable range of estimates of GFR. In certain clinical situations, clearance measures may be necessary to estimate GFR (Table 52).

All individuals should be informed about their estimated level of GFR. Individuals with an estimated GFR below 60 mL/min/1.73 m^2 are classified as having chronic kidney disease and should be educated about their diagnosis and the implications of decreased kidney function.

Individuals with a serum creatinine of 2.0 mg/dL have moderate to severe decrease in GFR, regardless of the equation used to estimate GFR. However, these individuals constitute only a minority of individuals with chronic kidney disease.

Review of the literature showed a paucity of data on the lower limit of a normal GFR in elderly populations. Therefore, older individuals with low GFR should be assessed for other markers of chronic kidney disease including hypertension and proteinuria.

When precise measures of GFR are necessary, or when muscle mass may deviate substantially from values predicted by age, race, sex in adults or height in children (eg, in malnourished patients[174,190-193]), clearance measures using exogenous filtration markers may be necessary. In patients with mild or moderate decreased GFR, post-cimetidine creatinine clearance may more closely approximate GFR, as cimetidine blocks tubular secretion of creatinine.[169,181] There is a growing literature on using serum cystatin C to estimate GFR. However, limited sample size, statistical methodology, lack of information on cystatin C assay calibration, and conflicting results make the available data inadequate for recommending cystatin C measurement for widespread clinical application.[116] Non-radiolabeled iothalamate can be used to decrease the cost and inconvenience of measuring GFR.[194]

IMPLEMENTATION ISSUES

Development and implementation of international standardization and calibration of serum creatinine assays will be important in allowing for the accurate diagnosis of mild and moderate kidney disease. The importance of accurate measurement of serum creatinine needs to be recognized by clinical chemistry laboratories and equipment manufacturers.

RESEARCH RECOMMENDATIONS

Estimating GFR

Although existing equations based on serum creatinine provide an excellent cost-effective method for estimating GFR, their precision is limited. New methods are needed, particularly for detecting mild and moderate kidney disease, but their value in terms of bias, precision, and practicality should be well tested in large samples of subjects with and without kidney disease. In adults, new measures will have to perform substantially better than the 12.1% median difference (~90% of estimates within 30%) from GFR obtained with serum creatinine, age, sex, and race using the MDRD Study equation. In children, standardization of creatinine measurement across studies, use of gold standard GFR measures for reference, and inclusion of larger samples of children of different ages and ethnicities will allow refinement of the constants which should be used in estimating GFR in future modifications of the Counahan-Barratt or Schwartz formula.

While the MDRD Study equation has many advantages, it needs further validation. In particular, further studies should focus on individuals with diabetes, mild decreases in kidney function or normal GFR, Mexican-Americans (whose average serum creatinine is lower than Caucasians), and non-US populations. The extent to which averaging multiple estimates improves precision needs further study. Including a direct measure of body composition by bioelectric impedance or dual-energy X-ray absorptiometry scanning may provide promising directions for improving on the prediction of GFR using serum creatinine.

Definition of "Normal" GFR Across Ages and Ethnicities

The definition of decreased GFR relies on an understanding of the "normal" GFR range. The amount of data in healthy individuals of different ethnicities and children is limited. GFR may differ across ethnic groups but data are very sparse. It is also unknown to what extent a mild decrease in GFR among individuals without hypertension is indicative or kidney disease or "normal" aging.

Prediction Equations for Creatinine Excretion

It would be useful in clinical practice to be able to estimate creatinine excretion from physiologic variables related to creatinine generation and extra-renal elimination, such as age, gender, race, body size, and GFR. This might be done in cross-sectional studies that measured these physiologic variables as well as 24-hour urine creatinine excretion. This would allow improved estimates of daily excretion of some urine solutes from measurements of solute-to-creatinine ratio in spot urine samples.

GUIDELINE 5.   ASSESSMENT OF PROTEINURIA

Normal individuals usually excrete very small amounts of protein in the urine. Persistently increased protein excretion is usually a marker of kidney damage. The excretion of specific types of protein, such as albumin or low molecular weight globulins, depends on the type of kidney disease that is present. Increased excretion of albumin is a sensitive marker for chronic kidney disease due to diabetes, glomerular disease, and hypertension. Increased excretion of low molecular weight globulins is a sensitive marker for some types of tubulointerstitial disease. In this guideline, the term "proteinuria" refers to increased urinary excretion of albumin, other specific proteins, or total protein; "albuminuria" refers specifically to increased urinary excretion of albumin. "Microalbuminuria" refers to albumin excretion above the normal range but below the level of detection by tests for total protein. Guidelines for detection and monitoring of proteinuria in adults and children differ because of differences in the prevalence and type of chronic kidney disease.

Guidelines for Adults and Children

- Under most circumstances, untimed ("spot") urine samples should be used to detect and monitor proteinuria in children and adults.
- It is usually not necessary to obtain a timed urine collection (overnight or 24-hour) for these evaluations in either children or adults.
- First morning specimens are preferred, but random specimens are acceptable if first morning specimens are not available.
- In most cases, screening with urine dipsticks is acceptable for detecting proteinuria:
  - Standard urine dipsticks are acceptable for detecting increased total urine protein.
  - Albumin-specific dipsticks are acceptable for detecting albuminuria.
- Patients with a positive dipstick test (1 + or greater) should undergo confirmation of proteinuria by a quantitative measurement (protein-to-creatinine ratio or albumin-to-creatinine ratio) within 3 months.
- Patients with two or more positive quantitative tests temporally spaced by 1 to 2 weeks should be diagnosed as having persistent proteinuria and undergo further evaluation and management for chronic kidney disease as stated in Guideline 2.
- Monitoring proteinuria in patients with chronic kidney disease should be performed using quantitative measurements.

Specific Guidelines for Adults

- When screening adults at increased risk for chronic kidney disease, albumin should be measured in a spot urine sample using either:
  - Albumin-specific dipstick;
  - Albumin-to-creatinine ratio.
- When monitoring proteinuria in adults with chronic kidney disease, the protein-to-creatinine ratio in spot urine samples should be measured using:
  - Albumin-to-creatinine ratio;
  - Total protein-to-creatinine ratio is acceptable if albumin-to-creatinine ratio is high (>500 to 1,000 mg/g).

Specific Guidelines for Children Without Diabetes

- When screening children for chronic kidney disease, total urine protein should be measured in a spot urine sample using either:
  - Standard urine dipstick;
  - Total protein-to-creatine ratio.
- Orthostatic proteinuria must be excluded by repeat measurement on a first morning specimen if the initial finding of proteinuria was obtained on a random specimen.
- When monitoring proteinuria in children with chronic kidney disease, the total protein-to-creatinine ratio should be measured in spot urine specimens.

Specific Guidelines for Children With Diabetes

- Screening and monitoring of post-pubertal children with diabetes of 5 or more years of duration should follow the guidelines for adults.
- Screening and monitoring other children with diabetes should follow the guidelines for children without diabetes.

BACKGROUND

The measurement of urinary protein excretion provides a sensitive marker of many types of kidney disease from early to advanced stages. The most pertinent question with respect to screening for proteinuria is whether early detection of kidney disease associated with this abnormality will result in a more timely introduction of therapy that may slow the course of disease? The answer is "yes"—at least for some chronic kidney diseases. For example, in diabetic kidney disease, early detection of albuminuria appears to permit effective therapy early in the course of disease.

The American Diabetes Association[8] and the NKF-PARADE[6,7] have recommended assessment of proteinuria to detect chronic kidney disease. These recommendations largely agree in the methods for assessment of proteinuria. The purpose of this guideline is to review the rationale for methods of assessment of proteinuria and to determine whether detection and monitoring of proteinuria using untimed ("spot") urine samples is as accurate as using timed (overnight or 24-hour) urine specimens. Algorithms for screening and evaluation of proteinuria in asymptomatic, healthy individuals and in patients at increased risk for chronic kidney disease recommended by NKF-PARADE are given in Part 9.

RATIONALE

Criterion Standard

It is important to consider the timing of urine specimens and the methods for detection of urine proteins. Although the basic concepts of measuring and interpreting urinary protein excretion have changed little over several decades, clinicians must now decide whether simple qualitative or more cumbersome quantitative tests are necessary and whether albumin or total protein should be measured. In clinical practice, most screening (*qualitative*) methods use a commercial dipstick, which measures total protein or albumin. These dipsticks, which are of course simple to use, usually afford high specificity; ie, they have relatively few false positive results, thereby creating a practical advantage for the clinician. However, they afford low sensitivity; ie, they may fail to detect some forms of kidney disease during the early stages, when the level of proteinuria is below the sensitivity of the test strip used.

Timed urine collections versus untimed ("spot") urine samples. When screening tests are positive, measurement of protein excretion in a 24-hour collection has been the longstanding "gold standard" for the *quantitative* evaluation of proteinuria. However, in recent years some studies have advocated that the measurement of protein excretion should be done on an overnight specimen. The rationale for measuring proteinuria in timed overnight urine collections rather than 24-hour specimens relates to the lack of consistency when hourly protein excretion rates are examined in the same individual at different times during the day. This inconsistency results from varying levels of activity and possibly other factors that are not well documented. The high intra-individual variability that ensues makes serial comparisons in individual patients very difficult unless multiple measurements are taken. This problem is particularly troublesome for individuals with orthostatic proteinuria—who may excrete more than 1 g of protein during waking hours, but less than 100 mg during sleep. Indeed, evaluation for postural (orthostatic) proteinuria requires comparison of a measurement of protein excretion in an overnight ("recumbent") collection to a daytime ("upright") collection.

An alternative method for quantitative evaluation of proteinuria is measurement of the ratio of protein or albumin to creatinine in an untimed "spot" urine specimen. These ratios correct for variations in urinary concentration due to hydration and provide a more convenient method of assessing protein and albumin excretion than that involved with timed urine collections. The issue to be explored in this section is whether this increased level of convenience can be achieved without a reduced level of precision. Based on the review of evidence accumulated over three decades, the Work Group proposes that the time has come to forego the traditional "timed urine collections" and adopt the use of "spot" urine measurements that compare the concentration of protein to the concentration of creatinine.

Total protein versus albumin. The assessment of protein excretion in the urine can be accomplished by several different techniques. In addition to standard methods of measuring total protein, there are now multiple versions of immunoassays capable of detecting albumin levels at concentrations present in the majority of normal people. In general, the literature does not provide substantial information concerning the relative merits of measuring total protein versus albumin to detect and monitor kidney damage. Different guidelines for children and adults reflect differences in the prevalence of specific types of chronic kidney disease.

Strength of Evidence
Rationale for ADULTS and CHILDREN
This section will describe the rationale for using "spot" urine samples to estimate protein excretion individuals of all ages, timing of urine samples, and dipstick for quantitative assessment. The two subsequent sections will review data for adults and children separately.

Table 53. Spot Urine Protein vs. Timed Urine Protein in Adults

Author, Year	No. of Subjects (Measurements)*	Method of Spot Urine (Length)	Applic-ability	Proteinuria Range	Correlation to Timed Specimen (R^2)	Quality
Zelmanovitz,[195] 1998	86 (105/105)	AM, not first (24 hr)	♦♦	6.5–12,000 mg/24 hr	0.59	●

* (X/Y): X = number of timed urine collections; Y = number of spot urine collections

Rationale for Using "Spot" Urine Samples

Collection of a timed urine sample is inconvenient and may be associated with errors (R, O). Twenty-four-hour urine collections may be associated with significant collection errors, largely due to improper timing and missed samples, leading to over-collections and under-collections. Timed overnight collections or shorter timed daytime collections may reduce the inconvenience of a 24-hour collection, but are still associated with collection errors. In addition, errors due to incomplete bladder emptying are relatively more important in shorter collection intervals.

Concentration of protein in a spot urine sample provides a rough index of the protein excretion rate, but is also affected by hydration (R, C). The concentration of protein in the urine is affected by urine volume as well as protein excretion rate. Urine volume is dependent primarily on the state of hydration. For example, in a patient with urine protein excretion of 500 mg per day the protein concentration may vary from 100 mg/dL (2+ on the dipstick) in a patient with urine volume of 500 mL/d to 20 mg/dL (trace on the dipstick) in a patient with urine volume of 2500 mL/day. Despite this, there is a rough correlation between protein concentration in a spot urine sample and protein excretion rate (Tables 53, 54, and 55).

Table 54. Spot Urine Albumin vs. Timed Urine Albumin in Adults

Author, Year	No. of Subjects (Measurements)*	Method of Spot Urine (Length)	Applic-ability	Albuminuria Range	Correlation to Timed Specimen (R^2)	Quality
Zelmanovitz,[196] 1997	95 (123/123)	AM, not first (24 hr)	♦♦	Median 61.5 (0.2–5,840) mg/24 hr[a]	0.83	●
Ahn,[197] 1999	105 (105/105)	Random (24 hr)	♦♦	<30 mg/24 hr ->300 mg/24 hr[b]	0.66	○
Schwab,[198] 1992	94 (94/188)	First AM (24 hr) Random (24 hr)	♦♦	0- -800 mg/24 hr	0.62 0.62	○
Ng,[199] 2000	65 (65/65)	AM (24 hr)	♦♦	34–300 mg/24 hour	Sn = 86%[c] Sp = 86%[c]	○
Ciavarella,[200] 1989	119 (119/119)	First AM (4 hr)	♦♦	<30 mg/24 hr ->300 mg/24 hr[b]	0.92	○

* (X/Y): X = number of timed urine collections; Y = number of spot urine collections

[a] Reported as 42.7 (0.13–4,057) µg/min.
[b] Reported as <20 µg/min – >200 µg/min.
[c] Test threshold = 13.3 mg/L (threshold nearest to the intersection of the receiver operating characteristics curve at the 100%-to-100% diagonal)

Abbreviations: Sn, sensitivity; Sp, specificity

Table 55. Spot Urine Dipstick Albumin vs. Timed Urine Albumin in Adults

Author, Year	No. of Subjects (Measurements)*	Method of Spot Urine (Length)	Applic- ability	Albuminuria Range	Sensitivity	Specificity	Quality
Webb,[201] 1996	492 (984/984)	Overnight (Overnight)	↟↟	ND	67%[a]	86%[a]	●
Poulsen,[202] 1992	183 (183/183)	Random (24 hr)	↟↟	0– ~220 mg/24 hr	86%[b]	97%[b]	●
Gerber,[203] 1998	170 (170/170)	Random (Overnight) Random (24 hr)	↟↟	6.5–12,100 mg/24 hr	75%[c] 92%[c]	90%[c] 63%[c]	○

* (X/Y): X = number of timed urine collections; Y = number of spot urine collections

[a] Test threshold = 20 mg/L; microalbuminuria ≥20 μg/min
[b] Test threshold = 15 mg/L; microalbuminuria ≥30 mg/24 hr (R^2 = 0.62)
[c] Test threshold = 20 mg/L; microalbuminuria ≥20 mg/L

Urine protein-to-creatinine and albumin-to-creatinine ratios provide accu- rate estimates of the urinary protein and albumin excretion rate, and are not affected by hydration (R, C). Several studies have addressed the relationships between total excretion of protein or albumin and the ratio of either to creatinine in patients of all ages (Tables 56, 57, 58, and 59). Since urine proteins and creatinine are highly soluble in water, they will undergo similar, if not identical, dilution in urine. In principle, if the excretion of creatinine is relatively constant throughout the day, and similar among individuals, then the ratio of protein-to-creatinine in an untimed sample would reflect the excretion of protein. Although creatinine excretion varies among individuals according to age, gender, race, and body size, the results from these studies in adults and children demonstrate a strong correlation between these measures.

Rationale for Timing of Sample Collection

A first morning urine specimen is preferred, but random urine specimens are acceptable if first morning urine specimens are not available (R, O). A first morning urine specimen is preferred because it correlates best with 24-hour protein excretion and is required for the diagnosis of orthostatic proteinuria. In children, ortho-

Table 56. Spot Urine Protein-to-Creatinine Ratio vs. Timed Urine Protein in Adults

Author, Year	No. of Subjects (Measurements)*	Method of Spot Urine (Length)	Applic- ability	Proteinuria Range	Correlation to Timed Specimen (R^2)	Quality
Schwab,[204] 1987	101 (101/101)	Midday (24 hr)	↟↟↟	0–9,600 mg/24 hr	0.92	●
Ginsberg,[205] 1983	76 (76/76)	Random (24 hr)	↟↟↟	~ 0–25,000 mg/24 hr	0.94	●
Rodby,[206] 1995	229 (262/262)	Random (24 hr)	↟↟	50–13,300 mg/24 hr	0.81[a]	●
Zelmanovitz,[195] 1998	86 (105/105)	AM, not first (24 hr)	↟↟	6.5–12,000 mg/24 hr	0.52	●
Wilson,[207] 1993	236 (236/236)	First AM (24 hr)	↟↟↟	~ 0–290 mg/24 hr	0.83	○
Chu,[208] 1990	41 (41/164)	Aliquots (24 hr)	↟↟	1,610 ± 1,970 mg/24 hr/1.73 m²	0.72–0.83	○
Steinhauslin,[209] 1995	133 (520/520)	AM (24 hr)	↟	240 (20–12,100) mg/24 hr/1.73 m²	0.86	○

* (X/Y): X = number of timed urine collections; Y = number of spot urine collections

[a] After log/log transformation of data

Author, Year	No. of Subjects (Measurements)*	Method of Spot Urine (Length)	Applic- ability	Albuminuria Range	Correlation to Timed Specimen (R^2)	Quality
Zelmanovitz,[196] 1997	95 (123/123)	AM, not first (24 hr)	↟↟	Median 61.5 (0.2–5,840) mg/24 hr[a]	0.85	●
Nathan,[210] 1987	35 (35/100)	Aliquots (24 hr)	↟↟	2.3–210 mg/24 hr	0.64	●
Ahn,[197] 1999	105 (105/105)	Random (24 hr)	↟↟	<30 mg/24 hr – >300 mg/24 hr[b]	0.56	◐
Ng,[199] 2000	65 (65/65)	AM (24 hr)	↟↟	34–300 mg/24 hour	Sn = 93%[c] Sp = 94%[c]	◐
Ciavarella,[200] 1989	119 (119/119)	First AM (4 hr)	↟↟	<30 mg/24 hr – >300 mg/24 hr[b]	0.96	○
Cottiero,[211] 1995	33 (66/ND)	Unclear (4 hr)	↟	≈ 0–220 mg/24 hr/1.73 m²	0.86	○

* (X/Y): X = number of timed urine collections; Y = number of spot urine collections

[a] Reported as 42.7 (0.13–4,057) µg/min.

[b] Reported as <20 – >200 µg/min.

[c] Test threshold = 13.3 mg/L (threshold nearest to the intersection of the receiver operating characteristics curve at the 100%-to-100% diagonal)

Abbreviations: Sn, sensitivity; Sp, specificity

static proteinuria must be excluded by a first morning urine protein measurement if the initial finding of proteinuria was obtained on a random specimen during the day. Otherwise, for ease and consistency of collection, a random urine specimen for protein or albumin to creatinine ratio is acceptable if a first-morning urine specimen is not available. This recommendation is consistent with the recommendations by the American Diabetes Association[8] and by the NKF PARADE,[6,7] which recommend a first-morning sample, but accept a random sample if a first-morning specimen is not available.

Table 60 compares the advantages and disadvantages of the various modalities of collecting urine for evaluating kidney function. For all procedures, identical methods

Table 58. Spot Urine Protein-to-Creatinine Ratio vs. Timed Urine Protein in Nondiabetic Children

Author, Year	No. of Subjects (Measurements)*	Method of Spot Urine (Length)	Applic- ability	Proteinuria Range	Correlation to Timed Specimen (R^2)	Quality
Yoshimoto,[212] 1990	44 (44/44)	Random (24 hr)	↟↟↟	20–16,800 mg/24 hr/m²	0.97	●
Iyer,[213] 1991	100 (100/100)	Random (24 hr)	↟↟↟	0–9,600 mg/24 hr	0.25 (normal & acute GN) 0.66 (nephrotic)	◐
Elises,[37] 1988	66 (71/71)	Early AM (Overnight)	↟↟↟	<24 – >2,400 mg/24 hr/m²[a]	0.93	◐
Chahar,[214] 1993	50 (50/50)	Random (24 hr)	↟↟↟	10–6,000 mg/24 hr	0.96–0.98	◐
Mir,[215] 1992	50 (50/50)	First AM (24 hr)	↟↟	20 ±10 – 70 ±20 mg/24 hr/kg	p < 0.01	◐
Houser,[216] 1984	20 (20/20)[b]	Aliquots (24 hr)	↟	15.4 – 8,500 mg/24 hr/m²	0.97	◐
Abitbol,[217] 1990	20 (20/20)	Midday (24 hr)	↟	ND	0.94	◐

* (X/Y): X = number of timed urine collections; Y = number of spot urine collections

[a] Reported as <1 – >100 mg/hr/m²

[b] 15 children (age 1 mo–18 y) and 5 adults

Abbreviation: GN, glomerulonephritis

Table 59. Spot Urine Albumin-to-Creatinine Ratio vs. Timed Urine Albumin in Children

Author, Year	No. of Subjects (Measure-ments)*	Diabetic vs. Nondiabetic	Method of Spot Urine (Length)	Applic-ability	Albuminuria Range	Correlation to Timed Specimen (R^2)	Quality
Cowell,[33] 1986	111 (111/111)	Nondiabetic	First AM (24 hr)	♟♟	1–45 mg/24 hr	0.59	●
	64 (64/64)	Diabetic		♟♟	1–38 mg/24 hr	0.86	◗
Sochett,[218] 1988	41 (41/41)	Diabetic	Random (24 hr)	♟♟	ND	0.17[a]	●
Jefferson,[45] 1985	40 (40/40)	Diabetic	Random (24 hr)	♟♟	1.4–43 mg/24 hr[b]	0.69–0.78	●
Barratt,[26] 1970	8 (71/71)	Nondiabetic	Random (24 hr)	♟	$U_{Alb/Cr}$ = 10^{-5}– 300 mg/g	0.94[c]	◗
Davies,[21] 1984	374 (374/374)	Nondiabetic	First AM (Overnight)	♟♟♟	Mean: 6.6–8.3 mg/1.73 m²/d	0.79	○
Gibb,[42] 1989	79 (ND)	Both	First AM (Overnight)	♟♟	ND	0.81	○
Houser,[39] 1986	17 (17/17)	Nondiabetic	First AM (24 hr)	♟	3.4–4,700 mg/24 hr/m²	0.92	○

* (X/Y): X = number of timed urine collections; Y = number of spot urine collections

[a] After log/log transformation of data.
[b] Reported as 1–30 µg/min.
[c] Spot urine albumin-to-creatinine ratio compared to 24 hr urine albumin-clearance-to-creatinine-clearance ratio, after log/log transformation.

Abbreviation: $U_{Alb/Cr}$, urine albumin-to-creatinine ratio

are utilized in the laboratory. The differences among these protocols balance ease of collection of samples with the need to collect urine to reflect kidney function over the course of the day or overnight.

Rationale for Measurement Methods

Screening for proteinuria with urine dipsticks is acceptable. Confirmation of proteinuria should be performed using quantitative measurements (R, O). Standard urine dipsticks detect total protein above a concentration of 10 to 20 mg/dL. The reagent pad contains a colorimetric pH indicator dye which changes color when

Table 60. Comparison of Methods for Urine Collection for Assessment of Proteinuria

Random Urine for Albumin-to-Creatinine Ratio	First Morning Urine for Albumin-to-Creatinine Ratio	Timed Overnight Urine for Albumin Excretion	Timed 24-Hour Albumin Excretion
Advantages			
A good estimate of albumin excretion over the whole day	A good estimate of overnight albumin excretion	Defines overnight albumin excretion	Defines albumin over the entire 24 hours
Easy assays to perform in most laboratories	Easy assays to perform in most laboratories	Easy assay to perform in most laboratories	Easy assay to perform in most laboratories
Directly relates to published results of random A/C	Directly relates to published results of first morning A/C	Directly relates to published results of overnight excretion	Directly relates to published results of 24 hour albumin excretion
Easiest single sample collection	Easier single sample collection	Easier collection of one or more samples	
Disadvantages			
Lower creatinine excretion in women: higher values of A/C in women	Lower creatinine excretion in women: higher values of A/C in women	More complex collection of sample(s)	Most complex collection of sample(s)
Lower creatinine excretion with age: higher values of A/C in older people	Lower creatinine excretion with age: higher values of A/C in older people	Frequent incomplete collections	Frequent incomplete collections
Greater creatinine excretion in people of African descent: lower values of A/C	Greater creatinine excretion in people of African descent: lower values of A/C		

Abbreviation: A/C, albumin-to-creatinine ratio

**Table 61. Common Causes of False Results
in Routine Measurements of Urinary Albumin or Total Protein**

	False Positive	False Negative
Fluid Balance	Dehydration increases concentration of protein in the urine	Excessive hydration decreases concentration of protein in the urine
Hematuria	Hematuria increases amount of protein in the urine[a]	
Exercise	Exercise increases the excretion of protein in the urine, especially albumin	
Infection	Urinary infection may cause production of proteins from the organism and the cellular reactions to them	
Urine proteins other than albumin		These proteins usually do not react as strongly as albumin with the routine methods for measuring protein on dipsticks
Pharmaceutical agents*	Extremely alkaline urine (pH >8) may react with the reagent pads on dipsticks to yield a color falsely indicating protein	

* Or other circumstances causing markedly increased alkalinity of the urine

[a] Hematuria is associated with the presence of proteins that may be measured by the sensitive methods (e.g., those measuring low levels of albumin). Dipsticks that have multiple reagent pads will often have a measurement of hemoglobin, thereby indicating hematuria as the cause of increased albuminuria/proteinuria.

bound by negatively charged serum proteins, including albumin and most globulins. The standard urine dipstick is insensitive for low concentrations of albumin that may occur in patients with microalbuminuria. In addition, the standard dipstick is also insensitive to positively charged serum proteins, such as some immunoglobulin light chains.

Albumin-specific dipsticks detect albumin above a concentration of 3 to 4 mg/dL and are useful for detection of microalbuminuria.

Consistent with recommendations by ADA and NKF-PARADE, the Work Group recommended screening using either standard or albumin-specific dipsticks, or protein-to-creatinine or albumin-to-creatinine ratio. Screening with a dipstick for proteinuria or albuminuria is often a satisfactory first approach to evaluation of kidney disease; however, clinicians need to be cognizant of causes of false positive and more importantly false negative results (Table 61), and in both instances repeat analyses of urine with quantitative total protein or albumin and creatinine analyses are strongly advised when a result may be inconsistent with the clinical evaluation. Special care should be taken to avoid false negative results which may delay implementation of treatment early in the course of kidney disease.

Monitoring proteinuria in patients with chronic kidney disease should be performed using quantitative measurements (O). Changes in proteinuria provide important prognostic information. Increasing proteinuria is associated with a higher risk of loss of kidney function. Decreasing proteinuria, either spontaneously or after treatment, is associated with a lower risk of loss of kidney function. Quantitative measurements provide a more accurate assessment of changes in proteinuria.

Rationale for Type of Protein: ADULTS
In adults, it is preferable to assess proteinuria as albumin, because:
- ***Albuminuria is a more sensitive marker than total protein for chronic kidney disease due to diabetes, hypertension, and glomerular diseases (R).***

In adults, the most common types of chronic kidney disease are due to diabetes, hypertension, and glomerular diseases. In patients with diabetes mellitus, there has been nearly a uniform adoption of albumin as the "criterion standard" in evaluating kidney damage. Thus, for this disease the same standards have been adopted for adults and children. Preliminary data suggest that elevated albumin excretion is also a marker of kidney damage in adults with hypertension. Proteinuria in glomerular diseases is primarily due to increased albumin excretion. Therefore, the Work Group concluded that albumin should be measured to detect and monitor kidney damage in adults.

The interpretation of albuminuria in kidney transplant recipients is more complicated than in other patients with chronic kidney disease. First, depending on the interval since transplantation, the patients' native kidneys may still excrete small amounts of protein, which may be sufficient to cause a positive test for albumin. Second, the main causes of damage in kidney transplant, rejection or toxicity from immunosuppressive drugs, are not characterized by proteinuria. However, diabetic kidney disease is the underlying cause for a large fraction of kidney transplant patients, which may recur in the transplant. Moreover, hypertension is very common after transplantation and is strongly associated with a more rapid loss of kidney function in transplant patients. Finally, recurrent glomerular disease may occur after transplantation and is associated with a greater risk of graft loss. Albuminuria is a better marker than total urine protein of kidney damage due to diabetes, hypertension, and glomerular disease. For these reasons, the Work Group recommends testing and monitoring for albuminuria, rather than total protein, in kidney transplant recipients, as well as in patients with other causes of chronic kidney disease.

The cost or technical difficulty of measuring albumin may exceed that for measuring total protein. It is acceptable to measure total protein-to-creatinine ratio as an index of proteinuria in adults when albumin-to-creatinine ratio is substantially elevated (eg, >500 to 1,000 mg/g). However, there is no reliable method to convert ratios of albumin-to-creatinine to total protein-to-creatinine or vice versa.

Rationale for Type of Protein: CHILDREN WITHOUT DIABETES
In children without diabetes, it is preferable to assess proteinuria as total protein, because:
- **Total protein detects albumin, which usually is present in large quantities in glomerular diseases of childhood (R).**
- **Total protein detects low molecular weight proteins which are present in other types of chronic kidney disease (non-glomerular diseases) in childhood (R).**

The prevalence of chronic kidney damage due to diabetes and hypertension is far lower in children than in adults. In contrast, the prevalence of kidney disease due to urinary tract abnormalities and congenital tubular disorders is far more common in children than in adults.[219] These latter diseases may be characterized by low molecular weight proteinuria, which would be detected by tests for total urine protein, but not by tests for albumin. Therefore, the Work Group recommends that total urine protein should be measured to detect and monitor kidney damage in most children, one exception being children with diabetes mellitus.

Rationale for Type of Protein: CHILDREN WITH DIABETES

In post-pubertal children with duration of diabetes greater than 5 years, it is preferable to assess proteinuria as albumin because:

- *Albuminuria is a more sensitive marker than total protein for chronic kidney disease due to diabetes (R).*

In other children with diabetes, it is preferable to assess proteinuria as total protein because:

- *Total protein detects albumin, which usually is present in large quantities in glomerular diseases of childhood (R).*
- *Total protein detects low molecular weight proteins which are present in other types of chronic kidney disease (non-glomerular diseases) in childhood (R).*

The risk of diabetic kidney disease in children is higher in post-pubertal children with duration of diabetes greater than 5 years than in other diabetic children. For these reasons, the American Diabetes Association recommends screening these children for chronic kidney disease, using the same algorithm as for adults. Other diabetic children are screened using the same algorithms as for other children.

LIMITATIONS

The main limitations of assessment of proteinuria as a marker of chronic kidney disease is potential misclassification of individuals due variability of levels of total protein or albumin in an individual over time and the extent to which conditions at the time of testing may obscure the true level. Excretion of total protein or albumin in the urine are highly variable in individuals with or without kidney disease. Most studies suggest that the standard deviation is about 40% to 50% of the mean. Examples of conditions that affect protein excretion other than kidney disease include activity, urinary tract infection, diet, and menstruation. Attempts to avoid these pitfalls include careful definition of events that should preclude the interpretation of abnormal results and consideration of repeat studies when abnormal results are obtained. Some authors have advocated that multiple (up to 5) specimens be obtained in order to obtain a reliable result.[42] The Work Group does not believe that such an approach is feasible in most instances. However, the Work Group acknowledges the need to repeat abnormal tests, especially low levels of total protein or albumin and the necessity to carefully consider the clinical setting in interpretation of urine protein measurements.

A limitation of this guideline is the use of correlation coefficients, rather than more detailed assessments of precision and bias, to assess the accuracy of spot urine measurements of protein-to-creatinine ratios as a measure of protein excretion rates. In most cases, data were not available to characterize the precision and bias. In addition, other than distinguishing normal from abnormal, the exact level of proteinuria is not usually required for clinical decision-making. In most circumstances, a "rough" approximation of the level of proteinuria or changes over time are sufficient. Thus, the Work Group concludes that the uniformly high correlation coefficients are sufficiently strong evidence to warrant the conclusions presented here.

CLINICAL APPLICATIONS
General considerations for adults and children

The identification of persistent proteinuria or albuminuria in patients of all ages has importance when considering diagnosis, prognosis, and therapeutic options. The relative ease with which proteinuria can be assessed and monitored allows clinicians to identify individuals with completely asymptomatic forms of progressive kidney disease during the early stages of their disease. Such patients may benefit from subsequent changes in management that forestall or prevent additional kidney problems.

Proteinuria is a key finding in the differential diagnosis of chronic kidney disease. The relationship between the level of proteinuria and the type (diagnosis) of chronic kidney disease is reviewed in Guideline 6 and in Part 9.

Proteinuria is a key prognostic finding in chronic kidney disease. The prognosis of patients with a variety of kidney disorders often correlates with their level of and persistence of proteinuria over time—even when other variables are controlled. This is important because of the obvious therapeutic implications for patients who are in the high risk category that is characterized by persistent, heavy proteinuria. The relationship between the level of proteinuria and risk for loss of kidney function is considered further in Guideline 13.

Finally, the most important clinical application of defining patients with proteinuria is potentially beneficial therapy. Many lines of evidence now indicate that medications that reduce proteinuria may provide significant long term benefits for patients with chronic kidney disease.

Specific considerations for children

The optimal frequency and timing of urine screening for proteinuria in children have not been well established. At one end of the spectrum, the governments of some countries have mandated that such screening be done on all school children every year. In Japan, for example, this has been in place for over 25 years.[220] In contrast, the American Academy of Pediatrics recommends that such screening be done on two occasions during childhood—once before starting school and then again during adolescence.[221] Some authors even consider this to be excessive and have proposed that urinalysis screening be limited to a single first morning dipstick done at school entry age in all asymptomatic children.[222]

The recommendations described in this section for children are consistent with other recent publications from the National Kidney Foundation PARADE[6,7] and the American Diabetes Association.[223] It should be noted, however, that the ADA position statement draws attention to the fact that microvascular disease may occur in prepubertal children and that "clinical judgment should be exercised when individualizing these recommendations."

IMPLEMENTATION ISSUES

The implementation of the guidelines in this section will encounter at least two potential obstacles. The first is the widely held belief that 24-hour urine collections provide "the only accurate method" of measuring protein or albumin excretion. This even applies to some pediatricians who continue to request 24-hour urine studies in small children despite the high degree of difficulty involved.

The second potential problem involves the adoption of urine protein measurements factored by urine creatinine. This approach has been developed to some extent for urine calcium-to-creatinine measurements, but many physicians are not aware of the accuracy and validity of protein-to-creatinine ratios. Many clinical laboratories may not report ratios of analytes to creatinine. A significant amount of education will be necessary to implement this approach.

A less obvious implementation issue relates to measuring albumin rather than total protein in the urine specimens. Assays for albumin may not be as available as those for total protein in some smaller communities. In such instances, the use of a spot urine and expression of the urine protein-to-creatinine ratio is still preferable to the 24-hour collection.

RESEARCH RECOMMENDATIONS

Evaluate novel approaches to measuring urine and blood abnormalities which may predate and possibly predict proteinuria/albuminuria. Examples include elevated levels of β_2-microglobulin and other tubular proteins in the urine of diabetic patients. Additional efforts should be instituted to identify constituents present in blood and/or urine that indicate normal kidney function with high specificity.

It would be useful to conduct prospective trials of the long-term efficacy of antihypertensive medications that reduce albumin/protein excretion in kidney disease. These studies should incorporate better procedures to examine the efficacy of sustaining kidney function in advanced kidney disease and in reducing the incidence of cardiovascular disease in patients with kidney disease.[224-227]

It would also be useful to determine the relationships between factors that may affect albumin/protein excretion and also increase the risk of macrovascular disease (eg, glucose intolerance/diabetes mellitus, rising blood pressure, elevated lipid levels, and obesity) and progressive kidney failure.[228,229]

GUIDELINE 6. MARKERS OF CHRONIC KIDNEY DISEASE OTHER THAN PROTEINURIA

Markers of kidney damage in addition to proteinuria include abnormalities in the urine sediment and abnormalities on imaging studies. Constellations of markers define clinical presentations for some types of chronic kidney disease. New markers are needed to detect kidney damage that occurs prior to a reduction in GFR in other types of chronic kidney diseases.

- Urine sediment examination or dipstick for red blood cells and white blood cells should be performed in patients with chronic kidney disease and in individuals at increased risk of developing chronic kidney disease.

- Imaging studies of the kidneys should be performed in patients with chronic kidney disease and in selected individuals at increased risk of developing chronic kidney disease.
- Although several novel urinary markers (such as tubular or low-molecular weight proteins and specific mononuclear cells) show promise of future utility, they should not be used for clinical decision-making at present.

BACKGROUND

Abnormal urinary excretion of albumin and total protein (Guideline 5) is a highly sensitive indicator of glomerular disease. The results of urine sediment examination and of imaging studies of the kidney, however, can also suggest other types of chronic kidney diseases, including vascular, tubulointerstitial, and cystic diseases of the kidney. In addition, proteins other than albumin in the urine may indicate tubulointerstitial injury. At present, there are no clinically proven markers specific for tubulointerstitial or vascular diseases of the kidney. The purpose of this guideline is to review: abnormalities of urine sediment and abnormalities of imaging studies associated with kidney damage; the relationships of these abnormalities to clinical presentations of kidney disease; and possible new markers of kidney damage.

RATIONALE

In some specific types of chronic kidney disease, abnormalities other than proteinuria are present prior to reduction in GFR. In general, urinalysis and ultrasound of the kidneys are helpful non-invasive tests to detect kidney damage. In addition, these assessments provide clues to the type (diagnosis) of chronic kidney disease.

Abnormalities of the Urinary Sediment

Examination of the urinary sediment, especially in conjunction with assessment of proteinuria, is useful in the detection of chronic kidney disease and in the identification of the type of kidney disease. Urinary sediment examination is recommended in patients with chronic kidney disease and should be considered in individuals at increased risk of developing chronic kidney disease.

Cells may originate from the kidneys or from elsewhere in the urinary tract, including the external genitalia. Casts form only in the kidneys and result from gelation within the tubules of Tamm-Horsfall protein, a high molecular weight glycoprotein derived from the epithelial surface of the distal nephron. Casts entrap material contained within the tubular lumen at the time of cast formation, including cells, cellular debris, crystals, fat, and filtered proteins. Gelation of Tamm-Horsfall glycoprotein is enhanced in concentrated urine and at acidic pH levels. Examination of the urinary sediment for casts requires careful preparation. A "fresh" first morning specimen is optimal, and repeated examination may be necessary.

The presence of formed elements in the urinary sediment may indicate glomerular, tubulointerstitial, or vascular kidney disease. Significant numbers of erythrocytes, leukocytes, or cellular casts in urinary sediment suggest the presence of acute or chronic kidney disease requiring further work-up. The differential diagnosis for persistent hematuria, for example, is quite broad, including glomerulonephritis, tubulointerstitial nephritis, vascular diseases, and urologic disorders. Therefore, as with proteinuria, specific diagnosis requires correlation of urinalysis findings with other clinical markers. The presence of red blood cell casts strongly suggests glomerulonephritis as the source of hematuria. Dysmorphic red blood cells may also indicate a glomerular disease. Pyuria (leukocyturia)—especially in the context of leukocyte casts—may be seen in tubulointerstitial nephritis, or along with hematuria in various forms of glomerulonephritis. Urinary eosinophils have been specifically associated with allergic tubulointerstitial nephritis. Examination of a single urinary sediment may be adequate in most cases. However, the finding of a negative urinary sediment in patients considered to be at high risk for chronic kidney disease should lead to a repeat examination of the sediment. Table 62 provides a brief guide to the interpretation of proteinuria and abnormalities in urine sediment.

Urine dipsticks include reagent pads that are sensitive for the detection of red blood cells (hemoglobin), neutrophils and eosinophils (leukocyte esterase), and bacteria (nitrites). Thus, urine sediment examination is generally not necessary for detection of these

Table 62. Interpretation of Proteinuria and Urine Sediment Abnormalities as Markers of Chronic Kidney Disease

Predominant Urinalysis Abnormality

RBC	RBC Casts*	WBC	WBC Casts	Tubular Cells	Cellular Casts	Granular Casts	Fat**	Total Protein-to-Creatinine Ratio†	Associated Kidney Disease
+	+								Proliferative glomerulonephritis or hereditary nephritis
+	−			+		+			Hereditary nephritis, or disease of small vessels (microangiopathy)
+	−			−		−			Cystic kidney disease, kidney neoplasms or urinary tract lesions other than kidney disease
±	−	+	+					200–1,000 mg/g	Tubulointerstitial nephritis
		+	−					<200 mg/g	Urinary tract lesions other than kidney disease
				+	+	+			May be present in all types of kidney disease, but most abundant in acute tubular necrosis (the most common kidney disease causing acute kidney failure)
−	−						+	>1,000 mg/g	Diabetic kidney disease and non-inflammatory glomerular diseases
−	−	−	−	−	−	−	−	200–1,000 mg/g	Non-inflammatory glomerular disease, non-inflammatory tubulointerstitial disease, or diseases affecting medium-sized arteries

Modified with permission.[230]

* Detection of red blood cell casts requires careful preparation and thorough and repeated examination of sediment from freshly obtained urine specimens. Even under ideal conditions, red blood cell casts may not always be detected in patients with proliferative glomerulonephritis.

** Oval fat bodies, fatty casts, free fat

† Cut-off values are not precise.

Abbreviations and symbols: RBC, red blood cells, WBC, white blood cells; +, abnormality present; −, abnormality not present; ±, abnormality may or may not be present formed elements. However, dipsticks cannot detect tubular epithelial cells, fat, or casts in the urine. In addition, urine dipsticks cannot detect crystals, fungi, or parasites. Urine sediment examination is necessary for detection of these abnormalities. The choice of urine sediment examination versus dipstick depends on the type of kidney disease that is being considered.

Imaging Studies

Abnormal results on imaging studies suggest either urologic or intrinsic kidney diseases. Imaging studies are recommended in patients with chronic kidney disease and in patients at increased risk of developing chronic kidney disease due to urinary tract stones, infections, obstruction, vesico-ureteral reflux, or polycystic kidney disease.

Hydronephrosis on ultrasound examination may be found in patients with urinary tract obstruction or with vesico-ureteral reflux. The presence of cysts—manifested either as multiple discrete macroscopic cysts or as bilaterally enlarged echogenic kidneys—suggests autosomal dominant or recessive polycystic kidney disease. Increased cortical echoes are a nonspecific but sensitive indicator of glomerular, interstitial, or vascular diseases. Imaging studies employing iodinated contrast agents can cause acute kidney damage and may present significant risks to some patients with decreased kidney function. The benefits of such studies must be weighed against potential risks. Baseline imaging studies will be appropriate in many patients. The appropriateness and frequency of follow-up studies will vary from case to case. Table 63 provides a brief overview of possible interpretations of abnormalities on imaging studies of the kidney.

Table 63. Interpretation of Abnormalities on Imaging Studies as Markers of Kidney Damage

Imaging Modality/Feature	Associated Kidney Disease
Ultrasonography	
General appearance	May show nephrocalcinosis or discrete stones, hydronephrosis, cysts or masses.
Increased echogenicity	May indicate cystic disease or "medical renal disease."
Small, "hyperechoic" kidneys	Generally indicate chronic kidney disease.
Large kidneys	Generally indicate tumors, infiltrating diseases or diseases causing nephrotic syndrome.
Size disparities and scarring	Suggest vascular, urologic or tubulointerstitial diseases due to stones or infection.
Doppler interrogation	May be useful in investigation of venous thrombosis, less so in arterial stenosis.
Intravenous pyelography (IVP)[a]	May reveal asymmetry of kidney size or function, presence of obstructing stones, tumors, scars, or dilated collecting ducts in medullary sponge kidney.
Computed tomography (CT)[b]	May show obstruction, tumors (e.g. angiomyolipoma), cysts or ureteral calculi. Helical CT with contrast may show sites of anatomic renal artery stenosis.
Magnetic resonance imaging (MRI)	May show mass lesions, renal vein thrombosis, cysts, etc. MR angiography using gadolinium may be useful in patients with decreased kidney function.
Nuclear scans[c]	May reveal asymmetry of kidney size or function, functional evidence of renal artery stenosis, acute pyelonephritis, or scars.

[a] This modality has been largely supplanted by computed tomography, although it remains useful to describe fine detail in the collecting system.

[b] With or without contrast

[c] Captopril renography, mercaptoacetyltriglycine (MAG3), dimercaptosuccinic acid (DMSA)

Clinical Presentations of Kidney Disease

Some constellations of abnormalities in blood and urine tests or imaging studies comprise specific clinical presentations of kidney disease. These presentations are often not defined precisely in textbooks and review articles. The major features are described below. Table 64 defines these presentations according to level of GFR, markers of kidney disease (urine protein excretion, urine sediment examination, imaging studies), and other clinical features. Decreased GFR and kidney failure are markers of more severe kidney disease (CKD Stages 2 through 5). The other presentations can occur without decreased GFR (CKD Stage 1) and can therefore serve as markers of kidney disease. Table 65 describes the most frequent presentations for each type of chronic kidney disease.

Decreased GFR and kidney failure. Either can be acute or chronic depending on duration, and due to any type (diagnosis) of kidney disease.

Nephritic and nephrotic syndromes. Nephritic syndrome (formerly "nephritis," also termed "acute glomerulonephritis") is an outdated term, characterized by hematuria with red blood cell casts, hypertension, and edema, with or without decreased GFR. Nephrotic syndrome (formerly "nephrosis") is defined as total urine protein excretion in excess of 3,500 mg/d (equivalent to a total protein-to-creatinine ratio greater than

Table 64. Clinical Presentations of Kidney Disease

Clinical Presentations	GFR (mL/min/1.73 m²)	Proteinuria	Urine Sediment	Imaging Studies	Other Features
Decreased GFR:	15–89	NA	NA	NA	Complications due to ↓ GFR
Kidney failure:	<15 or treated by dialysis	NA	NA	NA	Uremia
Nephritic syndrome ("nephritis"):	NA	Usually >1500 mg/d or >1000 mg/g creatinine	RBCs and RBC casts	NA	Edema, HBP
Nephrotic syndrome ("nephrosis"):	NA	>3500 mg/d or >3000 mg/g creatinine	Fatty casts, oval fat bodies, with or without RBCs and RBC casts	NA	Edema, low serum albumin, elevated serum lipids
Tubular syndromes:	Usually normal	Usually <1500 mg/d or <1000 mg/g creatinine	Usually normal	Usually normal	Fluid and electrolyte abnormalities, inability to concentrate urine
Kidney disease with urinary tract symptoms:	NA	Usually <1500 mg/d or <1000 mg/g creatinine	NA	Usually abnormal	Usually due to urinary tract infections, stones or obstruction
Asymptomatic urinalysis abnormalities (proteinuria, hematuria, pyuria or others):	≥90	<3500 mg/d or <3000 mg/g creatinine	RBCs with or without RBC casts, WBCs with or without WBC casts, tubular cells or casts	NA	No symptoms
Asymptomatic radiologic abnormalities:	≥90	Usually normal	Usually normal	Hydronephrosis, dilated calyces, dilated collecting ducts (on IVP), cysts, asymmetry of kidney size or function	No symptoms
Hypertension due to kidney disease:	NA	±	±	±	HBP

Modified with permission.[230]

Abbreviations and symbols: RBC, red blood cells; WBC, white blood cells; IVP, intravenous pyelogram; HBP, high blood pressure; NA, not applicable; ±, may be present or absent

Table 65. Relationship between Types of Kidney Disease and Clinical Presentations

Kidney Disease	Clinical Presentations
Diabetic kidney disease (type 1 and type 2)	Asymptomatic urinalysis abnormalities (proteinuria), nephrotic syndrome
Glomerular diseases Proliferative glomerulonephritis	Nephritic syndrome, asymptomatic urinalysis abnormalities (hematuria and proteinuria)
Noninflammatory diseases	Nephrotic syndrome, asymptomatic urinalysis abnormalities (proteinuria)
Vascular diseases Large vessels	HBP due to kidney disease, asymptomatic radiologic abnormalities
Medium-sized vessels	HBP due to kidney disease, asymptomatic urinalysis abnormalities (proteinuria)
Small vessels	HBP due to kidney disease, asymptomatic urinalysis abnormalities (hematuria)
Tubulointerstitial diseases Tubulointerstitial nephritis	Kidney disease with urinary tract symptoms, tubular syndromes, asymptomatic urinalysis abnormalities (pyuria, tubular cells), asymptomatic radiologic abnormalities, urine concentration effect
Noninflammatory diseases	Tubular syndromes, asymptomatic urinalysis abnormalities (proteinuria, pyuria, tubular cell or granular casts), asymptomatic radiologic abnormalities
Cystic diseases	Urinary tract symptoms, asymptomatic urinalysis abnormalities, asymptomatic radiologic abnormalities
Disease in the kidney transplant Chronic rejection	HBP due to kidney disease, asymptomatic urinalysis abnormalities (pyuria, proteinuria)
Drug toxicity	HBP due to kidney disease
Transplant glomerulopathy	Asymptomatic urinalysis abnormalities (proteinuria)
Recurrent disease	Nephrotic syndrome, asymptomatic urinalysis abnormalities (proteinuria, hematuria)

approximately 3,000 mg/g), reduced serum albumin concentration, and edema, with or without decreased GFR. Both syndromes indicate the presence of a glomerular disease.

Tubular Syndromes. There are disorders resulting from abnormal tubule handling of water or solutes, without decreased GFR. They include diverse disorders such as renal tubular acidosis, nephrogenic diabetes insipidus, hyporeninemic hypoaldosteronism and other potassium secretory defects, renal glycosuria, renal phosphaturia, renal aminoaciduria, and many others. These syndromes often indicate a tubular interstitial disease.

Kidney disease with urinary tract symptoms. Most kidney diseases are asymptomatic, but in some tubulointerstitial diseases symptoms are associated with the kidneys or lower urinary tract. The most common causes include urinary tract infections, obstruction, and stones.

Asymptomatic urinalysis abnormalities. Abnormalities in urinary protein excretion or in urinary sediment without decreased GFR or urinary tract symptoms. Principal abnormalities include hematuria with red blood cell casts (due to glomerular diseases), pyuria with white blood cell casts, renal tubular cells, coarse granular casts, or nonnephrotic proteinuria.

Asymptomatic radiologic abnormalities. These include structural abnormalities of the kidney observed on imaging studies, without decreased GFR, urinary tract symptoms, or abnormal urinalysis.

High blood pressure due to kidney disease. Sustained elevation of arterial blood pressure as the result of disease of the parenchyma or major vessels of the kidney, with or without decreased GFR, but usually with either urinary abnormalities or radiologic abnormalities. Large vessel diseases (unilateral or bilateral) are included as chronic kidney diseases.

Strength of Evidence: New Urinary Markers

Increased urinary excretion of some low molecular weight (LMW) proteins and N-acetyl-β-D-glucosaminidase (NAG) are key diagnostic indicators in a number of specific tubular diseases and may identify patients at higher risk of GFR decline in other kidney diseases (Tables 66, 67, 68, and 69) (C). Low molecular weight proteinuria is a defining feature in several uncommon diseases of the kidney (Dent's disease, autosomal dominant and cystinotic Fanconi syndrome, Lowe syndrome, Chinese herbs nephropathy).[231] The urinary excretion of retinol-binding protein (RBP), but not albumin, increases with the presence of kidney scarring in reflux nephropathy in children.[232] Increased urinary excretion rates of the LMW protein RBP and the tubular injury marker NAG are found in many patients with type I diabetes, even in the absence of albuminuria.[38,42] Excretion of these markers appears to correlate with the degree of glycemic control in some studies,[38,42] but not in others.[233] In children with type I diabetes and normal albumin excretion, the presence of abnormal urinary NAG excretion at baseline indicates increased risk of developing microalbuminuria within 5 years (19.5% versus 0%, $P < 0.05$).[234] In elderly patients with type 2 diabetes, individuals who developed macrovascular disease after 7 years of follow-up tended to have higher baseline NAG urinary excretion rates ($P = 0.07$).[233] Elevated urinary excretion of β-2-microglobulin (>500 ng/min) at baseline predicted deterioration of kidney function over a mean follow-up period of more than 4 years in adult patients with membranous nephropathy.[235] In adult and pediatric patients with a variety of kidney diseases (focal segmental glomerular sclerosis, membranous nephropathy, membranoproliferative glomerulonephritis), a pattern of "very low" molecular weight proteinuria by sodium dodecyl sulfate-polyacrylamide gel electrophoresis (SDS-PAGE) was associated with a higher rate of development of decreased kidney function at follow-up than was a pattern of "low" molecular weight proteinuria (50% versus 12.5%; $P = 0.0001$).[236] In adult and pediatric patients with IgA nephropathy and normal kidney function at baseline, the presence of a low molecular weight pattern of proteinuria by SDS-PAGE at presentation was associated with an approximately 4-fold increase in their risk of developing a decreased GFR after 6 years of follow-up.[237]

Urinary excretion of mononuclear cells may reflect the presence and/or degree of glomerular injury in some glomerular diseases, including diabetic nephropathy and IgA nephropathy (Table 70) (C). In children with various kidney diseases, semiquantitative evaluation of urinary podocyte excretion correlated with the severity of mesangial proliferation, extracapillary proliferation, tubulointerstitial changes,

Table 66. Retinol Binding Protein (RBP): Association with Various Outcomes

Author, Year	No. of Subjects	Outcome	Applic-ability	GFR Range* (mL/min/1.73 m^2)	Association with Outcome**	Quality
Ginevri,[38] 1993	621	Micro-albuminuria	♦♦	GFR >120	+	◯
Tomlinson,[232] 1994	143	Kidney scarring	♦♦	ND	+	◯
Gibb,[42] 1989	105	IDDM	♦♦	(0–120 scale)	+	◯

* At baseline

** Indicates whether urinary marker was associated (+) or not associated (–) with outcome.

Abbreviation: IDDM, insulin dependent diabetes mellitus

Table 67. N-Acetyl-β-D-Glucosaminidase (NAG): Association with Various Outcomes

Author, Year	No. of Subjects	Outcome	Applic-ability	GFR Range* (mL/min/1.73 m^2)	Association with Outcome**	Quality
Kordonouri,[234] 1998	64	Micro-albuminuria	♦♦	ND	+	●
Weitgasser,[233] 1999	124	CVD	♦♦	S_{cr} <1.5 mg/dL	–	◯
Gibb,[42] 1989	105	IDDM	♦♦	(0–120 scale)	+	◯

* At baseline

** Indicates whether urinary marker was associated (+) or not associated (–) with outcome.

Abbreviations: CVD, cardiovascular disease; IDDM, insulin dependent diabetes mellitus

Table 68. β-2-Microglobulin (β-2-MG): Association with Various Outcomes

Author, Year	No. of Subjects	Outcome	Applic-ability	GFR Range* (mL/min/1.73 m^2)	Association with Outcome**	Quality
Gibb,[42] 1989	105	IDDM	♦♦	(0–120 scale)	+	◯
Reichert,[238] 1995	30	Kidney function deterioration	♦♦	(0–120 scale)	+	◯

* At baseline

** Indicates whether urinary marker was associated (+) or not associated (–) with outcome.

Table 69. Sodium Dodecyl Sulfate-Polyacrylamide Gel Electrophoresis (SDS-PAGE): Association with Decreased GFR

Author, Year	No. of Subjects	Outcome	Applic-ability	GFR Range* (mL/min/1.73 m^2)	Association with Outcome**	Quality
Bazzi,[236] 1997	142	↓ GFR	♦♦♦	S_{cr} <1.4 mg/dL in 71%	+	◯
Woo,[237] 1991	60	↓ GFR	♦♦	(0–120 scale)	+	◯

* At baseline

** Indicates whether urinary marker was associated (+) or not associated (–) with outcome.

Table 70. Urinary Cell Excretion: Association with Various Outcomes

Author, Year	No. of Subjects	Urinary Cell	Outcome	Applic-ability	GFR Range* (mL/min/1.73 m²) 0 30 60 90 120	Association with Outcome**	Quality
Hotta,[241] 1993	79	CD14/CD56	IgA nephropathy	↑↑	|	+	●
Nakamura,[243] 2000b	60	Podocyte	Albuminuria	↑↑	$S_{Cr} \approx 0.4$–5.2 mg/dL	+	●
Nakamura,[242] 2000a	26	Podocyte	SLE	↑↑	$S_{Cr} \approx 0.7$–2.4 mg/dL	+	●
Hara,[239] 1998b	87	Podocyte	Various kidney diseases	↑↑	ND	+	○
Hara,[240] 1998a	84	Podocyte	Glomerular disease	↑↑	ND	+	○

* At baseline
** Indicates whether urinary marker was associated (+) or not associated (–) with outcome.

Abbreviations: IgA₁, immunoglobulin A; SLE, systemic lupus erythematosus

and proteinuria.[239] In pediatric patients with Henoch-Schönlein nephritis or IgA nephropathy followed for 12 months, the patients with resolution of podocyturia had the greatest resolution of acute inflammatory changes in their biopsies.[240] In adult patients with biopsy-proven IgA nephropathy, the extent of active crescents correlated strongly with the number of CD14⁺ cells (macrophages) and CD56⁺ cells (NK cells) in urinary sediment.[241]

In adult patients with either clinically stable systemic lupus erythematosus (SLE) nephritis (WHO classes IIIa, b, IVb, c) or clinically active SLE nephritis (WHO classes IVb, c), only the patients with active disease showed evidence of podocyturia.[242] In adult patients with type 2 diabetes, podocytes were present in the urine of 53% of microalbuminuric subjects and 80% of macroalbuminuric subjects, but in none of the normoalbuminuric subjects. Treatment with an angiotensin-converting enzyme inhibitor (ACE-inhibitor) reduced both urinary albumin excretion and podocyturia.[243]

LIMITATIONS

The findings of hematuria, pyuria, and casts on urinalysis, or of cystic or echogenic kidneys on ultrasound, are well established as indicators of various chronic kidney diseases. In the proper setting, these findings are sensitive markers for the presence of chronic kidney disease, although they may not suggest a specific diagnosis. Since the novel markers described above (eg, low molecular weight proteinuria, mononuclear cyturia) have only been correlated with various chronic kidney diseases in a few studies to date, their application in clinical practice has not been established. In particular, inasmuch as these markers may correlate strongly with proteinuria, it is not certain that they can yet be considered *independent* indicators of disease or predictors of risk of disease progression.

CLINICAL APPLICATIONS

In patients known to have chronic kidney disease on the basis of a decreased GFR, urinalysis and imaging studies may yield important diagnostic information. For example, the finding of red blood cell casts in the urine indicates a high likelihood of a proliferative glomerulonephritis. This finding would lead to a serological work-up and probably a kidney biopsy. The finding of diffuse nephrocalcinosis and nephrolithiasis on ultrasound in a patient with decreased GFR could suggest the possible diagnosis of hyperoxaluria, leading to specific blood tests.

In patients not previously known to have chronic kidney disease but presenting with symptoms suggestive of kidney disease (eg, edema, hematuria, or flank pain), examination of the urinary sediment may confirm the presence of kidney disease. Abnormalities in the sediment will be present in a large proportion of patients with chronic kidney disease. On ultrasound examination, the presence of a kidney stone and findings of obstruction may help to explain acute flank pain. Radiologic assessment may help to clarify other aspects of the nature of the kidney involvement. For example, bilateral small echogenic kidneys in a patient presenting with newly detected decreased kidney function can suggest a chronic rather than an acute process.

Examination of the urinary sediment may lead to the detection of kidney disease in patients presenting for evaluation of symptoms related to other organ systems. The evaluation of the urine in patients with signs of vasculitis or with carcinomas may result in detection of associated kidney disease. Findings suggestive of kidney disease may be expected to occur frequently in the evaluation of individuals presenting with hypertension, especially younger individuals.

In selected individuals with a normal GFR, but known to be at risk of chronic kidney disease, markers may serve as screening tests. For example, a patient at risk on the basis of a positive family history of polycystic kidney disease should undergo a screening kidney ultrasound one or more times before adulthoood. See Guideline 3.

Application of the newer urinary markers (mononuclear cells and specific proteins such as NAG) described herein must await their validation in more extensive clinical studies.

RESEARCH RECOMMENDATIONS

Novel and expanded uses of established methodologies (such as Doppler or functional MRI) should be pursued in clinical research studies. Several novel urinary markers show promise of noninvasive demonstration of kidney damage or prediction of disease progression. None appears to be ready at this time for widespread application in clinical practice. Longitudinal and follow-up studies are necessary to verify whether abnormal NAG and possibly retinol-binding protein excretion in normoalbuminuric diabetic patients reliably predict later development of microalbuminuria and diabetic nephropathy. Similar studies are needed to confirm whether increased β-2-microglobulin excretion predicts development of kidney failure in patients with idiopathic membranous nephropathy. Longitudinal studies of urinary excretion of specific cell types (macrophages, NK cells, podocytes) in diabetic nephropathy, Henoch-Schönlein nephropathy, and IgA nephropathy are also necessary in order to confirm preliminary findings that cyturia is strongly associated with activity in these diseases. Preliminary work on the urinary excretion of podocyte-specific marker proteins such as podocalyxin and nephrin should be validated by further studies.

PART 6. ASSOCIATION OF LEVEL OF GFR WITH COMPLICATIONS IN ADULTS

Many of the complications of chronic kidney disease can be prevented or delayed by early detection and treatment. The goal of Part 6 is to review the association of the level of GFR with complications of chronic kidney disease to determine the stage of chronic kidney disease when complications appear. As described in Appendix 1, Table 153, the Work Group searched for cross-sectional studies that related manifestations of complications and the level of kidney function. Data from NHANES III were also analyzed, as described in Appendix 2.

Because of different manifestations of complications of chronic kidney disease in children, especially in growth and development, the Work Group limited the scope of the review of evidence to adults. A separate Work Group will need to address this issue in children.

The Work Group did not attempt to review the evidence on the evaluation and management of complications of chronic kidney disease. This is the subject of past and forthcoming clinical practice guidelines by the National Kidney Foundation and other groups, which are referenced in the text.

Representative findings are shown by stage of chronic kidney disease in Figs 15 and 16. Figure 15 shows a higher prevalence of each complication at lower GFR. Figure 16

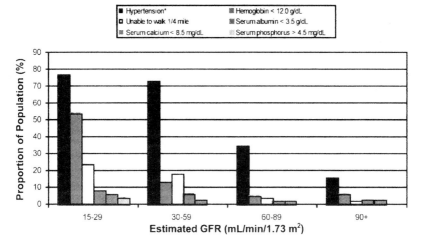

*≥140/90 or antihypertensive medication   p-trend <0.001 for each abnormality

Fig 15. Estimated prevalence of selected complications, by category of estimated GFR, among participants age ≥20 years in NHANES III, 1988 to 1994. These estimates are not adjusted for age, the mean of which is 33 years higher at an estimated GFR of 15 to 29 mL/min/1.73 m² than at an estimated GFR of ≥90 mL/min/1.73 m².

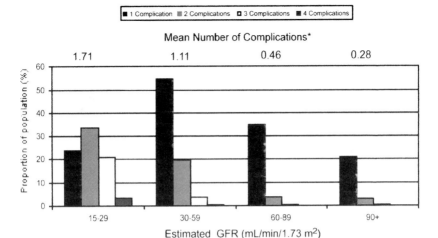

Fig 16. Estimated distribution of the number of complications, by category of estimated GFR among participants age ≥20 years in NHANES III, 1988 to 1994. These estimates are not adjusted for age, the mean of which is 33 years higher at an estimated GFR of 15 to 29 mL/min/1.73 m² than at an estimated GFR of ≥90 mL/min/1.73 m².

shows a larger mean number of complications per person and higher prevalence of multiple complications at lower GFR. These and other findings support the classification of stages of chronic kidney disease and are discussed in detail in Guidelines 7 through 12.

GUIDELINE 7.   ASSOCIATION OF LEVEL OF GFR WITH HYPERTENSION

High blood pressure is both a cause and a complication of chronic kidney disease. As a complication, high blood pressure may develop early during the course of chronic kidney disease and is associated with adverse outcomes—in particular, faster loss of kidney function and development of cardiovascular disease.

- Blood pressure should be closely monitored in all patients with chronic kidney disease.
- Treatment of high blood pressure in chronic kidney disease should include specification of target blood pressure levels, nonpharmacologic therapy, and specific antihypertensive agents for the prevention of progression of kidney disease (Guideline 13) and development of cardiovascular disease (Guideline 15).

BACKGROUND

High blood pressure can be either a cause or a consequence of chronic kidney disease. Adverse outcomes of high blood pressure in chronic kidney disease include faster decline in kidney function and cardiovascular disease. The appropriate evaluation and management of high blood pressure remains a major component of the care of patients with chronic kidney disease.

High blood pressure is a well-recognized public health problem in the United States. Based on epidemiological data from the National High Blood Pressure Education Program and the National Health and Nutrition Examination Surveys, the rates of detection, treatment, and control of high blood pressure have improved dramatically over the past five decades. Concomitantly, the rates of stroke, myocardial infarction, and heart failure have decreased by approximately 15% to 40%.[244] However, during the same time, high blood pressure as a cause of ESRD has increased at an annualized rate of 10% for the last several years, and cardiovascular disease is the leading cause of death in ESRD.[4,245,246] In part this may be due to inadequate control of high blood pressure in patients with chronic kidney disease.

In 1998, the NKF published the Report of the Task Force on Cardiovascular Disease in Chronic Renal Disease.[9] One of the major goals of the Task Force was to assess current knowledge about the association of high blood pressure and cardiovascular disease in chronic kidney disease. Portions of the Task Force Report are reproduced in this guideline with permission of the authors.[247,248] More recently, the NKF published a Report on Management of Hypertension in Adults with Renal Diseases and Diabetes from the Executive Committees of the Councils on Hypertension and Diabetic Kidney Disease.[249]

In July of 2001, the NKF initiated a K/DOQI Work Group specifically to conduct a detailed review of evidence and to develop clinical practice guidelines for the management of blood pressure in chronic kidney disease to prevent progression of kidney disease and development and progression of cardiovascular disease in chronic kidney disease. The goal of this guideline is to provide a selected review of the literature relating high blood pressure to adverse outcomes of chronic kidney disease and to describe the association of the level of GFR with high blood pressure, as reported in NHANES III. Guideline 13 describes the relationship of high blood pressure to progression of kidney disease.

RATIONALE

Definition

Consensus panels in the United States and other countries have defined hypertension in adults as systolic blood pressure greater than 140 mm Hg and/or diastolic blood pressure greater than 90 mm Hg. The Sixth Report of the Joint National Committee for the Prevention, Detection, Evaluation and Treatment of High Blood Pressure (JNC-VI) classifies categories of blood pressure levels as shown in Table 71.

JNC-VI recommends a goal blood pressure of <140/90 mm Hg for individuals with high blood pressure without diabetes, cardiovascular disease, or chronic kidney disease.

Table 71. Classification of Blood Pressure for Adults Age ≥18 Years (JNC-VI)

Category	Systolic Blood Pressure (mm Hg)		Diastolic Blood Pressure (mm Hg)
Optimal	<120	*and*	<80
Normal	<130	*and*	<85
High-Normal	130–139	*or*	85–89
High	≥140	*or*	≥90
Stage 1	140–159	*or*	90–99
Stage 2	160–179	*or*	100–109
Stage 3	≥180	*or*	≥110

Reprinted with permission.[247]

For individuals with high blood pressure and decreased kidney function, the recommended goal is <130/85 mm Hg.

Strength of Evidence

High blood pressure develops during the course of chronic kidney disease (R). High blood pressure is a well-described complication of chronic kidney disease. The prevalence of high blood pressure is approximately 80% in hemodialysis patients and 50% in peritoneal dialysis patients.[250,251] In patients with earlier stages of kidney disease, high blood pressure is also highly prevalent, varying with patient characteristics such as the cause of kidney disease and level of kidney function.[252] There are many causes of high blood pressure in chronic kidney disease. The clinically more important pathogenetic mechanisms of high blood pressure are listed in Table 72.[248]

High blood pressure is associated with worse outcomes in chronic kidney disease (R). In the general population, there is a strong, graded relationship between the level of blood pressure and all-cause mortality and fatal and nonfatal cardiovascular disease. Optimal levels of systolic and diastolic blood pressure are defined as less than 120 and 80 mm Hg, respectively. Among patients with chronic kidney disease, there is also substantial evidence of a relationship between elevated levels of blood pressure and cardiovascular risk. In addition, high blood pressure is associated with a greater rate of decline in kidney function and risk of development of kidney failure. However, the optimal level of blood pressure to minimize adverse outcomes for cardiovascular and kidney disease has not been established.

Progression of kidney disease. This subject is reviewed in more detail in Guideline 13. The following represent a few of the many studies that demonstrate these relationships.

Table 72. Pathogenetic Mechanisms of High Blood Pressure in Chronic Kidney Disease

Pre-existing essential hypertension

Extracellular fluid volume expansion

Renin-angiotensin aldosterone system stimulation

Increased sympathetic activity

Endogenous digitalis-like factors

Prostaglandins/bradykinins

Alteration in endothelium-derived factors (nitric oxide/endothelin)

Increased body weight

Erythropoietin administration

Parathyroid hormone secretion/increased intracellular calcium/hypercalcemia

Calcified arterial tree

Renal vascular disease and renal arterial stenosis

Chronic allograft dysfunction

Cadaver allografts, especially from a donor with a family history of hypertension

Cyclosporine, tacrolimus, other immunosuppressive and corticosteroid therapy

Reprinted with permission.[248]

Diabetic kidney disease. Numerous epidemiological studies and clinical trials have shown a relationship between the level of blood pressure and faster progression of diabetic kidney disease. Figure 17 shows the relationship in one of the earliest randomized trials.[253]

Nondiabetic kidney diseases. The Modification of Diet in Renal Disease Study showed a significant relationship between the rate of decline in GFR and level of blood pressure among patients with predominantly nondiabetic kidney disease. This relationship was affected by the baseline level of urine protein (Fig 18).[255]

Diseases in the kidney transplant. A relationship between level of blood pressure and progression of kidney disease has now been shown among kidney transplant recipients. The Collaborative Transplant Group documented that higher blood pressure after kidney transplantation is associated with more rapid development of graft failure[256] (Fig 19).

Cardiovascular disease and mortality. The prevalence of cardiovascular disease and related outcomes in patients with decreased GFR has not been evaluated in large-scale epidemiological studies, and little is known about CVD mortality and morbidity in these patients. Several studies have shown a high prevalence of left ventricular hypertrophy (LVH) in patients with decreased GFR and patients beginning dialysis. In one study, a higher level of systolic blood pressure, lower level of kidney function, more severe anemia, and older age were independently associated with higher left ventricular mass index.[257] A few studies have shown a relationship between higher systolic blood pressure and clinical cardiovascular disease events.[258,259] Among dialysis patients, higher blood pressure is clearly associated with development of cardiovascular disease. Table 73 shows

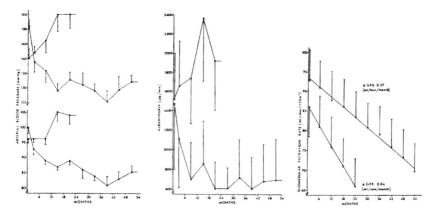

Fig 17. Relationship between blood pressure and progression of diabetic kidney disease. Mean arterial blood pressure, albumin excretion rate, and GFR in patients with type 1 diabetes randomly assigned to a reduction in mean arterial pressure of 10 mm Hg using metoprolol at 100 to 400 mg/d, hydralazine at 50 to 200 mg/d, and furosemide at 80 to 500 mg/d versus no antihypertensive therapy. Solid circles represent the treated group. Open circles represent the control group. Vertical lines represent standard error. Study was stopped earlier in the control group because of faster decline in GFR. Reprinted with permission.[253]

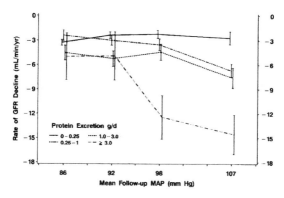

Fig 18. Relationship between mean arterial blood pressure and GFR decline. Mean GFR decline and achieved follow-up blood pressure in MDRD Study A (patients with baseline GFR 25 to 55 mL/min/1.73 m²). Regression lines relating the estimated mean GFR decline over 3 years to mean follow-up MAP for groups of patients defined according to baseline proteinuria. Within each group, a 3-slope model was used with break points at 92 and 98 mm Hg. Reprinted with permission.[255]

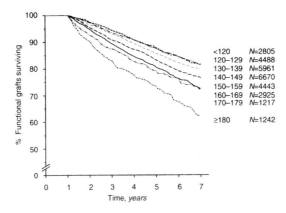

Fig 19.   Relationship between systolic blood pressure and graft survival. Association of systolic blood pressure at 1 year with subsequent graft survival in recipients of cadaveric kidney transplants. Ranges of systolic blood pressure value in mm Hg and number of patients studied in the subgroups are indicated. The association of systolic blood pressure with graft survival at seven years was statistically significant ($P < 0.0001$). Reproduced with permission.[256]

Table 73. Association of Mean Arterial Pressure and Cardiovascular Disease Events in Incident Dialysis Patients

Outcome	Relative Risk*	P-value
Normal LV (reference)	—	—
Concentric LVH	1.48	0.02
LV dilatation	1.48	0.06
Systolic dysfunction	—	NS
Ischemia	1.39	0.05
CHF	1.44	0.007
Death	0.82	0.009

* Relative risks are for 10 mm Hg higher mean follow-up monthly mean arterial pressure before the index event, controlling for age, diagnosis of diabetes, ischemic heart disease at onset of ESRD, follow-up monthly mean serum albumin and hematocrit. Data from Foley et al.[261] Reprinted with permission.[248]

Abbreviations: CVD, cardiovascular disease; LV, left ventricle; LVH, left ventricular hypertrophy; CHF, congestive heart failure; NS, not significant

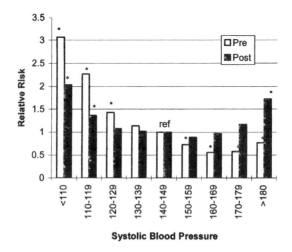

Fig 20. Mortality versus systolic blood pressure in hemodialysis patients. Dialysis Clinic, Inc. prevalent cohort (1992 to 1996, n = 5433).[262] Cox regression analysis including age, race, gender, and diagnosis as baseline covariates, and predialysis or postdialysis systolic blood pressure, albumin, and Kt/V as time-dependent covariates. Reprinted with permission.[248]

the relationship between mean arterial pressure and various cardiovascular disease outcomes in a prospective cohort of incident dialysis patients.[260] Left ventricular hypertrophy and congestive heart failure were both strongly associated with subsequent mortality. However, lower rather than higher blood pressure was associated with a higher risk of death.

The association between level of blood pressure and mortality does not appear to be consistent, with a number of studies reporting either positive or negative associations.[248] One recent study showed a bimodal distribution ("U-shaped" relationship) with excess risk in hemodialysis patients with normal or low blood pressure, as well as in patients with very high blood pressure[262] (Fig 20). It is likely that excess risk in patients with low blood pressure reflects confounding effects of underlying or pre-existing cardiovascular disease on mortality, while the true relationship of blood pressure to mortality is reflected in the excess risk in patients with very high blood pressure as in the general population.

Overall, these studies demonstrate that high blood pressure is associated with faster progression of chronic kidney disease, development of cardiovascular disease, and, likely, higher mortality in patients with chronic kidney disease.

Prevalence of high blood pressure is related to the level of GFR. Patients with chronic kidney disease have a high prevalence of high blood pressure, even when GFR is only mildly reduced (S). Figure 21 shows the relationship between GFR and prevalence of hypertension among 1,795 patients in the baseline cohort of the

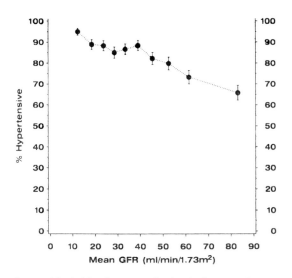

Fig 21. Prevalence of high blood pressure by level of GFR in the MDRD Study. High blood pressure was defined as classification by study investigators based on patient history (including the use of antihypertensive drugs) and review of medical records. GFR was measured by urinary clearance of ^{125}I-iothalamate. Patients were ranked by GFR into 10 groups, each containing 179 or 180 patients. Data are presented as mean values ± standard errors.

MDRD Study.[263] At GFR levels of 60 to 90 mL/min/1.73 m^2, the prevalence of high blood pressure was approximately 65% to 75%. In this study, high blood pressure was defined by patient history (including the use of antihypertensive medications) and medical records, rather than the level of blood pressure. In addition to GFR level, the prevalence of high blood pressure was significantly greater among men and individuals with higher body mass index, black race, and older age.

Figure 22 shows the prevalence of high blood pressure by level of GFR among 15,600 patients participating in the NHANES III. Two levels of high blood pressure are depicted: JNC Stage 1 or greater (systolic blood pressure ≥140 mm Hg or diastolic blood pressure ≥90 mm Hg, or taking medications for high blood pressure); and JNC Stage 2 or greater (systolic blood pressure ≥160 mm Hg or diastolic blood pressure ≥100 mm Hg).

In NHANES III, the approximately 40% prevalence of high blood pressure among individuals with GFR of approximately 90 mL/min/1.73 m^2 was lower than in the MDRD Study, presumably because not all patients with GFR in this range in NHANES III had chronic kidney disease. Among patients with lower GFR, the prevalence of high blood pressure is similar to that observed in the MDRD Study. Notably, the prevalence of JNC Stage ≥2 high blood pressure is approximately 20% among individuals with GFR 15 to 30 mL/min/1.73 m^2, which is approximately 2-fold greater than among patients with higher GFR.

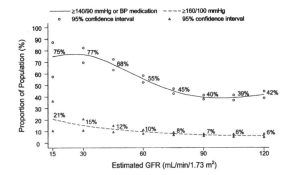

Fig 22.   Prevalence of high blood pressure by level of GFR, adjusted to age 60 years (NHANES III). Predicted prevalence of high blood pressure among adult participants age 20 years and older in NHANES III, 1988 to 1994. Values are adjusted to age 60 years using a polynomial regression. 95% confidence intervals are shown at selected levels of estimated GFR.

High blood pressure is not optimally controlled in patients with chronic kidney disease (S). A recent analysis of the NHANES III database assesses the level of blood pressure control among individuals with decreased kidney function.[5] Decreased kidney function was defined as elevated serum creatinine (≥ 1.6 mg/dL in men or ≥ 1.4 mg/dL in women).

An estimated 3% (5.6 million) of the US population had elevated serum creatinine according to this definition, and of these 70% had high blood pressure. Among individuals with decreased kidney function and high blood pressure, 75% received treatment. However, only 11% of individuals with high blood pressure and elevated serum creatinine had blood pressure <130/85 mm Hg, and 27% had blood pressure <140/90. Treated

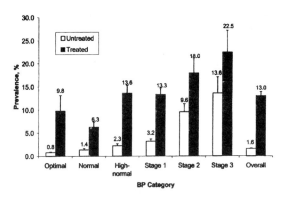

Fig 23.   Prevalence of elevated serum creatinine by JNC-VI blood pressure category and self-reported treatment with anti-hypertensive medications (NHANES III). Bars indicate standard errors. Reprinted with permission.[5]

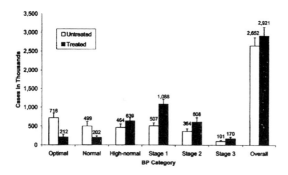

Fig 24. Estimated number of individuals with elevated serum creatinine by JNC-VI blood pressure category and self-reported treatment with anti-hypertensive medications (NHANES III). Bars indicate standard errors. Reprinted with permission.[5]

individuals had a mean blood pressure of 147/77 mm Hg, with 48% prescribed only one antihypertensive medication. Thus, it appears that additional efforts will be necessary to lower systolic blood pressure. Multi-drug therapy may be necessary in the majority of patients.

Figures 23 and 24 show the prevalence and number of individuals with elevated serum creatinine among patients receiving and not receiving antihypertensive therapy, according to blood pressure category. The largest number of treated and untreated individuals have JNC Stage 1 high blood pressure (140 to 159/90 to 99 mm Hg).

Treatment of high blood pressure in chronic kidney disease should include specification of target blood pressure levels, nonpharmacologic therapy, and specific antihypertensive agents for the prevention of progression of kidney disease (Guideline 13) and development of cardiovascular disease in patients with chronic kidney disease (Guideline 15) (R). Specific recommendations for evaluation and management of high blood pressure in chronic kidney disease are beyond the scope of this guideline. The investigation of antihypertensive agents to prevent or delay the progression of chronic kidney disease and development of cardiovascular disease is a rapidly evolving. A number of guidelines and recommendations have been developed. In addition, the role of non-pharmacologic therapy for the treatment of high blood pressure, and as adjuncts in the prevention and treatment of cardiovascular disease, are also under investigation. Recommendations by other groups and recent studies are reviewed in Guidelines 13 and 15.

LIMITATIONS

Unlike other guidelines in Part 6, this guideline is not based on a systematic review of the literature. Another limitation is the lack of large-scale cohort studies and clinical trials correlating blood pressure levels to subsequent loss of GFR and cardiovascular disease events. Since both chronic kidney disease and cardiovascular disease are chronic illnesses, observational studies are subject to confounding by "survival bias," whereby patients with more severe risk factors may not have survived to be entered into the study, thereby minimizing the apparent association between risk factors and outcomes. Thus, clinical trials may be required to determine the optimal level of blood pressure to prevent or slow progression of chronic kidney and development of cardiovascular disease.

A major limitation of cross-sectional studies has been the absence of a clear definition of chronic kidney disease. Since many patients with chronic kidney disease are not detected until late in the course, studies that rely on clinical diagnosis are subject to misclassification. The strong relationship between prevalence of high blood pressure and GFR level observed in NHANES III, irrespective of diagnosis of chronic kidney disease, is especially important in confirming the link between decreased GFR and high blood pressure. However, cross-sectional studies do not permit determination of the causal relationship between these variables. Thus, they cannot determine whether high blood pressure is a cause or a complication of chronic kidney disease, or whether both high blood pressure and decreased GFR are caused by a third factor, such as aging. Nonetheless, the data from both the MDRD Study and NHANES III show a high prevalence of high blood pressure among persons with decreased GFR, justifying the emphasis on monitoring and treatment of high blood pressure in patients with chronic kidney disease.

CLINICAL APPLICATIONS

Detection, evaluation and management of high blood pressure should be the goal for all health care providers for patients with chronic kidney disease. Providers must be aware of lower recommended target levels for blood pressure for patients with chronic kidney disease, specific recommendations for classes of antihypertensive agents, and the role of nonpharmacologic therapy.

IMPLEMENTATION ISSUES

Measuring blood pressure at routine health encounters is widely recommended and practiced. The large number of individuals with blood pressure above the target goal suggests a number of possible obstacles to implementation, such as:

- Limited access to or utilization of health care for many patients with chronic kidney disease
- Inadequate recognition of chronic kidney disease in patients with high blood pressure
- Inadequate education of patients and providers regarding lower blood pressure goals, specific classes of antihypertensive agents, and appropriate nonpharmacologic therapy for patients with chronic kidney disease
- Difficulty in attaining blood pressure control in patients with chronic kidney disease.

The high prevalence of earlier stages of chronic kidney disease requires a coordinated national effort by governmental agencies and nongovernmental organizations to address these issues.

RESEARCH RECOMMENDATIONS

A broad set of recommendations for research on high blood pressure in chronic kidney disease was developed by the NKF Task Force on Cardiovascular Disease in Chronic Renal Disease.[248] Recommendations for observational studies are reproduced in Table 74 and for clinical trials in Table 75.

Table 74. Recommended Research on High Blood Pressure in Chronic Kidney Disease: Observational Studies

Study Population (Stage of CKD)	Recommended Goals
General population:	Genetic studies to determine reasons for racial differences in high blood pressure, prevalence of chronic kidney disease, and prevalence of cardiovascular disease.
CKD patients: (Stages 1–5)	Determine the prevalence of stages of high blood pressure, as defined by JNC-VI
	Determine the relationship of abnormal ambulatory blood pressure monitoring results (for example, loss of diurnal blood pressure rhythm, "non-dipping") to level of GFR, body water content, and antihypertensive agents.
CKD patients & subgroups[a]: (Stages 1–5)	Determine the relationship of blood pressure level (systolic blood pressure, diastolic blood pressure, mean arterial pressure, and pulse pressure) to mortality and cause of death.
	Determine the relationship of blood pressure level to progression of kidney disease.
	Develop and standard methods to assess body water content.
	Compare blood pressure levels from ambulatory blood pressure monitoring to office and dialysis unit blood pressure levels.
Hemodialysis patients: (CKD Stage 5)	Determine relationships between blood pressure measurements taken at different times (predialysis, postdialysis, intradialysis, ABPM), in different postures (sitting, standing, reclining) and according to different methods (JNC-VI recommendations for office blood pressure measurements, dialysis unit "routine" blood pressure measurement).
	Determine relationship among interdialytic weight gain, intradialytic hypotension, class of antihypertensive agents, and blood pressure levels.
	Determine relationship between changes in blood pressure and serum electrolytes during dialysis with myocardial function and potential for arrhythmias.
	Determine relationships of intradialytic hypotension to coronary heart disease and atherosclerotic disease in other vascular beds (cerebrovascular disease and peripheral vascular disease).
Peritoneal dialysis patients: (CKD Stage 5)	Determine the relationship of residual kidney function, ultrafiltration capacity, and blood pressure levels over time.

[a] "Subgroups" refers to subgroups of the chronic kidney disease population defined by age, gender and race.

Table 75. Recommended Research on High Blood Pressure in Chronic Kidney Disease: Clinical Trials

Study Population (Stage of CKD)	Recommended Goals
CKD patients & subgroups[a]: (Stages 1–5)	Compare the effect of antihypertensive agents on blood pressure control and side effects in different types (diagnosis) of chronic kidney disease.
CKD patients without kidney failure: (Stages 1–4)	Determine the effect of blood pressure level and class of antihypertensive agents on preclinical outcomes of coronary heart disease and left ventricular hypertrophy, and on clinical cardiovascular disease agents.
	Determine the effect of nonpharmacologic therapy (dietary modification, exercise) on body water content, blood pressure control and side effects in different types of chronic kidney disease.
	Compare the effect of antihypertensive agents on progression of different types (diagnosis) of chronic kidney disease.
	Compare the effect of immunousppressive agents on blood pressure levels in kidney transplant recipients.
Hemodialysis patients: (CKD Stage 5)	Determine the effect of class of antihypertensive agents and timing of administration of the antihypertensive agents on intradialytic symptoms.
	Compare control of fluid intake and ultrafiltration vs. antihypertensive agents on blood pressure level and cardiovascular outcomes.
	Determine the feasibility maintaining blood pressure less than 140/90 mm Hg (effect on intradialytic and postdialysis blood pressures).
	Determine the effect of the dialysis membrane and reprocessing techniques on blood pressure level.
	Determine the effect of strategies to minimize intradialytic hypotension on subsequent preclinical and clinical cardiovascular disease outcomes.
Peritoneal dialysis patients: (CKD Stage 5)	Determine the feasibility of maintaining blood pressure less than 140/90 mm Hg.
Hemodialysis & peritoneal dialysis patients: (CKD Stage 5)	Determine the effect of dialysis dose and residual kidney function on blood pressure level.

[a] "Subgroups" refers to subgroups of the chronic kidney disease population defined by age, gender and race.

GUIDELINE 8. ASSOCIATION OF LEVEL OF GFR WITH ANEMIA

Anemia usually develops during the course of chronic kidney disease and may be associated with adverse outcomes.

- Patients with GFR <60 mL/min/1.73 m^2 should be evaluated for anemia. The evaluation should include measurement of hemoglobin level.
- Anemia in chronic kidney disease should be evaluated and treated — see K/DOQI Clinical Practice Guidelines for Anemia of Chronic Kidney Disease, Guidelines 1 through 4, as shown in Fig 25.

BACKGROUND

It is well established that anemia develops in the course of chronic kidney disease and is nearly universal in patients with kidney failure.[264] The development of effective therapeutic options, such as erythropoietin therapy, has provided for the effective treatment

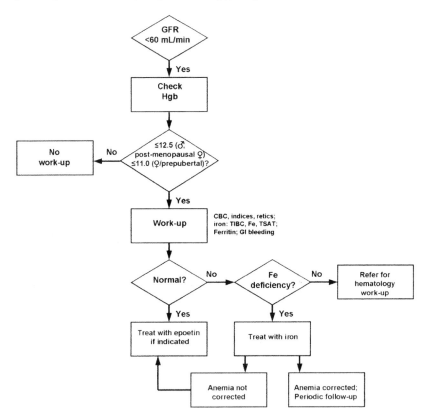

Fig 25. Anemia work-up for patients with chronic kidney disease. Modified and reproduced with permission.[265,266]

of anemia. An earlier K/DOQI clinical practice guideline is devoted to this topic[265,266]; however, that guideline focused primarily on patients treated by dialysis. This guideline addresses anemia in the earlier stages of chronic kidney disease.

Importantly, past guidelines have relied on serum creatinine levels >2 mg/dL as the criterion to test for the presence of anemia. The Work Group recommends that the K/DOQI Anemia guideline be updated to in corporate estimated GFR <60 mL/min/1.73 m² to trigger the ascertainment of anemia, rather than the previously cited serum creatinine levels (Fig 25).

RATIONALE
Definition of Anemia

Measures used to assess anemia and its causes include hemoglobin, hematocrit, and iron stores (as measured directly by bone marrow biopsy, or indirectly as measured by serum ferritin, transferrin saturation levels, and percentage of hypochromic red blood cells or reticulocytes). Erythropoietin levels are less useful as a measure of anemia in chronic kidney disease, since it is now well established that they are often not appropriately elevated despite low hemoglobin levels.[267-271]

Measurement of hemoglobin, rather than hematocrit, is the preferred method for assessing anemia. Unfortunately, this issue has been confused due to the use of hematocrit in a number of studies. Hematocrit is a derived value, affected by plasma water, and thus subject to imprecision as a direct measure of erythropoiesis. Measurement of hemoglobin gives an absolute value and, unlike hematocrit, is not affected greatly by shifts in plasma water, as may occur with diuretics or with dialysis therapy. Hemoglobin levels are directly affected by lack of erythropoietin production from the kidney and thus serve as a more precise measurement of erythropoiesis.

While decreased hemoglobin often accompanies chronic kidney disease, there is no quantitative definition of anemia in chronic kidney disease, since "acceptable" (normal) hemoglobin levels have not been defined for patients with kidney disease. Instead, anemia is defined according to physiological norms. All patients with chronic kidney disease who have hemoglobin levels lower than physiological norms are considered anemic.

The definition of anemia in chronic kidney disease is further complicated by gender differences in hemoglobin levels. In the normal population, hemoglobin levels vary between genders and also as a function of menopausal status. The World Health Organization defines anemia to be that level of hemoglobin and gender-determined normal ranges without reference to age or menopausal status.[272] Thus, for males, anemia is defined as hemoglobin level <13.0 g/dL, while in women, anemia is defined as hemoglobin level <12.0 g/dL. The WHO is in the process of updating these definitions to expand and refine them with specific levels in pregnant women and children of different ages. In most studies of anemia related to the level of kidney function, these issues have not been taken into account.

The operational definition of anemia in patients with kidney disease has also been influenced by health policy. In the past, national reimbursements (such as Medicare and

Medicaid in the United States) have required the attainment of specific levels of hemoglobin or hematocrit, leading investigators and clinicians to define anemia relative to those regulatory levels. As stated in the European Best Practice Guidelines for the Management of Anaemia,[273] it is important to define anemia relative to physiological norms rather than payment rules.

Some studies have arbitrarily defined the "anemia" of kidney disease as a hemoglobin level below some discretionary level (eg, 10 g/dL) that is well below the normative values in the general population. The low hemoglobin level that is often seen in chronic kidney disease should not lead to the acceptance of lower than normal hemoglobin levels as appropriate in patients with chronic kidney disease.

Strength of Evidence

Anemia develops during the course of chronic kidney disease (R). Lower hemoglobin may result from the loss of erythropoietin synthesis in the kidneys and/or the presence of inhibitors of erythropoiesis. Numerous articles document the association of anemia with kidney failure and describe its various causes.[267,268,274-276] The severity of anemia in chronic kidney disease is related to the duration and extent of kidney failure. The lowest hemoglobin levels are found in anephric patients and those who commence dialysis at very severely decreased levels of kidney function.[271,277,278]

Anemia is associated with worse outcomes in chronic kidney disease (R). As yet it is undetermined whether the presence of anemia in chronic kidney disease directly worsens prognosis or whether it is a marker for the severity of other illnesses. Definitive studies have not been concluded. The available evidence, consisting of large database analysis and population studies, clearly show that low hemoglobin levels are associated with higher rates of hospitalizations, cardiovascular disease, cognitive impairment, and other adverse patient outcomes, including mortality.[279-284]

Erythropoietin deficiency is the primary cause of anemia in chronic kidney disease (R). Anemia in patients with chronic kidney disease is due to a number of factors, the most common of which is abnormally low erythropoietin levels. Other causes include: functional or absolute iron deficiency, blood loss (either occult or overt), the presence of uremic inhibitors (eg, parathyroid hormone, spermine, etc), reduced half life of circulating blood cells, deficiencies of folate or Vitamin B_{12}, or some combination of these with a deficiency of erythropoietin.[267-269,274,275] Patients with kidney disease may have concurrent underlying hematological problems such as thalassemia minor, sickle cell disease, or acquired diseases such as myelofibrosis or aplastic anemia.

The causative role of erythropoietin deficiency in anemia of chronic kidney disease includes: (1) anemia is responsive to treatment with erythropoietin in all stages of chronic kidney disease; and (2) in patients with chronic kidney disease, circulating levels of erythropoietin are not sufficient to maintain hemoglobin within the normal range. North American (United States and Canada) and European studies have demonstrated these points.[270,271,282,285-287]

Table 76. Hemoglobin and Kidney Function

Author, Year	No. of Subjects	Applicability	GFR Range (mL/min/1.73 m²) 0 30 60 90 120	Results*/ Mean Level	Quality
Levin,[289] 1999	318	↑↑↑		↑	⬤
Taralov,[289] 1998	63	↑↑	S_D 5.1 mg/dL	↑	⬤
Clyne,[290] 1993	58	↑↑		⇧	⬤
Ishimura,[291] 1998	40	↑↑	S_C 2–8 mg/dL	↑	⬤
Nankivell,[141] 1995	123	↑		↑	◯
de Klerk,[292] 1982	99	↑		⇧	◯
Urabe,[293] 1987	17	↑	S_D 7–15 mg/dL	⇔	◯
Silverberg,[294] 1996	33	↑↑		10.0 g/dL	⬤
Lin,[295] 1996	51	↑↑		12.5 g/dL	◯
Clyne,[296] 1994	12	↑		8.9 g/dL	◯
Portoles,[297] 1997	11	↑		9.0 g/dL	◯
Dimitrakov,[298] 1994	6	↑	S_D 4.5±0.4 mg/dL	7.6 g/dL	◯

Unshaded studies reported the strength of association between the outcome measure (in this case, hemoglobin) and kidney function; shaded studies reported mean or median levels of the outcome measure in the study sample.

* ↑ = higher GFR associated with higher hemoglobin (statistically significant);
 ⇧ = higher GFR associated with higher hemoglobin;
 ⇔ = GFR *not* associated with hemoglobin.

Onset and severity of anemia are related to the level of GFR; below a GFR of approximately 60 mL/min/1.73 m², there is a higher prevalence of anemia (Tables 76 and 77 and Figs 26, 27, 28, and 29) (C, S). Studies reviewed for the purposes of this guideline include those of patients with chronic kidney disease prior to dialysis, those with kidney transplants, and those on dialysis.

The reviewed literature spans almost 30 years of investigation and describes the clinical findings of researchers as they explore the relationships between hemoglobin and kidney function (Tables 76 and 77). The majority of available data have been derived from studies of small sample size, most of which are cross-sectional studies or baseline data from clinical trials of variable size and robustness. These studies are predominantly of only moderate or modest quality from a methodological standpoint. The consistency of the information they provided does, however, indicate a trend toward lower hemoglobin levels at lower levels of GFR and a variability in hemoglobin levels across GFR levels.

In 12 of the 22 studies reviewed, there was an association between the level of hemoglobin or hematocrit and the selected measure of kidney function. Data obtained from the NHANES III analysis (Fig 26) demonstrates an association between hemoglobin and level of GFR at GFR levels <90 mL/min/1.73 m². While the increase in prevalence of anemia is most notable in the population studied at GFR levels <60 mL/min/1.73 m², anemia can be present in patients with higher GFR levels. Due to the sparcity of data

Table 77. Hematocrit and Kidney Function

Author, Year	No. of Subjects	Applicability	GFR Range (mL/min/1.73 m²)	Results*/ Mean Level	Quality
Klahr,[299] 1995	840	↟↟↟	(bar 30–60)	↑	◐
Radtke,[288] 1979	194	↟↟	(bar 0–60)	↑	◐
Howard,[300] 1989	106	↟↟	(+ at ~30)	↑	◐
Lim,[301] 1990	26	↟↟	S₀ 2–12 mg/dL	↑	○
Besarab,[302] 1985	102	↟	S₀ 1.5–2.1 mg/dL	⇧	○
Brod,[303] 1967	17	↟	(+ at 0)	⇧	○
Urabe,[293] 1987	17	↟	S₀ 7–15 mg/dL	⇔	○
Silverberg,[294] 1996	33	↟↟	(bar 30–60)	30%	●
Roth,[304] 1994	83	↟	(+ at ~20)	27%	●
Kuriyama,[305] 1997	66	↟↟	(+ at ~40)	32%	○
Lin,[295] 1996	51	↟↟	(bar 30–60)	35%	○
Portoles,[297] 1997	11	↟	(+ at ~20)	26%	○
Hayashi,[306] 2000	9	↟	S₀ 6.2 ±0.7 mg/dL	24%	○
Schwartz,[307] 1991	7	↟	(+ at ~20)	29%	○
Dimitrakov,[298] 1994	6	↟	S₀ 4.5 ±0.4 mg/dL	23%	○

* ↑ = higher GFR associated with higher hematocrit (statistically significant);
⇧ = higher GFR associated with higher hematocrit;
⇔ = GFR *not* associated with hematocrit.

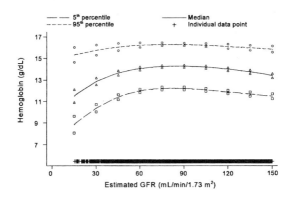

Fig 26. Blood hemoglobin percentiles by GFR adjusted to age 60 (NHANES III). Median and 5th and 95th percentiles of hemoglobin among adult participants age 20 years and older in NHANES III, 1988 to 1994. Values are adjusted to age 60 years using a polynomial quantile regression. The estimated GFR for each individual data point is shown with a plus sign (+) near the abscissa. 95% confidence intervals at selected levels of estimated GFR are demarcated with triangles, squares, and circles.

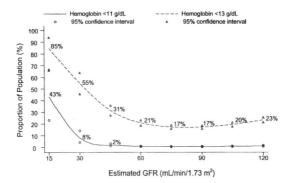

Fig 27. Adjusted prevalence in adults of low hemoglobin by GFR (NHANES III). Predicted prevalence of hemoglobin <11 and <13 g/dL among adult participants age 20 years and older in NHANES III, 1988 to 1994. Values are adjusted to age 60 years using a polynomial regression. 95% confidence intervals are shown at selected levels of estimated GFR.

points at values <30 mL/min/1.73 m² in the NHANES III database, the Canadian Multicentre Study[288] was utilized to demonstrate trends in a large cohort of patients prior to dialysis (Fig 28). Note in Fig 29 the increase in prevalence of anemia at lower levels of GFR, but the existence of up to 20% of patients with anemia at higher, though still abnormal levels of GFR (30 to 44 mL/min/1.73 m²). Thus, the NHANES III data are consistent with data derived from populations with kidney disease and lower GFR[288] (Figs 28 and 29).

Published studies cited in Tables 76 and 77 demonstrate a variability in the levels of

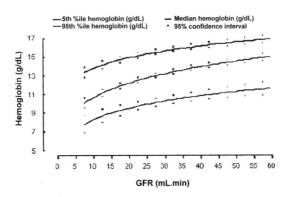

Fig 28. Hemoglobin percentiles by GFR. These data are based on the results of 446 patients enrolled in the Canadian Multicentre Longitudinal Cohort study of patients with chronic kidney disease. All patients were referred to nephrologists between 1994 and 1997. No patient was receiving erythropoietin therapy at the time of enrollment, and no patient had an AV fistula. Adapted and reprinted with permission.[288]

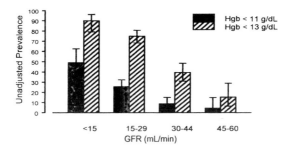

Fig 29.   Prevalence of low hemoglobin by GFR category. These data are based on the results of 446 patients enrolled in the Canadian Multicentre Longitudinal Cohort study of patients with chronic kidney disease. All patients were referred to nephrologists between 1994 and 1997. No patient was receiving erythropoiten therapy at the time of enrollment, and no patient had an AV fistula. Adapted and reprinted with permission.[288]

hemoglobin or hematocrit at each level of kidney function, whether assessed by serum creatinine concentration, creatinine clearance, or GFR. These observations underscore the need to measure hemoglobin levels in every individual with GFR <60 mL/min/1.73 m^2 and to individualize the assessment of anemia. The population-based trend toward lower hemoglobin levels as GFR falls does not yield a predictable progression that can be applied to individual patients. Thus, anemia should be considered in some patients with chronic kidney disease and GFR >60 mL/min/1.73 m^2.

Erythropoietin levels are not consistently associated with the level of GFR (Table 78) (C). Erythropoietin levels in patients with chronic kidney disease have not been well characterized in studies to date and do not appear to be directly related to level of kidney function. The majority of studies have been performed in patients already receiving dialysis, though some studies describe the relationship of erythropoietin levels to GFR in diabetics and in patients not on di!-!alysis.[275,308,309]

The consistent finding apparent from these studies is that, for any given level of kidney function and anemia, the erythropoietin levels are lower in individuals with kidney disease than in those with anemia but normal kidney function.

The interpretation of these findings is that patients with kidney disease, as compared to normal individuals, do not have an appropriate rise in the levels of erythropoieten in the presence of anemia; while levels may be higher than non-anemic chronic kidney disease patients, the rise in erythropoietin levels is not commensurate with that seen in

Table 78. Erythropoietin Level and Kidney Function

Author, Year	No. of Subjects	Applic- ability	GFR Range	Results*	Quality
Besarab,[310] 1987	65	👥	ND	⟺	○
Urabe,[293] 1987	17	👤	S$_a$ 7–15 mg/dL	⟺	○

* ⟺ = GFR *not* associated with erythropoietin.

Table 79. Ferritin and Kidney Function

Author, Year	No. of Subjects	Applic-ability	GFR Range (mL/min/1.73 m^2) 0 30 60 90 120	Results*/ Mean Level	Quality
Taralov,[289] 1998	63	♀♀	S$_0$ 5.1 mg/dL	↑	◑
Lin,[295] 1996	51	♀♀		296 µg/L	○
Dimitrakov,[296] 1994	6	♀	S$_0$ 4.5±0.4 mg/dL	247 µg/L	○

* ↑ = higher GFR associated with higher ferritin (statistically significant).

patients with the same degree of anemia but without kidney disease. Table 77 shows the paucity of data in this area and the weakness of the association demonstrated by published studies between erythropoiten levels and level of kidney function.

Measures of iron stores, including ferritin and transferrin saturation, are not consistently associated with the level of GFR (Tables 79 and 80) (C). Several measures of iron stores have been studied in patients with kidney disease. Most of these measures, unlike bone marrow biopsy, do not directly quantify the amount of iron available for use in erythrocyte synthesis, relying instead on indirect or surrogate measures. Ferritin levels in patients with reduced GFR may represent total body iron status, or they may simply be markers of inflammation. Given the "chronic inflammatory state" that may characterize chronic kidney disease, ferritin levels are not useful in measuring iron stores, nor in predicting the relation of hemoglobin to kidney function.

Transferrin saturation, in combination with serum iron and ferritin levels, may be helpful in diagnosing functional iron deficiency—just as low serum ferritin levels are helpful in diagnosing iron deficiency anemia.[311,312] However, there is little correlation of iron measurements with stages of kidney disease.

LIMITATIONS

This analysis is limited by a lack of data about the relationship of levels of hemoglobin and kidney function in a truly representative sample of patients with chronic kidney disease. Many of the published studies describe patients entered into clinical trials or seen by nephrologists. The reasons for these differences are incompletely studied but noted in conventional texts and review articles.[277,313]

Table 80. Miscellaneous Hematological Measures and Kidney Function

Author, Year	No. of Subjects	Applic-ability	GFR Range (mL/min/1.73 m^2) 0 30 60 90 120	Results*/ Mean Level	Quality
Taralov,[289] 1998	63	♀♀	S$_0$ 5.1 mg/dL	↑	◑
Silverberg,[294] 1996	33	♀♀		Iron saturation = 22%	◑
Lin,[295] 1996	51	♀♀		Transferrin saturation = 31%	○
Dimitrakov,[296] 1994	6	♀	S$_0$ 4.5±0.4 mg/dL	Transferrin = 2.8 g/L Fe = 72 mg/dL	○

* ↑ = higher GFR associated with higher iron (statistically significant).

Interestingly, specific subgroups of patients (such as those with polycystic kidney disease) may have erythropoietin synthesis that is better preserved than other subgroups (such as diabetics). In the subgroup of patients who have kidney transplants, there are multiple causes for anemia in addition to decreased kidney function. The use of immuno-suppressive agents or other medications, or chronic inflammation due to transplant rejection, may further confound the assessment of the etiology of declining hemoglobin. However, it is clear that at given levels of compromised GFR, kidney transplant patients do demonstrate reduced levels of hemoglobin, consistent with findings in patients with native diseased kidneys, and with those who have impaired kidney function.[310]

Another limitation of the current analysis is the variety (and lack of precision) of methods by which kidney function was measured in studies that assessed hemoglobin in patients with chronic kidney disease. Methods used included: measured GFR (iothala-mate or other methods), calculated GFR (using different equations), measured or calcu-lated creatinine clearance (using different equations). It is therefore difficult to determine whether the variability in hemoglobin at levels of kidney function is due to variability in measurements of kidney function or to variability associated with chronic kidney disease itself. While true variability between patients is the more likely possibility, the magnitude of variability is unknown.

CLINICAL APPLICATIONS

Available data permit the description of mean levels of hemoglobin (with wide standard deviations) at different levels of GFR and support the following recommendations. Physi-cians treating patients with chronic kidney disease should:

- Follow hemoglobin levels over time in all individuals with chronic kidney disease and expect some degree of decline over time as kidney function worsens
- Evaluate anemia in all patients with GFR <60 mL/min/1.73 m^2
- Assess the relationship of anemia to the patient's symptoms and findings and the impact of anemia on the patient's comorbid conditions and other complications of decreased kidney function
- As in anemia from any cause, treatments appropriate to the etiology of the anemia (iron or other supplement deficiency) should be implemented. The issues of timing of intervention and specific target of hemoglobin are beyond the scope of this guideline.

These recommendations are consistent with published K/DOQI Clinical Practice Guidelines on Anemia of Chronic Kidney Disease.[266] While there are no "normal"/ex-pected values of hemoglobin at any specific level of GFR, available data suggest that individual patients do trend toward a fall in hemoglobin as kidney function declines. The characterization of severity of anemia for any individual with chronic kidney disease should be made in light of changes in hemoglobin from previous levels. The decline in hemoglobin is most likely associated with a reduction in erythropoietin effectiveness or production, which accompanies the decline in GFR.

Treatment and assessment recommendations are beyond the scope of this guideline but are provided in the K/DOQI Clinical Practice Guidelines on Anemia of Chronic Kidney Disease[266] and the European Best Practice Guidelines for the Management of Anaemia in Patients with Chronic Renal Failure.[273]

RESEARCH RECOMMENDATIONS

Clearly, more information is needed on hemoglobin levels in chronic kidney disease—especially in patients in the early stages of kidney disease and as kidney function declines. Future studies should include:

- Evaluation of the relationships between erythropoietin levels, hemoglobin and iron stores in patients with chronic kidney disease at each stage of the disease
- Description of changes in these hematological parameters in specific subgroups, such as diabetics and patients with failing transplant grafts
- Evaluation of the impact of treatment of anemia in stages of kidney disease prior to dialysis (CKD Stages 1–4) on kidney function decline, cardiac function, and general well-being
- Economic evaluations of therapeutic strategies which include maintenance of hemoglobin versus correction from low levels at different stages of chronic kidney disease.

GUIDELINE 9. ASSOCIATION OF LEVEL OF GFR WITH NUTRITIONAL STATUS

Protein energy malnutrition develops during the course of chronic kidney disease and is associated with adverse outcomes. Low protein and calorie intake is an important cause of malnutrition in chronic kidney disease.

- Patients with GFR <60 mL/min/1.73 m^2 should undergo assessment of dietary protein and energy intake and nutritional status — see K/DOQI Clinical Practice Guidelines for Nutrition in Chronic Renal Failure (CRF), Guidelines 23 and 26:

Guideline 23. Panels of Nutritional Measures for Nondialyzed Patients: "For individuals with CRF (GFR <20 mL/min) protein-energy nutritional status should be evaluated by serial measurements of a panel of markers including at least one value from each of the following clusters:

(1) Serum albumin;

(2) Edema-free actual body weight, percent standard (NHANES II) body weight, or subjective global assessment (SGA); and

(3) Normalized protein nitrogen appearance (nPNA) or dietary interviews and diaries. (Evidence and Opinion)"

Guideline 26. Intensive Nutritional Counseling for Chronic Renal Failure: "The nutritional status of individuals with CRF should be monitored at regular intervals."

- Patients with decreased dietary intake or malnutrition should undergo dietary modification, counseling, and education or specialized nutrition therapy — see K/DOQI

Clinical Practice Guidelines for Nutrition in Chronic Renal Failure (CRF), Guidelines 24 and 25:

Guideline 24. Dietary Protein Intake for Nondialyzed Patients: "For individuals with chronic renal failure (GFR <25 mL/min) who are not undergoing maintenance dialysis, the institution of a planned low-protein diet providing 0.60 g protein/kg/d should be considered. For individuals who will not accept such a diet or who are unable to maintain adequate dietary energy intake with such a diet, an intake of up to 0.75 g protein/kg/d may be prescribed. (Evidence and Opinion)."

Guideline 25. Dietary Energy Intake (DEI) for Nondialyzed Patients: "The recommended DEI for individuals with chronic renal failure (GFR <25 mL/min) who are not undergoing maintenance dialysis is 35 kcal/kg/d for those who are younger than 60 years old and 30–35 kcal/kg/d for individuals who are 60 years of age or older. (Evidence and Opinion)."

BACKGROUND

Anorexia is evidenced by decreased dietary protein intake (DPI) and decreased dietary energy intake (DEI), which are hallmarks of kidney failure (K/DOQI Clinical Practice Guidelines for Nutrition in Chronic Renal Failure,[75] Guideline 6). As limitation of protein intake reduces the accumulation of toxic substances derived from the metabolism of protein, decreased DPI may be viewed as adaptive in patients with kidney failure. However, decreased DPI is also associated with worsening of indices of nutritional status. Thus, the overall outcome of this adaptive process may be the increased prevalence of protein energy malnutrition (PEM) in patients with chronic kidney disease.

The stage of chronic kidney disease at which decreased dietary nutrient intake and associated PEM become prevalent has not been adequately documented, due in part to the fact that no single measure provides a complete overview of nutritional status. The optimal monitoring of protein-energy nutritional status requires the collective evaluation of multiple parameters (ie, assessment of visceral protein, muscle mass or somatic protein, body composition). As a result, data for appropriate assessment of nutritional status in patients with chronic kidney disease have not been adequately collected and often the onset and progression of malnutrition is obscured by the progressive loss of kidney function. This guideline provides evidence on the association of the level of GFR with dietary intake and nutritional status and provides recommendations on how to approach this specific complication of chronic kidney disease.

RATIONALE
Markers of Protein-Energy Malnutrition

PEM is characterized by the insidious loss of body fat and somatic protein stores, diminished serum protein concentrations, and poor performance status and function. Serum albumin, serum pre-albumin, and serum transferrin levels are used to measure visceral protein. Anthropometry and dual-energy x-ray absorptiometry assess somatic protein and fat stores. In addition, edema-free weight, body mass index (BMI), and subjective global assessment (SGA) are valid and clinically useful tools for overall nutritional assessment.

Serum albumin concentration, even when only slightly less than 4.0 g/dL, is one of the most important markers of PEM in patients with chronic kidney disease. It is a very reliable indicator of visceral protein, although its concentration is also affected by its rate of synthesis and catabolism (half-life 20 days), which is altered negatively in the presence of inflammation.[314] The distribution of albumin between extra-cellular and intravascular spaces may be variable depending on the etiology of kidney disease, magnitude of proteinuria, and the state of extra-cellular fluid volume. In chronically malnourished patients, albumin tends to shift out of the intravascular compartment.

Several markers of visceral protein, other than albumin, have a shorter half-life and may be useful markers of early malnutrition. Among these are serum transferrin (half-life 8 days) and serum pre-albumin (half-life 2 days).[315] Iron stores affect serum transferrin, while pre-albumin is excreted by the kidneys and its concentration can be falsely elevated in patients with advanced kidney disease. All these markers are also affected by the presence of inflammation.

Anthropometry (edema-free weight, BMI, assessment of arm fat and muscle) has been used to estimate body composition and nutritional adequacy. Reproducibility of anthropometry measurements is poor and is dependent upon the skill of the observer. SGA has been proposed as an easy, useful, and clinically valid method for nutritional assessment. SGA includes subjective data (disease state, weight changes), indicators of poor nutritional status (appetite, food intake, gastrointestinal symptoms), and the clinical judgment of the clinician. The limitation of SGA is its reliance on subjective data. There are no studies which correlate anthropometric measurements or SGA with clinical outcome in patients with chronic kidney disease.

Serum bicarbonate concentration (also measured as total carbon dioxide content or CO_2), as a measure of acid-base balance, has been used to assess malnutrition in chronic kidney disease. Studies show that uremic acidosis causes an increase in protein degradation. Correction of acidosis is accompanied by a decrease in protein tissue breakdown.[316]

Assessment of nutrient intake can be useful in identifying PEM and several measures of dietary intake have been utilized in patients with chronic kidney disease. These include measurement of protein equivalent of total nitrogen appearance (PNA) as a marker of dietary protein intake, measurement of basal energy expenditure (BEE) as a measure of dietary energy needs, and dietary interviews or diaries as markers of overall intake. Additionally, total serum cholesterol can be a useful marker for energy intake, but not for protein intake.

The challenge for the clinician is to appropriately monitor the nutritional indices in patients with chronic kidney disease. While each marker has its own advantage in terms of precision and predictability, it is recommended that these markers be used in a complementary fashion to optimize assessment of patients with chronic kidney disease and to tailor specific interventions.[75]

It is also important for the clinician to educate patients about a proper diet, since hyperphosphatemia, hyperkalemia, and metabolic acidosis may develop during chronic kidney disease.

Medical Nutrition Therapy and Nutrition Counseling

As of January 2002, Medicare will provide payment for medical nutrition therapy (MNT) for patients with chronic kidney disease.[317]

"Medical nutrition therapy involves the assessment of the nutritional status of patients with a condition, illness, or injury that puts them at risk. This includes review and analysis of medical and diet history, laboratory values, and anthropometric measurements. Based on the assessment, nutrition modalities most appropriate to manage the condition or treat the illness or injury are chosen and include the following:

- *Diet modification, counseling, and education leading to the development of a personal diet plan to achieve nutritional goals and desired health outcomes.*
- *Specialized nutrition therapies including supplementation with medical foods for those unable to obtain adequate nutrients through food intake only; enteral nutrition delivered via tube feeding into the gastrointestinal tract for those unable to ingest or digest food; and parenteral nutrition delivered via intravenous infusion for those unable to absorb nutrients."*

Presently, it is proposed that patients will be eligible to receive reimbursement for medical nutrition therapy if they have GFR 15 to 50 mL/min/1.73 m^2, or if they have received a kidney transplant within the previous 6 months. These criteria are roughly equivalent to patients with CKD Stages 3–4 and Stage 5 who do not yet require dialysis. Most patients with CKD Stage 5 who are treated by dialysis are eligible for medical nutrition therapy from their dialysis providers.

Strength of Evidence

PEM develops during the course of chronic kidney disease (R). When compared to the demographically adjusted general population, dialysis patients experience greater signs and symptoms of wasting, malnutrition, morbidity, and mortality. It is estimated that 50% to 70% of dialysis patients suffer from PEM.[314] Abnormalities in nutritional markers are common and include decreased serum proteins, lower body mass as assessed by anthropometric measurements and SGA, and decreased nutrient intake. Reasons for PEM include disturbances in protein and energy metabolism, hormonal derangements, anorexia, and nausea and vomiting related to uremic toxicity. Comorbid conditions such as diabetes, vascular disease, and superimposed infections and inflammation are contributory.[318]

Malnutrition is associated with worse outcomes in chronic kidney disease (R). Among maintenance dialysis patients, PEM has been recognized as one of the most significant predictors of adverse outcomes. Risk of hospitalizations and mortality is inversely correlated to nutritional markers.[319] Recently, attention has focused on the characteristics of patients with chronic kidney disease at the time they begin maintenance dialysis. Studies have suggested that apart from the severity of uremic symptoms as well as the biochemical findings related to the extent of metabolic and hormonal abnormalities, the nutritional status of the patient at the initiation of dialysis is a clinically significant risk factor for subsequent clinical outcomes (morbidity and mortality) on dialysis.[320,321] The association between nutrition intake or status and clinical outcome does not prove a causal relationship. It is possible that comorbid conditions independently impair both nutritional intake or status and increase morbidity and mortality. In addition studies suggest that a combined state of poor nutritional status and inflammation predispose patients with chronic kidney disease to poor clinical outcomes.[322,323]

Low protein and calorie intake is an important cause of malnutrition in chronic kidney disease (R). While there are possibly multiple factors that contribute to the development of PEM in chronic kidney disease, low protein and calorie intake (decreased from usual intake) are certainly important contributors in this catabolic process. This relationship is evident from multiple studies, which show a strong relationship between the amount of dietary intake of nutrients, especially protein intake, and the stage of malnutrition in patients with chronic kidney disease.[324,325] Concentrations of serum albumin and transferrin, edema free weight, and percent lean body mass have all been directly related to dietary protein intake in patients with chronic kidney disease.

The mechanism by which chronic kidney disease leads to this decline in nutrient intake has not been defined. Accumulation of uremic toxins due to loss of kidney function is a potential explanation. Metabolic and hormonal derangements predispose patients with chronic kidney disease to decreased appetite and dietary nutrient intake.[326,327] Specific comorbid conditions, such as diabetes mellitus, cardiovascular disease, and depression, can facilitate the worsening of decreased nutrient intake in patients with chronic kidney disease. The mechanisms associated with these conditions are multiple and include gastrointestinal abnormalities, decreased appetite, effects of concomitant medication use, and role of inflammation.

Other causes of malnutrition in chronic kidney disease (R). Several factors other than low protein and calorie intake can also predispose chronic kidney disease patients to malnutrition. These include several hormonal and metabolic derangements related to loss of kidney function. Metabolic acidosis is commonly seen in chronic kidney disease patients and shown to be associated with increased protein catabolism in these patients. Specifically, the degradation of the essential, branched-chain amino acids and muscle protein is stimulated during metabolic acidosis. Further, metabolic acidosis suppresses albumin synthesis.[328] Worsening kidney function is also associated with resistance to insulin, growth hormone and insulin-like growth factor 1, all of which are known to be anabolic hormones. Of note, these abnormalities are most prominent in pediatric chronic kidney disease patients with apparent growth failure.[329-331]

Recent studies point to the increased concentrations of proinflammatory cytokines and acute phase reactants in chronic kidney disease patients.[323,332] Analysis of the data from NHANES III demonstrates increasing C-reactive protein concentrations as GFR decreases.[333] Thus, available evidence suggests a chronic inflammatory state in chronic

Table 81. Daily Calorie Intake and Kidney Function

Author, Year	No. of Subjects	Applic-ability	GFR Range (mL/min/1.73 m²)	Results/ Mean Level	Quality
Kopple,[324] 2000	1,785	♦♦♦		⬆	●
Kopple,[338] 1989	89	♦♦		⬄ (men) ⬆ (women)	●
Chauveau,[343] 1999	10	♦		27.8 Kcal/kg/d	○
Williams,[344] 1991	6	♦		38.3 Kcal/kg/d	○

Unshaded studies reported the strength of association between the outcome measure (in this case, daily calorie intake) and kidney function; shaded studies reported mean or median levels of the outcome measure in the study sample.

* ⬆ = higher GFR associated with higher daily caloric intake (statistically significant);
⬄ = GFR *not* associated with daily caloric intake.

kidney disease patients, especially for patients in Stages 3 to 5. The metabolic and nutritional effects of chronic inflammation are many and include anorexia, increased skeletal muscle protein breakdown, increased whole body protein catabolism, cytokine-mediated hypermetabolism, and disruption of the growth hormone and IGF-1 axis leading to decreased anabolism.[334-336] These findings suggest that chronic inflammation observed in chronic kidney disease patients is an important causative factor for poor nutritional status observed in these patients.

The level of dietary intake of protein and energy intake is related to the level of GFR; below a GFR of approximately 60 mL/min/1.73 m², there is a higher prevalence of reduced dietary protein and energy intake (Tables 81 and 82 and

Table 82. Daily Protein Intake and Kidney Function

Author, Year	No. of Subjects	Applic-ability	GFR Range (mL/min/1.73 m²)	Results*/ Mean Level	Quality
Kopple,[324] 2000	1,785	♦♦♦		⬆	●
Ikizler,[325] 1995	90	♦♦♦		⬆	●
Kopple,[338] 1989	89	♦♦		⬆	●
Coggins,[339] 1994	33	♦♦		⬆	●
Park,[340] 1997	64	♦♦♦		⬆	○
Pollock,[341] 1997	439	♦♦		⬆	○
Aparicio,[345] 2000	239	♦♦		0.84 g/kg/d	●
Walser,[346] 1993	16	♦♦		0.82 g/kg./d	●
Mazouz,[347] 1999	49	♦♦		0.87 g/kg/d	○
Chauveau,[343] 1999	10	♦		0.78 g/kg/d	○
Williams,[344] 1991	6	♦		82.2 g/d	○

* ⬆ = higher GFR associated with higher daily protein intake (statistically significant).

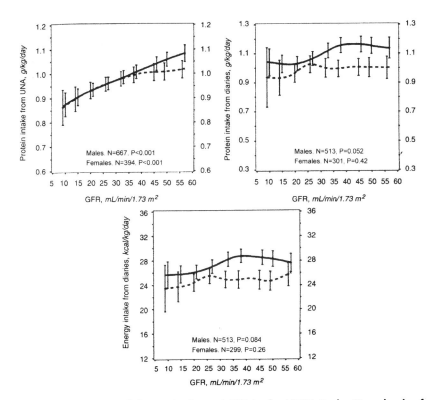

Fig 30. Association of dietary intake and GFR in the MDRD Study. Mean levels of protein and energy intake as a function of GFR based on 24-hour urine collections and diet diaries (males, solid lines; females, dashed lines). Data depict MDRD Study enrollees not on restricted diets. Abbreviation: UNA, urea nitrogen appearance. Reprinted with permission.[324]

Fig 30) (C, S). One of the most significant clinical indicators of kidney failure is an apparent decrease in appetite. Spontaneous decrease in dietary protein and energy intake can be regarded as an early index of uremia. This begins to occur when GFR falls below 60 mL/min/1.73 m². As protein and calorie intake decline, markers of nutrition health indicate worsening nutritional status.

K/DOQI Nutrition Guideline 24 recommends consideration of a protein intake of 0.60 g/kg/d for individuals with GFR <25 mL/min (corresponding approximately to CKD Stages 4–5), but does not address recommendations for patients with higher GFR. The recommended dietary allowance (RDA) of protein for normal adults is 0.75 g/kg/d. The MDRD Study was inconclusive regarding the benefits of protein restriction on kidney disease progression (see CKD Guideline 13), but there was no evidence of a beneficial effect from DPI higher than the RDA. A DPI of 0.75 g/kg/d therefore appears reasonable for patients with CKD Stages 1–3 (in the absence of evidence of malnutrition), but data are inconclusive, and individualized decision-making is advised. Patients with DPI less than approximately 0.75 g/kg/d should have more close monitoring of nutritional status.

K/DOQI Nutrition Guideline 25 recommends age-dependent DEI intakes of 30 to 35 kcal/kg/d for individuals with GFR <25 mL/min (corresponding approximately to CKD Stages 4-5), but does not address recommendations for patients with higher GFR. The RDA for energy intake in normal adults depends on energy expenditure. Average energy intake in adults in the United States is less than that recommended in the K/DOQI Nutrition Guideline. The rationale for higher DEI in patients with GFR <25 mL/min is based on studies demonstrating more efficient nitrogen utilization at higher energy intakes. For patients with CKD Stages 1-3, it would be reasonable to recommend higher energy intakes only if they have abnormally low body weight or show other signs of malnutrition.

Patients with DPI less than the RDA (0.75 g/kg/d) should be targeted for frequent follow-up to monitor nutritional status more closely. Some studies indicate that intensive nutrition counseling may help maintain calorie intake and to preserve markers of good nutrition as GFR declines.[299,324,325,337-342]

The onset and severity of PEM is related to the level of GFR; below a GFR of approximately 60 mL/min/1.73 m[2], there is a higher prevalence of impaired nutritional status (C, S). K/DOQI Nutrition Guideline 23 states that protein-energy nutritional status should be evaluated by serial measurements for individuals with GFR <20 mL/min.[75] An updated literature review supports the recommendation that evaluations of nutritional status should begin when GFR falls below approximately 60 mL/min/ 1.73 m[2]. Population studies show that albumin begins to decline once GFR reaches this level.[333] Other markers of nutritional status at this level of kidney function have not been as well studied.

K/DOQI Nutrition Guideline 23 recommends a panel of nutrition measures for evaluation of nutrition status in nondialyzed patients which includes serum albumin, body weight, subjective global assessment and assessment of protein intake through nPNA or dietary interviews. Other markers of nutritional status (eg, serum total proteins, serum prealbumin, serum transferrin, serum total bicarbonate, serum total cholesterol, and serum lipids) appear to be related to the level of GFR.

The calculation of standard body weight (SBW) requires a formula that uses elbow breadth to determine the patient's frame size. For many clinicians, this measurement is not feasible. The calculation of healthy weight range can be made with the simpler Body Mass Index (BMI) formula:

$$BMI = \frac{Weight\ (kg)}{Height\ (m)^2}$$

It is recommended that the BMI of maintenance dialysis patients be maintained in the upper 50th percentile for normal individuals, which would mean a BMI for men and women no lower than approximately 23.6 to 24.0 kg/m[2]. This recommendation also appears appropriate for chronic kidney disease patients with significant GFR reductions (Stages 3-5)—see K/DOQI Nutrition Guideline, Appendix VII.

K/DOQI Nutrition Guideline 26 recommends monitoring of nutritional status at 1- to 3-month intervals in patients with GFR <20 mL/min. It is the opinion of the CKD Work Group that this recommendation is appropriate for patients with GFR less than 30 ml/min/1.73 m^2 (CKD Stages 4-5) and less frequent monitoring (eg, every 6 to 12 months) may be acceptable for patients with GFR 30 to 60 mL/min/1.73m^2 (CKD Stage 3) if there is no evidence of malnutrition.

The high prevalence of malnutrition in chronic kidney disease, the association between malnutrition and clinical outcomes, and new evidence that nutrient intake begins to decline at GFR <60 mL/min/1.73 m^2 support the recommendation that nutritional status should be assessed and monitored earlier in the course of chronic kidney disease.

Serum albumin level is lower in patients with decreased GFR (Tables 83 and 84 and Figs 31 and 32) (C, S). Serum albumin is lower at levels of GFR below 60 mL/

Table 83. Serum Albumin and Kidney Function

Author, Year	No. of Subjects	Applic-ability	GFR Range (mL/min/1.73 m^2)	Results*/ Mean Level	Quality
Kopple,[324] 2000	1,785	↟↟↟		↑	●
Ikizler,[325] 1995	90	↟↟↟		⇔	●
Kopple,[338] 1989	89	↟↟		⇔	●
Monteon,[348] 1986	22	↟↟	S_{Cr} = 8.0 ± 2.4 mg/dL	⇔	●
Park,[346] 1997	64	↟↟↟		↑	○
Ando,[349] 1979	20	↟↟		⇑	○
Pollock,[341] 1997	439	↟↟		↑	○
Aparicio,[345] 2000	239	↟↟		3.8 g/dL	●
Stenvinkel,[325] 1999	109	↟↟		3.4 g/dL	●
Stenvinkel,[350] 1998	83	↟↟		3.3 g/dL	●
Walser,[351] 1999	23	↟		4.1 g/dL	●
Cupisti,[352] 1990	51	↟↟		3.8 g/dL	○
Sugimoto,[353] 1991	14	↟↟		3.3 g/dL	○
Guarnieri,[354] 1986	12	↟↟	S_{Cr} 2.1 ± 0.7 mg/dL	4.3 g/dL	○
Chauveau,[343] 1999	10	↟		4.1 g/dL	○
Williams,[344] 1991	6	↟		3.9 g/dL	○
Di Landro,[355] 1990	69	↟↟	S_{Cr} 4.3 mg/dL	4.2 g/dL	○
Vetter,[356] 1990	59	↟		4.2 g/dL	○

* ↑ = higher GFR associated with higher serum albumin (statistically significant);
⇑ = higher GFR associated with higher serum albumin;
⇔ = GFR *not* associated with serum albumin.

Table 84. Serum Protein & Pre-albumin and Kidney Function

Author, Year	No. of Subjects	Applicability	GFR Range (mL/min/1.73 m²)	Results*/ Mean Level	Quality
Serum Protein					
Ando,[349] 1979	20	♁♁	╂	⇧	◐
Barsotti,[357] 1988	8	♁	╂━	6.0 g/dL	●
Cupisti,[352] 1990	51	♁♁	╂	6.7 g/dL	◐
Williams,[344] 1991	6	♁	╂	6.6 g/dL	◐
Pre-albumin					
Ikizler,[325] 1995	90	♁♁♁	━╂━━	⇧	●
Park,[340] 1997	64	♁♁♁	╂━	⇧	◐
Chauveau,[343] 1999	10	♁	╂	3.9 g/dL	◐

* ⇧ = higher GFR associated with higher serum protein or pre-albumin.

min/1.73 m², indicating a decline in circulating protein levels or serum protein concentrations, protein losses or inflammation.[324,325,338,340,341,348,349] An acceptable goal level for albumin is >4.0 g/dL (bromcresol green method).

Similar findings have been reported for serum total proteins and pre-albumin.

Serum transferrin level is lower in patients with decreased GFR (Table 85 and Fig 33) (C, S). Serum transferrin is lower at lower GFR levels. This is evidenced

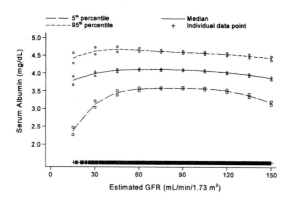

Fig 31. Serum albumin percentiles by GFR adjusted to age. Median and 5th and 95th percentiles of serum albumin among adult participants age 20 years and older in NHANES III, 1988 to 1994. Values are adjusted to age 60 years using a polynomial quantile regression. The estimated GFR for each individual data point is shown with a plus near the abscissa. 95% confidence intervals at selected levels of estimated GFR are demarcated with triangles, squares, and circles.

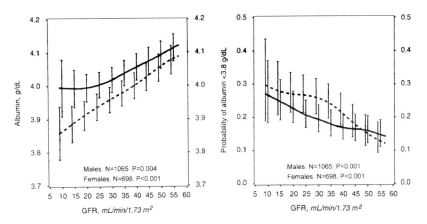

Fig 32. Association of serum albumin and GFR in the MDRD Study. Mean levels of serum albumin and the probability of serum albumin concentrations <3.8 g/dL as a function of GFR (males, solid lines; females, dashed lines). Reprinted with permission.[324]

Table 85. Transferrin and Kidney Function

Author, Year	No. of Subjects	Applicability	GFR Range (mL/min/1.73 m²)	Results*/ Mean Level	Quality
Kopple,[324] 2000	1,785	♂♂♂		⬆	●
Ikizler,[325] 1995	90	♂♂♂		⬆	●
Kopple,[338] 1989	89	♂♂		⬌	●
Park,[340] 1997	64	♂♂♂		⬆	○
Walser,[351] 1999	23	♂		233 mg/dL	●
Cupisti,[352] 1990	51	♂♂		244 mg/dL	◐
Guarnieri,[354] 1986	12	♂♂	Sᴄᵣ 2.1 ± 0.7 mg/dL	223 mg/dL	◐
Chauveau,[343] 1999	10	♂		216 mg/dL	◐
Vetter,[356] 1990	59	♂		210 mg/dL	○

* ⬆ = higher GFR associated with higher transferrin (statistically significant);
⬌ = GFR level *not* associated with transferrin.

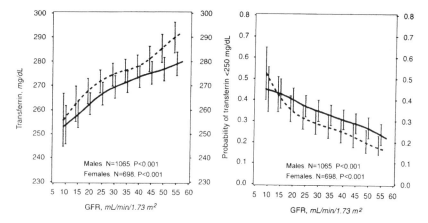

Fig 33. Association of serum transferrin and GFR in the MDRD Study. Mean levels of serum transferrin and the probability of serum transferrin concentrations <250 mg/dL as a function of GFR (males, solid lines; females, dashed lines). Reprinted with permission.[324]

in patients with chronic kidney disease, with no sign of inflammation, infection, and with stable iron status.[324,325,338,340]

Serum bicarbonate concentration is lower in patients with decreased GFR (Table 86) (C). As GFR falls to <60 mL/min/1.73 m², serum bicarbonate decreases. Low serum bicarbonate is an indicator of acidemia and associated with protein degradation. Low serum bicarbonate has been correlated to low serum albumin.[325,340] See K/DOQI Clinical Practice Guidelines for Nutrition in Chronic Renal Failure, Guideline 14, Treatment of Low Serum Bicarbonate:

Table 86. Serum Bicarbonate and Kidney Function

Author, Year	No. of Subjects	Applicability	GFR Range (mL/min/1.73 m²)	Results*/ Mean Level	Quality
Ikizler,[325] 1995	90	♦♦♦		↑	●
Park,[340] 1997	64	♦♦♦		↑	○
Aparicio,[345] 2000	239	♦♦		HCO₃⁻ = 23 mEq/L	●
Walser,[351] 1999	23	♦		HCO₃⁻ = 21 mEq/L	●
Mazouz,[347] 1999	49	♦♦		HCO₃⁻ = 24 mEq/L	○
Jenkins,[358] 1989	11	♦♦		HCO₃⁻ = 19 mEq/L	○
Williams,[344] 1991	6	♦		HCO₃⁻ = 17 mEq/L	○

* ↑ = higher GFR associated with higher serum bicarbonate (statistically significant).

Table 87. Lipids and Kidney Function

Author, Year	No. of Subjects	Applicability	GFR Range (mL/min/1.73 m²) 0 30 60 90 120	Results*/ Mean Level**	Quality
Total Cholesterol					
Kopple,[324] 2000	1,785	♦♦♦		⬆ (men) ⇧ (women)	●
Ikizler,[325] 1995	90	♦♦♦		⬆	●
Kopple,[338] 1989	89	♦♦		⇔	●
Coggins,[339] 1994	33	♦♦		⇔	●
Pollock,[341] 1997	439	♦♦		⇔	○
Triglycerides					
Pollock,[341] 1997	439	♦♦		⬆	○
LDL or HDL					
Coggins,[339] 1994	33	♦♦		⬇ (LDL)	●
Coggins,[339] 1994	33	♦♦		⇧ (HDL)	●
Total Cholesterol					
Stenvinkel,[350] 1998	83	♦♦		230 mg/dL	●
Huang,[359] 1998	83	♦♦		210 mg/dL	●
Zeller,[360] 1991	35	♦♦		200 mg/dL	●
Walser,[351] 1999	23	♦		204 mg/dL	●
Mazouz,[347] 1999	49	♦♦		240 mg/dL	◐
Guarnieri,[354] 1986	12	♦♦	S_D 2.1 ±0.7 mg/dL	196 mg/dL	◐
Jenkins,[358] 1989	11	♦♦		210 mg/dL	◐
Williams,[344] 1991	6	♦		290 mg/dL	◐
Di Landro,[355] 1990	69	♦♦	S_D 4.3 mg/dL	235 mg/dL	○
D'Amico,[361] 1990	108	♦	S_D 3.3 ±1.9 mg/dL	217 mg/dL	○

"Predialysis or stabilized serum bicarbonate levels should be maintained at or above 22 μmol/L."[75]

Serum cholesterol concentration is lower in patients with decreased GFR (Table 87 and Fig 34) (C, S). As GFR decreases to <60 mL/min/1.73 m², serum cholesterol falls, even when controlling for inflammation and comorbid conditions.[324,325,338, 339,341]

Body weight, body mass index, percentage body fat, and skin fold thickness are lower in patients with decreased GFR (Tables 88, 89, 90, and 91 and Fig 35) (C, S). As GFR falls to <50 mL/min/1.73 m², measurements of body mass show

Table 87. Lipids and Kidney Function (cont.)

Author, Year	No. of Subjects	Applicability	GFR Range (mL/min/1.73 m²)	Results/ Mean Level*	Quality
Triglycerides					
Stenvinkel,[350] 1998	83	♦♦		210 mg/dL	●
Huang,[359] 1998	83	♦♦		174 mg/dL	●
Zeller,[360] 1991	35	♦♦		162 mg/dL	●
Walser,[351] 1999	23	♦		158 mg/dL	●
Mazouz,[347] 1999	49	♦♦		180 mg/dL	○
Guarnieri,[354] 1986	12	♦♦	S_{Cr} 2.1 ±0.7 mg/dL	115 mg/dL	○
Jenkins,[358] 1989	11	♦♦		220 mg/dL	○
Williams,[344] 1991	6	♦		260 mg/dL	○
D'Amico,[361] 1990	108	♦	S_{Cr} 3.3 ±1.9 mg/dL	158 mg/dL	○
Di Landro,[355] 1990	69	♦♦	S_{Cr} 4.3 mg/dL	182 mg/dL	○
Miscellaneous					
D'Amico,[361] 1990	108	♦	S_{Cr} 3.3 ±1.9 mg/dL	43 mg/dL (HDL)	○
Zeller,[360] 1991	35	♦♦		2.9 (LDL:HDL ratio)	●

* ⬆ = higher GFR associated with higher level of indicated lipid (statistically significant);
  ⇧ = higher GFR associated with higher level of indicated lipid;
  ⇔ = GFR level *not* associated with level of indicated lipid;
  ⇩ = higher GFR associated with lower level of indicated lipid.

** Units conversion: to convert from mg/dL to mmo/L for cholesterol (total, LDL and HDL) multiply by 0.02586; for triglycerides multiply by 0.01129.

Abbreviations: HDL, high density lipoprotein; LDL, low density lipoprotein

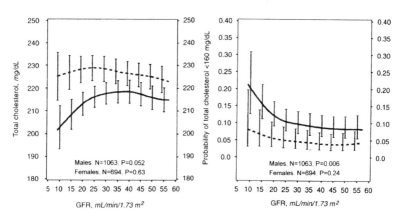

Fig 34. Association of serum cholesterol and GFR in the MDRD Study. Mean levels of serum cholesterol and the probability of serum cholesterol concentrations <160 mg/dL as a function of GFR (males, solid lines; females, dashed lines). Reprinted with permission.[324]

Table 88. Body Mass Index and Kidney Function

Author, Year	No. of Subjects	Applicability	GFR Range (mL/min/1.73 m²)	Results*/ Mean Level	Quality
Kopple,[324] 2000	1,785	♟♟♟		⬆ (men) ⬄ (women)	●
Kopple,[338] 1989	89	♟♟		⬄	●
Pollock,[341] 1997	439	♟♟		⬆	○
Aparicio,[349] 2000	239	♟♟		22.3 kg/m²	●
Stenvinkel,[323] 1999	109	♟♟		24.4 kg/m²	●
Stenvinkel,[350] 1998	83	♟♟		24.6 kg/m²	●
Huang,[359] 1998	83	♟♟		30.6 kg/m²	●
Guarnieri,[354] 1986	12	♟♟	S_{cr} 2.1 ± 0.7 mg/dL	24.0 kg/m²	◐
Chauveau,[349] 1999	10	♟		24.6 kg/m²	◐
Parillo,[362] 1988	6	♟	S_{cr} = 3.8 ± 1.9 mg/dL	27.6 kg/m²	◐

* ⬆ = higher GFR associated with higher body mass index (statistically significant);
⬄ = GFR *not* associated with body mass index.

declines in total mass, fat, and muscle. The correlations may be stronger in men than women. Assessment of body composition, especially with serial measurements can provide valuable information concerning long term adequacy of protein energy nutrition. Changes in body weight, BMI, and body fat in patients with chronic kidney disease and GFR >60 mL/min/1.73 m² have not been assessed.[324,338,341]

LIMITATIONS

There are certain limitations to the information presented herein. The design of most studies measuring nutrition markers in chronic kidney disease is based on data derived from cross-sectional studies. There are very few longitudinal studies available. In addition, there is a lack of uniform collective evaluation of the multiple markers of nutritional status in patients with chronic kidney disease. Although it is known that dietary nutrient intake decreases with GFR, there is only limited evidence that decreased dietary protein

Table 89. Ideal or Standard Body Weight and Kidney Function

Author, Year	No. of Subjects	Applicability	GFR Range (mL/min/1.73 m²)	Results*/ Mean Level	Quality
Kopple,[324] 2000	1,785	♟♟♟		⬆ (men) ⬄ (women)	●
Kopple,[338] 1989	89	♟♟		⬆ (men) ⬄ (women)	●
Goodship,[343] 1990	10	♟		110%	◐
D'Amico,[361] 1990	108	♟	S_{cr} 3.3 ± 1.9 mg/dL	110%	○

* ⬆ = higher GFR associated with higher body weight (statistically significant);
⬄ = GFR *not* associated with body weight.

Table 90. Body Tissue Composition (Muscle) and Kidney Function

Author, Year	Measurement	No. of Subjects	Applic- ability	GFR Range (mL/min/1.73 m^2)	Results*/ Mean Level	Quality
Kopple,[324] 2000	Arm muscle area	1,785	↟↟↟		↟ (men) ⟺ (women)	●
Kopple,[338] 1989	Arm muscle area	89	↟↟		↟ (men) ⟺ (women)	●
Guarnieri,[354] 1986	Arm muscle area	12	↟↟	S_{cr} 2.1 ±0.7 mg/dL	4,861 mm^2	○
Guarnieri,[354] 1986	Arm muscle circumference	12	↟↟	S_{cr} 2.1 ±0.7 mg/dL	24.6 cm	○
Chauveau,[343] 1999	Arm muscle circumference	10	↟		30.9 cm	○
Williams,[344] 1991	Arm muscle circumference	6	↟		28.5 cm	○
Cupisti,[352] 1990	Arm muscle circumference	51	↟↟		23.7 cm (men) 21.8 cm (women)	○
Jenkins,[356] 1989	Arm muscle circumference	11	↟↟		25.2 cm	○

Bold horizontal line divides studies by type of measurement (arm muscle area vs. arm muscle circumference).

* ↟ = higher GFR associated with greater muscle mass (statistically significant);
⟺ = GFR *not* associated with muscle mass.

Table 91. Body Tissue Composition (Fat) and Kidney Function

Author, Year	Measurement	No. of Subjects	Applic- ability	GFR Range (mL/min/1.73 m^2)	Results*/ Mean Level	Quality
Kopple,[324] 2000	Triceps skinfold thickness	1,785	↟↟↟		↟	●
Kopple,[338] 1989	Triceps skinfold thickness	89	↟↟		⟺	●
Kopple,[324] 2000	Biceps skinfold thickness	1,785	↟↟↟		↟	●
Monteon,[348] 1986	% Body fat	22	↟↟	S_{cr} 8.0 ±2.4 mg/dL	↟	●
Cupisti,[352] 1990	Triceps skinfold thickness	51	↟↟		11 mm (men) 16 mm (women)	○
Guarnieri,[354] 1986	Triceps skinfold thickness	12	↟↟	S_{cr} 2.1 ±0.7 mg/dL	13.2 mm	○
Chauveau,[343] 1999	Triceps skinfold thickness	10	↟		14.5 mm	○
Williams,[344] 1991	Triceps skinfold thickness	6	↟		17.2 mm	○
Guarnieri,[354] 1986	Arm fat area	12	↟↟	S_{cr} 2.1 ±0.7 mg/dL	1,792 mm^2	○
Woodrow,[364] 1996	Total body fat	23	↟	S_{cr} > 5.6 mg/dL	22%–25%	○

Bold horizontal lines divide studies by type of measurement used.

* ↟ = higher GFR associated with greater body fat (statistically significant);
⟺ = GFR *not* associated with body fat.

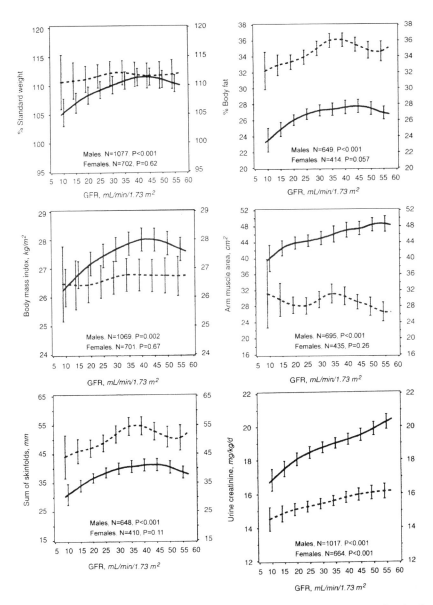

Fig 35. Association of body composition and GFR in the MDRD Study. Mean levels of anthropometric measures of nutritional status as a function of GFR (males, solid lines; females, dashed lines). Reprinted with permission.[324]

intake per se causes poor nutritional status. However, research indicates that when patients receive intensive nutrition therapy and monitoring while the GFR is declining, nutrition status can be maintained.[337,343,345,351,358,365-367]

CLINICAL APPLICATIONS

- Dietary protein prescription in chronic kidney disease is complicated by potential conflict between goals to slow the progression of kidney disease and preserve protein nutritional status. There is insufficient evidence to recommend for or against routine prescription of dietary protein restriction to slow progression (see Guideline 13). Thus, the RDA for protein of 0.75 g/kg/d appears reasonable in patients with GFR >30 mL/min/1.73 m^2 (CKD Stages 1-3). A lower protein intake of 0.6 g/kg/d can be considered for patients with lower GFR (Stages 4 and 5) to slow progression and minimize accumulation of uremic toxins. Individual decision-making is recommended after discussion of risks and benefits.

- Maintaining adequate energy intake is essential at all stages of chronic kidney disease.

- Assessment of nutritional status in chronic kidney disease requires multiple markers to assess protein status, fat stores, body composition, and dietary protein and energy intake.

- The nutritional status of patients with chronic kidney disease should be monitored at regular intervals: every 1 to 3 months for patients with GFR <30 mL/min/1.73 m^2 (CKD Stages 4 and 5) and every 6 to 12 months for patients with GFR 30 to 59 mL/min/1.73 m^2 (CKD Stage 3).

- The extent of PEM can be considered as an indication for the initiation of kidney replacement therapy. If PEM develops or persists despite vigorous attempts to optimize protein and energy intake, and there is no apparent cause for malnutrition other than low nutrient intake, initiation of maintenance dialysis or kidney transplant is recommended. See CKD Guideline 1, p. 43. In general, this guideline applies to patients with GFR <15 mL/min/1.73 m^2 (CKD Stage 5) but may apply to some patients with higher GFR levels.

IMPLEMENTATION ISSUES

In the United States, implementation of the medical nutrition therapy law for reimbursement through Medicare will allow for the provision of nutrition monitoring as described in these guidelines. Studies show that the most effective nutrition interventions in patients with chronic kidney disease involve patient training in self management skills and frequent, ongoing feedback, and interventions with the nutrition team.[368-371] Medical nutrition therapy for patients with chronic kidney disease must therefore include adequate time for nutrition assessment and education and regular, scheduled nutrition appointments.

Although occasionally a care provider, or other individual, may possess the expertise and time to conduct nutritional assessment, use dietary interviews and records to assess protein energy intake, assess body muscle and fat stores, interpret biochemical markers of nutrition status and relate to dietary intake, and provide nutritional therapy (develop a plan for nutritional management, counsel the patient and family on appropriate dietary protein energy intake, monitor nutrition intake, and provide encouragement to maximize dietary adherence)—a registered dietitian, trained and experienced in CKD nutrition, is best qualified to carry out these tasks. Such an individual not only has undergone all of the training required to become a registered dietitian, including in many instances a dietetic internship, but has also received formal or informal training in CKD nutrition. Such a person is particularly experienced in working with patients with chronic kidney disease and the nephrology team (see K/DOQI Clinical Practice Guidelines for Nutrition in Chronic Renal Failure, Appendix IV, *Role of the Renal Dietitian*[75]).

Research Recommendations

Although the data presented herein is compelling, more research, especially prospective studies evaluating the impact of kidney disease on nutritional parameters, is needed. Importantly, studies to define the optimal methods to evaluate nutritional status in chronic kidney disease patients are critical. Prospective studies evaluating the impact of different levels of nutritional status on subsequent outcome in chronic kidney disease patients should also be performed. Finally, prospective studies evaluating the impact of intensive nutritional counseling on nutritional status and possibly clinical outcome in chronic kidney disease patients should be carried out.

GUIDELINE 10. ASSOCIATION OF LEVEL OF GFR WITH BONE DISEASE AND DISORDERS OF CALCIUM AND PHOSPHORUS METABOLISM

Bone disease and disorders of calcium and phosphorus metabolism develop during the course of chronic kidney disease and are associated with adverse outcomes.

- Patients with GFR <60 mL/min/1.73 m^2 should be evaluated for bone disease and disorders of calcium and phosphorus metabolism.
- Patients with bone disease and disorders of bone metabolism should be evaluated and treated — see forthcoming K/DOQI Clinical Practice Guidelines on Bone Metabolism and Disease in Chronic Kidney Disease.

BACKGROUND

Chronic kidney disease is associated with a variety of bone disorders and disorders of calcium and phosphorus metabolism. The major disorders of bone can be classified into those associated with high parathyroid hormone (PTH) levels (osteitis fibrosa cystica) and those with low or normal PTH levels (adynamic bone disease). The hallmark lesion of chronic kidney disease is osteitis fibrosa, due to secondary hyperparathyroidism. However, with the advent of intensive treatments for secondary hyperparathyroidism, the prevalence of disorders associated with low or normal PTH levels has increased.

Irrespective of the cause, bone disease can lead to pain and an increased incidence of fractures. Abnormal calcium-phosphorus metabolism and hyperparathyroidism can also lead to calcification of blood vessels and potentially an increased risk of cardiovascular events.

The stage of chronic kidney disease at which bone disease begins to develop has not been well documented, nor has a consensus been developed regarding the best screening measures for detecting early abnormalities of calcium-phosphorus metabolism and bone disease. The aim of this guideline is to provide evidence on the association of level of GFR with disorders of calcium-phosphorus metabolism and bone disease and to provide recommendations on how to approach this complication of chronic kidney disease.

RATIONALE
Bone Disease in Chronic Kidney Disease

Bone disease associated with chronic kidney disease is composed of a number of abnormalities of bone mineralization. The major disorders can be classified into those associated with high bone turnover and high PTH levels (including osteitis fibrosa, the hallmark lesion of secondary hyperparathyroidism, and mixed lesion) and low bone turnover and low or normal PTH levels (osteomalacia and adynamic bone disease).[372] Osteomalacia may be related to vitamin D deficiency, excess aluminum, or metabolic acidosis; whereas adynamic bone disease may be related to over-suppression of PTH with calcitriol.[372-374]

The pathophysiology of bone disease due to secondary hyperparathyroidism is related to abnormal mineral metabolism: (1) decreased kidney function leads to reduced phosphorus excretion and consequent phosphorus retention; (2) elevated serum phosphorus can directly suppress calcitriol (dihydroxyvitamin D_3) production; (3) reduced kidney mass leads to decreased calcitriol production; (4) decreased calcitriol production with consequent reduced calcium absorption from the gastrointestinal tract contributes to hypocalcemia, as does abnormal calcium-phosphorus balance leading to an elevated calcium-phosphorus product.[375,376] Hypocalcemia, reduced calcitriol synthesis, and elevated serum phosphorus levels stimulate the production of PTH and the proliferation of parathyroid cells,[377-379] resulting in secondary hyperparathyroidism. High PTH levels stimulate osteoblasts and result in high bone turnover. The hallmark lesion of secondary hyperparathyroidism is osteitis fibrosa cystica. High bone turnover leads to irregularly woven abnormal osteoid, fibrosis, and cyst formation, which result in decreased cortical bone and bone strength and an increased risk of fracture.

Low turnover bone disease has two subgroups, osteomalacia and adynamic bone disease. Both lesions are characterized by a decrease in bone turnover or remodeling, with a reduced number of osteoclasts and osteoblasts, and decreased osteoblastic activity. In osteomalacia there is an accumulation of unmineralized bone matrix, or increased osteoid volume, which may be caused by vitamin D deficiency or excess aluminum. Adynamic bone disease is characterized by reduced bone volume and mineralization and may be due to excess aluminum or oversuppression of PTH production with calcitriol.[372]

Other Complications of Abnormal Calcium-Phosphorus Metabolism

In addition to abnormalities in bone metabolism, abnormal calcium-phosphorus metabolism may lead to calciphylaxis or extraosseous calcification of soft tissue and vascular tissue. This complication in its full manifestation has been reported to affect approximately 1% of dialysis patients.[380] However, in studies of coronary artery calcification using electron beam computed tomography, dialysis patients had coronary calcification scores that were several-fold higher than those of patients with known coronary artery disease.[381] The pathogenesis remains unclear, but hyperphosphatemia, hypercalcemia, elevated calcium-phosphorus product, and increased PTH levels are probable contributors.

Markers of Bone Disease and Abnormal Calcium-Phosphorus Metabolism in Chronic Kidney Disease

Bone biopsy following double-tetracycline labeling is the gold standard for the diagnosis of bone disease in chronic kidney disease and is the only means of definitively differentiating them. Five bone lesions associated with chronic kidney disease have been classified based on bone formation rate, osteoid area, and fibrosis on bone biopsy of patients with kidney failure[372,382] (Table 92).

Bone biopsy is not easy, nor necessary in routine clinical practice. Classically, bone resorption can be seen on plain radiographs in cases of advanced osteitis fibrosa, but radiological studies, including densitometry, have not been conclusively shown to differentiate the various types of bone disease associated with kidney failure. Bone biopsy is currently recommended only for patients with symptomatic disease in whom interventions are being contemplated (such as parathyroidectomy or desferoxamine treatment for elevated aluminum levels)[383] or for research of the effectiveness of therapies or alternative diagnostic tests.[384] In the absence of direct pathologic studies, clinicians have relied on biochemical data to determine the probable presence of, or assess the risk for, bone abnormalities. Low calcitriol (dihydroxyvitamin D_3) and calcium levels, and high phosphorus and PTH levels, are the classic abnormalities which develop with decreased

Table 92. Histologic Classification of Bone Lesions Associated with Kidney Disease

Lesions	Bone Formation Rate ($\mu m^2/mm^2$ tissue area/day)	Osteoid Area (%)	Fibrosis (%)
Aplastic (adynamic):	<108	<15%	<0.5%
Osteomalacia:	<108	>15%	<0.5%
Mild:	>108	<15%	<0.5%
Osteitis Fibrosa:	>108	<15%	>0.5%
Mixed:	>108	>15%	>0.5%

GFR.[385] The biochemical studies in common use are serum phosphorus, calcium, and PTH levels. Calcitriol levels can also be measured, but this is not commonly done in clinical practice. Serum phosphorus and calcium levels are used in screening for abnormalities of mineral metabolism that may lead to PTH excess; however, PTH levels may begin to rise even before there is appreciable hyperphosphatemia.[379] Hence, the recommendation to obtain PTH levels in the assessment of bone disease in chronic kidney disease.

An ideal serologic marker would be unique to bone and would be well correlated to histologic findings on biopsy. Two markers studied more extensively include PTH and bone alkaline phosphatase (bAP). PTH secretion is directly correlated with bone turnover, but PTH levels are not reliably correlated with bone turnover among dialysis patients, especially in the middle ranges.[386,387] PTH levels <65 pg/mL were found to be predictive of normal bone or low turnover lesions, and PTH levels >450 pg/mL were predictive of high turnover lesions, but levels in between did not have good predictive value. Overall bone turnover could not be predicted in 30% of HD and 50% of PD patients.[387] In another study, low turnover lesions were noted in the majority of patients with PTH levels <100 pg/mL and high turnover lesions in the majority of patients with PTH levels >200 to 300 pg/mL.[386] High bAP levels have been associated with high bone turnover and low levels with adynamic bone disease in dialysis patients. In one study, the combination of high bone alkaline phosphatase levels with high PTH levels increased the sensitivity of diagnosis of high turnover lesions; conversely, low levels of both of these markers result in increased sensitivity for diagnosis of low turnover lesions. However, specific cut-off levels for bAP have varied in the few studies examining the relationship to bone histology.[383]

Other markers of bone disease not yet fully investigated nor in widespread clinical use include osteocalcin, β2 microglobulin, procollagen type I carboxy-terminal propeptides (PICP), and type I collagen cross linked telopeptides (ICTP), among others. PICP has been correlated with bone formation, and ICTP and osteocalcin been correlated with bone resorption. However, levels of many of these markers are affected by age, diet, liver function, and kidney function; thus, interpretation of levels is difficult.[383]

Thus, abnormalities of bone mineral metabolism are present if there is an elevated serum phosphorus or PTH level or reduced serum calcium or calcitriol level. Given the possibility of an elevated PTH level in the face of normal serum calcium and phosphorus levels, the diagnosis of early abnormality of mineral metabolism requires measurement of PTH levels. Extreme elevations of serum PTH levels are more convincingly associated with high turnover lesions than low levels with low turnover lesions. Definitive diagnosis of type of bone disease requires bone biopsy.

Strength of Evidence

Bone disease and disorders of calcium and phosphorus metabolism develop during the course of chronic kidney disease (R). Radiologic and histologic changes of bone disease can be demonstrated in about 40% and nearly 100%, respectively, of patients with severely decreased kidney function and kidney failure.[388,389] However, the abnormalities that lead to bone disease begin to occur at earlier stages of chronic kidney disease. Elevated levels of PTH and phosphorus, reduced levels of calcium, and reduced urinary phosphate excretion have been described among patients with GFR <70 mL/min or lower.[372,379,386,390,391] Histologic changes have also been shown to occur at earlier stages of chronic kidney disease. In a study of 176 patients with creatinine clearances of 15 to 50 mL/min, 75% had "important histological abnormalities, with the majority having osteitis fibrosa with or without osteomalacia."[392] In another study of patients with creatinine clearances of 20 to 59 mL/min, 87% of patients had abnormal bone histology, and the majority had lesions of high bone formation rate associated with hyperparathyroidism.[374]

Bone disease and disorders of bone metabolism are associated with worse outcomes in chronic kidney disease (R). The consequences of abnormal bone mineral metabolism have been studied primarily in patients without kidney disease and in patients with kidney failure.[393,394] Hyperparathyroidism has been associated with abnormal bone histology, bone pain, and fractures among patients with either primary and secondary hyperparathyroidism,[395-397] and low PTH levels have been more recently recognized to result in an increased risk of vertebral and pelvic fractures.[398,399]

Calcification of cardiac muscle and coronary vasculature may lead to arrhythmia, left ventricular dysfunction, ischemia, congestive heart failure, and death. Calciphylaxis results in skin lesions that may become infected or gangrenous, leading to significant morbidity and mortality among patients on dialysis.[380,394,400] Elevated phosphorus and calcium-phosphorus product has also been linked to increased mortality among patients on dialysis.[400,401] It has been hypothesized that elevated phosphorus levels may hasten the loss of kidney function, possibly via calcium-phosphorus precipitation.[402]

In addition, there is some experimental evidence that elevated PTH levels may be associated with myocardial dysfunction, and impaired skeletal muscle, neurological, and hematopoietic function.[393] The impact of PTH levels on mortality appears conflicting. One study of dialysis patients reported an increased risk of death among dialysis patients with low serum PTH levels,[400,403] while another study of patients in an emergency room reported an increased risk of death among patients with high PTH levels.[404]

Onset and severity of bone disease and abnormalities of bone mineral metabolism are related to the level of GFR; below a GFR of approximately 60 mL/min/1.73 m², there is a higher prevalence of abnormalities of bone metabolism (C, S).

PTH levels are elevated in patients with decreased GFR and likely are the earliest marker of abnormal bone mineral metabolism (Tables 93 and 94 and Figs 36, 37, and 38) (C, S). The studies relating PTH levels to kidney function date back to the 1960s, with sample sizes ranging from 6 to over 200 subjects with kidney disease. Each of the 23 studies on this topic reviewed for this guideline consistently demonstrated the expected relationship of increasing serum PTH levels with decreasing levels of kidney function. Further details of these studies are presented in Table 93.

Table 93. Parathyroid Hormone and Kidney Function

Author, Year	No. of Subjects	Applicability	GFR Range (mL/min/1.73 m^2)	Results*	Quality
Martinez,[405] 1997	157	†††		⬇	●
Pitts,[406] 1988	72	†††		⬇	●
St. John,[407] 1992	51	†††		⬇	●
Reichel,[408] 1991	85	††		⬇	●
von Lilienfeld-Toal,[409] 1982	81	††		⬇	●
Cheung,[410] 1983	39	†††	S_{Cr} 3.4 ±0.3 mg/dL	⬇	◐
Fajtova,[411] 1995	39	†††		⬇	◐
Rix,[412] 1999	202	††		⬇	◐
Yumita,[413] 1996	195	††	S_{Cr} <1– >8 mg/dL	⬇	◐
Christensen,[414] 1977	188	††		⬇	◐
Kates,[378] 1997	84	††		⬇	◐
Malluche,[415] 1976	72	††		⬇	◐
McGonigle,[416] 1984	60	††	S_{Cr}: 5–11.5 mg/dL	⬇	◐
Saha,[417] 1994	50	††		⬇	◐
Messa,[418] 1995	43	††		⬇	◐
Tessitore,[419] 1987	41	††		⇩	◐
Coen,[420] 1989	32	††	S_{Cr} 6.5 ±2.9 mg/dL	⬇	◐
Tougaard,[421] 1977	24	††		⬇	◐
Madsen,[422] 1976	15	††		⇩	◐
Bedani,[423] 1985	61	††		⬇	○
Arata,[424] 1976	31	††		⇩	○
Arnaud,[425] 1973	~124[a]	†		⇩	○
Reiss,[426] 1968	6	†		⇩	○

GFR Range scale: 0, 30, 60, 90, 120

* ⬇ = higher GFR associated with lower parathyroid hormone (statistically significant);
⇩ = higher GFR associated with lower parathyroid hormone.

[a] No data given on exact number of subjects; 124 points counted on graph; no information on whether data-points each represent individual subjects.

Table 94. Fractional Excretion of Phosphorus and Kidney Function

Author, Year	No. of Subjects	Applicability	GFR Range (mL/min/1.73 m²)	Results*	Quality
Pitts,[406] 1988	72	↑↑↑	├──── (0–120)	⬇	●
Massry,[427] 1973	105	↑↑	├────	⇩	◑
Slatopolsky,[428] 1968	30	↑↑	────	⬇	○

* ⬇ = higher GFR associated with lower fractional excretion of phosphate (statistically significant);
  ⇩ = higher GFR associated with lower fractional excretion of phosphate.

Because of the variety of assays used to measure PTH and methods used to estimate level of kidney function, no attempt was made to combine data from different studies. However, it is evident and currently accepted that the intact PTH test provides the most consistently reliable measure of PTH levels.

There were four separate studies that examined the threshold creatinine clearance or GFR levels at which PTH levels begin to rise; these threshold levels ranged from <70 mL/min to <40 mL/min.[406,411,415,425] In addition, analyses of data from a single study[288] demonstrate an inverse correlation between level of GFR and PTH (Figs 36 and 37) and an increasing prevalence of abnormally elevated PTH levels with decreasing GFR (Fig

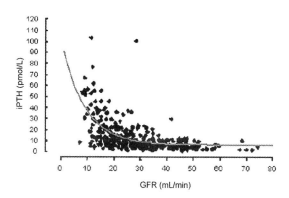

Fig 36. Scatterplot of iPTH versus GFR. These data are based on the results of 446 patients enrolled in the Canadian Multicentre Longitudinal Cohort study of patients with chronic kidney disease. All patients were referred to nephrologists between 1994 and 1997. No patient was receiving erythropoiten therapy at the time of enrollment, and no patient had an AV fistula. Intact molecule PTH assay is reported in pica moles per liter, and GFR is calculated using the modified MDRD formula (using age, race, gender, and serum creatinine). Adapted and reprinted with permission.[288]

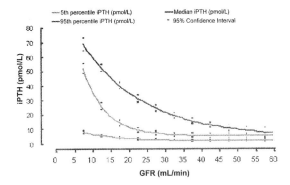

Fig 37. iPTH percentiles by GFR. These data are based on the results of 446 patients enrolled in the Canadian Multicentre Longitudinal Cohort study of patients with chronic kidney disease. All patients were referred to nephrologists between 1994 and 1997. No patient was receiving erythropoiten therapy at the time of enrollment, and no patient had an AV fistula. Intact molecule PTH assay is reported in pica moles per liter, and GFR is calculated using the modified MDRD formula (using age, race, gender, and serum creatinine). Data are presented as median iPTH and 5th and 95th percentiles. Adapted and reprinted with permission.[288]

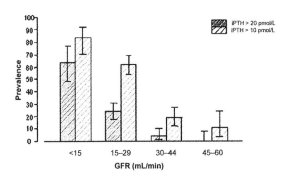

Fig 38. Prevalence of high iPTH by GFR category. These data are based on the results of 446 patients enrolled in the Canadian Multicentre Longitudinal Cohort study of patients with chronic kidney disease. All patients were referred to nephrologists between 1994 and 1997. No patient was receiving erythropoietin therapy at the time of enrollment, and no patient had an AV fistula. Intact molecule PTH assay is reported in pico moles per liter, and GFR is calculated using the modified MDRD formula (using age, race, gender, and serum creatinine). Adapted and reprinted with permission.[288]

38). Therefore, the preponderance of data support that serum PTH levels are increased in patients with decreased GFR.

Consistent with these observations, fractional excretion of phosphorous is higher at lower GFRs (Table 94).

Serum calcium levels are frequently, but not consistently, abnormal with decreased GFR (Table 95 and Figs 39 and 40) (C, S). The studies relating serum total or ionized calcium levels to kidney function date back to the 1960s, with sample sizes ranging from 15 to over 125 subjects with kidney disease. The studies were conflicting

Table 95. Serum Calcium and Kidney Function

Author, Year	No. of Subjects	Applicability	GFR Range (mL/min/1.73 m²)	Results*	Quality
Martinez,[405] 1997	157	↟↟↟		⇔	●
Pitts,[406] 1988	72	↟↟↟		↑	●
St. John,[407] 1992	51	↟↟↟		↑	●
Reichel,[408] 1991	85	↟↟		⇔	●
von Lilienfeld-Toal,[409] 1982	81	↟↟		↑	●
Cheung,[410] 1983	39	↟↟↟	S_{Ca} 3.4 ±0.3 mg/dL	⇔	○
Fajtova,[411] 1995	39	↟↟↟		↑	○
Coburn,[429] 1973	256	↟↟	S_{Ca} 11.1 ±7.6 mg/dL	⇧	○
Rix,[412] 1999	202	↟↟		↑	○
Yumita,[413] 1996	195	↟↟	S_{Ca} <1->8 mg/dL	⇔	○
Christensen,[414] 1977	188	↟↟		↑	○
Coburn,[430] 1969	126	↟↟		⇧	○
Massry,[427] 1973	105	↟↟		⇧	○
Kates,[378] 1997	84	↟↟		↑	○
Saha,[417] 1994	50	↟↟		⇔	○
Messa,[418] 1995	43	↟↟		⇔	○
Coen,[420] 1989	32	↟↟	S_{Ca} 6.5 ±2.9 mg/dL	↑	○
Tougaard,[421] 1977	24	↟↟		↑	○
Madsen,[422] 1976	15	↟↟↟		⇔	○
Arata,[424] 1976	31	↟↟		⇧	○

* ↑ = higher GFR associated with higher serum calcium (statistically significant);
⇧ = higher GFR associated with higher serum calcium;
⇔ = GFR *not* associated with serum calcium.

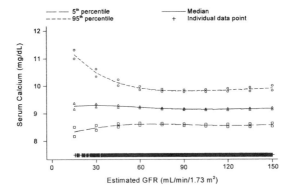

Fig 39. Serum calcium levels (adjusted for albumin) versus GFR. Median and 5th and 95th percentiles of serum calcium, adjusted for serum albumin, among adult participants age 20 years and older in NHANES III, 1988 to 1994. Values are adjusted to age 60 years using a polynomial quantile regression. The estimated GFR for each individual data point is shown with a plus near the abscissa. 95% confidence intervals at selected levels of estimated GFR are demarcated with triangles, squares, and circles.

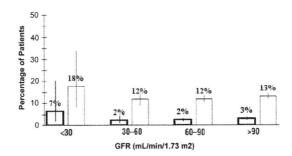

Fig 40. Prevalence of hypocalcemia (adjusted for albumin) versus GFR. These data are based on the results of 446 patients enrolled in the Canadian Multicentre Longitudinal Cohort study of patients with chronic kidney disease. All patients were referred to ne-phrologists between 1994 and 1997. No patient was receiving erythropoietin therapy at the time of enrollment, and no patient had an AV fistula. GFR is calculated using the modified MDRD formula. Hypocalcemia was defined as serum calcium levels (adjusted for albumin) of <8.5 mg/dL. Adapted and reprinted with permission.[288]

in that about one third (7/20) did not demonstrate the expected relationship between serum calcium levels and kidney function, that is, they did not show lower serum calcium levels among patients with worse kidney function. The remaining studies (13/20) showed that serum calcium levels were lower with lower levels of kidney function.

These data do not consistently show that there is a decrease in calcium levels with declining kidney function. This was not as expected based on the "known" pathophysiology of bone mineral metabolism. The studies showing conflicting results are of similar methodological quality and sample size. In summary, there is not a clear relationship of the level of serum calcium to the level of kidney function over a wide range of kidney function in the reviewed studies.

Similarly, analysis of data from NHANES III does not demonstrate a convincing relationship between serum calcium levels (adjusted for albumin) and level of GFR, although few patients had GFR below 30 ml/min/1.73 m^2 (Fig 39).

However, analyses of data from a single study with a large number of individuals with decreased GFR[288] demonstrate lower serum calcium levels and higher prevalence of lower serum calcium levels among individuals with lower GFR, in particular below a GFR of < 30 mL/min/1.73 m^2 (Fig 40).

The combination of the available information regarding pathophysiology of bone disease in chronic kidney disease and the available evidence reviewed herein would suggest that serum calcium levels are affected by the level of kidney function, though abnormalities in serum calcium levels may not become evident until GFR is <30 mL/min/1.73 m^2.

Serum phosphorus levels are elevated in patients with decreased GFR (Table 96 and Figs 41, 42, and 43) (C, S). There were 21 studies relating serum phosphorus levels to kidney function reviewed for this guideline. The sample sizes ranged from 15 to over 250 subjects with kidney disease. Fifteen studies showed the expected association of higher serum phosphorus levels with lower kidney function. The remaining 6 studies did not show an association of kidney function with serum phosphorus levels, although one did find a trend for increasing phosphorus levels when creatinine clearance was below 50 mL/min.[405] There were four studies that provided sufficient information to determine a threshold level of kidney function at which phosphorus levels start to rise. The apparent threshold GFR ranged from 20 to 50 mL/min/1.73 m^2.

In addition, analyses of data from a single study[288] and from an analysis of data from NHANES III, demonstrate an increase in serum phosphorus levels (Fig 41) and an increasing prevalence of abnormally elevated serum phosphorus (Fig 42), with lower GFR. Concomitantly, NHANES III data showed that calcium-phosphorus product and prevalence of elevated calcium phosphorus product were higher in individuals with lower GFR (Fig 43).

Overall, these data confirm that serum phosphorus level is higher in individuals with decreased kidney function and suggest that serum phosphorus levels become abnormal in some patients at GFR below approximately 60 mL/min/1.73 m^2.

Table 96. Serum Phosphate and Kidney Function

Author, Year	No. of Subjects	Applicability	GFR Range (mL/min/1.73 m²)	Results*	Quality
Martinez,[405] 1997	157	↟↟↟		⇔	●
Pitts,[406] 1988	72	↟↟↟		↓	●
St. John,[407] 1992	51	↟↟↟		↓	●
Reichel,[408] 1991	85	↟↟		⇔	●
von Lilienfeld-Toal,[409] 1982	81	↟↟		↓	●
Cheung,[410] 1983	39	↟↟↟	S_{cr} 3.4 ±0.3 mg/dL	↓	◐
Fajtova,[411] 1995	39	↟↟↟		↓	◐
Coburn,[429] 1973	256	↟↟	S_{cr} 11.1 ±7.6 mg/dL	⇩	◐
Rix,[412] 1999	202	↟↟		↓	◐
Yumita,[413] 1996	195	↟↟	S_{cr} <1 – >8 mg/dL	↓	◐
Christensen,[414] 1977	188	↟↟		⇔	◐
Coburn,[430] 1969	126	↟↟		⇩	◐
Massry,[427] 1973	105	↟↟		⇩	◐
Kates,[378] 1997	84	↟↟		↓	◐
Saha,[417] 1994	50	↟↟		⇩	◐
Messa,[418] 1995	43	↟↟		⇔	◐
Coen,[420] 1989	32	↟↟	S_{cr} 6.5 ±2.9 mg/dL	↓	◐
Tougaard,[421] 1977	24	↟↟		↓	◐
Madsen,[422] 1976	15	↟↟		⇔	◐
Arata,[424] 1976	31	↟↟		⇩	○
Slatopolsky,[428] 1968	30	↟↟		⇔	○

* ↓ = higher GFR associated with lower serum phosphate (statistically significant);
 ⇩ = higher GFR associated with lower serum phosphate;
 ⇔ = GFR *not* associated with serum phosphate.

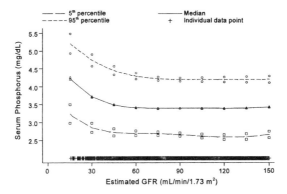

Fig 41. Serum phosphorus levels versus GFR (NHANES III). Median and 5th and 95th percentiles of serum phosphorus among adult participants age 20 years and older in NHANES III, 1988 to 1994. Values are adjusted to age 60 years using a polynomial quantile regression. The estimated GFR for each individual data point is shown with a plus near the abscissa. 95% confidence intervals at selected levels of estimated GFR are demarcated with triangles, squares, and circles.

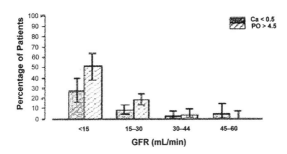

Fig 42. Prevalence of low calcium and high phosphate by GFR category. These data are based on the results of 446 patients enrolled in the Canadian Multicentre Longitudinal Cohort study of patients with chronic kidney disease. All patients were referred to nephrologists between 1994 and 1997. No patient was receiving erythropoiten therapy at the time of enrollment, and no patient had an AV fistula. Intact molecule PTH assay is reported in picomoles per liter, and GFR is calculated using the modified MDRD formula (using age, race, gender, and serum creatinine). Low calcium levels are defined as levels 8.5 mg/dL, adjusted for albumin, and high phosphate levels are defined as >4.5 mg/dL. Adapted and reprinted with permission.[288]

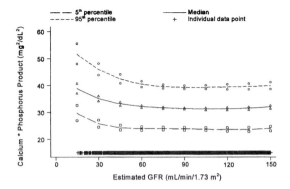

Fig 43. Calcium-phosphorus product percentiles by GFR (NHANES III). Median and 5th and 95th percentiles of serum calcium-phosphorus product, adjusted for serum albumin, among adult participants age 20 years and older in NHANES III, 1988 to 1994. Values are adjusted to age 60 years using a polynomial quantile regression. The estimated GFR for each individual data point is shown with a plus near the abscissa. 95% confidence intervals at selected levels of estimated GFR are demarcated with triangles, squares, and circles.

Vitamin D₃ levels are decreased among patients with decreased GFR (Table 97) (C). There were 14 studies relating vitamin D₃ (calcitriol) levels to kidney function reviewed for this guideline, with sample sizes ranging from 39 to over 200 subjects with kidney disease. Thirteen of the 14 studies evaluated 1,25 dihydroxyvitamin D levels, three of these also evaluated 24,25 dihydroxyvitamin D (2 studies) and/or 25 hydroxyvitamin D levels (3 studies), and one study evaluated only 25 hydroxyvitamin D levels. Each of the 13 studies noted that 1,25 dihydroxyvitamin D levels were lower with decreased kidney function. The two studies evaluating 24,25 dihydroxyvitamin D levels noted lower levels with lower kidney function. The four studies evaluating 25 hydroxyvitamin D levels showed conflicting results.

These data confirm that 1,25 dihydroxyvitamin D levels are lower in patients with decreased kidney function. There is limited information to suggest that 24,25 dihydroxyvitamin D levels are lower in patients with decreased kidney function. The studies do not provide data on the association between level of kidney function and 25 hydroxyvitamin D levels.

Bone histology is abnormal in the majority of patients with kidney failure (Table 98) (C). Six articles that related bone biopsy findings to level of kidney function among patients with chronic kidney disease not yet on dialysis were reviewed. The sample sizes ranged from 20 to 176 individuals. The levels of kidney function ranged from nearly normal (creatinine clearance of 117 mL/min) to the initiation of dialysis. Among patients with kidney failure immediately prior to initiation of dialysis, 98% to 100% had abnormal bone histology, with the majority of the biopsies showing either

Table 97. Vitamin D_3 and Kidney Function

Author, Year	No. of Subjects	Applicability	GFR Range (mL/min/1.73 m²)	Results*	Quality
Pitts,[406] 1988	72	↑↑↑	(graph)	↑	●
St. John,[407] 1992	51	↑↑↑	(graph)	↑ (1,25) ⟺ (25)	●
Reichel,[408] 1991	85	↑↑	(graph)	↑ (1,25)	●
Ishimura,[431] 1999	76	↑↑↑	(graph)	↑ (1,25; 24,25) ⟺ (25)	○
Cheung,[410] 1983	39	↑↑↑	S_{Cr} 3.4 ±0.3 mg/dL	↑ (1,25)	○
Fajtova,[411] 1995	39	↑↑↑	(graph)	↑ (1,25)	○
Rix,[412] 1999	202	↑↑	(graph)	↑ (1,25)	○
Yumita,[413] 1996	195	↑↑	S_{Cr} <1–>8 mg/dL	↑ (1,25)	○
Kates,[378] 1997	84	↑↑	(graph)	↑ (1,25)	○
Nielsen,[432] 1976	81	↑↑	(graph)	⬇ (25)	○
Saha,[417] 1994	50	↑↑	(graph)	⇧ (1,25; 24,25; 25)	○
Messa,[418] 1995	43	↑↑	(graph)	↑ (1,25)	○
Tessitore,[419] 1987	41	↑↑	(graph)	↑ (1,25)	○
Coen,[420] 1989	32	↑↑	S_{Cr} 6.5 ±2.9 mg/dL	⬇ (1, 25) ⟺ (25)	○

* ↑ = higher GFR associated with higher level of indicated Vitamin D_3 (statistically significant);
⇧ = higher GFR associated with higher level of indicated Vitamin D_3;
⟺ = GFR *not* associated with level of indicated Vitamin D_3;
⬇ = higher GFR associated with lower level of indicated Vitamin D_3.

osteitis fibrosa or adynamic bone disease[389,433] (data not shown). The studies evaluating patients with varying levels of kidney function demonstrated: (1) a direct relationship between bone mineralization and kidney function[415,421]; (2) an inverse relationship between kidney function and bone osteoid/resorption[415]; or (3) a higher prevalence of abnormalities on bone biopsy (osteomalacia, resorption, osteoid) among patients with reduced kidney function.[392,419,434,435] In two studies of patients with varying levels of kidney function not yet receiving treatment with vitamin D agents, one[374] with 76, the other[392] with 176 subjects, 75% to 85% had significant abnormalities on bone biopsy. The majority had osteitis fibrosa, with or without osteomalacia.

There were 4 studies of bone densitometry reviewed for this topic, which demonstrated that bone mineralization is reduced with decreased kidney function. One study presented the results as a higher prevalence of reduced bone mineral content with decreased levels of kidney function. Other studies noted a reduced bone mineral content among patients with decreased kidney function compared to controls. This is insufficient evidence to make firm statements regarding the relationship between bone density and level of kidney function.

Table 98. Bone Disease and Kidney Function

Author, Year	Measurement	No. of Subjects	Applic-ability	GFR Range (mL/min/1.73 m²)	Results*	Quality
Biopsy Studies:						
Hamdy,[392] 1995	Abnormal bone histology	176	↑↑		⇩	●
Coen,[435] 1996	Bone disease severity by biopsy	76	↑↑		↓	●
Malluche,[415] 1976	Osteoid %	72	↑↑		↓	●
Malluche,[415] 1976	Osteoclastic surface resorption	72	↑↑		↓	●
Bedani,[423] 1985	Osteoclastic surface resorption	61	↑↑		⇩	○
Tessitore,[419] 1987	Proportion with osteomalacia	41	↑↑		⇔	●
Tessitore,[419] 1987	% bone resorption	41	↑↑		⇩	●
Suzuki,[434] 1980	Osteoid surface area	20	↑↑		⇩	●
Radiology Studies:						
Madsen,[436] 1978	Bone mineral content	279	↑↑↑		↑	●
Nielsen,[432] 1976	Bone mineral content	81	↑↑		⇩	●
Tougaard,[421] 1977	Bone mineral content	24	↑↑		↑	●
Bedani,[423] 1985	Acro-osteolysis	61	↑↑		⇩	○
Rix,[412] 1999	Hip DEXA	202	↑↑		↑	●
Other Studies:						
Tougaard,[421] 1977	Phosphorus: hydroxyproline ratio	24	↑↑		↑	●

Bold horizontal lines divide studies by type of measurement used.

* ↑ = higher GFR associated with higher level of indicated bone measurement (statistically significant);
⇔ = GFR *not* associated with indicated bone measurement;
↓ = higher GFR associated with lower level of indicated bone measurement (statistically significant);
⇩ = higher GFR associated with lower level of indicated bone measurement.

LIMITATIONS

These guidelines are limited by the inability to provide a definitive quantitative or semi-quantitative assessment of the relationship between level of kidney function and marker of bone disease. This is in part due to the lack of comparability of many of the studies given the diversity of the laboratory assays or tests for the particular abnormality. This was particularly true for PTH and vitamin D_3 (calcitriol) levels, but also applies to bone densitometry. Similarly, the interpretation of bone biopsies and radiographic tests likely has a range of error, in this case related to inter-observer variability.

In addition, as with most of the Guidelines in Part 6, the results are difficult to compare as they use different measures for kidney function: measured GFR or creatinine clearance, estimation equations for GFR or creatinine clearance, or simply serum creatinine.

Lastly, many of the studies involved only few patients with GFR >60 mL/min/1.73 m². This leads to the extrapolation of the results from other studies to such patients with variable levels of confidence for the various markers.

CLINICAL APPLICATIONS

The data reviewed here suggest that abnormalities of bone/mineral metabolism begin to occur early in kidney disease; thus, the implications are that:

- Indices of bone/mineral metabolism should be measured when there is indication of any level of kidney dysfunction—PTH, phosphorus and ionized calcium levels are the most commonly used biomarkers.
- Biomarkers of bone/mineral metabolism should be followed longitudinally in individual patients as it is expected that abnormalities may develop or become more severe as kidney function deteriorates.
- There are currently no convincing data to suggest that there is benefit to routinely obtaining bone biopsies or bone densitometry. Bone biopsy may be indicated if there is symptomatic disease or if "aggressive" interventions such as parathyroidectomy or desferoxamine therapy are being contemplated.

The applications suggested above are based on review of the available literature presented herein and on opinion. The suggestion to follow the biomarkers over time is based on the hypothesis that a change in some of these biomarkers may occur even when there is no change in GFR. In fact, changes in the biomarkers may provide an earlier indication of worsening kidney function.

Treatment recommendations are beyond the scope of this guideline, and will be addressed elsewhere (see K/DOQI Bone Metabolism and Disease in CKD Guidelines).

IMPLEMENTATION ISSUES

Medicare at present does not cover payment for PTH levels for screening for hyperparathyroidism among patients with chronic kidney disease, unless they have a diagnosis specific to hyperparathyroidism.[437] Calcium and ionized calcium tests are also not covered for the evaluation of patients with chronic kidney disease, while phosphate and alkaline phosphate tests are covered.[437]

Clearly, since the evidence shows that there may be elevation in the PTH level in the setting of normal phosphorus and calcium levels, and high PTH levels are deleterious to bone and non-osseous tissue, policies regarding testing and reimbursement need to be reassessed.

RESEARCH RECOMMENDATIONS

Much of the available information regarding abnormalities of mineral metabolism is derived from studies of patients with kidney failure or severely decreased kidney function. Clearly, more information is needed on the abnormalities of bone mineral metabolism among patients with earlier stages of chronic kidney disease. Moreover, research on outcomes related to abnormal mineral metabolism or bone disease is lacking in both patients with mildly, as well as severely decreased kidney function. In addition to bone complications, there is increasing evidence relating abnormal calcium-phosphorus metabolism and hyperparathyroidism to vascular calcification and cardiovascular complications.

The relationship between levels of the available markers, and levels of kidney function, should be more accurately characterized. In addition, the relationship between such levels and kidney function should be separately studied among patients with additional risks of bone complications, that is, patients treated for prolonged periods with corticosteroids and transplant recipients.

Research should also focus on the impact of interventions on levels of available markers and outcomes, specifically of interest would be comparing patients cared for by nephrologists with those not under the care of nephrologists, patients treated for some specified period of time for hyperparathyroidism compared to those not treated, and patients treated with corticosteroids compared to those never treated with such drugs.

GUIDELINE 11. ASSOCIATION OF LEVEL OF GFR WITH NEUROPATHY

Neuropathy develops during the course of chronic kidney disease and may become symptomatic.

- Patients with chronic kidney disease should be periodically assessed for central and peripheral neurologic involvement by eliciting symptoms and signs during routine office visits or exams.
- Specialized laboratory testing for neuropathy in patients with chronic kidney disease is indicated only in the presence of symptoms.

BACKGROUND

Neuropathy is a common complication of patients with kidney failure.[438-440] Neuropathy may be manifested as encephalopathy, peripheral polyneuropathy, autonomic dysfunction, sleep disorders, and, less commonly, peripheral mononeuropathy. Occurrence of neuropathy is related to the level of kidney function, but not the type of kidney disease. However, there are certain causes of chronic kidney disease that also affect the central and/or peripheral nervous system. These are amyloidosis, diabetes, systemic lupus erythematosus, polyarteritis nodosa, and hepatic failure.[438,439] In addition, there are congenital disorders that affect both the kidneys and nervous system, such as Von Hippel Lindau disease, Wilson's disease, and Fabry's disease.[438]

The pathophysiology of uremic neuropathy is not well understood. Levels of urea, creatinine, PTH, "middle molecules," and others have been correlated with reduction of nerve conduction velocity (NCV) and peripheral manifestations of neuropathy.[438,439] In advanced stages there is evidence of histopathological damage with axonal degeneration and secondary demyelination of peripheral nerves.[438]

RATIONALE
Markers of Neuropathy

Uremic neuropathy may affect the central, peripheral, or autonomic nervous systems. Early uremic encephalopathy may present with fatigue, impaired memory, or concentration. With more advanced uremia delirium, visual hallucinations, disorientation, convulsions, and coma may develop.[438] Generally, uremic polyneuropathy is a symmetrical, mixed sensory and motor polyneuropathy, with distal nerves more severely affected. Patients may complain of pruritus, burning, muscle irritability, cramps, or weakness.[438,439] Autonomic function abnormalities include impaired heart rate and blood pressure variability in response to respiratory cycle, postural change, and valsalva.

Signs on examination include muscle atrophy, loss of deep tendon reflexes, poor attention span, impaired abstract thinking, abnormal or absent reflexes (in particular ankle jerk), and impaired sensation (vibratory, light touch pressure, and pain).[438,439] Later signs include meningismus, myoclonus, and asterixis.[438] Electroencephalography (EEG) has generalized slowing, and bilateral spike and wave complexes have been described in up to 14% of patients, even in the absence of evident clinical seizure activity.[438] EEG measures of sleep also are disturbed in dialysis patients.[441] CT scan or MRI is not helpful, though there may be cerebral atrophy.[438,442-444] The most sensitive test for detection of asymptomatic peripheral neuropathy is slowed sensory NCV; although motor NCV is slowed, there is a wide intra-individual day-to-day variation, and these findings occur with more advanced kidney dysfunction.[438,439,445]

Strength of Evidence

Neuropathy develops during the course of chronic kidney disease (R). Neuropathy is present in up to 65% of patients at the initiation of dialysis[438,439]; thus, it must begin to develop during an earlier phase of kidney disease. Symptoms of peripheral neuropathy generally do not present unless the GFR is under 12 to 20 mL/min, or uremia has been present for at least 6 months.[438,439] Encephalopathy may become evident with less prolonged impairment of kidney function and can be seen with acute decline in GFR, although the correlation of central nervous system manifestations with level of kidney function is poor.[438] Autonomic neuropathy is present in 20% to 80% of patients with diabetic nephropathy,[442,444] in 66% of patients with severely impaired kidney function (creatinine clearance <8 mL/min), and in 50% of patients on dialysis.[443]

Objective findings of peripheral neuropathy as evaluated by NCV studies are present in 15% to 85% of individuals with decreased GFR.[446-449] Sensory NCV is decreased in over 90% of patients, whereas motor NCV is decreased in only 40%.[445] Among patients on dialysis, objective evidence of neuropathy is present in 50% to 100%,[440,446] and the prevalence appears to increase with duration of dialysis.[440]

Objective evidence of central nervous system (CNS) dysfunction is not uniformly evident. EEG has been described to be minimally abnormal in a "small percentage" of patients[445] or as slowed in most patients,[450] with the degree of slowing more pronounced with more advanced dysfunction. EEG findings have been reported to improve after initiation of dialysis or with transplant.[450] Tests of cognitive function were abnormal in all patients and were more impaired with increasing creatinine. Transplant and dialysis patients had somewhat better, but not normal, scores.[450]

Treatment with dialysis improves the more severe symptoms and findings of CNS involvement and improves the symptoms of polyneuropathy; however, NCV remains abnormal in up to 60% to 80%.[440] The symptoms and findings of peripheral neuropathy are dramatically improved by transplantation.[438]

Neuropathy is associated with worse outcomes in chronic kidney disease (R). No articles were found that specifically related the presence of neuropathy to other outcomes among patients with chronic kidney disease. However, it is self-evident that impaired cognition and sleep, dysesthesias, and impaired autonomic function would at least lead to reduced quality of life and inability to function normally. If the neuropathy leads to skin ulcers, then certainly this would result in objective morbidity and potentially mortality. Advanced encephalopathy may result in seizures, coma, and death.[438]

Objective findings of neuropathy can be detected before symptoms arise (C, R). Several of the articles reviewed note that the majority of patients who have abnormalities in tests of nervous system function are asymptomatic.[445,447,448] However, abnormalities are more profound among patients with symptoms.[447,448]

Onset and severity of neuropathy is associated with the level of GFR; there is insufficient evidence to define a specific threshold level of GFR that is associated with an increased prevalence or severity of neuropathy (C). The articles reviewed varied greatly in the levels of kidney function assessed, as well as in the measure of kidney function used, as some used only serum creatinine levels and other used GFR or creatinine clearance. Most studies demonstrated a relationship between kidney function and the particular marker of neuropathy. However, several studies only compared the particular marker with the normal or reference standard for the test or compared grouped data on patients with kidney disease with controls or patients on dialysis/transplant without providing data at various levels of kidney function. Summaries of the studies reviewed are presented in Tables 99 and 100.

Table 99. Nerve Conduction Velocity and Kidney Function

Author, Year	No. of Subjects	Applicability	GFR Range (mL/min/1.73 m²) 0 30 60 90 120	Results*	Quality
Teschan,[450] 1979	177	↟↟	S_Cr 2–29 mg/dL	⇔	O
Di Paolo,[445] 1982	129	↟↟	(0–60)	↑	O
Savazzi,[451] 1980	100	↟↟	(0–30)	⇧	O
Nielsen,[446] 1973	56	↟↟	(0–30)	↑	O
Goel,[447] 1978	40	↟↟	(30–60)	⇔	O
Knoll,[449] 1980	210	↟	S_Cr 1–12 mg/dL	⇔	O

* ↑ = higher GFR associated with faster nerve conduction velocity (statistically significant);
 ⇧ = higher GFR associated with faster nerve conduction velocity;
 ⇔ = GFR *not* associated with nerve conduction velocity.

Table 100. Miscellaneous Neurological Measurements and Kidney Function

Author, Year	Measurement	No. of Subjects	Applic-ability	GFR Range (mL/min/1.73 m²) 0 30 60 90 120	Results*	Quality
Teschan,[450] 1979	EEG slowing	177	�♦	S_{Cr} 2–29 mg/dL	⬇	O
Teschan,[450] 1979	Cognition/memory test score	177	♦♦	S_{Cr} 2–29 mg/dL	⬆	O
Goel,[447] 1978	Peripheral neuropathy symptoms	40	♦♦	——+——	⇔	O
Knoll,[449] 1980	Reflex response latency	210	♦	S_{Cr} 1–12 mg/dL	⬆	O
Di Paolo,[445] 1982	Abnormal EMG	129	♦♦	—+—	100%	O

* ⬆ = higher GFR associated with higher level of indicated neurological measurement (statistically significant);
⇔ = GFR *not* associated with indicated cognitive measurement;
⬇ = higher GFR associated with lower level of indicated neurological measurement (statistically significant).

Abbreviations: EEG, electroencephalogram; EMG, electromyography

Nerve conduction velocity (NCV) is slower in patients with decreased GFR (Table 99) (C). There were 6 studies relating NCV to level of kidney function. The studies had sample sizes ranging from 40 to 210 subjects, with 29 to 72 patients with decreased kidney function not yet on dialysis. All but one[450] of the studies showed that NCV was decreased below normal levels among patients with decreased kidney function. In three of the studies, the correlation between kidney function level and NCV was significant; in the other two correlation was suggested but lacked statistical significance. A threshold level of kidney function for abnormal motor NCV was only mentioned or deducible from three studies. Below a GFR of 8 to 13[446,448] or serum creatinine above 7 to 8 mg/dL,[445] 50% or more patients with decreased kidney function had abnormal NCV. The threshold level at which 50% or more of patients have abnormal sensory NCV velocity was evaluated in only two studies and noted to be approximately 8 to 20 mL/min.[445,448]

These data generally confirm that NCV is decreased among patients with decreased kidney function. The reviewed studies do suggest a correlation between level of GFR and NCV, but they do not offer sufficient information to convincingly demonstrate a threshold level of GFR at which NCV becomes abnormal.

Memory and cognition are impaired in patients with decreased GFR (Table 100) (C). Only one study was found that evaluated memory and cognition among patients with decreased kidney function prior to the availability of erythropoietin.[450] In this study of 177 subjects, of whom 72 had decreased kidney function not yet on dialysis, several cognitive functions were assessed, including sustained attention, selective attention, speed of decision-making, short-term memory, and mental manipulation of symbols. Each of these test measures was significantly lower among patients with decreased kidney function, correlated with level of dysfunction, and was improved to varying degrees among patients on dialysis and to a greater degree among patients with a kidney transplant.

Table 101. Autonomic Function and Kidney Function

Author, Year	Measurement	No. of Subjects	Applicability	GFR Range (mL/min/1.73 m²) 0 30 60 90 120	Results*	Quality
Campese,[443] 1981[a]	HR responses	112	↟↟	▬————┼	↑	●
Weinrauch,[442] 1995	HR responses	42	↟↟	———┼———	⇔	●
Sterner,[444] 1997	HR responses	123	↟↟	———	⇧	○
Campese,[443] 1981[a]	BP responses	112	↟↟	▬————┼	↑	●
Weinrauch,[442] 1995	Day:night BPI	42	↟↟	——┼——	⇔	●

Bold horizontal lines divide studies by measurement used.

* ↟ = higher GFR associated with higher level of indicated autonomic function measurement (statistically significant);
⇧ = higher GFR associated with higher level of indicated autonomic function measurement;
⇔ = GFR *not* associated with level of indicated autonomic function measurement.

[a] Study included two separate populations.

Abbreviations: BP, blood pressure; BPI, blood pressure index; HR, heart rate

***Autonomic function is impaired in patients with decreased GFR (Table 101)
(C).*** Only three studies were found that objectively evaluated autonomic function among patients with kidney disease. These studies had between 42 and 123 subjects and between 21 and 67 patients with decreased kidney function not yet on dialysis. Each of these studies noted that autonomic function was impaired in more than 50% of patients with chronic kidney disease; however, only one of them found an association between level of kidney function and measures of autonomic nerve function.

The results of these studies cannot be extrapolated with confidence to the general population of patients with chronic kidney disease, as two were limited to patients with diabetes[442,444] and thus confounded by the neuropathy ascribable to diabetes, and the third only had patients with very decreased kidney function (GFR <8 mL/min) or on dialysis.[443]

Symptoms of neuropathy, including sleep disturbances, are increased in patients with decreased GFR (C). Symptoms or clinical signs of peripheral neuropathy were evaluated or mentioned in four of the six studies of peripheral neuropathy reviewed for this guideline.[445-448,450] The method of ascertaining the presence of symptoms or clinical findings was mentioned in only one of these studies[447] as a "detailed neurological examination was carried out to find. . . evidence of clinically manifest neuropathy." The prevalence of symptoms or clinical findings ranged from 0% to 52%. Individuals with clinical symptoms had a greater reduction in NCV as compared to those without such symptoms in 2 studies,[446,448] whereas there was no significant correlation between NCV and symptoms in one of the studies.[447] None of the studies commented on the correlation between symptoms and level of kidney function; however, from a single study it was estimated that patients with symptoms had a lower mean level of kidney function (GFR = 6 mL/min) than patients without symptoms (GFR = 16 mL/min).[446]

The reviewed studies do not offer sufficient information to convincingly delineate a progressive increase in prevalence of symptoms with decreasing GFR.

LIMITATIONS

Several of the reviewed articles included patients who had started dialysis or received a kidney transplant; information on these patients was used for background information and comparison. More articles than were reviewed were found with the literature search, but were not exhaustively reviewed as preliminary review suggested the lack of or inability to extract the necessary information. This may have led to the omission of some articles that may have provided further information.

These guidelines are limited by the inability to provide a definitive quantitative or semi-quantitative assessment of the relationship between level of kidney function and markers of neuropathy. This is in part due to the dearth of studies, the use of different measures of kidney function, the limited presentation of methods, and the failure to present adequate correlation data. In particular, there was extremely limited information on cognitive function and symptoms of neuropathy.

Lastly, many of the studies involved only a limited number of patients with mildly to moderately decreased kidney function, and two of the studies were limited to diabetics, confounding the results with the presence of diabetic neuropathy.

CLINICAL APPLICATIONS

The data reviewed here suggest that symptoms of neuropathy begin to occur at very low levels of GFR. The inconclusive evidence presented herein has the implications that:

- Indices of neuropathy are not useful to monitor progression of chronic kidney disease.
- Symptoms or indices of neuropathy are evidence of kidney failure, and may be useful to determine need to initiate dialysis.
- There are currently no convincing data to suggest that there is benefit to obtaining nerve conduction studies or nerve biopsies in asymptomatic patients.

The applications suggested above are based on review of the available literature presented herein and opinion based on others' reviews of the problem. Treatment and assessment recommendations are beyond the scope of this guideline.

IMPLEMENTATION ISSUES

The only implementation issue arising from this guideline is to provide education regarding the prevalence of neuropathy, and the need to elicit symptoms and signs of this condition during routine office visits.

RESEARCH RECOMMENDATIONS

Much of the available information regarding neuropathy is derived from studies of patients with kidney failure. More information on neuropathy among patients with chronic kidney disease with earlier stages of chronic kidney disease may provide other means to follow progression of chronic kidney disease. In addition, if neuropathy were to be more carefully described and noted to have a high prevalence in earlier stages of chronic kidney disease and a relationship to kidney function, treatments to delay its progression could be considered.

The relationship between subjective and objective measures of neuropathy, and levels of kidney function, should be more accurately characterized. In addition, the relationship between neuropathy and kidney function should be separately studied among patients with additional risks of neuropathy, such as diabetics and patients with amyloidosis.

GUIDELINE 12. ASSOCIATION OF LEVEL OF GFR WITH INDICES OF FUNCTIONING AND WELL-BEING

Impairments in domains of functioning and well-being develop during the course of chronic kidney disease and are associated with adverse outcomes. Impaired functioning and well-being may be related to sociodemographic factors, conditions causing chronic kidney disease, complications of kidney disease, or possibly directly due to reduced GFR.

- Patients with GFR <60 mL/min/1.73 m^2 should undergo regular assessment for impairment of functioning and well-being:
- To establish a baseline and monitor changes in functioning and well-being over time
- To assess the effect of interventions on functioning and well-being.

BACKGROUND

When there is no cure for a chronic illness, an essential healthcare goal must be to maximize quality of life. The purpose of this guideline is to identify stages and complications of kidney disease that place adult patients at greater risk for reduced quality of life. This guideline is not intended to cover all the quality of life concerns that apply to children and adolescents, nor is it intended to recommend interventions to improve quality of life in any age group. For the purpose of this guideline, concepts that embody pertinent components of quality of life will be referred to as "functioning and well-being." Recent studies show that the functioning and well-being of individuals with chronic kidney disease is related to such factors as: late referral and inadequate pre-dialysis care[80]; symptoms; effects of illness on physical, psychological, and social functioning; and satisfaction with health and care.[452] Complications of chronic kidney disease, such as anemia, malnutrition, bone disease, neuropathy, and comorbid conditions, such as diabetes and cardiovascular disease, can negatively affect functioning and well-being. To improve functioning and well-being, patients must be referred sooner and complications and comorbid conditions must be managed appropriately.

This guideline describes the association between the level of kidney function and domains of functioning and well-being in patients with chronic kidney disease. One must analyze the full continuum of stages of chronic kidney disease to understand the risks for compromised functioning and well-being. Armed with this knowledge, clinicians can more quickly identify stages of chronic kidney disease at which deficits are likely to occur and develop strategies to treat higher risk patients and ameliorate or eliminate deficits before they become severe or irreversible.

RATIONALE

Definitions

Health status outcomes experts recommend defining "quality of life" to include variables that health professionals can identify, quantify, and modify: (1) health status (signs and symptoms, lab values, death); (2) functional status (physical, mental, social, and role functioning), and (3) well-being (energy/fatigue, pain, health perceptions, and satisfaction).[453,454] Self-report is preferable to staff report since outcomes are dependent on the lived experience and expectations of the individual patient.

Difficulties in measuring this poorly understood concept have led researchers in the articles reviewed to study several variables using different methods and instruments (Table 102). Use of different instruments has impeded comparing findings, interpreting results, and drawing conclusions.

Strength of Evidence

Indices of functioning and well-being are impaired in chronic kidney disease (R). Dialysis patients report significantly more bodily pain, lower vitality, poorer general health, greater physical, mental, and social dysfunction, and greater limitations in their ability to work and participate in activities due to their health and emotions than the US reference norm. At least 25% are depressed.[455] Dialysis patients' exercise capacity is

Table 102. Domains of Functioning and Well-being Measured by Specific Instruments

Instrument	Symptoms & Health Perception	Physical Function	Mental Health Function	Employment	Social Function
Beck Depression Inventory (BDI)	Depressive	No	Yes	Yes	Yes
Center for Epidemiological Studies-Depression (CES-D)	Yes	No	Yes	No	No
Cognitive Depression Index (CDI)	No	No	Yes	No	No
ESRD Severity Coefficient	Yes	No	No	No	No
EuroQol	Yes	Yes	Yes	Yes	Yes
Health Index (HI)	Yes	Yes	Yes	No	No
Illness Effects Questionnaire (IEQ)	Yes	No	Yes	No	Yes
Karnofsky Performance Scale (KPS)	Yes	Yes	No	Yes	Yes
MOS Short Form 36 (SF-36)	Yes	Yes	Yes	Yes	Yes
Multidimensional Scale of Perceived Social Support (MSP)	No	No	No	No	Yes
NHANES Adult Questionnaire (NHANES)	Yes	Yes	Yes	Yes	Yes
Quality of Well-being Scale (QWB)	Yes	Yes	Yes	Yes	Yes
Rand Health Insurance Experiment instrument (RHIE)	No	Yes	Yes	Yes	Yes
Satisfaction with Life Scale (SLS)	No	No	Yes	No	No
Sense of Coherence Scale	No	No	Yes	No	No
Sickness Impact Profile (SIP)	Yes	Yes	Yes	Yes	Yes
Social Adjustment Scale Self-Report (SAS-SR)	No	Yes	Yes	Yes	Yes
State Trait Anxiety Inventory (STAI)	Anxiety	No	Yes	No	No
Symptom Checklist-90R (SCL-90R)	Yes	No	Yes	No	No

significantly worse than that of healthy controls.[456] Kidney failure negatively affects sense of control and health outlook in those on dialysis.[457] About 39% of those who worked full or part-time 6 months before dialysis do not continue working when they start dialysis.[4] Elderly people on dialysis engage in few previously enjoyed activities outside their homes and many leave home only for dialysis because of weakness.[458]

Impairment in indices of functioning and well-being are associated with worse outcomes in chronic kidney disease (R). Impaired functioning and well-being in dialysis patients is linked to increased risk of death and hospitalization while improvement in scores has been associated with better outcomes. Patients with SF-36 Physical Component Summary (PCS) scores <34.6 had a 2.03 relative risk of dying and a 1.67 relative risk of being hospitalized. Each 5-point improvement in PCS scores was associated with 10% longer survival and 6% fewer hospital days. On the SF-36, a Mental Health scale score ≤52 and a Mental Component Summary (MCS) score ≤42 indicate depression. Each 5-point improvement in the MCS score is associated with 2% fewer hospital days.[455]

Impairment in functioning and well-being are associated with sociodemographic characteristics (R). Low income and low education were associated with greater impairments in functioning and well-being in patients with chronic kidney disease.[459]

Impairment in functioning and well-being may be due to conditions that cause chronic kidney disease (such as diabetes or hypertension) or complications of decreased GFR (such as anemia, malnutrition, bone disease, or neuropathy) (R). Hypertension, diabetes with angina, prior cardiac infarction,[460] osteoporosis, bone fractures,[461] and malnutrition[462] have been shown to impair functioning and well-being in those with no known kidney disease. Among veterans with diabetes, neuropathy and kidney disease have been associated with the greatest decrease in functioning and well-being.[463]

Anemia has been linked to poor functioning and well-being in patients with severely decreased GFR and dialysis patients, and improving anemia with erythropoietin has been linked to improvement in functioning and well-being.[284,464-468]

Indices of functioning and well-being are related to the level of GFR; below a GFR of approximately 60 mL/min/1.73 m², there is a higher prevalence of impairments in indices of functioning and well-being (S, C). Data from cross-sectional studies and baseline data from longitudinal studies were reviewed to assess the relationship between level of kidney function and level of functioning and well-being. Populations studied include those with decreased kidney function, including those with functioning transplants, and dialysis patients when compared with healthy subjects or kidney transplant recipients. While much of the data on functioning and well-being related to outcomes have been obtained in dialysis patients, there is convincing evidence that abnormalities in functioning and well-being begin earlier in chronic kidney disease and may well be related to declining GFR.

Table 103. Symptoms & Health Perception and Kidney Function

Author, Year	Instrument/ QoL Parameters	No. of Subjects	Applic-ability	GFR Range (mL/min/1.73 m^2)	Results*	Quality
Rocco,[469] 1997	SCL-90R	1,284	♯♯		↑	●
	MDRD Symptom Form: Symptoms					
Korevaar,[470] 2000	SF-36: Pain, General health	301	♯♯		↑	●
	EuroQol: Pain, Discomfort, Health valuation					
Shidler,[471] 1998	IEQ: Perception of illness	50	♯♯		⇔	●
Klang,[472] 1996	HI: General health, Fatigue, Energy, Sleep problems, Mobility, Mood, Loneliness	38	♯♯		↑	●
Harris,[459] 1993	SIP: Perceived illness	360	♯♯		⇔	○
Fujisawa,[473] 2000	SF-36: General health	231	♯♯	S$_{Cr}$ 1.2 ±0.5 mg/dL	↑	○
Griep,[474] 1997	Odor perception	202	♯♯		↑	○
Sacks,[475] 1990	IEQ: Perception of illness	73	♯♯	S$_{Cr}$ 5.4 ±3.4 mg/dL	↑	○
Manninen,[476] 1991	Satisfaction with health	226	♯	ND	↑ (transplant vs. dialysis)	○

* ↑ = higher GFR associated with better functioning and well-being (statistically significant);
 ⇔ = GFR *not* associated with level of functioning and well-being.

Abbreviations: SCL-90R, Symptom Checklist-90R; SF-36, Medical Outcomes Study Short Form 36; IEQ, Illness Effects Questionnaire; HI, Health Index; SIP, Sickness Impact Profile

Symptoms (Table 103 and Fig 44). Reduced kidney function is associated with increasing symptoms such as tiring easily, weakness, low energy, cramps, bruising, bad tasting mouth, hiccoughs, and poor odor perception. This is true in patients with native kidney disease and those with kidney transplants. Diabetic dialysis and transplant patients are more likely to report poor health than dialysis or transplant patients who do not have diabetes.

Physical Functioning (Table 104 and Figs 45 and 46). Decreased GFR in NHANES III subjects is associated with impaired walking and lifting ability. In transplant recipients, reduced kidney function is also associated with poorer physical function scores. In one study of patients with decreased GFR, impairment in physical function was not significantly related to the level of kidney function, but physical impairment was 8 times worse than in the general population. Dialysis patients report greater physical dysfunction than transplant recipients and diabetic dialysis and transplant patients are more likely to report physical dysfunction than those patients who do not have diabetes.

Depression (Table 105). Reduced kidney function is associated with poorer psychosocial functioning, higher anxiety, higher distress, decreased sense of well-being, higher depression, and negative health perception. Depressed patients are more likely to report poor life satisfaction, irrespective of kidney function. Dialysis patients report significantly lower "happiness with personal life" and lower psychosocial functioning than transplant

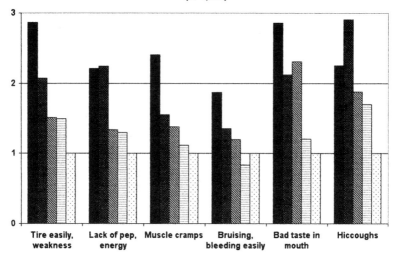

(N=1,284)

| | GFR 10-20 | GFR 20-30 | GFR 30-40 | GFR 40-50 | GFR 50-60 |

Fig 44. Kidney function (GFR) and odds of having symptoms affecting quality of life and well-being in the MDRD Study, controlled for age, gender, race, kidney diagnosis, education, income, and smoking status. Reprinted with permission.[469]

Table 104. Physical Functioning and Kidney Function

Author, Year	Instrument/ QoL Parameters	No. of Subjects	Applic- ability	GFR Range (mL/min/1.73 m²)	Results*	Quality
Rocco,[469] 1997	QWB: Physical activity, Mobility	900	👫	0 — 30 — 60 — 90 — 120	⬆	●
Korevaar,[470] 2000	SF-36: Physical function EuroQol: Mobility, Self-care	301	👫	⊢	⬆	●
Shidler,[471] 1998	KPS: Physical function	50	👫	—⊢—	⬆	●
Klang,[472] 1996	SIP: Physical dimension	38	👫	⊢	⬆	●
Harris,[459] 1993	SIP: Physical dimension	360	👫	⊢—	⬄	○
Fujisawa,[473] 2000	SF-36: Physical function	231	👫	S₀ 1.2 ±0.5 mg/dL	⬆	◑
Churchill,[477] 1987	RHIE: Physical function	171	👫	ND	⬆ (transplant vs. dialysis)	○
Manninen,[476] 1991	SIP: Physical dimension, Weight carrying	226	👤	ND	⬆ (transplant vs. dialysis)	○

* ⬆ = higher GFR associated with better physical functioning (statistically significant);
⬄ = GFR *not* associated with level of physical functioning.

Abbreviations: QWB, Quality of Well-Being Scale; SF-36, Medical Outcomes Study Short Form 36; KPS, Karnofsky Performance Scale; SIP, Sickness Impact Profile; RHIE, Rand Health Insurance Experiment instrument

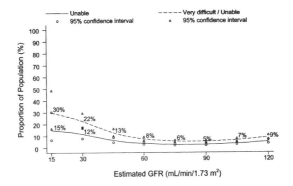

Fig 45. Adjusted prevalence of physical inability to walk by GFR category (NHANES III). Predicted prevalence of physical inability to walk one-quarter mile among adult participants age 20 years and older in NHANES III, 1988 to 1994. Values are adjusted to age 60 years using a polynomial regression. 95% confidence intervals are shown at selected levels of estimated GFR.

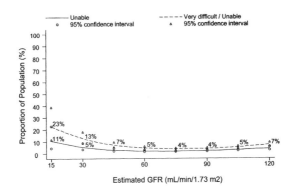

Fig 46. Adjusted prevalence of physical inability to lift by GFR category (NHANES III). Predicted prevalence of physical inability to lift 10 pounds among adult participants age 20 years and older in NHANES III, 1988 to 1994. Values are adjusted to age 60 years using a polynomial regression. 95% confidence intervals are shown at selected levels of estimated GFR.

Table 105. Mental Health, Depression & Well-Being and Kidney Function

Author, Year	Instrument/ QoL Parameters	No. of Subjects	Applic- ability	GFR Range (mL/min/1.73 m²)	Results*	Quality
Rocco,[469] 1997	SCL-90R: Psychological distress	936	♀♀	(GFR plot)	⬆	●
Korevaar,[470] 2000	SF-36: Mental health EuroQol: Anxiety/Depression	301	♀♀	(GFR plot)	⬆	●
Shidler,[471] 1998	BDI: Depression CDI: Depression SWLS: Life satisfaction	50	♀♀	(GFR plot)	⬌	●
Klang,[472] 1996	SIP: Psychosocial dimension STAI: Anxiety	38	♀♀	(GFR plot)	⬆	●
Harris,[459] 1993	SIP: Psychosocial subscale, Mental & emotional dysfunction	360	♀♀	(GFR plot)	⬌	○
Fujisawa,[473] 2000	SF-36: Mental health, Role emotional	231	♀♀	S_{cr} 1.2 ±0.5 mg/dL	⬌	○
Sacks,[475] 1990	BDI: Depression CDI: Depression	73	♀♀	S_{cr} 5.4 ±3.4 mg/dL	⬆	○
Black,[478] 1998	CES-D: Depression	2,823 (19[a])	♀♀	ND	⬆	○
Churchill,[477] 1987	RHIE: Happiness with personal life	171	♀♀	ND	⬆ (transplant vs. dialysis)	○
Manninen,[476] 1991	SIP: Psychosocial dimension, Emotional behavior	226	♀	ND	⬆ (transplant vs. dialysis)	○

* ⬆ = higher GFR associated with better functioning and well-being (statistically significant);
⬌ = GFR *not* associated with functioning and well-being.

[a] Only 19 subjects had self-reported chronic kidney disease.

Abbreviations: SCL-90R, Symptom Checklist-90R; SF-36, Medical Outcomes Study Short Form 36; BDI, Beck Depression Inventory; CDI, Cognitive Depression Index; SWLS, Satisfaction with Life Scale; SIP, Sickness Impact Profile; CES-D, Center for Epidemiological Studies Depression Scale; RHIE, Rand Health Insurance Experiment instrument

recipients. In elderly Mexican Americans, kidney disease has been found to be predictive of depressive symptoms.

Employment and Usual Activities (Table 106). Reduced kidney function is associated with lower employment. In those with chronic kidney disease and GFR <50, the presence of physical dysfunction is significantly related to unemployment, but the association to kidney function is not significant since physical dysfunction is not uniformly present. Full-time employment is higher for those with decreased GFR (mean serum creatinine 5.4 mg/dL, 69%) compared with those with kidney failure (mean serum creatinine 13.7 mg/dL, 12%). More dialysis patients report their health limits work and other activities than those with functioning transplants. Dialysis and transplant patients with diabetes are more likely to report difficulty working than dialysis and transplant patients without diabetes.

Social Functioning (Table 107). Reduced kidney function is associated with reduced social activity, social functioning, and social interaction. Dialysis patients report fewer neighborhood acquaintances, social contacts, and worse social well-being than healthy individuals while transplant recipients report higher social function and social

Table 106. Employment, Home Management, Recreation & Pastimes and Kidney Function

Author, Year	Instrument/ QoL Parameters	No. of Subjects	Applic-ability	GFR Range (mL/min/1.73 m^2)	Results*	Quality
Korevaar,[470] 2000	SF-36: Role physical, Role emotional EuroQol: Usual activities	301	♛♛	+ (0–30)	⬆	●
Shidler,[471] 1998	KPS: Functional status	50	♛♛	(30–90)	⬆	●
Klang,[472] 1996	SIP: Work, Home management	38	♛♛	+ (0–30)	⬆	◗
Harris,[469] 1993	SIP: Unemployment	360	♛♛	(0–60)	⇔	◯
Fujisawa,[473] 2000	SF-36: Role physical, Role emotional	231	♛♛	S_{cr} 1.2 ±0.5 mg/dL	⇔	◯
Sacks,[475] 1990	SAS-SR: Role disruption, Employment	73	♛♛	S_{cr} 5.4 ±3.4 mg/dL	⬆	◯
Churchill,[477] 1987	RHIE: Heavy work	171	♛♛	ND	⬆ (transplant vs. dialysis)	◯
Manninen,[476] 1991	SIP: Work ability, Seeing to read, inspect	226	♛	ND	⬆ (transplant vs. dialysis)	◯

* ⬆ = higher GFR associated with better functioning and well-being (statistically significant);
⇔ = GFR *not* associated with functioning and well-being.

Abbreviations: SF-36, Medical Outcomes Study Short Form 36; KPS, Karofsky Performance Scale; SIP, Sickness Impact Profile; SAS-SR, Social Adjustment Scale Self-Report; RHIE, Rand Health Insurance Experiment instrument

Table 107. Social Functioning and Kidney Function

Author, Year	Instrument/ QoL Parameters	No. of Subjects	Applic-ability	GFR Range (mL/min/1.73 m^2)	Results*	Quality
Rocco,[469] 1997	QWB: Social activity	900	♛♛	(30–60)	⬆	●
Korevaar,[470] 2000	SF-36: Social function EuroQol: Usual activities	301	♛♛	+ (0–30)	⬆	●
Shidler,[471] 1998	MSP: Social support	50	♛♛	(30–90)	⇔	●
Klang,[472] 1996	SIP: Social interaction	38	♛♛	+ (0–30)	⬆	●
Fujisawa,[473] 2000	SF-36: Social functioning, Role emotional	231	♛♛	S_{cr} 1.2 ±0.5 mg/dL	⬆	◯
Sacks,[475] 1990	SAS-SR: Social & leisure activities	73	♛♛	S_{cr} 5.4 ±3.4 mg/dL	⇔	◯
Churchill,[477] 1987	RHIE: Social contacts, Group participation, Social well being, Neighborhood acquaintance	171	♛♛	ND	⬆ (transplant vs. dialysis)	◯
Manninen,[476] 1991	SIP: Work ability, Seeing to read, inspect	226	♛	ND	⬆ (transplant vs. dialysis)	◯

* ⬆ = higher GFR associated with better functioning and well-being (statistically significant);
⇔ = GFR *not* associated with level of functioning and well-being.

Abbreviations: QWB, Quality of Well-Being Scale; SF-36, Medical Outcomes Study Short Form 36; MSP, Multidimensional Scale of Perceived Social Support; SIP, Sickness Impact Profile; SAS-SR, Social Adjustment Scale Self-Report; RHIE, Rand Health Insurance Experiment instrument interaction than those on dialysis. Diabetics on dialysis or with transplants are more likely to report problems with social interaction than nondiabetic patients. Level of perceived social support in chronic kidney disease is not associated with the level of kidney function.

LIMITATIONS AND EXCEPTIONS

Most study samples were not randomly selected. Medication usage was not reported even if medications (eg, anti-depressants) could affect outcomes. Seven of 12 studies did not provide full information on patient demographics. Three studies reported differences between groups of very unequal sizes and one reported percentages but did not report whether observed differences were statistically significant.

Historically, there has been no "gold standard" definition for quality of life or functioning and well-being. Researchers have studied multiple variables using standardized and non-standardized instruments. Thus, results are not comparable to one another.[479] With lack of instrument comparability, findings appear to be conflicting. Many studies have examined the relationships between functioning and well-being and treatment modalities after the onset of kidney failure. Few studies of persons with decreased GFR have examined the relationship between level of GFR and functioning and well-being. Three of the studies of individuals with decreased GFR had such severely restrictive inclusion criteria for level of kidney function that functioning and well-being deficits were already present. Of the 12 studies reported, 3 reported no measure of kidney function and 2 reported only serum creatinine, a less reliable measure of kidney function than GFR or creatinine clearance. Most of the studies reported only mean values for kidney function. Only the MDRD Study and NHANES III examined functioning and well-being at a wide range of levels of kidney function. Precise statements about how early deficits in domains of functioning and well-being occur as kidney function deteriorates require this essential data. Finally, since anemia has been shown to limit functioning and well-being, inadequate anemia management in studies conducted prior to the widespread use of erythropoietin could have affected outcomes. Therefore, recent functioning and well-being outcomes may not be comparable to outcomes reported in studies prior to 1989 even if the same instruments were used.

CLINICAL APPLICATIONS

The conferees at the Institute of Medicine (IOM) Workshop "Assessing Health and Quality of Life Outcomes in Dialysis" recommended that ESRD providers:

- Assess functioning and well-being in kidney disease using standardized survey instruments that are valid, reliable, responsive to changes, easily interpretable, and easy to use, such as the Dartmouth COOP Charts, the Duke Health Profile/Duke Severity of Illness (DUKE/DUSOI), Medical Outcomes Study 36-Item Short Form (SF-36), or the Kidney Disease Quality of Life (KDQOL).
- Assess patient functioning and well-being early in chronic kidney disease to establish a baseline, to maintain or improve health status, and to manage the disease

continuum by linking clinical and health outcomes with functional status outcomes.[454]

Data reported in the reviewed studies suggest that decreased kidney function affects patients' functioning and well-being through several dimensions. Deficits in functioning are reported by patients even at early stages of chronic kidney disease, and persist even after transplantation. The implications of these findings are:

- Clinicians should assess functional status and well-being as soon as possible after referral in order to obtain baseline data and enable early intervention to improve functioning and well-being.

- Clinicians should regularly reassess functioning and well-being to ascertain the patient's current status and the effectiveness of interventions to improve functioning and well-being. Reassessment is needed when a patient reports increased frequency or severity of symptoms, has a new complication of kidney disease, has an access for dialysis placed, starts dialysis, changes modality, or participates in a clinical or rehabilitation intervention (eg, counseling, peer support, education, physical therapy or independent exercise, or vocational rehabilitation).

These recommendations are based on the opinions expressed by the authors of most of the studies reviewed for this guideline, as well as those of recognized experts in functioning and health status outcomes measurement who attended the IOM Workshop.

IMPLEMENTATION ISSUES

Researchers may use any of a wide array of instruments to measure functioning and well-being throughout the course of chronic kidney disease. However, clinicians want to know what instrument to use, when to use it, and who should administer, score, and analyze the data. In general, it is practical for clinicians to use only a few instruments and to gain experience with them. Based on the literature reviewed for this guideline, it appears that any clinician treating patients with decreased GFR can administer the Dartmouth COOP Charts, DUKE Health Profiles, Kidney Disease Quality of Life, or SF-36 that have been used with dialysis and transplant patients (Table 108). In the clinical setting ease of use is essential. These surveys are recommended because each has an instructional manual and patients can complete them independently or with limited assistance. To assess specific limitations in functioning and well-being, clinicians can supplement these general instruments with more specific instruments including performance-based tests of physical functioning.

RESEARCH RECOMMENDATIONS

Research in dialysis patients has shown that functioning and well-being pre-treatment may predict post-treatment outcomes. Therefore, large-scale longitudinal studies are needed to evaluate the relationship between GFR and all domains of functional status and well-being throughout the course of progression of kidney disease. More research should be undertaken using the recommended standardized instruments and their outcomes compared. Whenever specific medications could affect outcomes, usage should

Table 108. Functioning and Well-Being Measures

Instrument (Applications)	Specifications	Ordering Information
Dartmouth COOP Functional Health Assessment Charts (Generic for youth, adult and elderly; one for dialysis)	Time: <10 min (youth & adult), 20 min. (elderly & dialysis) Domains: physical, emotional, daily activities, social activities, social support, pain, overall health quality of life, financial, diseases, symptoms/problems, burden of dialysis Cost: depends on choice of scoring Scoring/Analysis: several options Languages: unknown Version for Visually Impaired: large print, pictures	FNX Corporation 1 Dorset Lane Lebanon, NH 03766 (800) 369-6669 Attn: John Wasson, MD Web: *http://home.fnxnet.com*
Duke Health Profile (DUKE) (Generic)	Time: 5 min. Domains (generic): physical health, mental health, social health, general health, perceived health, self-esteem, anxiety, depression, anxiety-depression, pain, disability Cost: free for non-commercial use; manual $30 Automated version: Duke University Medical Center Languages: 19 Scoring/analysis: Duke University Medical Center Version for Visually Impaired: no	George R. Parkerson, Jr., MD Department of Community & Family Medicine Duke University Medical Center Box 3886 Durham NC 27710 (919) 681-6560 Email: *george.parkerson@duke.edu* Web: *www.qlmed.org/duke/*
Kidney Disease Quality of Life (KDQOL™) (Kidney-specific)	Time: 30 min. (long form) 16 min. (short form) Domains (generic): physical functioning, role limitations-physical, bodily pain, general health, vitality, social functioning, role limitations-emotional, mental health (ESRD/dialysis): symptoms/problems, effects of kidney disease on daily life, burden of kidney disease, cognitive function, work status, sexual function, quality of social interaction, sleep Cost: free single, can make unlimited copies Automated version: HDO at (770) 889-5558 Scoring/analysis: HDO at (770) 889-5558 Languages: multiple Version for visually impaired: large print	RAND Corp. 1333 H St., NW Washington, DC 20004-4792 Attn: Caren Kamberg E-mail: *caren_kamberg@rand.org* Web: *www.qlmed.org/KDQOL/index.html*
Medical Outcomes Study 36 Item Short Form (SF-36[a]) (Generic)	Time: 12-15 min. Domains (generic): physical functioning, role limitations-physical, bodily pain, general health, vitality, social functioning, role limitations-emotional, mental health Cost: free, copy with permission Scoring/analysis: Quality Metric, Inc. (401) 334-8800 Languages: multiple Version for visually impaired: unknown	QualityMetric Inc. 640 George Washington Hwy Ste 201 Lincoln, RI 02865 (888) 947-9800) Email: info@qmetric.com Web: *www.qlmed.org/SF-36/index.html* or *http://sf-36.com/*

[a] Shorter versions include the SF-12 and SF-8.

be assessed. Because conditions such as anemia, bone disease, cardiovascular, disease, and diabetes can affect functioning and well-being, researchers need to study whether appropriate management of these conditions improves functioning and well-being. Finally, researchers need to examine the effectiveness of rehabilitation interventions in earlier stages of chronic kidney disease. Doing so could provide further scientific evidence for the relationship of kidney function and treatment on patients' risk of dysfunction, hospitalization, and death and increase understanding of what interventions improve functioning and well-being and reduce the burden of chronic kidney disease on the patient, his or her family, and society.

PART 7. STRATIFICATION OF RISK FOR PROGRESSION OF KIDNEY DISEASE AND DEVELOPMENT OF CARDIOVASCULAR DISEASE

The major outcomes of chronic kidney disease are loss of kidney function, leading to complications and kidney failure, and development of cardiovascular disease. The goals of Part 7 are to define risk factors for progression of chronic kidney disease and to determine whether chronic kidney disease is a risk factor for cardiovascular disease. Because of the well-known association of cardiovascular disease and diabetes, the Work Group considered patients with chronic kidney disease due to diabetes separately from patients with chronic kidney disease due to other causes. As described in Appendix 1, Table 153, the Work Group searched primarily for longitudinal studies that related risk factors to loss of kidney function (Guideline 13) and that related proteinuria and decreased GFR to cardiovascular disease (Guidelines 14 and 15). It was beyond the scope of the Work Group to undertake a systematic review of studies of treatment. However, existing guidelines and recommendations were reviewed, as were selected studies, to provide further evidence of efficacy of treatment.

GUIDELINE 13. FACTORS ASSOCIATED WITH LOSS OF KIDNEY FUNCTION IN CHRONIC KIDNEY DISEASE

The level of kidney function tends to decline progressively over time in most patients with chronic kidney diseases.
- The rate of GFR decline should be assessed in patients with chronic kidney disease to:
  - Predict the interval until the onset of kidney failure;
  - Assess the effect of interventions to slow the GFR decline.
- Among patients with chronic kidney disease, the rate of GFR decline should be estimated by:
  - Computing the GFR decline from past and ongoing measurements of serum creatinine;
  - Ascertaining risk factors for faster versus slower GFR decline, including type (diagnosis) of kidney disease, nonmodifiable and modifiable factors.
- Interventions to slow the progression of kidney disease should be considered in all patients with chronic kidney disease.
  - Interventions that have been proven to be effective include:
    (1) Strict glucose control in diabetes;
    (2) Strict blood pressure control;
    (3) Angiotensin-converting enzyme inhibition or angiotensin-2 receptor blockade.
  - Interventions that have been studied, but the results are inconclusive, include:
    (1) Dietary protein restriction;

(2) Lipid-lowering therapy;

  (3) Partial correction of anemia.

- Attempts should be made to prevent and correct acute decline in GFR. Frequent causes of acute decline in GFR include:
  - Volume depletion;
  - Intravenous radiographic contrast;
  - Selected antimicrobial agents (for example, aminoglycosides and amphotericin B);
  - Nonsteroidal anti-inflammatory agents, including cyclo-oxygenase type 2 inhibitors;
  - Angiotensin-converting enzyme inhibition and angiotensin-2 receptor blockers;
  - Cyclosporine and tacrolimus;
  - Obstruction of the urinary tract.
- Measurements of serum creatinine for estimation of GFR should be obtained at least yearly in patients with chronic kidney disease, and more often in patients with:
  - GFR <60 mL/min/1.73 m^2;
  - Fast GFR decline in the past (≥4 mL/min/1.73 m^2 per year);
  - Risk factors for faster progression;
  - Ongoing treatment to slow progression;
  - Exposure to risk factors for acute GFR decline.

BACKGROUND

Kidney function progressively declines in most patients with chronic kidney disease after sufficient damage has occurred to lower the glomerular filtration rate (GFR).[480] This progressive decline has been attributed to a variety of mechanisms, including failure to resolve the initial injury and onset of self-perpetuating injury, ultimately leading to the typical pathologic features of the "end-stage" kidney and kidney failure. Although the factors responsible for progression of kidney disease are not known in each case, a variety of factors have been associated with more rapid progression and some therapies have been proven to slow the progression of disease.

The intent of this guideline is to examine the literature to determine factors associated with more rapid loss of kidney function in chronic kidney disease. Evidence primarily from longitudinal studies was used to formulate this guideline. Although some authors have performed a meta-analysis of studies, a quantitative data synthesis was not performed for this Guideline.

RATIONALE

Definitions of Outcome Measures

Progression of kidney disease is defined as either (1) decline in the level of kidney function, estimated by measuring GFR, creatinine clearance or serum creatinine, in a patient who has been followed longitudinally with reliable (and comparable) assays of kidney function, or (2) onset of kidney failure, defined by initiation of kidney replacement therapy, either for symptoms or complications of decreased kidney function. Kidney replacement therapy includes hemodialysis, peritoneal dialysis or kidney transplantation. For consideration of therapy for diabetic kidney disease, development and worsening of proteinuria was also included in the definition of progression of kidney disease.

Strength of Evidence

The natural history of most chronic kidney diseases is that GFR declines progressively over time (Fig 47) (R). Data from the MDRD Study during an average 2-year follow-up show that the average rate of decline in GFR was approximately 4 mL/min/year and was not related to the baseline level of GFR. Approximately 85% of patients had GFR decline during follow-up. The remaining patients experienced improvement or stabilization of GFR.[480]

Other studies have shown that certain types of kidney disease may undergo complete remission in a substantial number of patients. For example, up to 35% of patients with idiopathic membranous nephropathy[481] and up to 30% of patients with primary focal segmental glomerulosclerosis[482] may undergo remission of disease.

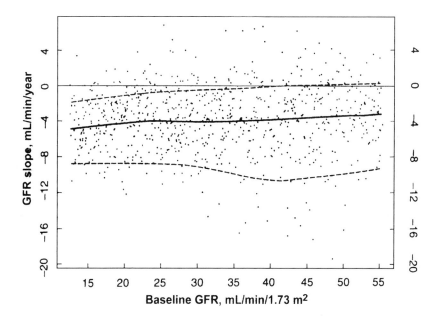

Fig 47. GFR slopes in the Modification of Diet in Renal Disease Study. The best linear unbiased estimates of GFR slope over 3 years in Study A or overall slope in Study B are shown as a function of baseline GFR. The lower, middle and upper lines represent the 10th, 50th (median), and 90th percentiles of the distribution of GFR slopes, respectively. The GFR slope estimates are not related to baseline GFR, but the variability in slope estimates is higher at higher levels of baseline GFR. Reprinted with permission.[480]

The rate of GFR decline is often relatively constant over time in an individual patient; however, the rate of GFR decline is highly variable among patients, ranging from slowly progressive over decades, to rapidly progressive over months (Table 109 and Fig 48) (R, C). Many studies have demonstrated that the rate of decline in the reciprocal of serum creatinine concentration ($1/S_{Cr}$) appears constant

Table 109. Mean Rate of Decline of GFR for Various Causes of Kidney Disease

Cause of Kidney Disease	Mean Rate of GFR* Decline (Per Year)	Mean GFR* at Baseline
Diabetes	**0–12.6 mL/min**	**36–117 mL/min**
Nielsen,[498] 1997	1.2 mL/min/1.73 m²	89 mL/min/1.73 m²
Yip,[494] 1996	1.5–2.5[d] mL/min/1.73 m²	>100 mL/min/1.73 m²
Huang,[359] 1998	1.7 mL/min/1.73 m²	117 mL/min/1.73 m²
Zeller,[360] 1991	3.1–12.1[b] mL/min/1.73 m²	47 mL/min/1.73 m²
Berrut,[497] 1997	0–4.8[c] mL/min	94 mL/min
Ellis,[495] 1996	5 mL/min	96 mL/min
Gall,[489] 1993	5.7 mL/min	83 mL/min
Dillon,[488] 1993	7.9 mL/min	36 mL/min
Biesenbach,[491] 1994a	10.9–12.6[d] mL/min/1.73 m²	81–89[d] mL/min/1.73 m²
Biesenbach,[505] 1994b	9.6–15.7[e] mL/min/1.73 m²	81 mL/min/1.73 m²
Austin,[487] 1993	1.2–13.2[f] mL/min/1.73 m²	91–53[f] mL/min/1.73 m²
Bakris,[506] 1996	1.9 mL/min/1.73 m²	63 mL/min/1.73 m²
Bakris,[507] 1997	2.6 mL/min/1.73 m²	70 mL/min/1.73 m²
Hovind,[508] 2001	4.0 mL/min/1.73 m²	89 mL/min/1.73 m²
Glomerular Diseases	**1.4–9.5 mL/min**	**<43–93 mL/min**
IgA Nephropathy (Rekola,[486] 1991)	1.4 mL/min	83 mL/min
Membranous nephropathy (Pei,[481] 1992)	3.2 mL/min/1.73 m²	93 mL/min/1.73 m²
Chronic glomerulonephritis, (Hannedouche,[501] 1993)	9.5 mL/min	Serum creatinine ≈ 5 mg/dL
Chronic glomerulonephritis, (Massy,[499] 1999)	4.6 mL/min	43 mL/min
Hypertension	**2–10.4 mL/min**	**15–41[g] mL/min**
Hannedouche,[490] 1993	10.4 mL/min	Serum creatinine ≈ 5 mg/dL
Massy,[499] 1999	2 mL/min	41 mL/min
Renal artery stenosis (Baboolal,[496] 1998)	4 mL/min	39 mL/min
Tubulointerstitial Diseases	**2–5.4 mL/min**	**15–41[g] mL/min**
Hannedouche,[501] 1993	5.4 mL/min	Serum creatinine ≈ 5 mg/dL
Massy,[499] 1999	2 mL/min	41 mL/min
Polycystic Kidney Disease	**3.8–5.4 mL/min**	**15–47[g] mL/min**
Hannedouche,[501] 1993	5.4 mL/min	Serum creatinine ≈ 5 mg/dL
Massy,[499] 1999	3.8 mL/min	47 mL/min
Diseases Other than Diabetes	**2.8–3.9 mL/min**	**42–43 mL/min**
Samuelsson,[509] 1996	2.8 mL/min/1.73 m²	42 mL/min/1.73 m²
Hunsicker,[480] 1997	3.9 mL/min/1.73 m²	43 mL/min/1.73 m²

* Or creatinine clearance
[a] Values for no hyperfiltration and hyperfiltration, respectively
[b] Values for low protein diet and normal protein diet, respectively
[c] Values for normoalbuminuria and microalbuminuria, respectively
[d] Values for Type 2 and Type 1 diabetes, respectively
[e] Mean SBP <160 and >160 mm Hg, respectively
[f] Values for subnephrotic and nephrotic, respectively
[g] Assumes serum creatinine of 5 mg/dL ≈ GFR of 15 mL/min

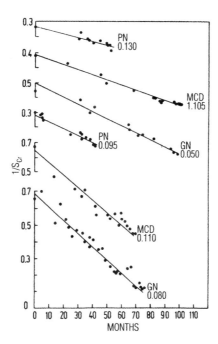

Fig 48. Composite plot of reciprocal serum creatinine versus time in six patients with chronic kidney disease. Units of reciprocal serum creatinine concentration are dL/mg. Vertical axis has uniform divisions of 0.1 dL/mg. Final value for each patient is shown. Abbreviations: PN, pyelonephritis; MCD, medullary cystic disease; GN, glomerulonephritis. Reprinted with permission.[485]

over time.[483,484] One of the earliest such studies is shown in Fig 48. Because of the reciprocal relationship between serum creatinine and GFR, it has been assumed that the constant rate of decline in $1/S_{Cr}$ would reflect a constant decline in GFR. Indeed, studies have shown that the GFR decline does appear relatively constant over time, although other studies have shown that other continuous relationships (such as the logarithm) or non-continuous (spline) relationships may fit the data better in some cases.

The studies reviewed for this guideline show a wide range in the rate of GFR decline among studies, as well as among individual patients (Table 109). The mean rate of decline in GFR varied widely, from no decline to over 12 mL/min/1.73 m^2 per year.[359,481,486-500] The standard deviations of GFR declines, expressed as a percent of the mean GFR decline, also vary widely, from approximately 25% to 150%.

The rate of decline in GFR can be used to estimate the interval until the onset of kidney failure (Table 110) (R). In principle, if the rate of GFR decline is constant over time, then the interval until the onset of kidney failure could be estimated from

Table 110. Years Until Kidney Failure (GFR <15 mL/min/1.73 m²)
Based on Level of GFR and Rate of GFR Decline

Level of GFR (mL/min/1.73 m²)	Rate of GFR Decline (mL/min/1.73 m² per year)					
	10	**8**	**6**	**4**	**2**	**1***
90	7.5	9.4	13	19	38	75
80	6.5	8.1	11	16	33	65
70	5.5	6.8	9.2	14	28	55
60	4.5	5.6	7.5	11	23	45
50	3.5	4.4	5.8	8.8	18	35
40	2.5	3.1	4.2	6.3	13	25
30	1.5	1.9	2.5	3.8	7.5	15
20	0.5	0.6	0.8	1.3	2.5	5.0

* Average age-related GFR decline after age 20–30 years

the current level of GFR and the rate of decline in GFR. An estimate of the time until kidney failure would be useful to facilitate planning for kidney replacement therapy, or may even suggest that concerns about kidney failure may be unwarranted if life expectancy is short. Table 110 shows the number of years until GFR declines to 15 mL/min/1.73 m², calculated from the current level of GFR and the estimated rate of decline of GFR. For patients with GFR <60 mL/min/1.73 m², the interval until kidney failure is approximately 10 years or less if the rate of decline is ≥4 mL/min/1.73 m² per year. This rate of decline can be considered "fast."

Although it is difficult to predict the rate of decline in GFR, either of the following two general approaches, or a combination of the two, is recommended:

Approach 1: Compute the GFR decline from past and ongoing measurements of serum creatinine; the GFR decline in the past provides a rough estimate of the expected GFR decline in the future (R). In principle, the GFR decline could be computed simply from the slope of the regression line relating estimated GFR versus time. However, there are a number of limitations to estimation of the slope and extrapolation of the rate of decline to predict the time to development of kidney failure. These limitations are related principally to whether the rate of decline is truly constant and the precision of the estimate of the rate of decline.

First, most of the studies that demonstrated a constant rate of decline in kidney function were retrospective, including only patients who had already progressed to kidney failure. The fraction of patients with decreased GFR in whom the subsequent decline in kidney function is constant is unknown.

Second, even among patients in whom the rate appears constant, the rate may change over time. In a pooled analysis of four studies of 77 patients with an apparently constant rate of decline in the reciprocal of the serum creatinine concentration, 32% to 51% of patients had a significant change in the slope[502] (Fig 49). The changes in slope were judged to be spontaneous, since they did not necessarily occur at the time of changes

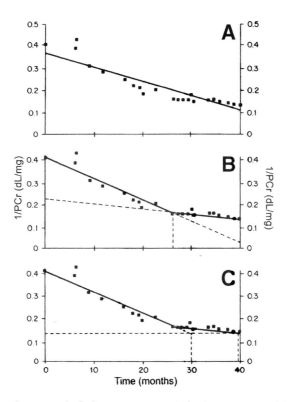

Fig 49. Plot of reciprocal of plasma creatinine ($1/P_{Cr}$) in a patient. (A) Solid line is single best fit regression line. (B) Solid lines are two best fit regression lines (spline) with an intersection (breakpoint) at 26 months (vertical dashed line). Diagonal dashed lines are extrapolations of the regression lines to earlier and later times. (C) Calculation of prediction error. Solid lines are two best fit regression lines. The diagonal dashed line is an extrapolation of the first regression line to the time when the final value for $1/P_{Cr}$ (0.132 dL/mg) was obtained. The interval predicted from the first regression line was 30 months (left vertical dashed line). The actual interval was 40 months (right vertical dashed line). The prediction error (difference between the actual and predicted intervals) was 10 months (25% of the actual interval). Reprinted with permission.[502]

in therapy. In that study, the second slope was less steep in 61% of cases and more steep in 39% of cases. The magnitude of the changes in slope was relatively large in comparison to the first slope (mean of 130% of the value of the first slope). Consequently, the mean error in the interval until reaching the final serum creatinine was also relatively large, 27% of the predicted interval (Fig 49).

Similar changes in slope of GFR decline have sometimes been observed in clinical trials, where they have been attributed to the effect of the interventions (for example,

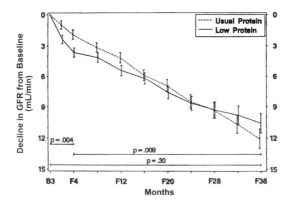

Fig 50. Comparison of GFR decline between diet groups in the Modification of Diet in Renal Disease Study. Estimated mean (± SEM) GFR decline from baseline (B) to selected follow-up times (F) in Study A are shown. From baseline to 4 months of follow-up, mean GFR decline was 1.6 mL/min faster in the low protein diet group (P = 0.004). From 4 months to the end of follow-up, mean GFR decline was 1.1 mL/min/month (28%) slower in the usual protein diet group (P = 0.009). From baseline to 3 years of follow-up, the projected mean GFR decline was 1.2 mL/min (10%) less in the low protein diet group (P = 0.30). Adapted from Klahr et al[315] and reprinted with permission.[492]

low protein diet, strict blood pressure control, ACE inhibition). Figure 50 shows data from MDRD Study A. GFR decline was faster in the first four months after randomization to a low protein diet and a slower decline thereafter compared to patients randomized to a usual protein diet.[492] The authors hypothesized that the greater decline soon after the intervention was related to a hypothesized beneficial effect of the intervention: an initial decrease in single nephron GFR, followed by a subsequent slowing in the rate of decline in the number of nephrons.[503]

Third, even if the rate of decline is constant, the precision of the estimate of the slope depends on a number of variables, including the true rate of decline, the number of measurements of kidney function, measurement error, biological variability, and the duration of follow-up. At least three previous measures of kidney function are necessary (more are better) to permit a precise estimate of the slope, especially if the rate of decline is slow.[504]

Approach 2: Ascertain factors associated with a "fast" or "slow" GFR decline; these factors include type (diagnosis) of kidney disease, nonmodifiable and modifiable factors (R). For this review, longitudinal studies were compiled to relate the rate of decline in kidney function with the potential associated factors. Observational studies and interventional trials were included. The effect of interventions on the rate of progression is summarized in a later section. The articles reviewed were published between 1984 and 2000. The studies varied in the levels of kidney function assessed,

Table 111. Kidney Disease Type as Predictor of Progression

Author, Year	No. of Subjects	Kidney Diseases Examined	Applic- ability	GFR Range* (mL/min/1.73 m²) 0 30 60 90 120	Association** (Uni- variate)	Association** (Multi- variate)	Quality†
Hunsicker,[480] 1997	826	No IDDM	↑↑	▬▬	PKD	PKD Glomerular	● (<3)
Massy,[499] 1999	138	All	↑↑↑	─┼─	GN PKD		○
Hannedouche,[501] 1993	223	No DM	↑↑	S$_{Cr}$ 5.1 ±0.4 mg/dL	GN HTN		○(ND)

* At baseline

** For each column, listed kidney diseases were associated with faster GFR decline of kidney function in univariate and/or multivariate analyses.

† A "<3" superscript indicates a mean or median duration of follow-up of 1–3 years; "ND" indicates that no data on duration were reported. No superscript indicates a mean or median duration of follow-up of 3 or more years.

Abbreviations for Tables 111–121: BP, blood pressure; DBP, diastolic blood pressure; DM, diabetes mellitus; FSGS, focal glomerulosclerosis; GN, glomerulonephritis; HgbA$_{1c}$, hemoglobin variant A$_{1c}$; HDL, high density lipoprotein; HTN, hypertensive nephrosclerosis; IDDM, insulin-dependent diabetes mellitus; LDL, low density lipoprotein; MAP, mean arterial pressure; NIDDM, non-insulin dependent diabetes mellitus; PKD, polycystic kidney disease; SBP, systolic blood pressure; SLE, systemic lupus erythematosus

sample sizes, and methodological quality. Duration of follow-up is a key component of studies of prognosis. Duration of follow-up between 1 and 3 years or less than 1 year is noted in the tables.

The rate of GFR decline is related to the type of kidney disease; diabetic kidney disease, glomerular diseases, polycystic kidney disease, and kidney disease in transplant recipients are associated with a faster GFR decline than hypertensive kidney disease and tubulointerstitial kidney diseases (Tables 109 and 111) (C, R).

Few studies specifically related rate of GFR decline to type of kidney disease (Table 111). The MDRD Study was the largest, with a sample size of 826, while the other two studies had between 138 and 223 subjects. These studies reported somewhat conflicting results. In the MDRD Study[480] and the study by Massy,[499] polycystic kidney disease was associated with a faster rate of progression, whereas in the study by Hannedouche,[490] polycystic kidney disease was associated with a slower rate of progression. Massy and Hannedouche both reported that glomerular disease was associated with a faster rate of progression than tubulointerstitial nephropathy. However, these two studies showed a conflicting result regarding the rate of progression associated with hypertensive kidney disease. These studies either excluded diabetics, or had a very small proportion of patients with diabetes in the study sample.

Additional information regarding different rates of GFR decline depending on underlying cause of kidney disease was extracted from studies of isolated causes of kidney disease or from studies which provided rates of progression for individual causes of kidney disease. Table 111 shows the reported or estimated rates of GFR decline that were described for different causes of kidney disease.

The data presented in Table 111 are not easily compared; the study methods varied (retrospective or prospective, observational, or interventional), different measures of kidney function were used, and the effect of interventions or other potential confounders cannot be determined. Nonetheless, the crude data suggest a trend for more rapid progression among patients with diabetes, especially those patients with proteinuria or decreased GFR, compared with other causes of kidney disease. There was a wide range of rates of decline among patients with nondiabetic kidney disease. Data on rates of GFR decline among kidney transplant recipients could not be found. However, the Work Group concluded that GFR decline is faster than in many other causes of chronic kidney disease given that graft survival rates are approximately 75% at 5 years for living donors and 60% at 5 years for cadaveric donors[509] or an approximate half-life until graft failure for kidney transplants of approximately 12 and 7, respectively. Loss of kidney function for transplant recipients is influenced by episodes of rejection, use of immunosuppressive agents, patient gender and size, and quality of the donor kidney, among other factors.

The rate of GFR decline is related to some nonmodifiable patient characteristics, irrespective of the type of kidney disease; African-American race, lower baseline level of kidney function, male gender, and older age are associated with a faster GFR decline (C).

Race (Table 112). Six studies addressed the association of race with the rate of GFR decline in either univariate or multivariate analyses. Half reported a faster rate of progression among blacks; however, only one study reported a significant association between black race and faster rates of progression in multivariate analysis.

Level of Kidney Function (Table 113). Twenty-one studies addressed the association of low baseline level of kidney function with the rate of GFR decline in either univariate or multivariate analyses. The majority of the studies reported a faster rate of progression among individuals with lower baseline kidney function, but about one third reported no association. No studies reported a slower rate of progression.

Table 112. Black Race as a Predictor of Progression

Author, Year	No. of Subjects	Kidney Diseases Examined	Applic-ability	GFR Range* (mL/min/1.73 m²)	Results** (Uni-variate)	Results** (Multi-variate)	Quality†
Shulman,[510] 1989	8,693	HTN	↑↑	S_{Cr} 1.08 ±0.38 mg/dL		⇔	●
Walker,[511] 1993	5,524	DM, HTN	↑↑	S_{Cr} 1.1 ±0.14 mg/dL		⇔	●
Hunsicker,[480] 1997	826	No IDDM	↑↑	▬▬▬	↑	↑	●(<3)
Krop,[512] 1999	1,434	DM	↑↑	S_{Cr} 1.1 mg/dL	↑	⇔	○
Breyer,[513] 1996	409	DM	↑↑	ND	↑		○
Dillon,[488] 1993	59	DM	↑↑	▬▬┼▬▬	⇔		○(<3)

* At baseline

** ↑ = black race associated with faster GFR decline (statistically significant);
⇔ = black race *not* associated with rate of GFR decline.

† A "<3" superscript indicates a mean or median duration of follow-up of 1–3 years. No superscript indicates a mean or median duration of follow-up of 3 or more years.

Abbreviations: see footnote for Table 111.

Table 113. Low Baseline Kidney Function as a Predictor of Progression

Author, Year	No. of Subjects	Kidney Diseases Examined	Applic-ability	GFR Range* (mL/min/1.73 m²)	Results** (Uni-variate)	Results** (Multi-variate)	Quality†
Shulman,[510] 1989	8,693	HTN	↑↑	S_Cr 1.08 ±0.38 mg/dL		↑	●
Hunsicker,[480] 1997	826	No IDDM	↑↑		⇔	⇔	● (<3)
Klein,[514] 1999	555	IDDM	↑↑		↑		●
Hovind,[508] 2001	301	IDDM	↑↑		⇔		●
Massy,[499] 1999	138	All	↑↑↑		↑	↑	○
Samuelsson,[515] 1996	49	All	↑↑↑		⇔		○
Krop,[512] 1999	1,434	DM	↑↑	S_Cr 1.1 mg/dL	↑		○
Breyer,[513] 1996	409	DM	↑↑	ND	↑		○
Nakano,[516] 1999	257	DM	↑↑			↑	○
Samuelsson,[517] 1997	73	No DM	↑↑			↑	◉
Ruggenenti,[518] 1998	65	NIDDM	↑↑	S_Cr 1.8 ±0.9 mg/dL	↑	↑	○(<3)
Berrut,[497] 1997	51	NIDDM	↑↑		⇔		○(<3)
Zeller,[360] 1991	35	IDDM	↑↑		↑		○(<3)
Nielsen,[498] 1997	32	DM	↑↑		↑	↑	○
Rekola,[486] 1991	153	IgA nephropathy	↑		↑		○
Dillon,[488] 1993	59	DM	↑↑		⇔		○(<3)
Tu,[519] 1984	117	Membranous GN	↑			⇔	○
Chitalia,[482] 1999	111	FSGS	↑	S_Cr 1.5 ±0.8 mg/dL	↑		○
Toth,[520] 1994	100	Membranous GN	↑			↑	○
Jacobsen,[521] 1999	94	SLE	↑	S_Cr 0.6–1.4 mg/dL	⇔		○
Reichert,[238] 1995	30	Membranous GN	↑		⇔		○(<1)

* At baseline

** ↑ = low baseline kidney function associated with faster GFR decline (statistically significant);
⇔ = low baseline kidney function *not* associated with rate of GFR decline.

† A "<3" superscript indicates a mean or median duration of follow-up of 1–3 years; "<1" indicates mean or median duration of follow-up <1 year. No superscript indicates a mean or median duration of follow-up of 3 or more years.

Abbreviations: see footnote for Table 111.

Table 114. Male Gender as a Predictor of Progression

Author, Year	No. of Subjects	Kidney Diseases Examined	Applic-ability	GFR Range* (mL/min/1.73 m^2) 0 30 60 90 120	Results** (Uni-variate)	Results** (Multi-variate)	Quality†
Shulman,[519] 1989	8,693	HTN	↑↑	S$_{Cr}$ 1.08 ±0.38 mg/dL		⬆	●
Hunsicker,[480] 1997	826	No IDDM	↑↑	[bar]	⬆	⇔	● $^{(<3)}$
Ravid,[522] 1998	574	DM	↑↑	ND	⬆		●
Klein,[514] 1999	555	IDDM	↑↑	[bar]	⬆	⇔	●
Hovind,[508] 2001	301	IDDM	↑↑	[bar]	⬆	⇔	●
Rosman,[523] 1989	153	All	↑↑↑	[bar]	⬆		◐
Massy,[499] 1999	138	All	↑↑↑	[bar]	⇔	⇧	◐
Krop,[512] 1999	1,434	DM	↑↑	S$_{Cr}$ 1.1 mg/dL	⇔		◐
Nakano,[516] 1999	257	DM	↑↑	[bar]		⬇	◐
Ruggenenti,[518] 1998	65	NIDDM	↑↑	S$_{Cr}$ 1.8 ±0.9 mg/dL	⇔	⇔	◐ $^{(<3)}$
Nielsen,[498] 1997	32	DM	↑↑	[bar]		⇔	◐
Rekola,[486] 1991	153	IgA nephropathy	↑	[bar]	⬆		◐
Locatelli,[524] 1991	456	No DM	↑↑	S$_{Cr}$ 1.3–7.0 mg/dL		⇔	○ $^{(<3)}$
Hannedouche,[501] 1993	223	No DM	↑↑	S$_{Cr}$ 5.1 ±0.4 mg/dL		⬆	○ $^{(ND)}$
Tu,[519] 1984	117	Membranous GN	↑	[bar]		⬆	○
Toth,[520] 1994	100	Membranous GN	↑	[bar]		⇔	○
Jacobsen,[521] 1999	94	SLE	↑	S$_{Cr}$ 0.6–1.4 mg/dL		⇔	○
Reichert,[238] 1995	30	Membranous GN	↑	[bar]	⇔		○ $^{(<3)}$

* At baseline

** ⬆ = male gender associated with faster GFR decline (statistically significant);

⇧ = male gender associated with faster GFR decline;

⇔ = male gender *not* associated with rate of GFR decline;

⬇ = male gender associated with slower GFR decline ()statistically significant.

† A "<3" superscript indicates a mean or median duration of follow-up of 1–3 years; "<1" indicates mean or median duration of follow-up <1 year; "ND" indicates that no data on duration were reported. No superscript indicates a mean or median duration of follow-up of 3 or more years.

Abbreviations: see footnote for Table 111.

Gender (Table 114). Eighteen studies addressed the impact of gender on the rate of GFR decline in either univariate or multivariate analyses. The data report either a faster rate of progression or no association with male gender, and a single study reported a faster rate of progression among females. The evidence is not conclusive, but suggests a faster rate of progression among men.

Age (Table 115). Twenty-one studies reported the association of age with the rate of GFR decline in either univariate or multivariate analyses. These data generally support either an association of older age with faster rates of GFR decline or no association, except among diabetics, where younger age at diagnosis of diabetes is associated with

Table 115. Older Age as a Predictor of Progression

Author, Year	No. of Subjects	Kidney Diseases Examined	Applic-ability	GFR Range* (mL/min/1.73 m^2)	Results** (Uni-variate)	Results** (Multi-variate)	Quality†
Shulman,[510] 1989	8,693	HTN	↑↑	S$_{Cr}$ 1.08 ±0.38 mg/dL		↑	●
Walker,[511] 1993	5,524	HTN	↑↑	S$_{Cr}$ 1.1 ±0.14 mg/dL		⇔	●
Hunsicker,[486] 1997	826	No IDDM	↑↑		↓	⇔	● [(<3)]
Klein,[514] 1999[a]	555	IDDM	↑↑			↓	●
Hovind,[508] 2001	301	IDDM	↑↑		⇔		●
Massy,[499] 1999	138	All	↑↑↑		⇔	⇔	○
Krop,[512] 1999	1,434	DM	↑↑	S$_{Cr}$ 1.1 mg/dL	↑		○
Breyer,[513] 1996	409	DM	↑↑	ND	↑	↑	○
Nakano,[516] 1999	257	DM	↑↑			↑	○
Ruggenenti,[518] 1998	65	NIDDM	↑↑	S$_{Cr}$ 1.8 ±0.9 mg/dL	⇔	⇔	○ [(<3)]
Berrut,[497] 1997	51	NIDDM	↑↑			⇔	○ [(<3)]
Nielsen,[498] 1997	32	DM	↑↑			⇔	○
Gall,[489] 1993	26	DM	↑↑			⇔	○
Rekola,[486] 1991	153	IgA nephropathy	↑		↑		○
Baboolal,[496] 1998	51	All	↑↑↑		⇔		○
Hannedouche,[501] 1993	223	No DM	↑↑	S$_{Cr}$ 5.1 ±0.4 mg/dL		↑	○ [(ND)]
Dillon,[488] 1993	59	DM	↑↑		↓	⇔	○ [(<3)]
Tu,[519] 1984	117	Membranous GN	↑			⇔	○
Toth,[520] 1994	100	Membranous GN	↑			⇔	○
Jacobsen,[521] 1999	94	SLE	↑	S$_{Cr}$ 0.6–1.4 mg/dL	⇔		○
Reichert,[238] 1995	30	Membranous GN	↑		⇔		○ [(<3)]

*At baseline

** ↑ = older age associated with faster GFR decline (statistically significant);
 ⇔ = older age *not* associated with rate of GFR decline;
 ↓ = older age associated with slower GFR decline (statistically significant).

† A "<3" superscript indicates a mean or median duration of follow-up of 1–3 years; "<1" superscript indicates a mean or median duration of follow-up <1 year; "ND" indicates that no data on duration were reported. No superscript indicates a mean or median duration of follow-up of 3 or more years.

[a] Younger age at diagnosis of diabetes mellitus associated with faster progression.

Abbreviations: see footnote for Table 111.

Table 116. Proteinuria or Albuminuria as Predictors of Progression

Author, Year	No. of Subjects	Kidney Diseases Examined	Applic-ability	GFR Range* (mL/min/1.73 m²)	Results** (Univariate)	Results** (Multivariate)	Quality†
Walker,[511] 1993	5,524	DM, HTN	↑↑	S_{Cr} 1.1 ±0.14 mg/dL	↑	⇔	●
Hunsicker,[490] 1997	826	No IDDM	↑↑	(bar)	↑	↑	●[(<3)]
Klein,[514] 1999	555	IDDM	↑↑	(bar)	↑	↑	●
Hovind,[508] 2001	301	IDDM	↑↑	(bar)	↑	↑	●
Massy,[499] 1999	138	All	↑↑↑	(bar)	↑	↑	◐
Samuelsson,[515] 1996	49	All	↑↑↑	(bar)	↑		◐
Breyer,[513] 1996	409	DM	↑↑	ND	↑		◐
Yokoyama,[525] 1997	182	DM	↑↑	(bar)	↑	↑	◐[(<3)]
Samuelsson,[517] 1997	73	No DM	↑↑	(bar)		↑	◐
Ruggenenti,[518] 1998	65	NIDDM	↑↑	S_{Cr} 1.8 ±0.9 mg/dL	↑	↑	◐[(<3)]
Berrut,[497] 1997	51	NIDDM	↑↑	(bar)	↑	↑	◐[(<3)]
Austin,[487] 1993	38	DM	↑↑	(bar)	↑		◐[(<3)]
Nielsen,[498] 1997	32	DM	↑↑	(bar)	⇔ ↑ on antihypertensive	⇔ ↑ on antihypertensive	◐
Gall,[489] 1993	26	DM	↑↑	(bar)	↑	⇔	◐
Rekola,[486] 1991	153	IgA nephropathy	↑	(bar)	↑		◐
Bazzi,[236] 1997	145	Primary GN	↑	Mean S_{Cr}: 1.0–2.5 mg/dL	↑		◐
Locatelli,[524] 1991	456	No DM	↑↑	S_{Cr} 1.3–7.0 mg/dL		↑	○[(<3)]
Dillon,[488] 1993	59	DM	↑↑	(bar)	↑	↑	○[(<3)]
Pei,[481] 1992	184	Membranous GN	↑	(bar)	↑	⇔	○[(<3)]
Tu,[519] 1984	117	Membranous GN	↑	(bar)		⇔	○
Chitalia,[482] 1999	111	FSGS	↑	S_{Cr} 1.5 ±0.8 mg/dL	⇔	⇔	○
Toth,[520] 1994	100	Membranous GN	↑	(bar)		⇔	○
Jacobsen,[521] 1999	94	SLE	↑	S_{Cr} 0.6–1.4 mg/dL	⇔	⇔	○
Reichert,[238] 1995	30	Membranous GN	↑	(bar)	↑		○[(<1)]

* At baseline

** ↑ = proteinuria or albuminuria associated with faster GFR decline (statistically significant); ⇔ = proteinuria or albuminuria *not* associated with rate of GFR decline.

† A "<3" superscript indicates a mean or median duration of follow-up of 1–3 years; "<1" superscript indicates a mean or median duration of follow-up <1 year; "ND" indicates that no data on duration were reported. No superscript indicates a mean or median duration of follow-up of 3 or more years.

Abbreviations: see footnote for Table 111.

a faster rate of GFR decline. Coupled with the fact that the elderly start from a lower baseline GFR, older individuals with chronic kidney disease deserve special attention and closer follow-up.

The rate of GFR decline is also related to modifiable patient characteristics, irrespective of the type of kidney disease. Higher level of proteinuria, lower serum albumin concentration, higher blood pressure level, poor glycemic control, and smoking are associated with a faster GFR decline. The associations of dyslipidemia and anemia with faster GFR decline are inconclusive (C).

Proteinuria (Table 116). Twenty-four studies addressed the association of proteinuria with the rate of GFR decline in univariate and/or multivariate analyses and showed conflicting results. Although these data do not unanimously show that proteinuria is associated with faster rate of GFR decline when controlling for other factors, the studies with larger sample sizes and higher methodological quality and applicability do support the association.

Low Serum Albumin (Table 117). Eight studies addressed the association of low baseline serum albumin with rate of GFR decline in either univariate or multivariate analyses. The association of low serum albumin with faster rate of GFR decline was more consistently noted in studies of diabetic patients. No studies reported a slower rate of GFR decline associated with low serum albumin.

Table 117. Low Serum Albumin as a Predictor of Progression

Author, Year	No. of Subjects	Kidney Diseases Examined	Applic-ability	GFR Range* (mL/min/1.73 m^2)	Results** (Uni-variate)	Results** (Multi-variate)	Quality†
Hunsicker,[480] 1997	826	No IDDM	⬆⬆		⬆	⬆	● [(<3)]
Breyer,[513] 1996	409	DM	⬆⬆	ND	⬆		○
Nakano,[516] 1999	257	DM	⬆⬆			⬌	○
Yokoyama,[525] 1997	182	DM	⬆⬆		⬆	⬆	○ [(<3)]
Dillon,[488] 1993	59	DM	⬆⬆		⬆	⬆	○ [(<3)]
Tu,[519] 1984	117	Membranous GN	⬆			⬆	○
Jacobsen,[521] 1999	94	SLE	⬆	S_{cr} 0.6–1.4 mg/dL	⬌		○
Reichert,[238] 1995	30	Membranous GN	⬆		⬌		○ [(<1)]

* At baseline

** ⬆ = low serum albumin associated with faster GFR decline (statistically significant);
  ⬌ = low serum albumin *not* associated with rate of GFR decline.

† A "<3" superscript indicates a mean or median duration of follow-up of 1–3 years; "<1" superscript indicates a mean or median duration of follow-up <1 year. No superscript indicates a mean or median duration of follow-up of 3 or more years.

Abbreviations: see footnote for Table 111.

Table 118. Blood Pressure as a Predictor of Progression

Author, Year	No. of Subjects	Kidney Diseases Examined	Applic-ability	GFR Range* (mL/min/1.73 m²) 0 30 60 90 120	Results** (Uni-variate)	Results** (Multi-variate)	Quality†
Elevated BP, MAP							
Walker,[511] 1993	5,524	HTN	↑↑	S₀ 1.1 ±0.14 mg/dL	↑		●
Hunsicker,[480] 1997	826	No IDDM	↑↑		↑	↑	● (<3)
Ravid,[522] 1998	574	DM	↑↑	ND		↑	●
Klein,[514] 1999	555	IDDM	↑↑			↑	●
Hovind,[508] 2001	301	IDDM	↑↑		↑	↑	●
Nakano,[516] 1999	257	DM	↑↑			↑	○
Gall,[489] 1993	26	DM	↑↑		↑	⇔	○
Breyer,[513] 1996	409	DM	↑↑	ND	↑		○
Rekola,[486] 1991	153	IgA nephropathy	↑		↑		○
Hannedouche,[490] 1993	223	No DM	↑↑	S₀ 5.1 ±0.4 mg/dL		↑	○(ND)
Toth,[520] 1994	100	Membranous GN	↑			⇔	○
Dillon,[488] 1993	59	DM	↑↑			↑	○(<3)
Reichert,[238] 1995	30	Membranous GN	↑		⇔		○(<1)

Blood Pressure (Table 118). Twenty-six studies related blood pressure levels to the rate of GFR decline in univariate and/or multivariate analyses. The studies differed in that they assessed systolic blood pressure, diastolic blood pressure, or mean arterial pressure—two of these or all of these. Most studies reporting multivariate analyses showed a significant association between elevated blood pressure, based on any measures of blood pressure, and faster rate of GFR decline. There were only 7 studies that reported no significant association between elevated blood pressure measures and faster rate of GFR decline in multivariate analysis. These data, though not unanimous, confirm that elevated blood pressure is associated with faster rate of GFR decline when controlling for other factors.

Glycemic Control in Diabetes (Table 119). Thirteen studies addressed the impact of poor glycemic control on the rate of GFR decline in univariate and/or multivariate analyses. There were 6 studies that reported in multivariate analyses a significant association between poor glycemic control, either an elevated fasting blood sugar and/or HgbA$_{1c}$ levels and faster rate of GFR decline; in one of these the association was noted only among patients on antihypertensive agents. A similar number of studies showed no significant association between poor glycemic control and faster rate of GFR decline in

Table 118. Blood Pressure as a Predictor of Progression (cont.)

Author, Year	No. of Subjects	Kidney Diseases Examined	Applic-ability	GFR Range (mL/min/1.73 m²) 0 30 60 90 120	Results** (Uni-variate)	Results** (Multi-variate)	Quality†
Elevated SBP							
Shulman,[510] 1989	8,693	HTN	↑↑	S_{Cr} 1.08 ±0.38 mg/dL		↑	●
Walker,[511] 1993	5,524	DM, HTN	↑↑	S_{Cr} 1.1 ±0.14 mg/dL	↑	↑	●
Klein,[514] 1999	555	IDDM	↑↑		↑		●
Hovind,[506] 2001	301	IDDM	↑↑		↑		●
Massy,[499] 1999	138	All	↑↑↑		⇔	⇔	○
Samuelsson,[515] 1996	49	All	↑↑↑		↑		○
Krop,[512] 1999	1,434	DM	↑↑	S_{Cr} 1.1 mg/dL	↑		○
Yokoyama,[525] 1997	182	DM	↑↑		↑	⇔	○ (<3)
Samuelsson,[517] 1997	73	No DM	↑↑			↑	○
Ruggenenti,[518] 1998	65	NIDDM	↑↑	S_{Cr} 1.8 ±0.9 mg/dL	⇔	⇔	○ (<3)
Berrut,[497] 1997	51	NIDDM	↑↑		⇔		○ (<3)
Gall,[489] 1993	26	DM	↑↑		↑	↑	○
Hannedouche,[490] 1993	223	No DM	↑↑	S_{Cr} 5.1 ±0.4 mg/dL		↑	○ (ND)
Dillon,[498] 1993	59	DM	↑↑		↑	⇔	○ (<3)
Biesenbach,[491] 1994a	32	DM	↑↑		↑	↑	○
Biesenbach,[505] 1994b	12	NIDDM	↑↑		↑		○
Tu,[519] 1984	117	Membranous GN	↑			⇔	○
Chitalia,[492] 1999	111	FSGS	↑	S_{Cr} 1.5 ±0.8 mg/dL	↑		○
Toth,[526] 1994	100	Membranous GN	↑		↑	⇔	○

multivariate analyses. Although these data do not unanimously show that poor glycemic control is associated with faster rate of GFR decline when controlling for other factors, the studies with larger sample sizes and higher methodological quality and applicability do support the association.

Smoking (Table 120). Ten studies reported the association of smoking on the rate of GFR decline in univariate and/or multivariate analyses. The reviewed studies reported conflicting results. However, the large sample sizes and adequate methodological quality and applicability of the studies supporting the association of smoking with faster rate of GFR decline provide reasonable evidence that there may be a deleterious effect of smoking on rate of progression.

Table 118. Blood Pressure as a Predictor of Progression (cont.)

Author, Year	No. of Subjects	Kidney Diseases Examined	Applic- ability	GFR Range* (mL/min/1.73 m²)	Results** (Uni- variate)	Results** (Multi- variate)	Quality†
Elevated DBP							
Shulman,[510] 1989	8,693	HTN	↑↑	S_Cr 1.08 ±0.38 mg/dL	↑	↑	●
Ravid,[522] 1998	574	DM	↑↑	ND		↑	●
Klein,[514] 1999	555	IDDM	↑↑		↑	↑	●
Hovind,[506] 2001	301	IDDM	↑↑		↑		●
Rosman,[523] 1989	153	All	↑↑↑		↑ (PKD only)		○
Massy,[499] 1999	138	All	↑↑↑		⇔		○
Samuelsson,[515] 1996	49	All	↑↑↑		⇔		○
Yokoyama,[525] 1997	182	DM	↑↑		↑	↑	○ (<3)
Samuelsson,[517] 1997	73	No DM	↑↑			↑	○
Ruggenenti,[518] 1998	65	NIDDM	↑↑	S_Cr 1.8 ±0.9 mg/dL	⇔	⇔	○ (<3)
Berrut,[497] 1997	51	NIDDM	↑↑		↑		○ (<3)
Gall,[489] 1993	26	DM	↑↑		⇔	⇔	○
Hannedouche,[490] 1993	223	No DM	↑↑	S_Cr 5.1 ±0.4 mg/dL		↑	○ (ND)
Dillon,[488] 1993	59	DM	↑↑		↑	↑	○ (<3)
Biesenbach,[491] 1994a	32	DM	↑↑		↑	↑	○
Chitalia,[482] 1999	111	FSGS	↑	S_Cr 1.5 ±0.8 mg/dL	↑		○
Toth,[520] 1993	100	Membranous GN	↑		↑	⇔	○

* At baseline

** ↑ = elevated blood pressure measurement associated with faster GFR decline (statistically significant);
⇔ = elevated blood pressure measurement *not* associated with rate of GFR decline.

† A "<3" superscript indicates a mean or median duration of follow-up of 1–3 years; "<1" superscript indicates a mean or median duration of follow-up <1 year; "ND" indicates that no data on duration were reported. No superscript indicates a mean or median duration of follow-up of 3 or more years.

Abbreviations: see footnote for Table 111.

Dyslipidemia (Table 121). Fifteen studies addressed the association of dyslipidemia with the rate of GFR decline in univariate and/or multivariate analyses. The studies evaluated one or more of the following factors: high levels of total cholesterol, triglycerides, or low density lipoprotein, and low levels of high density lipoprotein. The impact of dyslipidemia reported herein is based on whether any one of these factors was associated with a faster rate of progression. There were 7 studies that reported in multivariate analyses a significant association between dyslipidemia and faster rate of progression. There were 7 studies that reported no significant association between dyslipidemia and

Table 121. Dyslipidemia as Predictors of Progression

Author, Year	No. of Subjects	Kidney Diseases Examined	Applic-ability	GFR Range* (mL/min/1.73 m²)	Results** (Uni-variate)	Results** (Multi-variate)	Quality†
High Total Cholesterol							
Walker,[511] 1993	5,524	DM, HTN	↑↑	S_{cr} 1.1 ±0.14 mg/dL	⇔	⇔	●
Hunsicker,[490] 1997	826	No IDDM	↑↑	▬▬▬	⇔		●(<3)
Ravid,[522] 1998	574	DM	↑↑	ND		↑	●
Klein,[514] 1999	555	IDDM	↑↑		↑		●
Hovind,[508] 2001	301	IDDM	↑↑		↑	↑	●
Massy,[499] 1999	138	All	↑↑↑		⇔		○
Samuelsson,[515] 1996	49	All	↑↑↑		⇔		○
Yokoyama,[525] 1997	182	DM	↑↑		↑	⇔	○(<3)
Samuelsson,[517] 1997	73	No DM	↑↑			↑	○
Nielsen,[498] 1997	32	DM	↑↑			⇔	○
Gall,[489] 1993	26	DM	↑↑		⇔	⇔	○
Locatelli,[524] 1991	456	No DM	↑↑	S_{cr} 1.3–7.0 mg/dL		⇔	○(<3)
Dillon,[488] 1993	59	DM	↑↑		↑	↑	○(<3)
Biesenbach,[491] 1994a	32	DM	↑↑			⇔	○
Toth,[520] 1994	100	Membranous GN	↑			↑	○

Among patients with insulin dependent diabetes mellitus (IDDM), 80% who have sustained microalbuminuria develop overt nephropathy in 10 to 15 years, and among these, kidney failure develops in 50%. The DCCT, a prospective study comparing conventional with intensive treatment of 1,441 patients with IDDM followed for a mean of 6.5 years, firmly established the benefit of intensive glycemic control in reducing the occurrence of subclinical and overt nephropathy among patients with IDDM.[528] This trial demonstrated that the occurrence of nephropathy or its progression is reduced by 40% to 60%, depending on whether the outcome was microalbuminuria (40%), albuminuria (54%), or overt nephropathy (60%). The difference was observed with a mean HgbA$_{1c}$ of 7.2% in the intensively treated versus 9% in the conventionally treated patients.

The role of strict glycemic control in slowing the progression of diabetic kidney disease is less certain. A subgroup of patients within the DCCT with microalbuminuria at baseline (n = 73) showed a trend toward a beneficial effect.[528] Another study of 70 patients did not reveal a benefit.[529] Both of these studies may have been too small to detect a beneficial effect.

Among patients with non-insulin dependent DM (NIDDM), 20% to 40% of patients with microalbuminuria develop overt nephropathy, and among these, kidney failure

Table 121. Dyslipidemia as Predictors of Progression (cont.)

Author, Year	No. of Subjects	Kidney Diseases Examined	Applic- ability	GFR Range* (mL/min/1.73 m²)	Results** (Uni- variate)	Results** (Multi- variate)	Quality†
High Triglycerides							
Walker,[511] 1993	5,524	DM, HTN	↑↑	S_D 1.1 ±0.14 mg/dL	⇔		●
Massy,[499] 1999	138	All	↑↑↑		↑	⇧	○
Samuelsson,[515] 1996	49	All	↑↑↑		⇔		○
Yokoyama,[525] 1997	182	DM	↑↑		↑	⇔	○ (<3)
Samuelsson,[517] 1997	73	No DM	↑↑			⇔	○
Nielsen,[498] 1997	32	DM	↑↑			⇔	○
Biesenbach,[491] 1994a	32	DM	↑↑			⇔	○
Low HDL							
Hunsicker,[480] 1997	826	No IDDM	↑↑		↑	↑	● (<3)
Ravid,[522] 1998	574	DM	↑↑	ND		↑	●
Klein,[514] 1999	555	IDDM	↑↑		↑	↑	●
Massy,[499] 1999	138	All	↑↑↑		↑	⇔	○
Samuelsson,[515] 1996	49	All	↑↑↑		⇔		○
Yokoyama,[525] 1997	182	DM	↑↑			⇔	○ (<3)
Samuelsson,[517] 1997	73	No DM	↑↑			⇔	○
Nielsen,[498] 1997	32	DM	↑↑			⇔	○
Gall,[409] 1993	26	DM	↑↑		⇔	⇔	○
High LDL							
Hunsicker,[480] 1997	826	No IDDM	↑↑		⇔		● (<3)
Ravid,[522] 1998	574	DM	↑↑	ND		↑	●
Samuelsson,[515] 1996	49	All	↑↑↑		↑		○
Samuelsson,[517] 1997	73	No DM	↑↑			↑	○

* At baseline

** ↑ = dyslipidemia measurement associated with faster GFR decline (statistically significant);
  ⇧ = dyslipidemia measurement associated with faster GFR decline;
  ⇔ = dyslipidemia measurement *not* associated with rate of GFR decline.

† A "<3" superscript indicates a mean or median duration of follow-up of 1–3 years. No superscript indicates a mean or median duration of follow-up of 3 or more years.

Abbreviations: see footnote for Table 111.

Table 122. Anemia as a Predictor of Progression

Author, Year	No. of Subjects	Kidney Diseases Examined	Applic-ability	GFR Range* (mL/min/1.73 m²)	Results** (Uni-variate)	Results (Multi-variate)	Quality†
Kuriyama,[366] 1997	108	All	↑↑↑	S$_{Cr}$ 9 ±7 mg/dL	↑[a]		○[(<1)]

* At baseline

** ↑ = anemia associated with faster GFR decline (statistically significant).

† A "<3" superscript indicates a mean or median duration of follow-up of 1–3 years. No superscript indicates a mean or median duration of follow-up of 3 or more years.

[a] Untreated non-anemic subjects and anemic subjects treated with erythropoietin vs. untreated anemic subjects.

develops in 20%. Three randomized trials of strict glycemic control in type 2 diabetes also demonstrate a beneficial effect of strict glycemic control on the development and progression of diabetic kidney disease.

The United Kingdom Prospective Diabetes Study (UKPDS 33) compared strict glycemic control to standard therapy in diagnosed patients with type 2 diabetes.[530] The study employed a complex factorial design including diet, sulfonylureas, metformin, and insulin to achieve target fasting blood glucose values of <110 versus <270 mg/dL. Fasting blood glucose values rose over time in both groups; the mean HgbA$_{1c}$ was 11% lower in the intervention group. The intervention group had a 25% reduction in "microvascular" events, a combined endpoint that included both retinal and kidney disease. The data suggested a lower prevalence of microalbuminuria in the intervention group and a reduced incidence of declining kidney function.

The Kumamoto study compared intensive insulin therapy to standard therapy in 110 non-obese patients with type 2 diabetes, using a protocol similar to the DCCT.[531] Mean achieved HgbA$_{1c}$ levels were 7.1 versus 9.4% in the intervention and control groups, respectively. The results showed a lower incidence of the development and progression of microalbuminuria.

The Steno Type 2 Study compared an intensive multifactor intervention to standard therapy in 160 patients with type 2 diabetes and microalbuminuria.[532] The intervention included not only intensive insulin therapy, but also strict blood pressure control, ACE inhibition, dietary fat restriction, exercise, lipid-lowering drugs, anti-oxidants, and aspirin (in patients with coronary heart disease). There was 73% reduction in the incidence of clinical proteinuria in the intervention group. However, the relative importance of strict glycemic control and any of the other factors cannot be determined from this study.

The most recently updated Clinical Practice Recommendations (2001)[526] of the ADA regarding intensive glycemic control recommend the following treatment goals for patients with diabetes (Table 123).

"The desired outcome of glycemic control in type 1 diabetes is to lower HgbA$_{1c}$ (or any equivalent measure of chronic glycemia) so as to achieve maximum prevention of complications with due regard for patient safety. To achieve these goals with intensive management, the following may be necessary:

- *Frequent self-monitoring of blood glucose (at least three or four times a day);*

Table 123. Recommendations for Glycemic Control for People with Diabetes

	Normal	Goal	Additional Action Suggested
Whole blood values			
Average preprandial glucose (mg/dL)[a]	<100	80–120	<80/ >140
Average bedtime glucose (mg/dL)[a]	<110	100–140	<100/ >160
Plasma values			
Average preprandial glucose (mg/dL)[b]	<110	90–130	<90/ >150
Average bedtime glucose (mg/dL)[b]	<120	110–150	<110/ >180
HgbA$_{1C}$ (%)	<6	<7	>8

The values shown in this table are by necessity generalized to the entire population of individuals with diabetes. Patients with comorbid diseases, the very young and older adults, and others with unusual conditions or circumstances may warrant different treatment goals. These values are for nonpregnant adults. "Additional action suggested" depends on individual patients circumstances. Such actions may include enhanced diabetes self-management education, comanagement with a diabetes team, referral to an endocrinologist, change in pharmacological therapy, initiation or increase in self-monitoring of blood glucose (SMBG), or more frequent contact with the patient. HgbA$_{1C}$ is reference to a nondiabetic range of 4.0–6.0% (mean 5.0%, SD 0.5%). Adapted from 2001 ADA Clinical Practice Guidelines[526] (on the Internet, see *www.diabetes.org/clinicalrecommendations/Supplement101/S3.htm*).

[a] Measurement of capillary blood glucose
[b] Values calibrated to plasma glucose.

- *Medical nutrition therapy;*
- *Education in self-management and problem solving;*
- *Possible hospitalization for initiation of therapy.*

"In situations where resource are unavailable or insufficient, referral to a diabetes care team for consultation and/or comanagement is recommended."

Type 2 diabetes is addressed separately in the ADA guidelines:

"Daily self monitoring of blood glucose is especially important for patients treated with insulin or sulfonylureas to monitor for and prevent asymptomatic hypoglycemia. The optimal frequency of self monitoring of blood glucose for patients with type 2 diabetes is not known, but it should be sufficient to facilitate reaching glucose goals. The role of self-monitoring of blood glucose in stable diet-treated patients with type 2 diabetes is not known.

"Type 2 diabetes treatment methods should emphasize diabetes management as a multiple risk factor approach including medical nutrition therapy, exercise, weight reduction when indicated, and use of oral glucose-lowering agents and/or insulin, with careful attention given to cardiovascular risk factors, including hypertension, smoking, dyslipidemia, and family history. Whether treated with insulin or oral glucose-lowering agents, or a combination, goals remain those outlined in the table."

Strict blood pressure control slows the progression of chronic kidney disease (R). The Sixth Report of the Joint National Committee on Prevention, Detection, Evaluation and Treatment of High Blood Pressure (JNC-VI),[245] the most recently updated ADA Clinical Practice Recommendations (2001),[526] the NKF Task Force on Cardiovascular Disease in Chronic Renal Disease,[9] and a report from the NKF Hypertension and Diabetes Executive Committees Working Group[249] were reviewed for this section. This

Table 124. Risk Stratification and Indication for Antihypertensive Treatment

Blood Pressure Stage (Blood Pressure, mm Hg)	Risk Group A: No risk factors; TOD or CCD	Risk Group B: One or more risk factors (except diabetes); no TOD or CCD	Risk Group C: TOD or CCD; and/or diabetes
High-normal: (130–139/85–89)	Lifestyle modification	Lifestyle modification	Drug therapy and simultaneous lifestyle modification for CHF, diabetes, or CKD; lifestyle modification for other TOD or CCD
Stage 1: (140–159/90–99)	Drug therapy after 12 months of lifestyle modification	Drug therapy after 6 months of lifestyle modification	Drug therapy and simultaneous lifestyle modification
Stages 2–3: (>160/ >100)	Drug therapy and simultaneous lifestyle modification	Drug therapy and simultaneous lifestyle modification	Drug therapy and simultaneous lifestyle modification

Reprinted with permission.[245]

Abbreviations: TOD, target organ damage; CCD, clinical cardiovascular disease; CHF, congestive heart failure; CKD, chronic kidney disease

section will discuss primarily the target blood pressure level for patients with chronic kidney disease, with only brief reference to the role of specific antihypertensive agents. Angiotensin-converting enzyme (ACE) inhibitors and angiotensin-2 receptor blockers are discussed in the next section.

Recommendations for the general population are based on a large body of evidence from observational studies and clinical trials relating blood pressure levels to mortality and cardiovascular disease. There is general agreement that risk stratification should be used in deciding which patients with high blood pressure should be treated and how intensively[245] (Table 124). The recommended goal of antihypertensive therapy for patients at low or moderate risk for complications is to maintain systolic and diastolic blood pressure less than 140 and 90 mm Hg, respectively.[245] These definitions and goals do not differ according to age (among adults), gender, or race. Target blood pressure is lower in younger patients and related to age, weight and height.[533] Patients at greatest risk for complications or who already have evidence of cardiovascular disease are considered for the earliest and more aggressive treatment.

In the general population, the recommended antihypertensive agents are diuretics and beta-adrenergic blockers, because their efficacy in reducing cardiovascular mortality and morbidity has been proven in clinical trials. Recent studies show equal efficacy of angiotensin converting enzyme inhibitors (ACE-inhibitors) and calcium channel blockers in the general population.[534,535] In addition, alternative target blood pressure and medications may be preferred in those subgroups of patients with comorbid conditions. These subgroups include, among others, patients with chronic kidney disease, diabetes, and cardiovascular disease.

The knowledge base for chronic kidney disease is substantially smaller. Large-scale epidemiological studies of cardiovascular disease have included few patients with chronic kidney disease, and most clinical trials of antihypertensive agents to prevent cardiovascular disease have excluded patients with decreased kidney function. Some of the important randomized trials on the target level of blood pressure in patients with chronic kidney disease due to diabetes and other diseases are summarized below. The Work Group did not find randomized trials on target blood pressure levels in kidney transplant recipients.

Diabetic kidney disease. The benefit of blood pressure control to levels of approximately 140/90 mm Hg in retarding the decline in GFR in patients with type 1 diabetes was shown years ago.[536] The UKPDS has recently shown that better blood pressure control is also associated with decreased development of microalbuminuria in type 2 diabetes.[537] There have been no large-scale studies comparing even lower levels of target blood pressure ("strict blood pressure control") on the progression of diabetic kidney disease. However, a subgroup analysis of the Hypertension Optimal Trial (HOT) showed that patients with diabetes who were randomized to lower levels of blood pressure (diastolic blood pressure of <90 versus <85 versus <80 mm Hg) had lower mortality and fewer cardiovascular disease events than patients with higher blood pressure levels.[538] Thus, it seems reasonable to recommend even lower target blood pressure levels for patients with diabetic kidney disease.

Nondiabetic kidney diseases. The MDRD Study is the largest completed randomized trial on strict blood pressure on the rate of GFR decline in nondiabetic kidney disease. A total of 840 patients were randomized either to usual target blood pressure (mean arterial pressure <107 mm Hg, equivalent to blood pressure <140/90 mm Hg) versus a lower-than-usual target blood press (mean arterial pressure <92 mm Hg, equivalent to blood pressure <125/75 mm Hg). The mean separation between randomized groups was 4 to 5 mm Hg. Patients with higher levels of proteinuria at baseline had a greater beneficial effect of the low blood pressure goal. The investigators recommended a lower target blood pressure for patients with urine protein excretion less than approximately 1.0 g/d. At the time of preparation of these guidelines, the African American Study of Kidney Disease and Hypertension (AASK) is nearing completion, and additional information on the benefit of strict blood pressure control in nondiabetic kidney disease is expected in the near future.

Based largely on extrapolation from recommendations for the general population and limited observational studies and clinical trials in patients with chronic kidney disease, the NKF Task Force on Cardiovascular Disease recommended target blood pressure levels and strategies for treatment for patients with chronic kidney disease (Table 125). The

Table 125. Blood Pressure, Goals, Nonpharmacologic and Pharmacologic Therapy Recommended by the NKF Task Force on Cardiovascular Disease in Chronic Renal Disease

Population	BP Goal (mm Hg)	Nonpharmacologic Therapy	Pharmacological Therapy
General Population	<140/90	Reduction in dietary salt, Exercise	ß-blockers, diuretics
CKD Stages 1–4 with proteinuria (>1 g/d) or diabetic kidney disease:	<125/75	Reduction in dietary salt	ACE-inhibitors or angiotensin 2 receptor blockers (diuretics), or CCBs in kidney transplant recipients
CKD Stages 1–4 without proteinuria (<1 g/d):	<135/85	Reduction in dietary salt	ACE-inhibitors or angiotensin-II receptor blockers (diuretics), or CCBs in kidney transplant recipients
CKD Stage 5:	<140/90	Reduction in dietary salt. Reduction in fluid intake and ultrafiltration in dialysis patients	Any, except diuretics in dialysis patients

Modified with permission.[248]

Abbreviations: ACE, angiotensin-converting enzyme; CCB, calcium channel blocker

Task Force recommendations were meant to serve as a guide to clinicians until more definitive recommendations are available.

A K/DOQI Work Group has now been established to develop guidelines for the management of high blood pressure in patients with chronic kidney disease not requiring dialysis. The goals of the Work Group are to determine the recommended blood pressure targets, nonpharmacologic therapy, and antihypertensive drug classes for various causes of kidney disease (including diabetes), with additional recommendations for subgroups of patients based on level of kidney function, level of proteinuria, and, if available, age, gender, and race, for prevention of progression of kidney disease, atherosclerotic cardio-vascular disease, and heart failure (including LVH).

Angiotensin-converting enzyme inhibitors and angiotensin receptor antago-nists slow the progression of chronic kidney disease (R). For this Guideline, the Sixth Report of the Joint National Committee on Prevention, Detection, Evaluation and Treatment of High Blood Pressure (JNC-VI),[245] the most recently updated ADA Clinical Practice Recommendations (2001),[526] and results of a meta-analysis and selected random-ized clinical trials were reviewed. This section presents an overview of the main points of these guidelines and studies. In addition, preliminary results of clinical trials with angiotensin receptor antagonists are briefly discussed. Full detail of the recommendations of the ADA and JNC-VI is beyond the scope of this work, and the reader is referred to these sources for complete guidelines (ADA guidelines on diabetic kidney disease are available on the internet at *www.diabetes.org/clinicalrecommendations/Supple-ment101/S69.htm*).

In addition to lowering systemic blood pressure, ACE-inhibitors and angiotensin re-ceptor antagonists also lower glomerular capillary blood pressure and protein filtration, which may contribute to their beneficial effect in slowing progression.[539,540] They may also have a beneficial effect in reducing angiotensin II mediated cell proliferation and fibrosis.[540]

Diabetic kidney disease. The ADA recommends the use of ACE-inhibitors for dia-betic patients with any evidence of kidney disease (microalbuminuria or greater degree of proteinuria), regardless of the presence of hypertension, in the absence of contraindi-cations or complications:

"Many studies have shown that in hypertensive patients with type 1 diabetes, ACE-inhibitors can reduce the level of albuminuria and can reduce the rate of progression of renal disease to a greater degree than other antihypertensive agents that lower blood pressure by an equal amount. Other studies have shown that there is a benefit in reducing the progression of micro albuminuria in normotensive patients with type 1 diabetes and normotensive and hypertensive patients with type 2 diabetes.

"ACE-inhibitors may exacerbate hyperkalemia in patients with advanced renal insufficiency and/or hyporeninemic hypoaldosteronism. In older patients with bilat-eral renal artery stenosis and in patients with advanced renal disease even without renal artery stenosis, ACE-inhibitors may cause a rapid decline in renal function.

Cough may also occur. This class of agents is contraindicated in pregnancy and therefore should be used with caution in women of childbearing potential.

"Because of the high proportion of patients who progress from microalbuminuria to overt nephropathy and subsequently to ESRD, use of ACE-inhibitors is recommended for all type 1 patients with microalbuminuria (30–299 mg/24hr), even if normotensive. However, because of the more variable rate of progression from microalbuminuria to overt nephropathy and ESRD in patients with type 2 diabetes, the use of ACE-inhibitors in normotensive type 2 diabetic patients is less well substantiated. Should such a patient show progression of albuminuria or develop hypertension, then ACE-inhibitors would clearly be indicated. The effect of ACE-inhibitors appears to be a class effect, so choice of agent may depend of cost and adherence issues."

Two randomized trials comparing the impact of angiotensin receptor blockers with conventional antihypertensive treatment on the progression of diabetic kidney disease have recently been completed: Irbesartan in Diabetic Nephropathy (IDNT)[541] and Reduction of Endpoints in Non-Insulin Dependent Diabetes Mellitus with the Angiotensin II Antagonist Losartan (RENAAL).[542] Both studies showed a beneficial effect of the angiotensin-receptor antagonists. Comparison with ACE-inhibitors is not available to date.

It is important to note that ACE-inhibitors have been found to have beneficial effects on total mortality and cardiovascular disease in diabetic patients without chronic kidney disease.[543–545] Although most patients in these studies were hypertensive, the beneficial effect of ACE-inhibitor therapy appeared to be independent of its blood pressure lowering effect. Thus, patients with diabetes and hypertension or chronic kidney disease benefit from ACE-inhibitors. If blood pressure remains elevated after initiation of an ACE-inhibitor, other antihypertensive agents should be prescribed to achieve target blood pressure.

Nondiabetic kidney disease. The JNC-VI recommends ACE inhibitors as the drug of choice for treating hypertension among some types of patients with nondiabetic kidney disease:

"The most important action to slow progressive renal disease is to lower blood pressure to goal. All classes of antihypertensive drugs are effective, and, in most cases, multiple antihypertensive drugs may be needed. Impressive results have been achieved with ACE-inhibitors. . . in patients with proteinuria greater than 1 gram per 24 hours, and in patients with renal insufficiency. Consequently, patients with hypertension who have renal insufficiency should receive, unless contraindicated, an ACE-inhibitor (in most cases, along with a diuretic) to control hypertension and to slow progressive renal failure. In patients with creatinine level of 265.2 μmol/L (3 mg/dL) or greater, ACE-inhibitors should be used with caution.

"An initial transient decrease in GFR may occur during the first 3 months of treatment as blood pressure is lowered. If patients are euvolemic and creatinine rises 88.4 μmol/L (1 mg/dL) above baseline levels, creatinine and potassium should be remeasured after several days; if they remain persistently elevated, consideration should be given to the diagnosis of renal artery stenosis and ACE-inhibitors and angio-

tensin II receptor blockers discontinued because these drugs can markedly reduce renal perfusion in patients with bilateral renal artery stenosis or renal artery stenosis to a solitary kidney."

These recommendations are based on a number of randomized trials published over the past decade, which have been summarized recently in a meta-analysis of patient level data.[546] In that analysis, data on 1860 nondiabetic patients included in 11 randomized clinical trials of various ACE-inhibitors were pooled. The results showed better blood pressure control, lower urine protein excretion and an approximately 30% reduction in the risk of development of kidney failure and the combined endpoint of doubling of baseline serum creatinine or kidney failure in the ACE-inhibitor group. The beneficial effects of ACE-inhibitors to slow progression appeared to be independent of their effects on blood pressure and proteinuria. The results also showed an incrementally greater beneficial effect with greater degrees of proteinuria >0.5 g/d. The benefit to patients with proteinuria <0.5 g/d was inconclusive. A recent report from the African American Study of Kidney Disease and Hypertension (AASK) documents a beneficial effect of the ACE-inhibitor ramipril compared to the dihydropyridine calcium channel blocker amlodipine on the GFR decline in African Americans with nephrosclerosis and decreased GFR.[547] The beneficial effect was more pronounced in patients with proteinuria ≥300 mg/24 hr.

The available evidence suggests a benefit to using ACE-inhibitors to treat hypertension among proteinuric patients with nondiabetic kidney disease. The benefit may extend to patients without proteinuria but this is not established. The use of ACE-inhibitors must always be done with the consideration that it may have a detrimental effect on GFR in patients with renovascular disease or renal artery stenosis. Furthermore, in kidney transplant recipients, ACE-inhibitors may exacerbate hyperkalemia caused by cyclosporine or tacrolimus. Thus, treatment of patients with chronic kidney disease with ACE-inhibitors requires knowledge of the expected benefits and risks of therapy and careful attention to blood pressure, kidney function, serum electrolytes, and possible drug interactions.

The HOPE Study also demonstrated a beneficial effect of the ACE-inhibitor ramipril on total mortality and cardiovascular disease in nondiabetic patients without chronic kidney disease, but with a history of cardiovascular disease and one cardiovascular disease risk factor (including hypertension).[545] The beneficial effect of the ACE-inhibitor appeared to be independent of its blood pressure lowering effect. Thus, non-diabetic patients with chronic kidney disease (especially if they have proteinuria) or cardiovascular disease benefit from ACE-inhibitors. If blood pressure remains elevated after initiation of an ACE-inhibitor, other antihypertensive agents should be prescribed to achieve the target blood pressure.

There is insufficient evidence to recommend for or against routine prescription of dietary protein restriction for the purpose of slowing the progression of chronic kidney disease; individual decision-making is recommended, after discussion of risks and benefits (R). The MDRD Study was designed to determine the impact of protein restriction on rate of GFR decline, however the results of this study were inconclusive.[503] Study A compared a low protein diet (0.58 g/kg/d) to a usual protein diet (1.3 g/kg/d) among patients with moderately decreased GFR (25 to 55 mL/min/1.73 m²). As described earlier (Fig 50), there was an initial faster GFR decline in the low-protein diet group, followed by a slower GFR decline thereafter, but no significant benefit over a 3-year interval. Study B compared a very low protein diet (0.28 g/kg/d) supplemented with a mixture of essential ketoacids and amino acids (0.28 g/kg/d) to a low protein diet (0.58 g/kg/d) in patients with severely decreased GFR (13 to 24 mL/min/1.73 m²). There was no apparent benefit of the very low protein diet. There have been several secondary analyses of the data, which provide further information on the effectiveness of these interventions.[503] Specifically, comparisons of the distributions of GFR slopes between randomized groups in Study A were consistent with a beneficial effect of the low protein diet group. Analyses of the impact of achieved protein intake in Study B revealed a 49% reduction in risk of kidney failure or death for every 0.2 g/kg lower achieved total protein intake. In another report, it was noted that a specific ketoacid supplement with a very low protein diet may be more beneficial than the supplement with essential amino acids used in the MDRD study.[548] A meta-analysis of five randomized trials of 1,413 patients, including MDRD Study A, showed a 30% reduction in kidney failure or death in patients randomized to the low protein diet group.[549] A meta-analysis of randomized and uncontrolled trials and observational studies suggested that dietary protein restriction reduced the rate of decline of GFR by only 0.53 mL/min per year.[550] Patients in these studies did not reportedly develop hypoalbuminemia or other signs of malnutrition. However, they received intensive nutritional monitoring and counseling. It is thus unclear whether such severely restricted protein diets can be safely prescribed or even maintained in the absence of frequent dietitian involvement.

The Work Group concluded that there was insufficient information to recommend for or against a low protein diet (0.6 g/kg/d) for patients with chronic kidney disease. The lack of firm evidence regarding its impact, and the logistic and financial difficulties of providing intensive nutritional intervention, preclude recommendation of a low protein diet in all patients with chronic kidney disease. Individual decision-making is recommended, after discussion of risks and benefits. This is in agreement with the K/DOQI Clinical Practice Guidelines on Nutrition in Chronic Renal Failure,[75] which recommends consideration of a low protein diet (0.6 g/kg/d) for patients with GFR in the range of CKD Stage 4 and 5. Whether or not the decision is made to pursue a low protein diet, the Work Group re inforces the importance of maintaining a good nutritional status with advancing chronic kidney disease, which generally would involve evaluation and monitoring by a dietician, and refers the reader to Guideline 9.

There is insufficient evidence to recommend lipid-lowering therapy for the purpose of slowing the progression of chronic kidney disease (R). Some of observational studies have reported that various dyslipidemias are associated with decreased kidney function in the general population and in patients with chronic kidney disease.[480,551-554] However, it is impossible to determine from these studies whether dyslipidemias cause reduced kidney function, result from reduced kidney function, or whether other conditions such as proteinuria cause both reduced kidney function and dyslipidemias. Each of these explanations is plausible, and only randomized, controlled trials can adequately test the hypothesis that dyslipidemias cause a decline in kidney function.

Unfortunately, there are no large, adequately powered, randomized, controlled trials testing the hypothesis that treatment of dyslipidemia preserves kidney function. However, there have been several small studies[555-566] and a meta-analysis of these studies.[567] This meta-analysis included prospective, controlled trials published before July 1, 1999. Three trials published only in abstract form were included,[555,556,566] but one of these studies has subsequently been published in a peer-reviewed journal.[566] All patients were followed for at least 3 months, but in only 5 studies were patients followed for at least 1 year. Statins were used in 10 studies, gemfibrozil in 1 study, and probocol in 1 study. Altogether, 362 patients with chronic kidney disease were included in the meta-analysis. The results suggested that the rate of decline in GFR was significantly less in patients treated with a lipid-lowering agent compared to placebo.[567] No significant heterogeneity in treatment effect was detected between the studies. However, the quality of the studies was generally low, and their small sample sizes and relatively short duration of follow-up make it difficult to conclude that lipid-lowering therapies reduce the rate of decline in GFR in chronic kidney disease. Clearly, adequately powered, randomized controlled trials are needed to determine the role of lipid-lowering therapy in retarding the rate of decline in kidney function in patients with chronic kidney disease. The evaluation and management of dyslipidemia in patients with chronic kidney disease has been addressed by the NKF Task Force on Cardiovascular Disease in Chronic Renal Disease and is reviewed briefly in Guideline 15. The management of dyslipidemia in patients with kidney failure is the subject of an ongoing K/DOQI Work Group.

There is insufficient evidence to recommend for or against partial correction of anemia with recombinant human erythropoietin and or/iron for the purpose of slowing the rate of decline of GFR (R). There have been several studies evaluating the use of erythropoietin and/or iron among patients with chronic kidney disease prior to initiation of dialysis, with the intention of demonstrating effectiveness in improving anemia and lack of harm in terms of increasing the rate of decline of kidney function. Most patients enrolled in these studies had severely reduced kidney function. These studies have shown either no overall difference in the rate of decline of kidney function in treated compared to untreated groups[297,304,306] or compared to pre-treatment rates of decline,[568] or a slight benefit in terms of a slower rate of decline of GFR in the treated group[294,569] and prolongation of time to ESRD[569], or reduced proportion of patients who experienced doubling of baseline serum creatinine in the treated versus untreated groups.[305] Each of these studies, as well as a study comparing intravenous with oral iron and erythropoietin for the treatment of anemia in chronic kidney disease,[570] also concluded that normalization of hemoglobin or hematocrit had essentially no effect on the rate of decline of kidney function. In one study comparing intravenous iron with or without erythropoietin in patients with less severe reduction in kidney function (mean serum creatinine of 2.8 mg/dL), the authors concluded that "treatment of anemia was associated with a slowing of the rate of progression of renal failure" based on the fact that the GFR decline pre-treatment was faster than post-treatment in long term follow-up.[571] However, this study excluded patients who progressed to dialysis during the initial study period.

In summary, the reviewed studies were generally designed to demonstrate no difference/no harm of treatment of anemia, primarily among patients with severely reduced kidney function. The available evidence that partial correction of anemia with erythropoietin (and iron) results in improvement in the rate of decline of GFR is therefore inconclusive. Further studies specifically addressing the effects of anemia and its treatment on rate of GFR decline are necessary to clarify this issue. The evaluation and management of anemia should be undertaken as described in Guideline 8, and as previously detailed in the K/DOQI Clinical Practice Guidelines on Anemia of Chronic Kidney Disease.[265]

GFR decline may be irregular. Acute decline in GFR may be superimposed on chronic kidney disease. Risk factors for acute decline in GFR include (R):
- **Volume depletion;**
- **Intravenous radiographic contrast;**
- **Selected antimicrobial agents (for example, aminoglycosides and amphotericin B);**
- **Nonsteroidal anti-inflammatory agents (NSAIDs), including cyclo-oxygenase type 2 (COX 2) inhibitors;**
- **Angiotensin-converting enzyme inhibitors and angiotensin-receptor blockers;**
- **Cyclosporine and tacrolimus;**
- **Obstruction of the urinary tract.**

Selected review articles were used to formulate this section.[572,573]

Reduced blood flow to the kidney, toxic insult, obstruction, inflammation, or infection can result in acute deterioration of kidney function. Reduced blood flow to the kidney and intrinsic damage to the kidney because of a nephrotoxic or ischemic insult are the most common causes of acute deterioration of GFR.

Volume depletion accounts for the majority of community acquired cases of acute reduction in the blood flow to the kidney and a resultant reduction in GFR. The most common precipitants of volume depletion are vomiting, diarrhea, poor fluid intake, fever, and diuretic use. Heart failure can effectively result in a reduction of blood flow to the kidney due to reduced cardiac output, in the face of apparent volume overload. The risk of developing acute deterioration of kidney function due to volume depletion is highest in the elderly, as they may already have compromised blood flow to the kidneys due to atherosclerotic disease.

Common toxic insults encountered in clinical practice are radiocontrast dye, amino-glycoside antibiotics, and NSAIDs. In particular, these are likely to result in acute decline in GFR if there is an additional insult such as sepsis, volume depletion, heart failure, or treatment with ACE inhibitors. Toxins can cause kidney failure via a number of mechanisms including (not an exhaustive list): (1) alteration of kidney blood flow (NSAIDs, ACE inhibitors, cyclosporine, radiocontrast agents), (2) direct tubular injury (aminoglycosides, radiocontrast, amphotericin B), (3) intratubular obstruction (acyclovir, sulfonamides), (4) allergic interstitial nephritis (NSAIDs, penicillins, cephalosporins, sulfonamides). The avoidance of potential nephrotoxins, such as intravenous radiographic contrast, certain antibiotics, and NSAIDs must be based on an individualized assessment of the risks of acute decline in GFR versus the therapeutic benefits of treatment. For example, in a patient with debilitating arthritis, avoidance of NSAID use should be considered in light of the benefits of reducing pain and immobility; in a patient with coronary artery disease, the avoidance of intravenous radiocontrast should be weighed against the potential benefits of an angioplasty procedure.

Finally, obstruction can cause an acute decline in GFR if there is bilateral ureteral obstruction, unilateral ureteral obstruction in a person with a single functioning kidney, or obstruction at the level of the bladder. The most common causes of obstruction are prostatic hypertrophy, cancer of the prostate or cervix, or retroperitoneal disorders. In addition, kidney stones, blood, fungal infection, and bladder malignancy may result in obstruction. Unlike with toxic insults, acute decline in GFR due to obstruction is commonly seen in the outpatient setting.

In summary, there are numerous situations that may cause an acute deterioration in the GFR that are potentially avoidable. The clinician should become familiar with the most common causes, in order to prevent avoidable worsening of the course of chronic kidney disease.

LIMITATIONS

The formulation of this guideline was limited by a number of factors. Most notably, with many of the studies the results were difficult to compare as they use different measures for kidney function: measured GFR or creatinine clearance, estimation equations for GFR or creatinine clearance, or simply serum creatinine. Further limiting the comparability of the results across the studies is the wide variation in the selection of analytic techniques and presentation of data.

A major limitation of this guideline is its failure to provide a semi-quantitative assessment of the relationships between the factors assessed and the outcomes of rate of progression or risk for kidney failure. This review of these studies does not provide a conclusive answer to the causes underlying the more rapid rate of progression or increased risk for kidney failure.

CLINICAL APPLICATIONS

It is important to follow each individual's rate of progression, as there is a wide variation among individuals and disease types and in the response to interventions.

There is a broad range of factors that are associated with more rapid decline in kidney function, some of which are amenable to interventions.

Certain patient groups, defined by either type of kidney disease, clinical, gender, racial, or age characteristics, are at greater risk for progression of kidney disease—this denotes the need to increase awareness among patients and providers about proper care and the need to institute interventions to attempt to slow progression.

IMPLEMENTATION ISSUES

Patients with certain causes of kidney disease, and certain modifiable and nonmodifiable characteristics, may be at increased risk for faster rates of GFR decline. There is increasing evidence that certain interventions can slow the decline in GFR and prevent the development of kidney failure in both diabetic and nondiabetic patients.

It is thus critical to educate patients and providers regarding the risk factors and to facilitate providing aggressive interventions where indicated. This may require changing the policies of care providers and payers regarding frequency of follow-up and payment for medications.

RESEARCH RECOMMENDATIONS

It is evident that there is a large amount of data in studies of varying size and quality regarding the impact of underlying conditions, patient characteristics, and interventions. However, there are certain factors whose impact has not been conclusively determined, such as dietary protein intake, hyperlipidemia, and anemia and their treatment. Proteinuria as a risk factor deserves special consideration. Antihypertensive agents, especially ACE-inhibitors and angiotensin-receptor blockers, reduce proteinuria and slow the progression of kidney disease. However, the role of proteinuria per se has not been adequately studied. There is a need to develop alternative therapies to reduce urine protein.

Many of the conclusions regarding the impact of factors unrelated to intervention, such as age, gender, race, and cause of kidney disease, come from "small" interventional trials. Similarly, in the case of the impact of blood pressure control, conclusions largely come from the observations that patients with lower blood pressures have improved outcomes. In the case of cause of kidney disease, the conclusion that certain causes are associated with faster rates of progression come from the comparison of studies of single causes, using diverse methods to measure or estimate GFR. A noninterventional prospective cohort study including sufficient numbers of patients with all causes of kidney disease, undergoing similar testing for level of kidney function, would be ideal to evaluate the impact of cause of kidney disease on the rate of decline in GFR. Alternatively, a sufficiently large prospective interventional trial could achieve a similar goal.

GUIDELINE 14. ASSOCIATION OF CHRONIC KIDNEY DISEASE WITH DIABETIC COMPLICATIONS

The risk of cardiovascular disease, retinopathy, and other diabetic complications is higher in patients with diabetic kidney disease than in diabetic patients without kidney disease.

- Prevention, detection, evaluation, and treatment of diabetic complications in patients with chronic kidney disease should follow published guidelines and position statements.
- Guidelines regarding angiotensin-converting enzyme inhibitors or angiotensin-receptor blockers and strict blood pressure control are particularly important since these agents may prevent or delay some of the adverse outcomes of both kidney and cardiovascular disease.
- Application of published guidelines to diabetic patients with chronic kidney disease should take into account their "higher-risk" status for diabetic complications.

BACKGROUND

The onset of diabetes is characterized by metabolic and hemodynamic disturbances that increase vascular permeability, raise systemic blood pressure, and alter the regulation of intracapillary pressure. In the kidney, these changes may lead to increased trafficking of plasma proteins across the glomerular membrane and to the appearance of protein in the urine. The presence of urinary protein not only heralds the onset of diabetic kidney disease, but it may contribute to the glomerular and tubulointerstitial damage that ultimately leads to diabetic glomerulosclerosis.[574] The strong relationship between proteinuria and a constellation of other diabetic complications supports the view that elevated urinary protein excretion reflects a generalized vascular disturbance that affects many organs, including the eyes, heart, and nervous system.[575]

This guideline describes the association of cardiovascular (macrovascular), retinal (microvascular), and other (principally neuropathic) complications of diabetes with levels of albumin/protein in the urine. It highlights the strong relationship between progressive diabetic kidney disease and the development of other diabetic complications and emphasizes the importance of monitoring and treating diabetic chronic kidney disease patients for these other complications.

RATIONALE

Microalbuminuria refers to levels of urinary albumin excretion below those detected by standard dipstick methods and macroalbuminuria refers to higher levels of urinary albumin excretion. Microalbuminuria is present when the albumin excretion rate is 30 to 300 mg/24 hours (20 to 200 μg/min) or the albumin-to-creatinine ratio is 30 to 300 mg/g.[576] Proteinuria generally refers to a positive dipstick test for protein or to a daily output of protein above a certain cut point, typically $\geq$500 mg/d. Thus, macroalbuminuria and proteinuria may be relatively equivalent measures of urinary protein excretion (see Guideline 5). Nevertheless, differences in methods of measurement and the lack of standardized definitions or terminology often make comparisons between studies difficult.

Definitions of Diabetic Complications Other Than Chronic Kidney Disease

Cardiovascular disease. Cardiovascular disease is not a specific complication of diabetes per se, since it occurs frequently in nondiabetic individuals. Diabetes and an array of metabolic disorders associated with it, however, increase the risk of cardiovascular disease in diabetic patients and may accelerate the process of atherosclerosis. For the purposes of this guideline, cardiovascular disease refers to coronary heart disease, cerebrovascular disease, peripheral vascular disease, congestive heart failure, and left ventricular hypertrophy. The American Diabetes Association provides clinical practice recommendations for screening and treatment of cardiovascular disease in diabetes[526] which are available on the Internet (*www.diabetes.org/Clinicalrecommendations*)

The variety of measures of cardiovascular disease used in different studies may limit the interpretability of the findings reviewed for this guideline, although the nearly uniformly positive association suggests this may not be an important limitation. On the other hand, cardiovascular disease itself may increase the level of urinary albumin/protein. Thus, the extent to which chronic diabetic glomerulosclerosis is an independent risk factor for the development of cardiovascular disease may be difficult to determine with certainty, especially in congestive heart failure, without demonstrating diabetic kidney damage at the tissue level.

Retinopathy. The earliest change of diabetic retinopathy that can be seen with the ophthalmoscope is the retinal microaneurysm. Other changes found in nonproliferative retinopathy include retinal hemorrhages, hard exudates, cotton-wool spots, intraretinal microvascular abnormalities (IRMA), and venous abnormalities. Growth of abnormal blood vessels and fibrous tissue that extends from the retinal surface or optic nerve characterizes the proliferative stage of diabetic retinopathy. With experience, these changes can be identified readily by direct ophthalmoscopy, preferably through dilated pupils. Stereoscopic fundus photographs, however, produce a more reliable and reproducible assessment of diabetic retinopathy. The Airlie House Classification scheme, or a modification of this scheme, is commonly used to classify the level of retinopathy in epidemiological studies; the more severely involved eye is used for classification. The American Diabetes Association provides clinical practice recommendations for screening and treatment of diabetic retinopathy.[526]

Neither the diagnosis nor classification of retinopathy was uniform in the studies reviewed for this guideline. Some studies performed retinal photographs (from 2 to 7 fields, depending on the study) and others relied on ophthalmoscopic examinations through dilated pupils. Moreover, retinopathy was graded by the Airlie House Classification scheme (or a modification of this scheme) in some studies and by less precisely defined clinical criteria in others. Beyond methodological issues, the absence of retinopathy in some subjects with elevated albuminuria/proteinuria may reflect the presence of nondiabetic kidney disease, particularly in older type 2 diabetic patients. These factors undoubtedly contributed, at least in part, to the reported variability of the association between retinopathy and albuminuria/proteinuria.

Neuropathy. Diabetic neuropathy is perhaps one of the most difficult complications of diabetes to measure. Although 60% to 70% of people with either type of diabetes are affected, many investigators in the past used non-standardized methods for measuring neuropathy. The lack of standardized nomenclature and criteria for diabetic neuropathy

Table 126. Research Classification of Diabetic Polyneuropathy

| | | Clinical Assessments | |
	Symptom Score	Neurological Examination Score	Abnormal Physiological Tests
Class I			
A	0	0	0 *or* AFT or QST
B	0	0	EDX *or* AFT and QST
C	0	0	EDX *and* either AFT or QST or both
Class II			
A	+	0	0 *or* AFT or QST
B	0 or +	+	EDX *or* AFT and QST
C	0 or + +	+ 0 or +	EDX *and* either AFT or QST or both

Reprinted with permission.[577]

Abbreviations and symbols: +, abnormal result; 0, normal result; AFT, autonomic function testing; EDX, electrodiagnosis; QST, quantitative sensory testing

undoubtedly diminished the quality of the data available for review. Accordingly, studies examining the relationship between the level of urinary albumin/protein and diabetic neuropathy often yielded confusing and conflicting results.

In 1988, a joint conference of the American Diabetes Association and the American Academy of Neurology adopted standardized nomenclature and criteria for the diagnosis of neuropathy in diabetes.[577] The classification was divided into subclinical and clinical neuropathy (Table 126). Subclinical neuropathy is defined as an abnormal electrodiagnostic test, quantitative sensory threshold, or autonomic function test in the absence of clinical signs and symptoms. Clinical neuropathy is defined as an abnormal test associated with clinical signs and/or symptoms. The American Diabetes Association provides clinical practice recommendations for screening and treatment of diabetic neuropathy.[526]

Strength of Evidence

Given the numerous studies and general agreement on the relationship between proteinuria and complications of diabetes other than chronic kidney disease, review articles were used as the primary source of information for this guideline. Since reviews often reported the associations qualitatively, individual studies were included to provide quantitative estimates of the association. Reference was also made to individual studies of non-Caucasian patients, since many reviews reported only results from studies in Caucasians. Given the low rate or absence of type 1 diabetes in many non-Caucasians, the impact of ethnicity on the relationship between proteinuria and other diabetic complications was examined only in those with type 2 diabetes. Selection of individual studies for

Table 127. Prevalence of Atherosclerotic Cardiovascular Disease
According to the Stage of Kidney Disease in Various Racial/Ethnic Groups with Type 2 Diabetes

Author, Year	No. of Subjects	Applic-ability	Ethnicity	Definition of ASCVD	Crude Prevalence (%) by Stage of Kidney Disease*			Quality
					NAE	Micro	Clin Prot	
Stephenson,[597] 1994	3,421	⇈	Multiple[a]	CHD	20[b]	20[b]	26[b]	◉
Lee,[598] 1995	631	⇈	Korean	CHD	10	12	26	◉
				CVD	6	11	17	
				PVD	3	7	17	
John,[599] 1991	538	⇈	Asian Indian	CHD	15	26	29	◉
				CVD	2	6	10	
				PVD	0.5	0.9	2	
Howard,[600] 1995	1,500 (AZ)	⇡	American Indian	CHD	15	ND	26	○
	1,527 (OK)				28		40	
	1,522 (ND, SD)				29		48	

* NAE corresponds to individuals at increased risk for CKD, while microproteinuria and clinical proteinuria correspond to CKD Stage 1.

[a] Includes American Indians, Chinese, Japanese, whites, non-Hispanic whites.
[b] Proteinuria was measured by the salicylsulphonic acid test; light and heavy proteinuria were grouped into the clinical proteinuria category; some of those without proteinuria by this test may have had microalbuminuria.

Abbreviations: ASCVD, atherosclerotic cardiovascular disease; NAE, normal urinary albumin excretion; Micro, microproteinuria; Clin Prot, clinical proteinuria; CHD, coronary heart disease; CVD, cerebrovascular disease; PVD, peripheral vascular disease; AZ, Arizona; ND, North Dakota; OK, Oklahoma; SD, South Dakota

this guideline was not subject to the systematic review process used in other K/DOQI guidelines and is intended to be illustrative rather than comprehensive.

Cardiovascular disease is related to the level of proteinuria or albuminuria in diabetic kidney disease (Table 127 and Figs 51 and 52) (R, C). Increased cardiovascular mortality was linked with elevated urinary albumin excretion in type 2 diabetes in 1984[578,579] and with type 1 diabetes in 1987.[580] This association was confirmed subse-

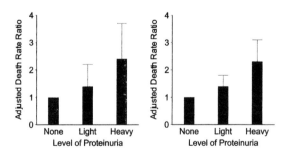

Fig 51. Cardiovascular mortality with diabetes. Relative cardiovascular mortality in type 1 (left panel) and type 2 (right panel) diabetes according to the level of urinary protein excretion in the WHO Multinational Study of Vascular Disease in Diabetes.[597] Death rate ratios were adjusted for age, duration of diabetes, systolic blood pressure, serum cholesterol concentration, and smoking history by Poisson regression.

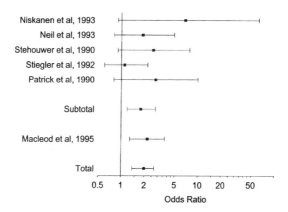

Fig 52. Microalbuminuria and cardiovascular morbidity with type 2 diabetes. Crude association of microalbuminuria and cardiovascular morbidity or mortality in type 2 diabetes. The results are presented with (total) and without (subtotal) the study that included subjects with clinical proteinuria. Adapted and reprinted with permission.[586]

quently in many studies and described in numerous review articles,[581-596] and it is reported in diverse racial/ethnic groups (Table 127).

The association between diabetic kidney disease and cardiovascular disease is generally considered stronger in type 2 than in type 1 diabetes at all levels of albuminuria/proteinuria, due in large part to the older age of the type 2 diabetic patients. In the WHO Multinational Study of Vascular Disease in Diabetes,[597] however, similar cardiovascular death rates were reported in the 1,188 patients with type 1 and the 3,234 patients with type 2 diabetes from ten centers worldwide (Fig 51). These results may be influenced by the racial/ethnic mix of the sample cohort, since some populations included in the cohort with high rates of type 2 diabetes, such as the Pima Indians, have lower rates of cardiovascular disease than Caucasians with type 2 diabetes.[601]

A meta-analysis of 11 cohort studies involving 2,138 patients with type 2 diabetes[586] provides compelling evidence that even modest elevations of urinary albumin excretion are associated with increased cardiovascular risk. In this review, patients with microalbuminuria had an overall crude odds ratio for cardiovascular morbidity and mortality of 2.0 (95% confidence interval, 1.4 to 2.7) compared to those with normal urinary albumin excretion (Fig 52).

Retinopathy is related to the level of proteinuria or albuminuria in diabetic kidney disease (Table 128) (R, C). Review articles evaluated for this guideline included patients from clinic and population-based studies of type 1 and type 2 diabetes.[581,585,590,591,595,602] These articles reflect the widely recognized positive association between the level of albuminuria/proteinuria and retinopathy in both types of diabetes. Discordance between these two diabetic complications, however, occurs fre-

---

Table 128. Prevalence of Retinopathy According to the Stage of Kidney Disease in Various Racial/Ethnic Groups with Type 2 Diabetes

Study	No. of Patients	Ethnicity	Definition of Retinopathy*	Crude prevalence (%) by Stage of kidney disease		
				NAE	Micro	Clin Prot
Lee,[598] 1995	631	Korean	Nonproliferative	20	39	48
			Proliferative	1	11	34
John,[599] 1991	538	Asian Indian	Retinopathy	8	12	50

* Retinopathy determined by ophthalmoscopy through dilated pupils.

Abbreviations: NAE, normal urinary albumin excretion; Micro, microproteinuria; Clin Prot, clinical proteinuria

quently,[603,604] particularly in type 2 diabetes, because of the coexistence of nondiabetic kidney disease. Nevertheless, the incidence of proliferative retinopathy increases dramatically with the development of elevated urinary albumin/protein excretion.[605] A greater frequency of retinopathy with higher levels of urinary albumin/protein excretion is also reported in various racial/ethnic groups (Table 128), and the relationship may be stronger in some groups than in others.[606]

Other diabetic complications (for example, neuropathy) may be related to the level of proteinuria or albuminuria in diabetic kidney disease (R). Less is known about the strength of the association between urinary albumin/protein excretion and neuropathy than about the other complications of type 1 and type 2 diabetes. The review articles evaluated for this guideline comment briefly that some studies found a relationship whereas others did not.[581,591] Much of the confusion is undoubtedly attributable to non-standardized definitions of diabetic neuropathy. In 1988, consensus was achieved on a standardized classification scheme (vide supra), but there are still few reviews available that comment on the relationship between albuminuria/proteinuria and diabetic neuropathy by these criteria.

A large number of published guidelines and position statements are available to guide the practitioner in the prevention, detection, evaluation and treatment of diabetic complications (Table 129). Guidelines regarding angiotensin-converting-enzyme inhibitors or angiotensin-receptor blockers and strict blood pressure control are particularly important since these agents may prevent or delay some of the adverse outcomes of both kidney and cardiovascular disease (R).

LIMITATIONS

Data in the elderly and in racial/ethnic groups other than non-Hispanic whites are sparse, particularly in review articles, making the findings reported in this guideline difficult to extrapolate with confidence to the elderly and to different populations around the world. Moreover, after the development of kidney failure, much of the available data do not differentiate type 1 from type 2 diabetes.

CLINICAL APPLICATIONS

Studies in both type 1[617] and type 2[618] diabetes indicate that nearly all of the excess mortality associated with diabetes is found in those with elevated urinary albumin/protein

Table 129. Guidelines and Position Statements on Care of Diabetic Complications

Cardiovascular Disease

National High Blood Pressure Education Program Working Group Report on Hypertension in Diabetes[607]

The Sixth Report of the Joint National Committee on Prevention, Detection, Evaluation, and Treatment of High Blood Pressure (JNC-VI)[245]

Executive Summary of the Third Report of the National Cholesterol Education Program (NCEP) Expert Panel on Detection, Evaluation and Treatment of High Blood Cholesterol in Adults (Adult Treatment Panel III[608]

Management of Dyslipidemia in Adults with Diabetes[609]

Aspirin Therapy in Diabetes[610]

Consensus Development Conference on the Diagnosis of Coronary Heart Disease in People with Diabetes[611]

Diabetes and Cardiovascular Disease. A Statement for Healthcare Professionals from the American Heart Association[612]

Retinopathy

Diabetic Retinopathy[613,614]

Care of the Patient with Diabetes Mellitus[615]

Neuropathy

Report and Recommendations of the San Antonio Conference on Diabetic Neuropathy[577]

Proceedings of a Consensus Development Conference on Standardized Measures in Diabetic Neuropathy[616]

General

Standards of Medical Care for Patients with Diabetes Mellitus[526]

---

excretion. Much of the excess mortality, particularly in type 2 diabetes, is attributable to cardiovascular disease rather than kidney failure, indicating the importance of identifying and treating the other complications of diabetes in these patients and the importance of close monitoring of proteinuria and kidney function to identify those at increased risk. The evidence reviewed to date suggests that the appearance of elevated albuminuria/proteinuria is associated with a higher risk of the non-kidney complications of diabetes even as patients progress towards chronic kidney disease. The association between albuminuria/proteinuria and cardiovascular disease, diabetic retinopathy, and diabetic neuropathy described in this guideline supports the recommendation that patients with diabetic nephropathy be carefully examined for the presence of other diabetic complications and that proper care for these complications be initiated. This recommendation is based on opinion derived from a review of the available evidence.

IMPLEMENTATION ISSUES

Implementation of coordinated patient management to address the diversity of potential complications is one of the greatest challenges of diabetes care. Recommendations regarding management of diet, exercise, glycemia, blood pressure, lipids, neuropathy, retinopathy, and cardiovascular disease must all be considered in addition to those for kidney disease. Although the challenges for health care providers are formidable, they may seem overwhelming to those with diabetes. One of the objectives of the National Diabetes Education Program, a Program managed jointly by the National Institute of Diabetes and Digestive and Kidney Diseases and the Centers for Disease Control and Prevention, is to promote an integrated patient-centered approach to diabetes care with the goal of reducing the morbidity and mortality associated with diabetes and its complications (*www.ndep.nib.gov*).

RESEARCH RECOMMENDATIONS

Much of the understanding about the relationships between diabetic nephropathy and cardiovascular disease, retinopathy, and neuropathy comes from studies in Caucasians. Yet the epidemic of diabetes affects many racial/ethnic groups worldwide. Since race/ethnicity may influence not only the risk of diabetes, but the severity and type of diabetic complications that develop, further characterization of the impact of diabetes in different populations is needed. Further characterization of these relationships in the elderly is also needed. Moreover, the extent to which aggressive treatment of diabetic complications modulates the progression of kidney disease needs to be examined, since recent studies suggest that improvements in the treatment of cardiovascular disease in patients with type 2 diabetes have contributed to an increase in diabetic kidney failure.[619]

GUIDELINE 15.   ASSOCIATION OF CHRONIC KIDNEY DISEASE WITH CARDIOVASCULAR DISEASE

Patients with chronic kidney disease, irrespective of diagnosis, are at increased risk of cardiovascular disease (CVD), including coronary heart disease, cerebrovascular disease, peripheral vascular disease, and heart failure. Both "traditional" and "chronic kidney disease related (nontraditional)" CVD risk factors may contribute to this increased risk.

- All patients with chronic kidney disease should be considered in the "highest risk" group for cardiovascular disease, irrespective of levels of traditional CVD risk factors.
- All patients with chronic kidney disease should undergo assessment of CVD risk factors, including:
  - Measurement of "traditional" CVD risk factors in all patients;
  - Individual decision-making regarding measurement of selected "CKD-related" CVD risk factors in some patients.
- Recommendations for CVD risk factor reduction should take into account the "highest-risk" status of patients with chronic kidney disease.

BACKGROUND

Similar to the general population, cardiovascular disease accounts for 40% to 50% of all deaths in the end-stage renal disease (ESRD) population, and CVD mortality rates in ESRD patients are approximately 15 times higher than the general population.[261] The burden of cardiovascular disease is evident upon the initiation of replacement therapy. Forty percent of patients starting dialysis already have evidence of coronary heart disease (CHD)[2] and only 15% are considered to have normal left ventricular structure and function by echocardiographic criteria.[620] Clearly, many manifestations of cardiovascular disease arise before the onset of kidney failure and the need for dialysis or transplantation.

Previously the National Kidney Foundation convened a Task Force to evaluate the epidemic of cardiovascular disease in patients with chronic kidney disease.[9] Highlighted in this report was the high mortality from cardiovascular disease in patients with kidney failure. The purpose of this guideline is to focus on the CVD risk associated with chronic kidney disease (excluding patients treated by dialysis). Guideline 14 addresses the risk of cardiovascular disease in patients with diabetic kidney disease. Therefore, this guideline focuses on the risk of cardiovascular disease in patients with nondiabetic kidney disease, and specifically to address the question whether chronic kidney disease is a risk factor for the development of cardiovascular disease. Guidelines for the evaluation and management of specific CVD risk factors in this population are currently being developed by other K/DOQI Work Groups.

RATIONALE

Definitions

For the purposes of this guideline, "cardiovascular disease" refers to coronary heart disease, cerebrovascular disease, peripheral vascular disease, and congestive heart failure. Left ventricular hypertrophy (LVH) was not always included, even though it is associated with chronic kidney disease and is a risk factor for clinical cardiovascular events. "Traditional" risk factors are those variables defined in the general population through prospective cohort studies such as the Framingham Heart Study (Table 130). "Chronic kidney disease (CKD)-related" risk factors include the hemodynamic and metabolic abnormalities associated with chronic kidney disease and complications of decreased kidney function. Some authors have subdivided CKD-related risk factors in those factors altered by the "uremic" state (for example, hypertension, dyslipidemia, homocysteine) and factors that are characteristic of the "uremic" state (for example, anemia, malnutrition, oxidative stress, and hyperparathyroidism).[621]

Strength of Evidence

Where possible, data from the NKF Task Force on Cardiovascular Disease in Chronic Renal Disease[9] has been used as the source of information for this guideline. Given the breadth of the topic and the extensive summary by the NKF Task Force, the current Work Group did not feel it was necessary to duplicate their effort. In addition to the Task Force summary, other recent review articles, where necessary, were used as a source of information for the following rationale statements. To determine the association of albuminuria and decreased GFR with incident cardiovascular disease, evidence tables were compiled after a systematic review of original articles.

Table 130. Traditional vs. Chronic Kidney Disease-Related Factors Potentially Related to an Increased Risk for Cardiovascular Disease

Traditional CVD Risk Factors	CKD-Related (Nontraditional) CVD Risk Factors
Older age	Type (diagnosis) of CKD
Male gender	Decreased GFR
White race	Proteinuria
Hypertension	Renin-angiotensin system activity
Elevated LDL cholesterol	Extra-cellular fluid volume overload
Decreased HDL cholesterol	
Diabetes mellitus	Abnormal calcium and phosphorus metabolism
Tobacco use	
Physical inactivity	Dyslipidemia
Menopause	Anemia
Psychosocial stress	Malnutrition
Family history of CVD	Inflammation
	Infection
	Thrombogenic factors
	Oxidative stress
	Elevated homocysteine
	Uremic toxins

Modified and reprinted with permission.[3]

Nondiabetic patients with chronic kidney disease have an increased prevalence of cardiovascular disease compared to the general population (R). Highlighted in the NKF Task Force Report was the high prevalence of cardiovascular disease in dialysis patients.[9] Data from the USRDS in 1997 show a 40% prevalence of either coronary artery disease or congestive heart failure in patients starting dialysis.[2] However, few studies have examined the prevalence of cardiovascular disease in a representative sample of patients with earlier stages of chronic kidney disease. In a report from the Framingham Heart Study, the prevalence of various manifestations of cardiovascular disease were examined in participants with elevated serum creatinine (serum creatinine 1.5 to 3.0 mg/dL and 1.4 to 3.0 mg/dL in men and women, respectively). In men, CVD prevalence was 17.9% and in women, CVD prevalence was 20.4%. This contrasts with the CVD prevalence reported in the same study in men (13.9%) and women (9.3%) with normal serum creatinine levels.[622] In another cross-sectional analysis, the prevalence of LVH by echocardiography was 27%, 31%, and 45% in patients with a creatinine clearance greater than 50, 25 to 50, and less than 25, respectively.[257] This high prevalence of LVH contrasts with a prevalence of less than 20% in Framingham Heart Study participants.[623]

Cardiovascular disease is the leading cause of death in nondiabetic patients with chronic kidney disease (R). Cardiovascular disease is the leading cause of death in patients with chronic kidney disease, regardless of stage of kidney disease. Approximately 40% of all deaths in the United States are secondary to cardiovascular disease.[624]

Studies involving patients with kidney disease are not dissimilar. In an ancillary analysis of the Hypertension Detection and Follow-up Program (HDFP) involving nearly 11,000 individuals, 58% of deaths in participants with baseline serum creatinine $\geq$1.7 mg/dL were secondary to cardiovascular causes.[510] In the British Regional Heart Study comprising 7690 men followed for more than 14 years, greater than 50% of all deaths in subjects within the upper decile of baseline serum creatinine were secondary to cardiovascular causes.[625] Although the HDFP and British Regional Heart Study analyses did not stratify by diabetes status, only a minority of subjects was known to be diabetic (16% within the HDFP study and <2.0% within the British Regional Heart Study).

Cardiovascular disease mortality is more likely than development of kidney failure in nondiabetic patients with chronic kidney disease (R). Most patients with chronic kidney disease do not develop kidney failure. The prevalence of chronic kidney disease by stage is shown in Table 4. The estimated prevalence of Stage 3 CKD is ~30 times greater than the prevalence of kidney failure (Stage 5 CKD). Although no prospective data on a cohort with Stage 3 CKD is available, indirectly it is evident that most of these individuals do not proceed to kidney failure, but likely die before the onset of kidney failure. From the discussion above, the cause of death is likely cardiovascular in origin. Further supportive data is available from the HDFP and Framingham analyses. In the HDFP trial, only 19% of deaths were attributable to kidney failure versus 58% from cardiovascular causes.[510] In the Framingham study, 198 deaths occurred in subjects with elevated serum creatinine values.[622] Only 10 of these deaths occurred when patients had already developed ESRD (unpublished data).

Nondiabetic patients with chronic kidney disease have an increased prevalence of "traditional" CVD risk factors compared to the general population (R).
Prevalence of risk factors with decreased GFR. Many patients with chronic kidney disease have a higher prevalence of traditional CVD risk factors compared to the general population. Data from NHANES III (Table 26) clearly illustrate the inverse association between older age and reduced GFR. Using the same dataset, the prevalence of diabetes and hypertension in subjects with elevated serum creatinine levels ($\geq$1.6 mg/dL in men and $\geq$1.4 mg/dL in women) in this database was recently reported. In this cross-sectional study, 19% of subjects with elevated serum creatinine were known to have diabetes mellitus, and 70% had high blood pressure. In contrast, the prevalence of diabetes mellitus and hypertension in the entire NHANES III sample was 4.8% and 22.8%, respectively.[5] A more extensive discussion on the association of hypertension with GFR is found under Guideline 7. Compared to the general population, the percent prevalence of lipoprotein abnormalities in patients with chronic kidney disease is also increased (Table 131). The prevalence of tobacco use in patients with chronic kidney disease does not appear to be markedly different from the prevalence in the general population.[626]

Prevalence of risk factors with proteinuria. Proteinuria is a strong independent predictor of GFR decline in patients with and without diabetes mellitus.[6] Therefore, it is not surprising that many of the same CVD risk factors associated with decreased GFR are also associated with increased urinary protein excretion. Proteinuria increases with

Table 131. Lipoprotein Abnormalities in the General Population and in Patients with Chronic Kidney Disease

	Total cholesterol >240 mg/dL (%)	LDL cholesterol >130 mg/dL (%)	HDL cholesterol <35 mg/dL (%)	Triglycerides >200 mg/dL (%)
General population:	20	40	15	15
CKD with nephrotic syndrome (includes diabetic kidney disease):	90	85	50	60
CKD without nephrotic syndrome:	30	10	35	40

Modified and reprinted with permission.[627]

age and the duration and severity of hypertension.[628] In patients with essential hypertension, the combined presence of proteinuria and dyslipidemia is frequent, and greater levels of urinary protein correlate significantly with greater serum levels of total cholesterol, triglycerides, and lipoprotein(a). Proteinuria is also inversely correlated with HDL cholesterol levels.[628] The positive correlation between proteinuria and blood pressure, total serum cholesterol, and triglycerides, and the inverse correlation with HDL cholesterol, have also been reported in a recent analysis of data from the MDRD Study.[629] These associations remained present even after adjustment for the presence of diabetes.

Table 132. Decreased GFR as a Predictor of Cardiovascular Disease

Author, Year	Outcome	No. of Subjects	Applic-ability	GFR Range (mL/min/1.73 m²)	Results*	Adjustment for Covariates	Quality
Ruilope,[634] 2001	Major cardiovascular events	18,597	♀♀	S_{Cr} 1.0 mg/dL[a]	↑	Multiple	●
Schillaci,[635] 2001	All cardiovascular events	1,829	♀♀	S_{Cr} 1.0 mg/dL[b]	↑	Multiple	◐
Pahor,[636] 1998	All cardiovascular events, All coronary events, Stroke	4,336	♀♀	S_{Cr} 0.4–2.4 mg/dL	↑	No	○
Mann,[637] 2001	Myocardial infarction	9,287	♀♀	S_{Cr} 1.1 mg/dL[c]	↑	Multiple	●
Jungers,[259] 1997	Myocardial infarction	147	♀♀		↑	Age	○
Sechi,[638] 1998	Coronary heart disease	417	♀♀		↑	No	◐
Sechi,[639] 1999	Coronary heart disease	250	♀♀		↑	No	○
Culleton,[622] 1999	Cardiovascular disease	6,223	♀♀♀		⇔ (men) ↑ (women)	Multiple	●
Mann,[637] 2001	Stroke	9,287	♀♀	S_{Cr} 1.1 mg/dL[c]	↑	Multiple	●
Sechi,[638] 1998	Cerebrovascular disease	417	♀♀		↑	No	◐
Sechi,[639] 1999	Cerebrovascular disease	250	♀♀		↑	No	○
Sechi,[638] 1998	Peripheral vascular disease	417	♀♀		↑	No	◐
Sechi,[639] 1999	Peripheral vascular disease	250	♀♀		↑	No	○

Bold horizontal lines divide listing of studies by cardiovascular outcome.

* ↑ = decreased GFR associated with higher rate of indicated cardiovascular disease (statistically significant);
⇔ = decreased GFR *not* associated with rate of indicated cardiovascular disease.

[a] Mean value for S_{Cr}; all subjects ≤3.0 mg/dL
[b] Mean value for S_{Cr}; all subjects <1.5 mg/dL (men) or <1.4 mg/dL (women)
[c] Mean value for S_{Cr}; all subjects <2.3 mg/dL

Evidence for abnormalities of the coagulation system with increased fibrinogen, increased von Willebrand factor, and reduced plasminogen activator inhibitor have also been described in patients with elevated levels of urinary protein.[630]

Nondiabetic patients with chronic kidney disease have a high prevalence of "chronic kidney disease-related" CVD risk factors (R). Numerous hemodynamic and metabolic factors associated with chronic kidney disease have been implicated as potential CVD risk factors (Table 130). The prevalence of many of these factors increases as GFR declines. The inverse association between anemia and GFR is reviewed in Guideline 8. The increased prevalence of abnormalities in PTH, and calcium and phosphate metabolism, are reviewed in Guideline 10. The reader is also referred to reviews which discuss factors such as homocysteine, inflammatory markers, thrombogenic factors, and oxidative stress in more detail.[3,631-633]

Chronic kidney disease is a risk factor for subsequent cardiovascular disease in individuals without diabetes (C).

Decreased GFR is a risk factor for cardiovascular disease in individuals without diabetes (Tables 132 and 133 and Fig 53) (C). Reduced GFR identifies

Table 133. Decreased GFR as a Predictor of Mortality

Author, Year	Outcome	No. of Subjects	Applic-ability	GFR Range (mL/min/1.73 m²)	Results*	Adjustment for Covariates	Quality
Ruilope,[634] 2001[a]	Total mortality	18,597	♦♦	S_Cr 1.0 mg/dL	↑	Multiple	●
Shulman,[310] 1989	Total mortality	10,768	♦♦	S_Cr 1.08 ±0.38 mg/dL	↑	Yes	●
Mann,[637] 2001[b]	Total mortality	9,287	♦♦	S_Cr 1.1 mg/dL	↑	Multiple	●
Wannamethee,[625] 1997	Total mortality	7,690	♦♦	S_Cr 0.9–1.5 mg/dL	↑	No	●
Fried,[640] 1998	Total mortality	4,165	♦♦	ND	↑	Yes	●
Matts,[641] 1993	Total mortality	416	♦♦	S_Cr 1.11 ±0.17 mg/dL	↑	Yes	●
Hemmelgarn,[642] 2001	Total mortality	16,989	♦♦	ND	↑	Multiple	○
Schillaci,[635] 2001[c]	Total mortality	1,829	♦♦	S_Cr 1.0 mg/dL	⇔	Multiple	○
Damsgaard,[643] 1990[d]	Total mortality	216	♦♦	┼	↑	Yes	○
Beattie,[644] 2001[d]	Total mortality	1,723	♦	┼	↑	Incomplete	○
Ruilope,[634] 2001[a]	CVD mortality	18,597	♦♦	S_Cr 1.0 mg/dL	↑	Multiple	●
Mann,[637] 2001[b]	CVD mortality	9,287	♦♦	S_Cr 1.1 mg/dL	↑	Multiple	○
Friedman,[645] 1991	Mortality following acute stroke	492	♦	S_Cr 1.4 ±0.5 mg/dL	↑	Yes	○
Matts,[641] 1993	CHD mortality	416	♦♦	S_Cr 1.11 ±0.17 mg/dL	↑	Yes	○

Bold horizontal lines divide listing of studies by cardiovascular outcome.

* ↑ = decreased GFR associated with higher rate of indicated cause of mortality (statistically significant);
⇔ = decreased GFR *not* associated with higher rate of indicated cause of mortality.

[a] Mean value for S_{Cr}; all subjects ≤3.0 mg/dL.
[b] Mean value for S_{Cr}; all subjects <2.3 mg/dL.
[c] Mean value for S_{Cr}; all subjects <1.5 mg/dL (men) or <1.4 mg/dL (women).
[d] Range refers to 25th to 75th percentiles.

Abbreviation: CVD, cardiovascular disease; CHD, coronary heart disease

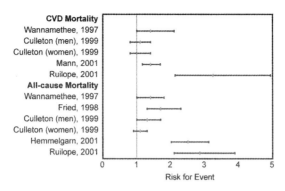

Fig 53. GFR and relative risk for death. Wannamethee[625]: risk is for S_{Cr} ≥1.5 mg/dL versus S_{Cr} ≤1.3 mg/dL. Upper limit for S_{Cr} was not defined. Culleton[622]: risk is for S_{Cr} ≥1.5 mg/dL and ≥1.4 mg/dL versus <1.5 and <1.4 in men and women respectively. Upper limit for S_{Cr} was 3.0 mg/dL for both men and women. Mann[637]: risk is for S_{Cr} ≥1.4 mg/dL versus <1.4 mg/dL. Upper limit for S_{Cr} was >2.3 mg/dL. Endpoint on this figure refers to the composite endpoint of cardiovascular death, MI, or stroke. Ruilope[634]: risk is for S_{Cr} >1.5 mg/dL versus ≤1.5 mg/dL. Upper limit for S_{Cr} was 3.0 mg/dL. Fried[640]: risk is for S_{Cr} ≥1.5 mg/dL versus S_{Cr} ≤0.9 mg/dL. Upper limit of S_{Cr} was not defined. Hemmelgarn[642]: risk is for S_{Cr} >2.3 mg/dL versus ≤2.3 mg/dL. Damsgaard[643] (1990), Friedman[645] (1991), Matts[641] (1993), Shulman[510] (1989), Beattie[644] (2001), and Schillaci[635] (2001): data not provided to present risk with confidence intervals.

individuals at greater risk for CVD events, including coronary heart disease, cerebrovascular disease and peripheral vascular disease, and death. The results of these studies are not entirely consistent. Some of this variability may be explained on differences in baseline demographics, severity of kidney disease, and the overall cardiovascular risk of the study sample. There is insufficient evidence to support an association with incident congestive heart failure, possibly because the number of congestive heart failure events is low.

Proteinuria is a risk factor for cardiovascular disease in individuals without diabetes (Tables 134, 135, and 136 and Figs 54, 55, and 56) (C). Likewise, proteinuria is also a risk factor for CVD events, CVD mortality, and all-cause mortality. Again, the results for all studies are not completely consistent but the weight of evidence is very supportive.

The identification of chronic kidney disease as a risk factor for cardiovascular disease does not prove causation. A temporal relation with chronic kidney disease and incident cardiovascular disease has been identified in many of these studies, but other criteria for causation are lacking, including consistency and biologic plausibility. Furthermore, although a dose-response relationship with proteinuria and cardiovascular disease may exist, such a relationship with reduced GFR has not been shown conclusively. An alternative hypothesis is that chronic kidney disease is a marker for the burden of exposure to

Table 134. Proteinuria as a Predictor of Cardiovascular Disease

Author, Year	Outcome	No. of Subjects	Applic-ability	GFR Range (mL/min/1.73 m^2)	Results*	Adjustment for Covariates	Quality
Wagener,[646] 1993	CVD	6,135	♦♦♦	ND	⬆ (men) ⬌ (women)	Multiple, including sex, age	●
Ljungman,[647] 1996	CVD	120	♦♦	⊢—⊣	⬆	BP, Smoking	○
Wagener,[646] 1993	IHD	6,135	♦♦♦	ND	⬆ (men) ⬌ (women)	Multiple, including sex, age	●
Culleton,[648] 2000	CHD	2,586	♦♦	ND	⬌	Multiple, including sex, age	●
Miettinen,[649] 1996	CHD	2,421	♦♦	ND	⇧	Multiple, including sex, age	●
Agewall,[650] 1997	AMI	439	♦♦	S$_{Cr}$ 1.13 mg/dL	⬆	Age, Prevalent CVD	●
Miettinen,[649] 1996	Stroke	2,421	♦♦	ND	⬆	Multiple, including sex, age	●
Agewall,[650] 1997	CVD	439	♦♦	S$_{Cr}$ 1.13 mg/dL	⬌	Age, Prevalent CVD	●

Bold horizontal lines divide listing of studies by cardiovascular outcome.

* ⬆ = proteinuria associated with higher rate of indicated cardiovascular disease (statistically significant);
⇧ = proteinuria associated with higher rate of indicated cardiovascular disease;
⬌ = proteinuria *not* associated with rate of indicated cardiovascular disease.

Abbreviations: CVD, cardiovascular disease; BP, blood pressure; IHD, ischemic heart disease; CHD, coronary heart disease; AMI, acute myocardial infarction

Table 135. Proteinuria as a Predictor of Cardiovascular Mortality

Author, Year	No. of Subjects	Applic-ability	GFR Range (mL/min/1.73 m^2)	Results*	Adjustment for Covariates	Quality
Wagener,[646] 1993	6,135	♦♦♦	ND	⬆ (men) ⬌ (women)	Multiple, including age	●
Grimm,[228] 1997	12,854	♦♦	ND	⬆	Multiple, including age	●
Culleton,[648] 2000	2,586	♦♦	ND	⬌ (men) ⬆ (women)	Multiple, including sex, age	●
Jager,[651] 1999	607	♦♦	⊢—⊣	⬌	Multiple, including sex, age	●
Agewall,[650] 1997	439	♦♦	S$_{Cr}$ 1.13 mg/dL	⬆	Age, Prevalent CVD	●
Kannel,[12] 1984	~5,100	♦♦♦	ND	⬆ (men) ⬌ (women)	Multiple, including sex, age	○

* ⬆ = proteinuria associated with higher rate of cardiovascular mortality (statistically significant);
⬌ = proteinuria *not* associated with rate of cardiovascular mortality.

Abbreviation: CVD, cardiovascular disease

Table 136. Proteinuria as a Predictor of Total Mortality

Author, Year	No. of Subjects	Applic- ability	GFR Range (mL/min/1.73 m²) 0 30 60 90 120	Results*	Adjustment for Covariates	Quality
Wagener,[646] 1993	6,135	⬆⬆⬆	ND	⬆	Multiple, including age	●
Grimm,[220] 1997	12,854	⬆⬆	ND	⬆	Multiple, including age	●
Culleton,[648] 2000	2,586	⬆⬆	ND	⬆	Multiple, including age	●
Miettinen,[649] 1996	2,421	⬆⬆	ND	⬆	Multiple, including sex, age	●
Jager,[651] 1999	607	⬆⬆	⟷	⟷	Multiple, including sex, age	●
Agewall,[650] 1997	439	⬆⬆	S_cr 1.13 mg/dL	⬆	Age, Prevalent CVD	●
Kannel,[12] 1984	~5,100	⬆⬆⬆	ND	⬆ (men) ⟷ (women)	Multiple, including sex, age	◐
Damsgaard,[643] 1990	216	⬆⬆	⊢╋⊣	⬆	Multiple, including sex	◐
Yudkin,[652] 1988	167	⬆⬆	ND	⬆	Multiple, including sex, age	○

* ⬆ = proteinuria associated with higher rate of total mortality (statistically significant);
⟷ = proteinuria *not* associated with rate of total mortality.

Abbreviation: CVD, cardiovascular disease

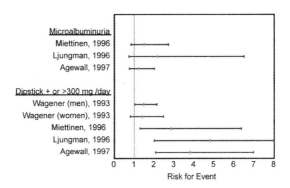

Fig 54. Proteinuria and relative risk for cardiovascular disease. Where possible, results presented are from multivariable analyses. Agewall[650], Ljungman[647]: Unadjusted results shown. Data not available to calculate age or multivariable adjusted risk.

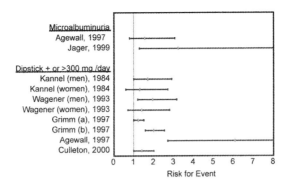

Fig 55. Proteinuria and relative risk for CVD death. Where possible, results presented are from multivariable analyses. Agewall[650]: unadjusted results shown. Data not available to calculate age or multivariable adjusted risk. Jager[651], Kannel[12], Culleton[648]: some diabetics included, but results shown are *adjusted* for diabetes. Grimm[228]: (a) proteinuria positive once; (b) proteinuria positive more than once over 6 years of follow-up.

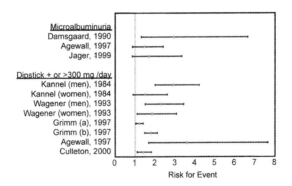

Fig 56. Proteinuria and relative risk for death. Where possible, results presented are from multivariable analyses. Damsgaard[643]: 4/216 subjects excreted more than 200 μg/min of albumin. Agewall[650]: unadjusted results shown. Data not available to calculate age or multivariable adjusted risk. Jager[651], Kannel[12], Culleton[648]: some diabetics included, but results shown are *adjusted* for diabetes. Grimm[228]: (a) proteinuria positive once; (b) proteinuria positive more than once over 6 years of follow-up. Miettinen[649]: Results not shown. Proteinuria predicted mortality but data was not provided to calculate risk.

"traditional" CVD risk factors. The relative contribution from "kidney disease-related" risk factors in this population remains uncertain.

Risk factor reduction is likely to be effective in reducing morbidity and mortality due to cardiovascular disease in patients with chronic kidney disease (O). Few patients with chronic kidney disease have been included in clinical trials with "hard" cardiovascular endpoints. In the absence of this high level evidence, extrapolation of evidence from clinical trial results in the general population to patients with chronic kidney disease is necessary. Several lines of reasoning support this process. First, "traditional" CVD risk factors can be modified in patients with chronic kidney disease. Clearly, antihypertensive agents are effective in lowering blood pressure. Lipid parameters can be improved with dietary and pharmacologic therapy. Smoking cessation programs should be no less effective in patients with chronic kidney disease than in the general population.

Second, adverse effects of risk factor reduction do not appear substantially greater in patients with chronic kidney disease than in the general population.

Third, the life span of most patients with chronic kidney disease often exceeds the duration of treatment required for beneficial effects. In the general population, the beneficial effect of risk factor reduction on morbidity and mortality begins to appear within 1 to 3 years or less in high risk groups. For example, survival curves for high risk patients randomized to lipid lowering therapy frequently diverge from placebo treated patients within 6 months of the start of treatment. The life-span of most patients with chronic kidney disease exceeds 1 to 3 years.

Treatment recommendations are beyond the scope of this guideline. The reader is referred to the NKF Task Force Report[9] for a summary of treatment recommendations for traditional CVD risk factors in chronic kidney disease, and to forthcoming K/DOQI guidelines on CKD-related CVD risk factors.

LIMITATIONS

The variety of measures used to assess kidney function has placed a significant limitation on this current review. This is particularly true for the assessment of CVD risk associated with reduced GFR. As a marker for GFR, serum creatinine was used in most studies. The limitations with serum creatinine measurements have been described previously. Few studies provided data on creatinine clearance, and no prospective studies provided a more accurate measure of GFR than serum creatinine. As a result, it was not possible to quantify the prevalence of cardiovascular disease or CVD risk factors by stage of kidney disease. Furthermore, the risk for future CVD events could not be defined by stage of kidney disease. A similar problem was found during the assessment of CVD risk associated with albuminuria. Older studies used dipsticks on random urines. Some dipsticks measured total protein, while others measured albumin excretion. More recent studies have quantified albumin excretion with more standardized techniques. The variability in urine protein measurement makes comparisons between studies difficult.

In addition, few studies provided analyses stratified by diabetes status. In contrast to the literature on CVD risk in diabetic kidney disease, few generalizable studies have been published on CVD risk specifically in nondiabetic individuals with chronic kidney disease. To our advantage, many of the studies reviewed included less than 10% diabetic patients. The Work Group agreed to extrapolate results from these mixed samples, limiting assessments to qualitative statements.

CLINICAL APPLICATIONS

"Traditional" CVD risk factors appear to be shared risk factors for both chronic kidney disease and cardiovascular disease and therefore are in high prevalence in chronic kidney disease. Therefore, it is essential to develop interdisciplinary programs for detection and treatment of traditional risk factors, emphasizing the inter-relationships among diabetes, cardiovascular disease, and kidney disease.

IMPLEMENTATION ISSUES

Physician, allied health, and patient education initiatives are necessary to ensure that patients with chronic kidney disease are recognized to be at high risk for future CVD events, irrespective of diagnosis. Coordinated patient management systems will be necessary to appropriately recognize and manage CVD risk factors in this patient population.

RESEARCH RECOMMENDATIONS

A large prospective multi-ethnic cohort study involving patients with Stage 3 and 4 chronic kidney disease is necessary to further examine the impact of "traditional" and "kidney disease-related" risk factors on incident cardiovascular disease. Emphasis should be placed on the recognition of potentially modifiable risk factors. Such a study could also determine the time course of cardiovascular disease in the chronic kidney disease population.

A predictive clinical tool, using kidney disease stage and diagnosis, risk factors, and/or other variables, should be developed to better predict risk in patients with chronic kidney disease.

Standards for the measurement of kidney function and albuminuria in observational and controlled trials should be established.

PART 8. RECOMMENDATIONS FOR CLINICAL PERFORMANCE MEASURES

Clinical practice guidelines (CPGs) are "systematically developed statements based on current professional knowledge to assist practitioner and patient decisions about appropriate health care for specific clinical circumstances." As such, guidelines define best clinical practices based on available evidence. Their translation into clinical practice for use in specific clinical circumstances is what makes guidelines relevant.

Passive dissemination of guidelines has proven to be of limited clinical utility. Nonadherence to best clinical practices, as articulated in CPGs, has been routinely observed. The translation of CPGs into clinical practice requires the development of a multi-component long-term implementation plan. A central component of such a plan is the linkage of selected guidelines to continuous quality improvement (CQI) programs to improve outcomes within a given local health care delivery system.

CQI efforts require measurement tools, both to quantify the current process of care and to monitor the success of changing practice patterns on clinical outcomes. Clinical performance measures (CPMs) are such tools. The rationale for CPMs, the essential steps in their development, and the attributes of well-designed CPMs have been described.[653,654]

The first step in the development of CPMs is the prioritization of CPGs, in collaboration with the Work Group that developed the guidelines. Following are guideline statements recommended by the CKD Work Group for potential use in CQI and CPM and examples of CPM that could be developed from them (Table 137). A special subcommittee of the Advisory Board, chaired by Alan S. Kliger, MD, is assessing feasibility and exploring opportunities for developing these recommendations for future use as CPMs.

PROPOSED CLINICAL PERFORMANCE MEASURES FOR CHRONIC KIDNEY DISEASE

Guideline 2

Preparation for kidney replacement therapy (dialysis and transplantation), as well as vascular access care, should be initiated when the estimated GFR declines to <30 mL/min/1.73 m^2.

Guideline 3

Individuals at increased risk for chronic kidney disease should be tested at the time of a health evaluations to determine if they have chronic kidney disease. These include individuals with:

- Diabetes;
- Hypertension;
- Autoimmune diseases;
- Systemic infections;
- Exposure to drugs or procedures associated with acute decline in kidney function;
- Recovery from acute kidney failure;

Table 137. K/DOQI CKD Clinical Practice Guidelines and Performance Measures

Guideline	Subject	Clinical Performance Measures?
1	Stages of Chronic Kidney Disease	
2	Evaluation and Treatment	Yes[a]
3	Individuals at Increased Risk for Chronic Kidney Disease	Yes[a]
4	Estimation of GFR	Yes[a]
5	Assessment of Proteinuria	Yes[a]
6	Markers of Kidney Damage Other than Proteinuria	
7	High Blood Pressure	Yes[b]
8	Anemia	Yes[a]
9	Malnutrition	Yes[a]
10	Bone Disease and Disorders of Calcium and Phosphorus Metabolism	Yes[a]
11	Neuropathy	
12	Functioning and Well-Being	Yes[a]
13	Loss of Kidney Function	Yes[b,c]
14	Diabetic Complications	Yes[b]
15	Cardiovascular Disease	Yes[a,b,c]

[a] Recommended for development of clinical performance measures based on CKD Guidelines.

[b] Recommended for development of clinical performance measures based on other guidelines such as those produced by JNC, ADA.

[c] Treatment recommendations in Guidelines 13 and 15 cannot be recommended for development of clinical performance measures, since such measures by definition depend on systematic review of the evidence, which was not performed for these guidelines.

- Age >60 years;
- Family history of kidney disease;
- Reduced kidney mass (includes kidney donors and transplant recipients).

Measurements should include:
- Serum creatinine for estimation of GFR;

- Assessment of proteinuria;
- Urinary sediment or urine dipstick for red blood cells and white blood cells.

Guideline 4

Estimated GFR should be the parameter used to evaluate the level of kidney function.

Guideline 5

The ratio of protein or albumin to creatinine in spot urine samples should be monitored in all patients with chronic kidney disease.

Guideline 7

Blood pressure should be monitored in all patients with chronic kidney disease.

High blood pressure should be evaluated and treated according to established guidelines, such as JNC-VI and ADA.

Guidelines 8–12

Patients with GFR <60 mL/min/1.73 m^2 should be evaluated and treated for complications of decreased GFR. This includes measurement of:

- Anemia (hemoglobin);
- Nutritional status (dietary energy and protein intake, weight, serum albumin, serum total cholesterol);
- Bone disease (parathyroid hormone, calcium, phosphorus);
- Functioning and well-being (questionnaires).

Guideline 13

Estimated GFR should be monitored yearly in patients with chronic kidney disease, and more frequently in patients with:

- GFR <60 mL/min/1.73 m^2
- Fast GFR decline in the past (≥ 4 mL/min/1.73 m^2)
- Risk factors for faster progression
- Ongoing treatment to slow progression
- Exposure to risk factors for acute GFR decline.

Guideline 14

Individuals with diabetic kidney disease are at higher risk of diabetic complications, including retinopathy, cardiovascular disease, and neuropathy.

They should be evaluated and managed according to established guidelines.

Guideline 15

Individuals with chronic kidney disease are at increased risk of cardiovascular disease.

They should be considered in the "highest risk group" for evaluation and management according to established guidelines.

Part 9. Approach To Chronic Kidney Disease Using These Guidelines

INTRODUCTION

The work group expanded on selected clinical topics that were not included in the scope of the review of evidence, but which nonetheless are relevant to the implementation of a clinical action plan for patients with chronic kidney disease. The clinical approach outlined below is based on guidelines contained within this report; the reader is cautioned that many of the recommendations in this section have not been adequately studied and therefore represent the *opinion* of members of the Work Group.

DETECTION OF CHRONIC KIDNEY DISEASE
Assessment of Risk

All individuals should be evaluated during health encounters to determine whether they are at increased risk of having or of developing chronic kidney disease. Guideline 3 lists risk factors for susceptibility to and initiation of chronic kidney disease ("CKD risk factors"). Ascertainment of risk factors through assessment of sociodemographic characteristics, review of past medical history and family history, and measurement of blood pressure would enable the clinician to determine whether a patient is at increased risk. Patients who are found to be at increased risk should be evaluated further.

Clinical Evaluation of Patients at Increased Risk

Clinical evaluation of patients at increased risk of chronic kidney disease includes assessment of markers of kidney damage, estimated GFR, and blood pressure (Table 138).

Unfortunately, these markers do not detect all types of chronic kidney damage. Thus, it may be difficult to detect the onset of some types of chronic kidney disease until GFR is decreased, for example, hypertensive nephrosclerosis and noninflammatory tubulointerstitial diseases.

Testing for Proteinuria

The algorithms recommended by NKF PARADE distinguish between individuals at increased for chronic kidney disease versus asymptomatic, healthy individuals. These algorithms have been modified by the Work Group with input from members of the PARADE Work Group (Fig 57). The algorithm for adults and children at increased risk (right side) begins with testing of a random "spot" urine sample with an albumin-specific dipstick. Alternatively, testing could begin with a spot urine sample for albumin-to-creatine ratio. The algorithm for asymptomatic healthy individuals (left side) does not require testing specifically for albumin. This algorithim is useful for children without diabetes, in whom universal screening is recommended. Universal screening is not currently recommended for adults.

DIFFERENTIAL DIAGNOSIS OF CHRONIC KIDNEY DISEASE
Clinical Presentation

Table 139 shows the relationship between stages of chronic kidney disease and clinical presentations. During the stage "At Increased Risk" and Stage 1 (Kidney Damage), spe-

Table 138. Clinical Evaluation of Patients at Increased Risk of Chronic Kidney Disease

All Patients

Measurement of blood pressure

Serum creatinine to estimate GFR

Protein-to-creatinine ratio or albumin-to-creatinine ratio in a first-morning or random untimed "spot" urine specimen

Examination of the urine sediment or dipstick for red blood cells and white blood cells

Selected Patients, Depending on Risk Factors

Ultrasound imaging (for example, in patients with symptoms of urinary tract obstruction, infection or stone, or family history of polycystic kidney disease)

Serum electrolytes (sodium, potassium, chloride and bicarbonate)

Urinary concentration or dilution (specific gravity or osmolality)

Urinary acidification (pH)

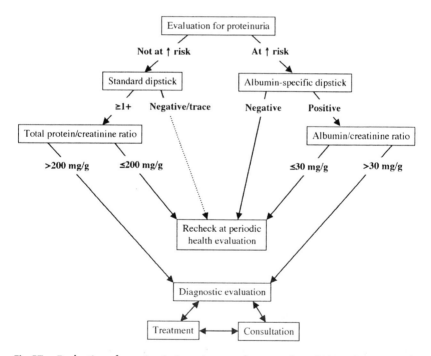

Fig 57.   Evaluation of proteinuria in patients not known to have kidney disease. Modified from NKF PARADE. NKF PARADE does not use gender-specific definitions for abnormal albumin-to-creatinine ratio. Modified with permission.[6]

Table 139. Stages of Chronic Kidney Disease: Clinical Presentations

Stage	Description	GFR Range (mL/min/1.73 m^2)	Clinical Presentations[*]
	At increased risk	≥90 (without markers of damage)	CKD risk factors
1	Kidney damage with normal or ↑ GFR	≥90	Markers of damage (Nephrotic syndrome, Nephritic syndrome, Tubular syndromes, Urinary tract symptoms, Asymptomatic urinalysis abnormalities, Asymptomatic radiologic abnormalities, Hypertension due to kidney disease)
2	Kidney damage with mild ↓ GFR	60–89	Mild complications
3	Moderate ↓ GFR	30–59	Moderate complications
4	Severe ↓ GFR	15–29	Severe complications
5	Kidney Failure	<15 (or dialysis)	Uremia, Cardiovascular disease

* Includes presentations from preceding stages. Chronic kidney disease is defined as either kidney damage or GFR <60 mL/min/1.73 m^2 for ≥3 months. Kidney damage is defined as pathologic abnormalities or markers of damage, including abnormalities in blood or urine tests or imaging studies

cific diseases are associated with specific risk factors and are manifested by specific clinical presentations, although markers for each diagnosis have not been discovered. During Stages 2 through 4 (Decreased GFR) and Stage 5 (Kidney Failure), different diseases may have similar clinical presentations, although markers of kidney damage may persist and provide clues to diagnosis.

Simplified Classification of Chronic Kidney Disease

Diseases of the kidney are classified according to etiology and pathology. A simplified classification is given in Table 140.

Table 140. Simplified Classification of Chronic Kidney Disease by Diagnosis

Disease	Major Types (Examples)
Diabetic kidney disease	Type 1 and type 2 diabetes
Nondiabetic kidney diseases	Glomerular diseases (autoimmune diseases, systemic infections, drugs, neoplasia)
	Vascular diseases (large vessel disease, hypertension, microangiopathy)
	Tubulointerstitial diseases (urinary tract infection, stones, obstruction, drug toxicity)
	Cystic diseases (polycystic kidney disease)
Diseases in the transplant	Chronic rejection
	Drug toxicity (cyclosporine or tacrolimus)
	Recurrent diseases (glomerular diseases)
	Transplant glomerulopathy

Definitive diagnosis often requires a biopsy of the kidney, which is associated with a risk, albeit usually small, of serious complications. Therefore, kidney biopsy is usually reserved for selected patients in whom a definitive diagnosis can be made only by biopsy and in whom a definitive diagnosis would result in a change in either treatment or prognosis. In most patients, diagnosis is assigned based on recognition of well-defined clinical presentations and causal factors based on clinical evaluation.

Clinical Evaluation

Chronic kidney disease is usually silent. Therefore, clinical assessment relies heavily on laboratory evaluation and diagnostic imaging. Nonetheless, a careful history will often reveal clues to the correct diagnosis (Table 141). Blood pressure measurement is essential, but other elements of the physical examination are usually not helpful, except to assess comorbid conditions and complications of decreased GFR. A number of drugs can be associated with chronic kidney damage, so a thorough review of the medication list (including prescribed medications, over-the-counter medications, "nontraditional" medications, vitamins and supplements, herbs, and drugs of abuse) is vital. Moreover, medications will require adjustment in dosage or discontinuation based on the level of GFR.

Table 141. Clues to the Diagnosis of Chronic Kidney Disease from the Patient's History

Clue	Potential Diagnosis
Review of Systems	
Symptoms during urination	Usually suggest disorders of the urinary tract such as infection, obstruction or stones
Recent infections	May suggest post-infectious glomerulonephritis or HIV-associated nephropathy
Skin rash or arthritis	Suggests autoimmune disease, such systemic lupus erythematosus or cryoglobulinemia
Risk factors for pareneterally transmitted disease	May suggest HIV, hepatitis B or hepatitis C infection and associated kidney diseases
Chronic Diseases	
Heart failure, cirrhosis, or gastrointestinal fluid losses	Usually suggest reduced kidney perfusion ("pre-renal factors").
Diabetes[a]	As a cause of chronic kidney disease: Diabetic kidney disease usually follows a typical clinical course after onset, first with microalbuminuria, followed by clinical proteinuria, hypertension and declining GFR.
Hypertension[a]	As a cause of chronic kidney disease: Hypertensive nephrosclerosis is usually characterized by severely elevated blood pressure readings over a long period of time, with associated end-organ damage in addition to kidney disease. Recent worsening of hypertension, in association with findings of diffuse atherosclerosis, suggests large vessel disease due to atherosclerosis. Recent onset of severe hypertension in young women suggests large vessel disease due to fibromuscular dysplasia
Past Medical History	
Findings from past "routine" examinations	May reveal a history of hypertension or proteinuria during childhood, during pregnancy, or on examinations for school, military service, or insurance.
Past urologic evaluations	Details may disclose radiologic abnormalities associated with kidney disease.
Family History of Kidney Diseases	
Every generation; equal susceptibility in males and females	Suggests an autosomal dominant disease, such as polycystic kidney disease.
Every generation; predominant male susceptibility	Suggests a sex-linked recessive disease, such as Alport's syndrome.
Less frequent than every generation	Suggests an autosomal recessive disease, such as medullary cystic kidney disease or autosomal recessive polycystic kidney disease.

[a] Extremely common in elderly patients, and often non-specific.

Table 142. Laboratory Evaluation of Patients with Chronic Kidney Disease

All Patients

Serum creatinine to estimate GFR

Protein-to-creatinine ratio or albumin-to-creatinine ratio in a first-morning or random untimed "spot" urine specimen

Examination of the urine sediment or dipstick for red blood cells and white blood cells

Imaging of the kidneys, usually by ultrasound

Serum electrolytes (sodium, potassium, choride and bicarbonate)

Laboratory Evaluation

Laboratory evaluation in *all* patients with chronic kidney disease should be performed (Table 142).

Guideline 6 provides a guide to interpretation of proteinuria and urine sediment abnormalities and findings on imaging studies as markers of kidney damage and a definition of clinical presentations.

Based on these measurements, the clinician can usually define the clinical presentation, thereby narrowing the differential diagnosis and guiding further diagnostic evaluation, decisions about kidney biopsy, and, often, decisions about treatment and prognosis with no need for kidney biopsy.

Relationships Among Type and Stage of Kidney Disease and Clinical Presentations

Tables 143, 144, and 145 show the relationships between stage of kidney disease and clinical features for diabetic kidney disease, nondiabetic kidney diseases, and diseases in the kidney transplant.

Table 143. Stages and Clinical Features of Diabetic Kidney Disease

Stage	Description	Clinical Features
	At Increased Risk	Diabetes mellitus, HBP, family history
1–2	Kidney Damage	Microalbuminuria: Diabetes duration 5–10 years, retinopathy, rising BP
		Albuminuria: Diabetes duration 10–15 years, retinopathy, HBP
3–4	Decreased GFR	HBP, retinopathy, CVD, other diabetic complications
5	Kidney Failure	Retinopathy, CVD, other diabetic complications, uremia

Abbreviations: HBP, high blood pressure, CVD, cardiovascular disease

Table 144. Stages and Clinical Features of Nondiabetic Kidney Disease

Table 144. Stages and Clinical Features of Nondiabetic Kidney Disease

CKD Stage Description	Clinical Features			
	Glomerular Diseases	Vascular Diseases	Tubulointerstitial Diseases	Cystic Diseases
At Increased Risk	Autoimmune diseases, systemic infections, drug exposure, neoplasia, family history	HBP, family history	Infections, stones, obstruction, drugs	Family history
1–2 Kidney Damage	Proteinuria, +RBCs	Micro-albuminuria	±WBCs, ±hydronephrosis	Cysts
3–4 Decreased GFR	HBP, complications	HBP, complications	HBP, complications	HBP, complications
5 Kidney Failure	Uremia, CVD	Uremia, CVD	Uremia, CVD	Uremia, CVD

Abbreviations: HBP, high blood pressure; RBCs, red blood cells; WBC, white blood cells; CVD, cardiovascular disease

Utility of Proteinuria in Diagnosis, Prognosis, and Treatment

Proteinuria is a key finding in the differential diagnosis of chronic kidney disease. Proteinuria is a marker of damage in diabetic kidney disease (Table 143), in glomerular diseases occurring in the native kidney (Table 144), and in transplant glomerular disease and recurrent glomerular disease in the transplant (Table 145). In these diseases, the magnitude of proteinuria is usually >1,000 mg/g (except in early diabetic kidney disease), and may approach nephrotic range (spot urine protein-to-creatinine ratio >3,000 mg/g). On the other hand, proteinuria is usually mild or absent in vascular diseases, tubulointerstitial diseases, and cystic diseases in the native kidney and in rejection and drug toxicity due to cyclosporine or tacrolimus in the transplant.

Proteinuria is also a key prognostic finding. It is well-known that nephrotic range proteinuria is associated with a wide range of complications, including hypoalbuminemia, edema, hyperlipidemia, and hypercoagulable state; faster progression of kidney disease; and premature cardiovascular disease. However, it is now known that elevated urine protein excretion below the nephrotic range is also associated with faster progression of kidney disease and development of cardiovascular disease. Furthermore, the reduction in proteinuria is correlated with a subsequent slower loss of kidney function.

Finally, proteinuria is also a guide to therapy. The benefit of antihypertensive therapy, especially with angiotensin-converting enzyme inhibitors, to slow the progression of kidney disease is greater in patients with higher levels of proteinuria compared to patients with lower levels of proteinuria.

Table 145. Stages and Clinical Features of Diseases in the Kidney Transplant

Stage Description	Clinical Features			
	Rejection	Drug Toxicity	Recurrent Disease	Transplant Glomerular Disease
At Increased Risk	All	Treatment with cyclosporine or tacrolimus	Glomerular diseases in native kidneys	All
1–2 Kidney Damage	HBP	HBP	Proteinuria	Proteinuria, HBP
3–4 Decreased GFR	HBP, Complications	HBP, Complications	HBP, Complications	HBP, Complications
5 Kidney Failure	Uremia, CVD	Uremia, CVD	Uremia, CVD	Uremia, CVD

Abbreviations: HBP, high blood pressure; CVD, cardiovascular disease

	Diabetic Kidney Disease	Nondiabetic Kidney Disease	Kidney Disease in the Transplant
Strict glycemic control	Yes[a]	NA	Not tested
ACE-inhibitors or angiotensin-receptor blockers	Yes	Yes (greater effect in patients with proteinuria)	Not tested
Strict blood pressure control	Yes <125/75 mm Hg	Yes <130/85 mm Hg (greater effect in patients with proteinuria) <125/75 mm Hg (in patients with proteinuria)	Not tested
Dietary protein restriction	Inconclusive	Inconclusive	Not tested

[a] Prevents or delays the onset of diabetic kidney disease. Inconclusive with regard to progression of established disease.

In summary, proteinuria is not only a marker of kidney damage, it is also a guide to the differential diagnosis, prognosis, and therapy of chronic kidney disease.

ESTIMATING AND SLOWING PROGRESSION OF CHRONIC KIDNEY DISEASE IN ADULTS

Guideline 13 reviews estimating decline in GFR and treatments to slow the GFR decline in adults. In general, GFR should be estimated from serum creatinine at least yearly in patients with chronic kidney disease and more often in patients with:

- GFR <60 mL/min/1.73 m^2
- Fast GFR decline in the past ($\geq$4 mL/min per year)
- Risk factors for faster progression
- Ongoing treatment to slow progression
- Exposure to risk factors for acute GFR decline.

Treatments to slow the progression of chronic kidney disease in adults in are shown in Table 146.

CARDIOVASCULAR DISEASE RISK ASSESSMENT AND REDUCTION

Guideline 15 concludes that patients with chronic kidney disease have a high risk of adverse outcomes of cardiovascular disease and should be considered in the "highest-risk group" for cardiovascular disease risk reduction. However, few patients with chronic kidney disease have been included in population-based epidemiologic studies of cardiovascular disease or long-term randomized clinical trials. The NKF Task Force on Cardiovascular Disease in Chronic Renal Disease recommended risk factor reduction for "traditional" risk factors based largely on extrapolation from the general population and evidence of safety and efficacy of interventions on risk factor levels in chronic kidney disease. It was the opinion of the CVD Task Force and the CKD Work Group that extrapolation from the general population to patients with chronic kidney disease is most appropriate for patients with higher levels of GFR (Stages 1 through 4) and less (but possibly still) appropriate for patients with kidney failure (Stage 5). A partial list of "traditional"

Table 147. "Traditional" Risk Factors for Chronic Kidney Disease and Associated Interventions

"Traditional" Risk Factors	Intervention
Family history of CVD	Screening
Hyperglycemia (in patients with diabetes)	Diet, insulin, and oral agents
Hypertension	Antihypertensive therapy
Meonpause	Possibly estrogen replacement
Physical inactivity	Exercise
Psychosocial stress	Possibly stress reduction
Renin-angiotensin system activity	Angiotensin-converting enzyme inhibitors or angiotensin-receptor blockers
Smoking (tobacco use)	Counseling and nicotine replacement
Thrombogenic factors	Antiplatelet agents
Total or LDL cholesterol	Lipid-lowering diets and drugs
Triglycerides	Lipid-lowering diets and drugs

cardiovascular disease risk factors and risk factor reduction strategies that are potentially safe and effective for patients with chronic kidney disease is shown in Table 147.

CLINICAL EVALUATION OF ADULTS WITH GFR <60 mL/min/ 1.73 m^2 (CKD STAGES 3–5)

Guidelines 7 through 12 show the associations between level of GFR and complications of chronic kidney disease in adults. Many complications begin to occur at GFR <60 mL/ min/ 1.73 m^2. Table 148 lists additional clinical evaluations (in addition to the ones listed in Tables 105 and 142) that should be performed in adults with GFR <60 mL/min/1.73 m^2.

DECREASED GFR AND CHRONIC KIDNEY DISEASE IN THE ELDERLY

Guideline 1 defines a decrease in GFR of 60 to 89 mL/min/1.73 m^2 as chronic kidney disease only if accompanied by a marker of kidney damage. GFR declines with age in normal individuals; therefore, it can be difficult to distinguish age-related decrease in GFR from chronic kidney disease in the elderly. Other causes of chronically decreased GFR in normal individuals without chronic kidney disease include a habitually low protein intake and unilateral nephrectomy.

Data from NHANES III suggest that almost 75% of individuals ≥70 years old may have

Table 148. Additional Clinical Interventions for Adults with GFR <60 mL/min/1.73 m^2

Clinical Problem	Parameters to Assess	Possible Additional Parameters to Assess (See Other Guidelines)
Anemia	Hemoglobin	If anemic: • Red blood cell indices • Reticulocyte count • Iron studies (serum iron, total binding capacity, percent transferrin saturation and ferritin) • Test for occult blood in stool • Medical evaluation for comorbid conditions
Malnutrition	Weight Serum albumin Dietary history Subjective global assessment (SGA)	If malnourished: • 24-hour urine collection for urea nitrogen excretion • Food recall/records for protein and total energy intake • Medical evaluation for comorbid conditions
Bone Disease	Serum PTH Serum calcium Serum phosphorus	If abnormal: • Consider Vitamin D levels • Consider bone x-rays • Consider DEXA scan
Neuropathy	Paresthesias Mental status abnormalities Sleep disturbances Restless legs	If symptomatic: • Neurologic exam, including mental status • Serum electrolytes • Medical evaluation for comorbid conditions • Consider nerve conduction velocity • Consider EEG/sleep studies
Reduced Functioning and Well-Being[a]	Standardized, self-administered instruments such as: Dartmouth COOP charts DUKE/DUSOI SF-36 KDQOL	If abnormal: • Medical evaluation for comorbid conditions • Self-management education • Physical rehabilitation • Mental health treatment • Social support • Vocational rehabilitation

Evaluations are in addition to those listed in Tables 141 and 142.

[a] Symptoms, physical functioning, depression, employment and usual activities, social functioning

Abbreviations: DEXA, dual energy x-ray absorptiometry (Bone densitometry); EEG, electroencephalogram

GFR <90 mL/min/1.73 m^2, and almost 25% may have GFR <60 mL/min/1.73 m^2. The fraction of elderly individuals with decreased GFR who truly have chronic kidney disease has not been systematically studied. Moreover, the health outcomes of decreased GFR in the elderly, with or without chronic kidney disease, are also not known.

Clinical evaluation of elderly individuals with GFR of 60 to 89 mL/min/1.73 m^2 should include an assessment for chronic kidney disease (Table 149).

Additional items for clinical evaluation of individuals with GFR <60 mL/min/1.73 m^2 are listed in Table 148.

It is the opinion of the members of the Work Group that clinical interventions for the elderly with chronic kidney disease should be based on diagnosis (as described above), severity of kidney function impairment, and stratification of risk for progression

Table 149. Clinical Evaluation of Elderly Individuals with GFR of 60–89 mL/min/1.73 m^2

All Individuals

Assessment of CKD risk factors

Measurement of blood pressure

Albumin-to-creatinine ratio in a "spot" urine specimen

Examination of the urine sediment of dipstick for red blood cells and white blood cells of kidney disease and cardiovascular disease. There is a spectrum of risk for adverse outcomes.

Patients with mild decreased GFR, low risk for progressive decline in GFR, and low risk for cardiovascular disease have a good prognosis and may require only adjustment of the dosage of drugs that are excreted by the kidney, monitoring of blood pressure, avoidance of drugs and pro!-!cedures with risk for acute kidney failure, and life-style modifications to reduce the risk of cardiovascular disease. Consultation with a nephrologist may be necessary to establish the diagnosis and treatment of the type of kidney disease. Kidney function should be monitored at least yearly.

Patients with moderately or severely decreased GFR or risk factors for faster decline in GFR or cardiovascular disease have a worse prognosis. In addition to the interventions mentioned above, they require assessment for complications of decreased GFR and dietary and pharmacologic therapy directed at slowing the progression of kidney disease and ameliorating cardiovascular risk factor levels. Consultation and/or co-management with a kidney disease care team is advisable during Stage 3, and referral to a nephrologist in Stage 4 is recommended. Kidney function may need to be monitored four times per year or more. A multidisciplinary team approach may be necessary to implement and coordinate care.

PART 10. APPENDICES

APPENDIX 1. METHODS FOR REVIEW OF ARTICLES

AIMS

The overall aim of the project was to develop a classification of the stages of chronic kidney disease, irrespective of the underlying cause of the kidney disease, and a clinical action plan for the evaluation and treatment of chronic kidney disease. This classification could then be transformed to an "evidence model" for future development of additional practice guidelines regarding specific diagnostic evaluations and therapeutic interventions (Executive Summary).

The Work Group sought to develop an "evidence base" for the classification and clinical action plan, derived from a systematic summary of the available scientific literature on: the evaluation of laboratory measurements for the clinical assessment of kidney disease; association of the level of kidney function with complications of chronic kidney disease; and stratification of the risk for loss of kidney function and development of cardiovascular disease.

Two products were developed from this process: a set of clinical practice guidelines regarding the classification and action plan, which are contained in this report; and an evidence report, which consists of the summary of the literature. Portions of the evidence report are contained in this report. The entire evidence report is on file with the National Kidney Foundation.

OVERVIEW OF PROCESS

Development of the guideline and evidence report required many concurrent steps:
- Form the Work Group and Evidence Review Team that would be responsible for different aspects of the process;
- Hold meetings to discuss process, methods, and results;
- Develop and refine topics;
- Define population of interest;
- Create draft guideline statements and rationales;
- Create draft summary tables;
- Create data extraction forms;
- Create and standardize quality assessment metrics;
- Develop literature search strategies;
- Perform literature searches;
- Screen abstracts and retrieve full articles;
- Review literature by primary and secondary reviewers;
- Extract data and perform critical appraisal of the literature;
- Tabulate data from articles into summaries and create summary graphics;
- Write guideline statements and rationales based on literature.

CREATION OF GROUPS

The Co-Chairs of the K/DOQI Advisory Board selected the Work Group Chair and Director of the Evidence Review Team, who then assembled groups to be responsible for the development of the guidelines and the evidence report, respectively. These groups collaborated closely throughout the project.

The Work Group consisted of "domain experts," including individuals with expertise in nephrology, epidemiology, laboratory medicine, nutrition, social work, pathology, gerontology, and family medicine. In addition, the Work Group had liaison members from the National Institute of Diabetes, Digestive and Kidney Diseases and from the National Institute on Aging. Midway through the project, at the request of the K/DOQI Advisory Board, the Work Group expanded the target population to include children and invited additional members with expertise in pediatric nephrology. The first task of the Work Group members was to define the overall topic and goals, including specifying the target condition, target population, and target audience. They then further developed and refined each topic, literature search strategy, and data extraction form (described below). The Work Group members were the principal reviewers of the literature, and from these detailed reviews they summarized the available evidence and took the primary roles of writing the guidelines and rationale statements.

The Evidence Review Team consisted of nephrologists (one senior nephrologist and three nephrology fellows) and methodologists from New England Medical Center with expertise in systematic review of the medical literature. They were responsible for coordinating the project, including coordinating meetings, refinement of goals and topics, creation of the format of the evidence report, development of literature search strategies, initial review and assessment of literature, and coordination of all partners. The Evidence Review Team also coordinated the methodological and analytic process of the report, coordinated the meetings, and defined and standardized the methodology of performing literature searches, of data extraction, and of summarizing the evidence in the report. They performed literature searches, retrieved and screened abstracts and articles, created forms to extract relevant data from articles, and tabulated results. Throughout the project, and especially at meetings, the Evidence Review Team led discussions on systematic review, literature searches, data extraction, assessment of quality of articles, and summary reporting. In addition, a member of the Evidence Review Team (BCA) at Johns Hopkins Medical Institutions assisted Dr. Coresh in analysis of NHANES III data.

DEVELOPMENT OF TOPICS

The goals of the Work Group spanned a diverse group of topics, which would have been too large for a comprehensive review of the literature. Based on their expertise, members of the Work Group focused on the specific questions listed in Table 8 and employed a selective review of evidence: a summary of reviews for established concepts (review of textbooks, reviews, guidelines, and selected original articles familiar to them as domain experts) and a review of primary articles and data for new concepts.

REFINEMENT OF TOPICS AND DEVELOPMENT OF MATERIALS

The Work Group and Evidence Review Team developed (a) draft guideline statements; (b) draft rationale statements that summarized the expected pertinent evidence; (c) mock summary tables containing the expected evidence; and (d) data extraction forms requesting the data elements to be retrieved from the primary articles to complete the tables. The development process included creation of initial mock-ups by the Work Group Chair and Evidence Review Team followed by iterative refinement by the Work Group members. The refinement process began prior to literature retrieval and continued through the start of reviewing individual articles. The refinement occurred by e-mail, telephone, and in-person communication regularly with local experts and with all experts during in-person meetings of the Evidence Review Team and Work Group members.

Data extraction forms were designed to capture information on various aspects of the primary articles. Forms for all topics included study setting and demographics, eligibility criteria, causes of kidney disease, numbers of subjects, study design, study funding source, population category (see below), study quality (based on criteria appropriate for each study design, see below), appropriate selection and definition of measures, results, and sections for comments and assessment of biases.

The various steps involved in development of the guideline statements, rationale statements, tables, and data extraction forms were piloted on one of the topics (bone disease) with a Work Group member at New England Medical Center. The "in-person" pilot experience allowed more efficient development and refinement of subsequent forms with Work Group members located at other institutions. It also provided experience in the steps necessary for training junior members of the Evidence Review Team to develop forms and to efficiently extract relevant information from primary articles. Training of the Work Group members to extract data from primary articles subsequently occurred by e-mail as well as at meetings.

RELEVANCE AND APPROPRIATENESS OF STUDY DESIGNS

Throughout the process of refinement of topics, the types of study design that would be relevant and appropriate to answer the questions posed in Table 8 were carefully considered.

Classification of Stages

Defining the stages of severity was an iterative process, based on expertise of the Work Group members and synthesis of evidence developed during the systematic review. After defining the stages of severity, it was necessary to estimate the prevalence of each stage (albuminuria or proteinuria as a marker of kidney damage, decreased GFR, kidney failure) in the general population. The ideal study design to assess prevalence would be a cross-sectional study of population representative of the general population. Criteria for evaluation of cross-sectional studies to assess prevalence are listed in Table 150. Data from NHANES III were fortunately available for some of these analyses. The methods for analysis of data from NHANES III are described in Appendix 2. In addition, articles from studies of community screening were included. For these studies, the relevant result is the

Table 150. Evaluation of Studies of Prevalence

Evaluation of Validity

- *Cross-sectional study design*
- *Was there a representative and well-defined sample of the population of interest?*
  - Minimize non-response
  - Define sampling strategy
  - Subgroups defined in advance
- *Were objective and unbiased criteria used to define cases and controls?*
- *Were methods for data collection applied equally to all study participants?*
- *Was there adjustment for important prognostic factors?*

Evaluation of Results

- *How large is the prevalence of cases?*
- *How precise are the estimates of prevalence?*
- *Are there important differences among subgroups?*

Evaluation of Clinical Applicability

- *Is the population, or subgroups of the population, under study similar to the population from which my patients are drawn?*
- *Were the definitions and measures useful in practice?*
- *Are the results useful for estimating probability of disease?*

estimate of prevalence, expressed as a percent, with the absolute number of individuals derived by extrapolation to the US population, where possible.

Evaluation of Laboratory Tests

Evidence was required to assess the performance of diagnostic tests (prediction equations for GFR, spot urine samples for protein-to-creatinine and albumin-to-creatinine ratios, and new urinary markers of kidney damage) for the evaluation of severity of chronic kidney disease. The ideal study design for diagnostic test evaluation would be a cross-sectional study of a representative sample of patients who are tested using the "gold"

Table 151. Diagnostic Test Evaluation

Evaluation of Validity

- *Cross-sectional study design*
- *Was there an independent, blind comparison with a reference standard?*
- *Did the patient sample include an appropriate spectrum of patients to whom the diagnostic test will be applied in clinical practice*
- *Did the results of the test being evaluated influence the decision to perform the reference standard?*
- *Were the methods for performing the test described in sufficient detail to permit replication?*

Evaluation of Results

- *Are likelihood ratios for the test results presented or data necessary for their calculation provided?*
- *Were calculations of sensitivity and specificity reported?*

Evaluation of Applicability

- *Will the reproducibility of the test result and its interpretation be satisfactory in my setting?*
- *Are the results applicable to my patient?*
- *Will the results change my management?*
- *Will patients be better off as a result of the test?*

Modified and reprinted with permission.[655]

(criterion) standard as well as the newer test. Criteria for evaluation of studies of diagnostic tests are listed in Table 151.[655] For these studies, the relevant result is the measure of performance (bias and precision) of the new test.

Association of Level of GFR With Complications

The appropriate study to assess the association of level of GFR with complications would be a cross-sectional study of a representative sample of patients with chronic kidney disease in whom the level of kidney function is related to the presence or absence or severity of a complication. In addition, baseline data from a longitudinal study would be appropriate. Principles of cross-sectional studies to assess associations are described in

Table 152. Evaluation of Clinical Associations

Evaluation of Validity

- *Case series or cross-sectional study design?*
- *Did the patient sample include an appropriate spectrum of patients for whom the associations are relevant?*
- *Were subgroups defined in advance?*
- *Were objective and unbiased criteria used to define outcomes and exposures?*
- *Were methods for data collection applied equally to all study participants?*
- *Was there adjustment for important prognostic factors?*

Evaluation of Results

- *How large is the prevalence of cases?*
- *How precise are the estimates of prevalence?*
- *Are there dose-response relationships between outcomes and exposures?*
- *How large is the relationship?*
- *How precise is the relationship?*
- *Are there important differences among subgroups in prevalence or relationships between outcomes and exposures?*

Evaluation of Clinical Applicability

- *Are the study patients similar to my own?*
- *Will the definitions and measures be useful in practice?*
- *Are the results useful for estimating probability of disease?*

Table 152. For some complications, data from NHANES III were available. However, the NHANES III database includes relatively few patients with severely decreased GFR (15 to 29 mL/min/1.73 m²); therefore, it was also desirable to use cross-sectional studies, baseline data from longitudinal studies, and case series of patients with decreased GFR. Data from baseline assessments of patients enrolled in the Canadian Multicentre cohort study of patients with chronic kidney disease were used for Figures 28, 29, 36, 37, 38, 40, and 42.[288] Data from all 446 patients enrolled from 1994 to 1997 were available.

Studies that provided data for various levels of kidney function were preferred; however, if data were sparse, studies that provided only the mean level of kidney function were included. Members of the Work Group provided individual patient data that were used for some analyses.

Stratification of Risk (Prognosis)

The appropriate study to assess the relationship of risk factors to loss of kidney function and development of cardiovascular disease would be a longitudinal study of a representative sample of patients with chronic kidney disease with prospective assessment of factors at baseline and outcomes during follow-up. Because it can be difficult to determine the onset of chronic kidney disease and cardiovascular disease, prospective cohort studies were preferred to case-control studies or retrospective studies. Clinical trials were included, with the understanding that the selection criteria for the clinical trial may have lead to a non-representative cohort. Criteria for evaluating studies of prognosis are described in Table 153.[656] Of particular importance is multivariable analysis to control for confounding by factors other than the variables of interest (for example, confounding by age in studies of factors related to cardiovascular disease events). Because of the well-

Table 153. Evaluation of Studies of Prognosis

Evaluation of Validity

- *Cohort study design*
- *Was there a representative and well-defined sample of patients at a similar point in the course of the disease?*
- *Was follow-up sufficiently long and complete?*
- *Were objective and unbiased outcome criteria used?*
- *Was there adjustment for important prognostic factors?*

Evaluation of Results

- *How large is the likelihood of the outcome event(s) in a specified period of time?*
- *How precise are the estimates of likelihood?*

Evaluation of Clinical Applicability

- *Are the study patients similar to my own?*
- *Will the results lead directly to selecting or avoiding therapy?*
- *Are the results useful for reassuring or counseling patients?*

Modified and reprinted with permission.[656]

known association between diabetes and cardiovascular disease, diabetic and nondiabetic patients were considered separately. The association between diabetic kidney disease and other diabetic complications was evaluated using reviews of cross-sectional studies and selected primary articles of cohort studies. The association between nondiabetic kidney disease and cardiovascular disease was evaluated using several strategies: reviews and selected primary articles of incidence rates of cardiovascular disease in patients with nondiabetic kidney disease; reviews and selected primary articles of cross-sectional studies of the prevalence of risk factor levels in patients with nondiabetic kidney disease; and a systematic search for cohort studies of the relationship between albuminuria or proteinuria and decreased GFR with subsequent cardiovascular disease events in nondiabetic individuals.

LITERATURE SEARCH

The Work Group and Evidence Review Team decided in advance that a systematic process would be followed to obtain information on topics that relied on primary articles. In general, only full journal articles of original data were included. Review articles, editorials, letters, or abstracts were not included (except as noted). Though reports of formal studies were preferred, case series were also included. No systematic process was followed to obtain textbooks and review articles.

Studies for the literature review were identified primarily through Medline searches of English language literature conducted between February and June 2000. These searches were supplemented by relevant articles known to the domain experts and reviewers.

The Medline literature searches were conducted to identify clinical studies published from 1966 through the search dates. Separate search strategies were developed for each topic. Development of the search strategies was an iterative process that included input from all members of the Work Group. Search strategies were designed to yield approximately 1,000 to 2,000 titles each. The text words or MeSH headings for all topics included kidney or kidney diseases or kidney function tests. The searches were limited to studies on humans and published in English and focused on either adults or children, as relevant. In general, studies that focused on hemodialysis or peritoneal dialysis were excluded. The Medline search strategies are included in the Evidence Report.

Medline search results were screened by clinicians on the Evidence Review Team. Potential papers for retrieval were identified from printed abstracts and titles, based on study population, relevance to topic, and article type. In general, studies with fewer than 10 subjects were not included (except as noted). After retrieval, each paper was screened to verify relevance and appropriateness for review, based primarily on study design and ascertainment of necessary variables. Some articles were relevant to two or more topics. A goal was set of approximately 30 articles per topic. In many cases, the goal was exceeded. Domain experts made the final decision for inclusion or exclusion of articles. All articles included were abstracted and contained in the evidence tables.

Table 154. Literature Search and Review by Topic

Guideline, Topic	Primary Reviewer	Abstracts Screened	Articles Retrieved	Articles Added	Articles Included
Classification					
1 Normal proteinuria levels, children	Hogg	640[a]	67[a]	20	27
1 Proteinuria prevalence, children	Hogg	640[a]	67[a]	14	20
1 Level kidney function at start hemodialysis	Kausz	767	34	3	7
Evaluation					
4 GFR prediction equations, adults	Coresh	2,490	96	31	64/12[b]
4 GFR prediction equations, children	Furth	815	120	14	42/12[b]
5 Spot urine samples, adults	Steffes	268	17	12	17
5 Spot urine samples, children	Hogg	640[a]	67[a]	8	14
6 Other markers	Lemley	1,277	112	4	13
Association of GFR with Complications					
8 Anemia	Levin	3,533	72	4	23
9 Malnutrition	Ikizler, Harvey	3,051	191	11	29
10 Bone disease	Kausz	1,496	74	2	33
11 Neuropathy	Kausz	1,144	40	2	9
12 Functioning and well-being	Witten	1,795	107	4	11
Stratification of Risk					
13 Loss of kidney function	Kausz	All[c]	80	13	36
14 Diabetic complications	Nelson	0	0	4	4
15 Cardiovascular disease	Culleton	877	35	19	25
Totals:		18,153	1,045	165	367[d]

[a] Same articles were screened and retrieved for normal proteinuria, proteinuria prevalence and spot urine samples in children.

[b] First number refers to total number of studies reviewed and included in the evidence table. Second number refers to the number of articles which met criteria for inclusion in the summary table (prediction equation of interest, >100 subjects (adult), >50 subjects (children), extractable data on bias and precision).

[c] From all other searches

[d] Articles included in different pediatric urine sample sections not double-counted.

Table 154 details the literature search and review for each topic. Overall, 18,153 abstracts were screened, 1,110 articles were reviewed, and results were extracted from 367 articles.

FORMAT FOR EVIDENCE TABLES

Two types of evidence tables were prepared. Detailed tables contain data from each field of the components of the data extraction forms. These tables are contained in the evidence report but are not included in the manuscript. Summary tables describe the strength of evidence according to four dimensions: study size, applicability depending on the type of study subjects, results, and methodological quality (see table on the next page, Example of Format for Evidence Tables). Within each table, studies are ordered first by methodological quality (best to worst), then by applicability (most to least), and then by study size (largest to smallest).

Study Size

The study (sample) size is used as a measure of the weight of the evidence. In general, large studies provide more precise estimates of prevalence and associations. In addition,

Author, Year	No. of Subjects	Applicability	GFR Range* (mL/min/1.73 m²) 0 30 60 90 120	Results	Quality
Smith, 1999	1,000	↟↟↟	——┼——	⬇	●
Jones, 1995	500	↟↟	S_{Cr} = 3.4 mg/dL	⇧	◐
Rodriguez, 1995	250	↟↟	━━━	⬆	◐
Johnson, 1995	500	↟↟↟	┄┼┄	⟺	○
Klein, 1995	1,500	↟↟	S_{Cr} ≈ 0.9–4.0 mg/dL	3.3 g/dL	◐
Roberts, 1995	500	↟	┊ │ ┊	3.7 g/dL	◐
Doe, 2000	500	↟↟	S_{Cr} = 2.9 ±0.6 mg/dL	3.2 g/dL	○

Shading is used to distinguish studies do not report on the association between GFR and the table's outcome measure (e.g., serum albumin levels); unshaded studies use arrows to represent the strength and direction of the reported association.

* Where GFR data were not available, S_{Cr} values (in mg/dL) are given.

large studies are more likely to be generalizable; however, large size alone does not guarantee applicability. A study that enrolled a large number of selected patients may be less generalizable than several smaller studies that included a broad spectrum of patient populations.

Applicability

Applicability (also known as generalizability or external validity) addresses the issue of whether the study population is sufficiently broad so that the results can be generalized to the population of interest at large. The study population is typically defined by the inclusion and exclusion criteria. The target population was defined to include patients with chronic kidney disease and those at increased risk of chronic kidney disease, except where noted. A designation for applicability was assigned to each article, according to a three-level scale. In making this assessment, sociodemographic characteristics were considered, as were the stated causes of chronic kidney disease and prior treatments. If a study is considered to be not fully generalizable, reasons for lack of applicability are reported in the detailed tables on file at the NKF.

GFR Range

For all studies, the range of GFR (or creatinine clearance [C_{Cr}]) is represented graphically when available. The mean or median GFR is represented by a vertical line, with a horizontal bar approximating the 95% coverage interval. Studies without a vertical or horizontal line did not provide data on the mean/median or range, respectively. When data were available, the range was calculated as: Range = mean GFR ± 1.96 × (standard deviation).

When sufficient data were not available, the range was estimated from the full range of GFR levels reported, from the median GFR, or from available graphs. For studies that reported creatinine clearance instead of GFR, the mean and range of creatinine clearance

♔♔♔	Sample is representative of the target population, or results are definitely applicable to general chronic kidney disease population irrespective of study sample.
♔♔	Sample is representative of a relevant sub-group of the target population. For example, sample is only representative of people with a narrow range of GFR, or only a specific relevant subgroup, such as elderly individuals or patients with diabetic kidney disease. In addition, studies of association of level of kidney function with complications that report serum creatinine levels rather than estimated GFR are assigned to this category.
♔	Sample is representative of a narrow subgroup of patients only, and not well generalizable to other subgroups. For example, the study includes only patients with a rare disease. However, studies of such narrow subgroups may be extremely valuable for demonstrating "exceptions to the rule."

were used to estimate GFR. For studies that reported neither GFR nor creatinine clearance, the mean level of serum creatinine ($\pm$ standard deviation and/or range) is listed as text (eg, $S_{Cr} = 3.4 \pm 0.3$ mg/dL).

Results

In principle, the study design determined the type of results obtained. For studies of prevalence, the result is the percent of individuals with the condition of interest. For diagnostic test evaluation, the result is the strength of association between the new measurement method and the criterion standard. In addition to evaluating the size of correlations and regression coefficients, bias and precision of GFR estimate equations were also considered. For studies of the association between the level of GFR and complications, the result is direction and strength of the association. In addition to examining continuous relationships (correlations and regressions), the prevalence of complications for levels of GFR corresponding to stages of chronic kidney disease were estimated. For studies of prognosis, the result is the factor and the direction and strength of the association between the risk factor and outcome. Associations were represented according to the following symbols:

⇧	Positive association (measurement increases or decreases in the same direction as GFR)
⇔	No association (measurement does *not* vary with level of GFR)
⇩	Negative association (measurement changes in inverse direction as GFR)
⬆ or ⬇	Statistically significant association (p <0.05)

The specific meaning of the symbols is included as a footnote for each table.

For studies that provided only single point estimates (such as the mean value) of complications, those values are presented instead of data on association with level of GFR. Studies that reported strength of association of an outcome with GFR are listed and ranked separately from those that simply reported mean levels, with shading used to visually distinguish them.

Quality

Methodological quality (or internal validity) refers to the design, conduct, and reporting of the clinical study. Because studies with a variety of types of design were evaluated, a three-level classification of study quality was devised:

- ● Least bias; results are valid. A study that mostly adheres to the commonly held concepts of high quality, including the following: a formal study; clear description of the population and setting; clear description of an appropriate reference standard; proper measurement techniques; appropriate statistical and analytic methods; no reporting errors; and no obvious bias.

- ◉ Susceptible to some bias, but not sufficient to invalidate the results. A study that does not meet all the criteria in category above. It has some deficiencies but none likely to cause major bias. Includes retrospective studies and case series.

O	Significant bias that may invalidate the results. A study with serious errors in design or reporting. These studies may have large amounts of missing information or discrepancies in reporting. Includes prospective and retrospective studies and case series.

SUMMARIZING REVIEWS AND SELECTED ORIGINAL ARTICLES

Work Group members had wide latitude in summarizing reviews and selected original articles for topics that were determined, a priori, not to require a systemic review of the literature. The use of published or derived tables and figures was encouraged to simplify the presentation.

TRANSLATION OF EVIDENCE TO GUIDELINES

Format

This document contains 15 guidelines. The format for each guideline is outlined in Table 155. Each guideline contains one or more specific "guideline statements," which are presented as "bullets" that represent recommendations to the target audience. Each guideline contains background information, which is generally sufficient to interpret the guideline. A discussion of the broad concepts that frame the guidelines is provided in the preceding section of this report. The rationale for each guideline contains definitions

Table 155. Format for Guidelines

Introductory Statement
- **Guideline Statement 1**
- **Guideline Statement 2**

Background

Rationale

    Definitions (*if appropriate*)

    Markers of Disease (*if appropriate*)

    Strength of Evidence

        Rationale Statement 1

        Supporting text

        Rationale Statement 2

        Supporting text

Limitations

Clinical Applications

Implementation Issues

Research Recommendations

Grading Rationale Statements

Grade	Level of Evidence
S	Analysis of individual patient data from a single large, generalizable study of high methodological quality (for example, NHANES III)
C	Compilation of original articles (evidence tables)
R	Review of reviews and selected original articles
O	Opinion

and classifications of markers of disease (if appropriate) followed by a series of specific "rationale statements," each supported by evidence. The guideline concludes with a discussion of limitations of the evidence review and a brief discussion of clinical applications, implementation issues and research recommendations regarding the topic.

Strength of Evidence

Each rationale statement has been graded according the level of evidence on which it is based (see the table, *Grading Rationale Statements*).

LIMITATIONS OF APPROACH

While the literature searches were intended to be comprehensive, they were not exhaustive. Medline was the only database searched, and searches were limited to English language publications. Hand searches of journals were not performed, and review articles and textbook chapters were not systematically searched. In addition, search strategies were generally restricted to yield a maximum of about 2,000 titles each. This approach required the exclusion of some topics from searches. However, important studies known to the domain experts that were missed by the literature search were included in the review. In addition, essential studies identified during the review process were also included.

Exhaustive literature searches were hampered by limitations in available time and resources that were judged appropriate for the task. The search strategies required to capture every article that may have had data on each of the questions frequently yielded upwards of 10,000 articles. The difficulty of finding all potentially relevant studies was compounded by the fact that in many studies, the information of interest for this report was a secondary finding for the original studies.

Due to the wide variety of methods of analysis, units of measurements, definitions of chronic kidney disease, and methods of reporting in the original studies, it was often very difficult to standardize the findings for this report.

APPENDIX 2. KIDNEY FUNCTION AND ASSOCIATED CONDITIONS IN THE UNITED STATES: METHODS AND FINDINGS FROM THE THIRD NATIONAL HEALTH AND NUTRITION EXAMINATION SURVEY (1988 TO 1994)

The Third National Health and Nutrition Examination Survey (NHANES III) data offer the first opportunity to study the prevalence and number of people with chronic kidney disease in a nationally representative sample of the United States. An initial analysis from NHANES III showed that the prevalence of elevated serum creatinine was higher among non-Hispanic blacks than non-Hispanic whites and among older compared to younger individuals.[1] The present analysis was undertaken to describe the distribution of estimated glomerular filtration rate (GFR) in the US population. Estimated GFR was calculated using an equation based on each participant's creatinine, age, sex, and race. The associations of estimated GFR with age, high blood pressure, anemia, and other metabolic and functional abnormalities are also examined to display the range of abnormalities associated with decreased kidney function. The prevalence of microalbuminuria and proteinuria by age, sex, race, and diabetes are tabulated to show the frequency with which these abnormalities are present in the population.

METHODS

Survey

The NHANES III survey, conducted during 1988 to1994 by the National Center for Health Statistics (NCHS) of the Centers for Disease Control and Prevention, provides cross-sectional, nationally representative data on the health and nutritional status of the civilian, non-institutionalized US population.[657,658] Non-Hispanic blacks, Mexican-Americans, as well as the elderly and children were deliberately oversampled in this survey. This oversampling makes it possible to obtain reliable estimates of the distribution of creatinine in the two largest minority groups of the civilian, non-institutionalized US population as well in a broad range of age groups. Standardized questionnaires were administered in the home, followed by a detailed physical examination at a Mobile Examination Center.

Serum Creatinine

Serum was collected at the Mobile Examination Center and creatinine measurements were performed by the modified kinetic Jaffe reaction[659] using a Hitachi 737 analyzer (Boehringer Mannheim Corp, Indianapolis, IN) and reported using conventional units (1 mg/dL = 88.4 μmol/L). The coefficient of variation for creatinine determination ranged from 0.2% to 1.4% during the 6 years of study. Data on physiologic variation in creatinine were obtained in a sample of 1,921 participants who had a repeat creatinine measurement. The percent difference between the two creatinine measurements, a mean of 17 days apart, had a mean of 0.2% and standard deviation of 9.7%.[5]

Estimation of GFR

Estimation of GFR using an equation requires that the calibration of the serum creatinine assay be the same as that in the laboratory where the equation was developed. In NHANES

III, serum creatinine was measured in the White Sands Laboratory, where quality control data shows stable calibration over time. The mean serum creatinine for 20 to 39-year-old participants without hypertension or diabetes was 1.14 mg/dL for men and 0.91 mg/dL for women. College of American Pathologists Survey data, released with permission of both laboratories, show that creatinine values in the White Sands laboratory measured during 1992 to 1995 using the Hitachi 737 instrument averaged 0.2 to 0.3 mg/dL higher than values in the Cleveland Clinic measured using the Beckman Astra and Synchron instruments. The latter values were similar to the overall mean of all laboratories for creatinine. These lower values were also close to a gold standard HPLC assay for creatinine in a small validation study.[660] This concern lead to a direct comparison of the two laboratories using frozen samples from 212 Modification of Diet in Renal Disease (MDRD) Study participants and 342 Third National Health and Nutrition Examination Survey (NHANES III) participants which were assayed for serum creatinine a second time in each of the study laboratories during the year 2000.[661] The GFR estimates in this report are based on creatinine values which were recalibrated using these results. This correction resulted in an estimated median GFR value of 119 mL/min/1.73 m^2 at age 20 years (5th and 95th percentiles of 88 and 180 mL/min/1.73 m^2). These values are a little lower than published data on normal GFR among young adults. Whether the equations for estimating GFR require further refinement in the normal GFR range is uncertain, but the associations observed support the utility of this estimated GFR. Individuals with very low creatinine values had an estimated GFR that was higher than physiologically plausible. These NHANES participants were assigned a GFR value of 200 mL/min/1.73 m^2 as an upper limit to avoid undue influence (0.5% of men, 2.3% of women, 0.7% of nonpregnant women). Pregnant women accounted for approximately half of the women with an estimated GFR>200 mL/min/1.73 m^2. Statistics focused on percentiles of the distribution to further decrease the influence of such outliers.

Proteinuria

A random spot urine sample was obtained from each participant aged 6 years and older, using a clear catch technique and sterile containers. Urine samples were placed on dry ice and shipped overnight to a central laboratory where they were stored at $-20°C$. Urinary albumin concentration was measured by solid-phase fluorescent immunoassay.[662] Urine albumin was not measured in specimens which contained blood or which tested positive for hemoglobin using qualitative test strips (Multistix). Urine creatinine concentration was measured by the modified kinetic rate Jaffe method using a Beckman Synchron AS/ASTRA analyzer. The inter-assay coefficients of variation for low (1.0 mg/L) and medium (15 mg/L) urine albumin quality control standards were 16% and 10%, respectively. The urinary albumin to urinary creatinine ratio is reported in mg/g. Sex specific cutoffs were used to define microalbuminuria and albuminuria in a single spot urine.

Our estimates reflect the prevalence of albuminuria based on a single untimed urine specimen and include individuals with persistent albuminuria and individuals with intermittent albuminuria. Repeat measurements were obtained in a subset of 1,241 NHANES III participants within 2 months of the initial examination. Agreement between the initial and repeat tests classified as normal, micro, and macro albuminuria was 91.2% (kappa 0.59). Microalbuminuria persisted in the second visit in 57% and macroalbuminuria was present in another 4% of the 110 participants with microalbuminuria on the first exam. The variation in persistence by age group and sex was: 45% at 20 to 39 (n = 22), 59% at 40 to 59 (n = 32), 70% at 60 to 79 (n = 43), and 44% at ≥80 years (n = 9), 65% among men (n = 48), and 52% among women (n = 62). Among 1,099 individuals without microalbuminuria at the first visit 5% (n = 56) had microalbuminuria or albuminuria on the second visit.

Biochemistry

A 22 analyte biochemistry panel, including serum creatinine, was performed with a Hitachi Model 737 multi-channel analyzer (Boehringer Mannheim Diagnostics, Indianapolis, IN).

Blood Pressure

Blood pressure measurements were obtained three times during the home interview and another three times during the examination and averaged. Individuals were classified as hypertensive if they had a mean blood pressure ≥140 mm Hg systolic, or ≥90 mm Hg diastolic, or reported being currently prescribed medication for hypertension treatment.[102]

Diabetes

Diabetes was defined by history as well as blood glucose values. The primary analysis stratified individuals based on a history of diagnosed diabetes mellitus since this information was available for nearly all individuals and could be used by physicians for risk stratification. Ancillary analyses examined the impact of using the American Diabetes Association (ADA) criteria[663] for diabetes mellitus in the subset of individuals who fasted at least 8 hours.

Dietary History

Dietary history was collected using a food frequency questionnaire.

STATISTICAL ANALYSIS

The complex survey design of NHANES III incorporates differential probabilities of selection. To derive national estimates, sampling weights are used to adjust for non-coverage and non-response. All prevalence estimates were weighted to represent the civilian, non-institutionalized US population and to account for over sampling and non-response to the household interview and the physical examination.[658] All data analyses were conducted using STATA svy commands for analyzing complex survey design data with 49 strata and 98 primary sampling units.[664] A total of 16,589 participants out of 20,050 (82.7%) examined had both blood pressure and serum creatinine data were used as the starting sample for all analyses. The missing data rate was higher in older individuals

(individuals missing data were 4 years older), among men than women (17.9% versus 16.7%), and lower among Mexican-Americans and other ethnic groups (14%) than among non-Hispanic whites (19%) and non-Hispanic blacks (18%). These differences were primarily due to missing phlebotomy data. To minimize bias the combined Mobile Examination Center and home exam weights were divided by the proportion of participants missing creatinine data in each of the design age, sex, and race ethnicity strata. This corrects differences in missing data across sampling strata but assumes that data are missing randomly within strata. Missing data rates for other covariates among these individuals varied from 0% for serum albumin to 4.3% for urinary albumin. Survey weights were not further adjusted for missing data in these variables.

Estimated GFR was calculated using the abbreviated MDRD Study equation using the corrected serum creatinine (S_{Cr}, mg/dL) as follows:

$$\text{Estimated } GFR \text{ (mL/min/1.73 m}^2) = 186 \times (S_{Cr})^{-1.154} \times (Age)^{-0.203} \times (0.742 \text{ if female}) \times (1.21 \text{ if African American})$$

This equation is also equivalent to:

$$\text{Estimated } GFR \text{ (mL/min/1.73 m}^2) = \exp(5.228 - 1.154 \times \ln(S_{Cr}) - 0.203 \times \ln(Age) - (0.299 \text{ if female}) + (0.192 \text{ if African American})$$

Estimated GFR was analyzed both as a continuous measure and divided into ranges as described in the guidelines summary of stages of chronic kidney disease.

Continuous Analysis

Continuous analysis of estimated GFR used quantile regression to avoid undue influence of outliers.[664] The medians, as well as 95th and 5th percentiles of each covariates (for example, percentiles of blood hemoglobin), were regressed on estimated GFR to show how the middle and top and bottom ends of the covariate distribution varied across the range of GFR. The shape of the association of each covariate with median estimated GFR was modeled using a fifth order polynomial to allow for deviation from a linear association. The regression was further adjusted for age to avoid confounding by age since older individuals have a much lower GFR than younger individuals and older age is also associated with abnormalities in many other covariates. To allow for non-linear associations with age, age adjustment used a fifth order polynomial. The regression was then used to predict values across the range of GFR while fixing age to 60 years. Regressions were weighted using the sampling weights but quantile regression did not allow for explicit incorporation of survey strata into calculation of standard errors. The results are presented in graphical format as regression along with 95% confidence intervals for selected points in the age-adjusted regression. Regressions include all of the relevant data but the graphs are displayed for estimated GFRs between 15 and 150 mL/min/1.73 m^2 where the results are most meaningful.

Categorical Analysis

Categorical analysis of estimated GFR divided estimated GFR into four categories according to the proposed stages of chronic kidney disease ($\geq$90, 60 to 89, 30 to 59, and 30 to 15 mL/min/1.73 m²). The prevalence of abnormality in each category was calculated for two cutoff values. For example, with blood hemoglobin as the covariate, the cutoffs were <11 g/dL and <13 g/dL. This shows the prevalence of more and less severe abnormalities. Prevalence estimates were age adjusted using logistic regression to avoid confounding by age. Logistic regressions incorporating sample weights and the complex survey design were fit separately for each outcome (for example serum albumin <3.4 g/dL coded as 0/1) with a fifth order polynomial in GFR to fit non-linear associations. The model adjusted for age by including a fifth order polynomial in age. The regression was then used to predict the prevalence for a 60-year-old person with all other covariates unchanged. Bar graphs show this age adjusted prevalence and 95% confidence intervals by estimated GFR.

GFR Estimation in the Canadian Multicentre Cohort

This calculation was made using the abbreviated MDRD formula similarly to methods in NHANES III. Some of the figures label this estimate as "mL/min," although it should more correctly be labeled "mL/min/1.73 m²."

APPENDIX 3. METHODOLOGICAL ASPECTS OF EVALUATING EQUATIONS TO PREDICT GFR AND CALCULATIONS USING 24-HOUR URINE SAMPLES

IMPORTANCE OF SAMPLE SIZE

Many of the studies reviewed were small. Since estimates of accuracy from smaller studies can be unreliable, studies presented have at least 100 adults or 50 children. A smaller sample size was permitted for pediatric studies because large pediatric studies are rare. Several large validation studies evaluating the newly developed MDRD Study equation were conducted recently and were only available in abstract form.[162,165] In order to capture these valuable data, the authors were contacted and asked to analyze their data and provide estimates of accuracy for this review.

EVALUATION OF BIAS, PRECISION, AND ACCURACY

Review of the literature showed great heterogeneity in how the performance of prediction equations was assessed. The mean difference between the actual measured GFR (gold standard) and the estimated GFR based on an equation provides a valid measure of bias. The median difference provides a measure that is valid and less susceptible to influence by outliers. The standard deviation of the difference between the measured and estimated GFR should be reported as a measure of precision. The difference from the gold standard can also be expressed as a relative difference, eg, percent difference from the measured GFR. This has the advantage of allowing for the decreased absolute precision in estimating higher values of GFR. Clinically this is relevant, as there is less concern about the difference between 100 and 130 mL/min/1.73 m² than between 30 and 60 mL/min/1.73 m².

Most studies had a plot of the predicted versus measured GFR, which provided for a common basis for comparison. A magnified copy of the graph was used to estimate the proportion of GFR estimates within 30% and 50% of the measured GFR by counting the number of points outside of these limits. The average percent bias for the study was estimated as well. In most studies this had to be done by comparing the percent difference between the average estimated and measured GFR since average percent bias at the individual level was rarely available.

ANALYSIS AND INTERPRETATION OF DATA

Correlation coefficients are frequently cited in the literature on prediction equations. However, they are inadequate for measuring the validity of a method in estimating GFR for two reasons. Although correlation coefficients (r) measure the association between prediction equation and measured GFR, the correlation coefficient is highly dependent on the distribution of GFRs in the study population selected. Even poor estimates can discriminate between a GFR of 20 and 120 very reliably. Second, correlation measures ignore bias and measure relative rather than absolute agreement. For example, in the MDRD Study the Cockroft-Gault equation had a similar correlation to GFR as the MDRD Study equation but overestimated GFR by 19%.[17] Analogous studies in children show similar limitations in assessing the utility of a prediction equation by virtue of its correlation coefficient.[124] The correlation between inulin clearance and estimated GFR by the Schwartz formula was 0.905, while in the same study, the standard deviation of the difference between the reference value (C_{in}) on the predicted value was 28.6%, indicating limited precision.

Regression equations are another commonly used measure of prediction equations. Regression equations relating an estimate of GFR and the measured GFR provide an estimate of systematic bias, in the relationship between the two variables, as well as the correlation and residual root mean error, measures of precision. However, such regression analyses have two drawbacks. First, ordinary least square regression does not allow for measurement error in the X-variable. As a result, the regression equation provides a prediction equation conditional of the X-value rather than an unbiased estimate of the relationship. For example, a regression of one GFR measure on a second GFR measure, using the same technique on another day, would have a slope that is substantially lower than 1.0 and an intercept greater than zero. The importance of measurement error in the X-values depends on the correlation, which in turn depends on the study population. Second, regression equations cannot be pooled across different studies. Finally, evaluation of the accuracy of any equation for estimating GFR must be made in an independent group from the group in which the equation itself was derived.

NOTES ON EVALUATION OF MDRD STUDY EQUATION

No peer-reviewed publications validating the MDRD Study equation were available. An analysis of 1,775 GFR measurements in participants of the African-American Study of Kidney Disease and Hypertension (AASK) indicates that the equation performs similarly in this study population.[162] Accuracy was also similar among 321 kidney transplant recipients.[165] Thus, the abbreviated MDRD Study equation provides a rigorously developed equation for estimating GFR, which may allow for improved prediction of GFR.

A direct comparison of the abbreviated MDRD Study equation with other equations developed in the same study that include other variables (serum urea nitrogen, serum albumin, and 24-hour creatinine clearance) shows only a marginal improvement in the prediction. The median percent difference from GFR was 12.1% versus 11.3% for a 6 variable equation, which includes serum urea nitrogen and albumin. Exclusion of these analytes decreases the cost of testing, the susceptibility to bias in calibration of these other analytes, and bias due to alteration of these analyses by diseases other than kidney disease. This abbreviated equation also predicted GFR better than 24-hour creatinine clearance, even after bias correction of the creatinine clearance. While the equation performed well in the AASK study where a substantial number of GFR values in the normal range were included, the equation was developed in a sample with few individuals with a GFR greater than 90 mL/min/1.73 m^2.

CALCULATIONS USING 24-HOUR URINE SAMPLES

The daily urea clearance ($U_{urea} \times V$)/P_{urea} and creatinine clearance ($U_{Cr} \times V$)/S_{Cr} can be calculated from the concentrations of urea and creatinine and the volume (converted to mL/min) of the 24-hour urine collection. The weekly Kt/V_{urea} is equal to the daily urea clearance multiplied by seven (Kt) divided by the estimated total body water (V). Total body water can be estimated in adults by the Watson formula[665] or the Mellits-Cheek method for children using measured weight and height.[16] If daily protein intake is relatively constant and the patient is in a steady state, then urinary nitrogen excretion is roughly equal to nitrogen intake. Therefore, using the urea nitrogen concentration in the 24-hour urine, protein intake can be estimated from[666]:

Urinary nitrogen excretion = Urine urea nitrogen + nonurea nitrogen

Nonurea nitrogen excretion is relatively constant at 30 mg/kg per day. Each gram of nitrogen is derived from 6.25 grams of protein. Therefore:

Estimated protein intake (g/d) = 6.25 ×
(Urine urea nitrogen (g/d) + 30 $mg/kg/d$ × Weight (kg)

For example, a 50-kg woman with a 24-hour urine urea nitrogen excretion of 7 g has an estimated protein intake = 6.25 (7 + 1.5) = 53.1 g.

These parameters are useful in evaluating the patient's nutritional status, need for dialysis, and prescription of dialysis dose and modality.[320,667]

PART 11. WORK GROUP MEMBERS

THE FOLLOWING are brief sketches that describe the professional training and experience, particularly as they relate to the K/DOQI CKD Clinical Practice Guidelines, as well as principal academic affiliations of the work group members. All work group members completed a disclosure statement certifying that any potential conflict of interest would not influence their judgment or actions concerning the K/DOQI.

ADULT WORK GROUP

Kline Bolton, MD, FACP, is Professor of Medicine at University of Virginia in Charlottesville, where he is Chief of the Division of Nephrology and Director of the Nephrology Clinical Research Center, Kidney Center and Renal Operations. He has received special honors from organizations ranging from the American Society for Clinical Investigation to the International Society of Nephrology. He has published many articles in journals ranging from *American Journal of Kidney Diseases* and *Kidney International* to *Immunologic Renal Diseases*, and contributed to numerous text books, including the *Textbook of the Autoimmune Diseases* and the *Textbook of Nephrology*. He is Chairman of the Renal Physicians Association Work Group on *Appropriate Preparation of Patients for Renal Replacement Therapy.* His research interests are in refining the epitope(s) involved in causing Goodpasture's syndrome, treating glomerulonephritis, and disease management of CKD and ESRD.

Josef Coresh, MD, PhD (*Work Group Co-Chair*), is Associate Professor of Epidemiology, Medicine and Biostatistics at Johns Hopkins Bloomberg School of Public Health, Baltimore. He currently serves on the National Analgesic Nephropathy Advisory Committee and is conducting research focussing on cardiovascular and kidney disease in the Atherosclerosis Risk in Communities Study and the CHOICE Study cohort of kidney failure patients as well as NHANES data. He has been active in the following organizations: the International Society of Nephrology, the American Society of Nephrology, the American Heart Association, the American Statistical Association, the Delta Omega Honor Society in Public Health (Alpha Chapter), the International Genetic Epidemiology Society, the American Society of Human Genetics, and the Society for Epidemiological Research. Dr Coresh directs a cardiovascular epidemiology training grant, and is an American Heart Association Established Investigator.

Bruce Culleton, MD, FRCPC, is Clinical Assistant Professor of Nephrology at the University of Calgary Foothills Medical Center, Alberta, Canada. He has been active in the following organizations: the American Society of Nephrology, the International Society of Nephrology, the Kidney Foundation of Canada, the Canadian Hypertension Society, and the Canadian Renal Disease Alliance. In addition to serving on the Medical Advisory Board for Amgen Canada, Dr Culleton is a member of the Canadian Hypertension Society subgroup on the pharmacologic management of hypertension. Recently, he completed a Research Fellowship at the Framingham Heart Study where he pursued his interest in cardiovascular epidemiology in patients with kidney disease. He has also published several journal articles, abstracts, and book chapters in the area of cardiovascular disease in patients with chronic kidney disease.

Kathy Schiro Harvey, MS, RD, CSR, is Chief Renal Dietitian at Puget Sound Kidney Centers in Everett, Washington. She is past Chair of the Renal Practice Group of the American Dietetic Association, and Renal Dietitian at Providence St. Peter Kidney Centers, Olympia, Washington, and at Northwest Kidney Centers, Seattle, Washington. As Board Certified Specialist in Renal Nutrition, she focuses on the areas of pre-ESRD, hemodialysis, and peritoneal dialysis. She currently serves on the Editorial Board of the Journal of Renal Nutrition and is on the Dietitian Advisory Board of Genzyme Therapeutics. Ms Schiro Harvey was the recipient of the Outstanding Service Award of the American Dietetic Association.

Talat Alp Ikizler, MD, is Assistant Professor of Medicine at Vanderbilt University Medical Center, and Medical Director of the Vanderbilt University Outpatient Dialysis Unit, Nashville, Tennessee. He is a member of several societies including the American Society of Nephrology and the International Society of Nutrition and Metabolism in Renal Disease. His ongoing research projects are focused on nutrition and metabolism in chronic kidney failure patients, effects of initiation of dialysis on nutritional parameters, clinical aspects of acute kidney failure, inflammation in end-stage kidney disease patients, and vascular access in chronic hemodialysis patients. He has published over 30 papers and 5 book chapters and presented multiple abstracts. Dr Ikizler is the recipient of several grant (federal and pharmaceutical) awards and is a member of the Medical Review Board Network 8 Inc. and second vice president of the National Kidney Foundation of Middle Tennessee.

Cynda Ann Johnson, MD, MBA, is professor and head of the Department of Family Medicine at the University of Iowa. She received her bachelor's degree in German (with honors) and Biology and Phi Beta Kappa at Stanford University and her MD degree from UCLA in 1977. She returned for residency training at the University of Kansas, followed by a part-time teaching fellowship at UNC. She continued on the faculty at KU for the next 19 years. She joined the Family Medicine faculty at the University of Iowa in October 1999 as department head. She is chair of the Board of Directors for University of Iowa Community Medical Services and a member of the Iowa Academy of Family Physicians Board of Directors. Dr Johnson recently completed a 5-year term on the American Board of Family Practice, and was President of the Board in 1999–2000. She currently serves on the Executive Committee of the American Board of Medical Specialties and is a member of the ABMS-ACGME Joint Initiative on Resident Evaluation. In addition, Dr Johnson serves as the family medicine representative on a number of other boards addressing subspecialty issues. Dr Johnson was a member of the Jacobs Institute of Women's Health Expert Panel on Menopause Counseling, which subsequently published *Guidelines for Counseling Women on the Management of Menopause* in 2000. She and her husband, Bruce Johnson, MD, Professor of Internal Medicine at the University of Iowa, are co-authors of *Women's Health Care Handbook*, 2nd edition. Dr Johnson serves on multiple editorial boards and also is a reviewer for granting agencies. She is the physician representative on the Lutheran Church's national Task Force on Health and Ethical Challenges in Health Care.

Annamaria Kausz, MD, MS, is Assistant Professor of Medicine at Tufts University School of Medicine, Boston. She completed her Fellowship in Nephrology and in Pediatric Nephrology at the University of Washington Children's Hospital and Medical Center, Seattle, and received her Masters Degree in Epidemiology at the University of Washington School of Public Health. She received a K08 grant to conduct research in the area of chronic kidney disease. Dr Kausz is a past recipient of the American Society of Transplant Physicians Young Investigator Award. She serves on the Medical Advisory Board of Amgen Inc.

Paul L. Kimmel, MD, is Professor of Medicine at George Washington University Medical Center, Washington, DC, and Director of the Diabetic Nephropathy and HIV Programs at the National Institute of Diabetes and Digestive and Kidney Diseases, National Institutes of Health, Bethesda, Maryland. He has served on the Editorial Board of several nephrology journals and has published over 250 papers, including abstracts and book chapters. He has been a member of several professional organizations, scientific societies, and academic committees. His commitment to community health led him to Chair the NKF's National Capital Chapter's Professional Advisory Board and be a Member of its Board of Directors. He is past Director of dialysis centers in Pennsylvania and Washington, DC. Dr Kimmel is the recipient of a Medal for Excellence in Research from George Washington University Medical Center and is listed in Who's Who in Science and Engineering. He has received several grants from the National Kidney Foundation and National Institutes of Health.

John Kusek, PhD, is the Clinical Trials Program Director for the Division of Kidney, Urologic and Hematologic Diseases of the National Institute of Diabetes and Digestive and Kidney Diseases, National Institutes of Health. His interests are in the epidemiology of chronic renal insufficiency and clinical trials to prevent progression of chronic renal disease and in improving survival of hemodialysis patients. He has been involved with a number of clinical trials including the Modification of Diet in Renal Disease (MDRD) Study, the African American Study of Kidney Disease and Hypertension (AASK), the Hemodialysis (HEMO) Study, the Dialysis Access (DAC) Consortium, and the Folic Acid for Vascular Outcome Reduction in Transplantation (FAVORIT) Trial. He is also co-project director for a newly initiated prospective cohort study of chronic renal insufficiency. Areas of particular interest include recruitment, adherence, and quality of life for nephrology clinical trials.

Andrew S. Levey, MD (*Work Group Chair*), is Dr Gerald J. and Dorothy R. Friedman Professor of Medicine at Tufts University School of Medicine and Chief of the William B. Schwartz, MD Division of Nephrology at New England Medical Center, Boston. His research is mainly in the areas of epidemiology of chronic kidney disease and cardiovascular disease in chronic kidney disease, clinical trials to slow the progression of chronic kidney disease, clinical assessment of kidney function, and assessment and improvement of outcomes in dialysis and transplantation. Dr Levey is currently Program Director for an NIDDK-funded clinical research training program, "Clinical Trials, Epidemiology and Outcomes Research in Nephrology." He is past Chair of the Clinical Science Committee of the American Society of Nephrology. He is past Chair of the National Kidney Foundation's Task Force on Cardiovascular Disease in Chronic Renal Disease and will Chair a forthcoming Work Group on Management of High Blood Pressure in Chronic Kidney Disease. Dr Levey is the recipient of the National Kidney Foundation's President Award of 1998.

Adeera Levin, MD, FRCPC, is Clinical Associate Professor of Nephrology at the University of British Columbia, St. Paul's Hospital, Vancouver, Canada. She is currently the Director of Clinical Research and Education for Nephrology and the Post Graduate Fellowship Director. She is the President of the Canadian Society of Nephrology (2000–2002) and has served on the Executive of the CSN for the last 4 years. Dr Levin has been a member of the Scientific Review committee for the Kidney Foundation of Canada and served as the Chair of the Medical Advisory Committee for Kidney Foundation of Canada. She is the Director of the BC Provincial Agency, an organization working with the government to enhance the care of patients with kidney disease. Her area of interest and publications include early kidney disease, comorbidity, anemia, and other nontraditional risk factors for cardiovascular disease. She is the principal investigator on a number of multicenter Canadian studies and has developed a group of investigators known as the Canadian Renal Disease Alliance Group. She is active in the following organizations: the American Society of Nephrology, the International Society of Nephrology, and the Kidney Foundation of Canada, as well as locally in the University of British Columbia, Research Advisory Committee at St. Paul's Hospital. She is the recipient of the UBC Martin Hoffman Award for Excellence in Research and the Dean Whitlaw award for Outstanding Grand Rounds. She is the Chief Medical Editor for an educational publication aimed at increasing awareness of kidney disease, entitled PROFILES. She is currently on the editorial board of *Nephrology Dialysis Transplantation* and for the *American Journal of Kidney Disease* (2001) and reviews articles for *Peritoneal Dialysis International, Kidney International, Journal of American Society of Nephrology,* and *Canadian Family Practice.* Also, she serves on the Medical Advisory Board for Amgen Canada, Amgen USA, Janssen Cilag International, Ortho Biotech Inc, Canada, and Roche International. She has received grants from the Kidney Foundation of Canada to study comorbidities associated with chronic kidney disease and, more recently, to study the variability in the care delivered across Canada to patients with CKD. She has also received grants from BC Health Research Foundation, BC Transplant Foundation, Janssen Cilag international, Ortho Biotech, Amgen, and Genzyme Inc.

Kenneth Lloyd Minaker, MD, FRCP(C), CSC(GM), UE, is Associate Professor of Medicine at Harvard Medical School, Boston, and Chief for the Geriatric Medicine Unit at Massachusetts General Hospital. He directs MGH Senior Health, is Co-Director of the Program for Lifelong Health Maintenance at Harvard University Health Services, is Senior Editor of Intelihealth, Harvard Health Publications, and is Gerontology Editor, the Harvard Health Letter. He has served as Board Member of the American Geriatric Society, as Editor of the Journal of Gerontology: Medical Sciences, and as Director of Grecc Brockton/West Roxbury VAMC. His research interests are in the area of physiology of aging, glucose/insulin physiology, and sarcopenia. He is Principal Investigator of a Program Project on the biomedical aspects of aging. He is listed in Who's Who in America and Best Doctors in America. He has received research funds from Accor Inc. for health promotion research and from BioNebraska Inc. for his work on GHRH and GLP-1.

Robert Nelson, MD, PhD, is Staff Clinician at the National Institute of Diabetes and Digestive and Kidney Diseases, Arizona. He has served as Scientific Reviewer of several nephrology journals and has over 90 publications. He is a member of the American Society of Nephrology and the American Diabetes Association. He has lectured all over the world and consulted for the NKF Consensus Conference on Proteinuria Albuminuria Risk Assessment Detection Elimination (PARADE), Nashville. Dr Nelson's research in diabetic nephropathy has been sponsored by the National Institute of Diabetes and Digestive and Kidney Diseases and by the Agency for Health Care Policy and Research. He is the recipient of the L.S. Goerke Memorial Award from UCLA School of Public Health.

Helmut Rennke, MD, is Director of the Renal Pathology Laboratory at Brigham and Women's Hospital and a professor of Pathology at Harvard Medical School, Boston, and the Harvard-MIT Division of Health Sciences and Technology at Massachusetts Institute of Technology. His research areas currently focus on areas of renal pathology, including key clinical and morphologic aspects of fibrillary glomerulopathy and collapsing glomerulopathy. He is a noted regional, national, and international lecturer on renal research and renal pathology, and he is a recipient of the Annual Irving M. London Teaching Award, among others. He is widely published in journals including the *Journal of Cell Biology* as well as the *American Journal of Physiology, Journal of the American Society of Nephrology, Journal of Clinical Investigation, Endocrinology*, and *Kidney International.*

Michael Steffes, MD, PhD, is Professor in Laboratory Medicine and Pathology at the University of Minnesota, Minneapolis, and Clinical Pathologist at Fairview University Medical Center, Minneapolis. His research areas include diabetes mellitus, diabetic nephropathy, and cardiovascular disease. He participates from the base of the central laboratory for several clinical trials and studies. He has reported receiving several grants to conduct research on diabetes, its complications, and macrovascular disease.

Beth Witten, MSW, ACSW, LSCSW, is a kidney disease rehabilitation consultant with Witten and Associates, LLC. She serves as patient education coordinator for the Missouri Kidney Program Center for Renal Education and staffs the Life Options Rehabilitation Resource Center. Ms Witten has published over 20 papers, co-authored a chapter on kidney disease in the Encyclopedia of Disability and Rehabilitation, and made numerous presentations on rehabilitation topics. She served as president of the National Kidney Foundation's Council of Nephrology Social Workers and on several affiliate and national NKF committees. She has consulted on projects for the Health Care Financing Administration, the Rehabilitation Services Administration, and the Social Security Administration. A past member of the Missouri Kidney Program Advisory Council, Life Options Rehabilitation Advisory Council, and the Network 12 Medical Review Board, Ms Witten is the recipient of the National Kidney Foundation's Distinguished Service Award and the Council of Nephrology Social Workers' Special Recognition.

PEDIATRIC WORK GROUP

Susan Furth, MD, PhD, is Assistant Professor of Pediatrics at Johns Hopkins University School of Medicine, Baltimore. She completed her PhD in Clinical Investigation from Johns Hopkins University School of Hygiene and Public Health. Dr Furth has served as a reviewer for several journals and published over 25 peer-review manuscripts and invited reviews, numerous abstracts, and book chapters. She has received extensive research support from several organizations for her investigations in pediatric nephrology. She is a member of the Clinical Affairs Committee of the American Society of Pediatric Nephrology Clinical Science Committee and a symposium speaker at the Congress of the International Society for Pediatric Nephrology Association. She has conducted seminars and lectures, and been interviewed for Reuters Health News On-Line. Dr Furth is the recipient of the Young Investigator Award and the Johns Hopkins Comprehensive Transplant Center Clinical Research Award.

Ronald J. Hogg, MD (*Pediatric Work Group Chair*), is Director of Pediatric Nephrology at North Texas Hospital for Children at Medical City and Director of the Southwest Pediatric Nephrology Study Group, Texas. He is current President of the National Kidney Foundation of North Texas Medical Advisory Board and member of the National Kidney Foundation K/DOQI Advisory Board. Dr Hogg has published over 94 original papers, book chapters, and invited reviews on children with chronic kidney failure. He is a member of the Nephrology Section of the American Academy of Pediatrics, the International Society of Nephrology, and the American Society of Nephrology. He is past Chief of the Department of Pediatrics at Baylor University Medical Center, past Director of Renal Micropuncture Laboratory at the University of Texas Health Center at Dallas, and past Clinical Associate Professor of Pediatrics at the University of Texas Southwestern Medical School. Dr Hogg has reported receiving research grants from Astra Zeneca, Merck, Novartis, Parke-Davis, and Pfizer.

Kevin V. Lemley, MD, PhD, is Assistant Professor of Pediatrics at Stanford University Medical Center and Attending Nephrologist at Lucile S. Packard Children's Hospital, California. He completed his Research Fellowship at the University of Heidelberg, Germany, and his Clinical Fellowship at Stanford University. His research interests are in the area of the progression of glomerular disease, glomerular pathology, and mechanisms of proteinuria. He has been an active reviewer for several journals and has published over 30 peer-reviewed articles. Dr Lemley served on the National Kidney Foundation's PARADE (Proteinuria, Albuminuria, Risk, Assessment, Detection, and Elimination) Initiative Committee and consults for Fibrogen, Inc. He has been a Fellow of the Alexander von Humboldt Foundation and is a member of the International Society of Nephrology, the American Society of Nephrology, the American Society of Pediatric Nephrology, the International Pediatric Nephology Association, and the Society for Pediatric Research.

Ronald J. Portman, MD, is Professor of Pediatrics and Director of the Division of Pediatric Nephrology and Hypertension at the University of Texas-Houston Medical School. He completed his Fellowship in Pediatric Nephrology at Washington University School of Medicine and St. Louis Children's Hospital. Dr Portman has been an active Journal Reviewer and has published over 100 papers. He is founding member and officer of the American Association of Medical Chronobiology and Chronotherapeutics. He is the Chairman of the Executive Committee of the International Pediatric Hypertension Association and is an ASH Clinical Hypertension Specialist. He is a member of the American Society of Nephrology, the Southwest Pediatric Nephrology Study Group, the American Society of Pediatric Nephrology, and the International Pediatric Nephrology Association. His community service has led him to Co-Direct Pediatric Dialysis Camp and be a member of the Medical Advisory Board of the National Kidney Foundation of Southeast Texas and of the Medical Review Board of ESRD Network 14 of Texas. He reports research grants from AstraZenica, Pfizer, and Novartis.

George John Schwartz, MD, is Chief of Pediatric Nephrology and Associate Chair for Academic Affairs at the University of Rochester School of Medicine and Dentistry. He has reviewed dozens of abstracts and manuscripts for many nephrology and physiology journals and is on the editorial boards of *Seminars in Nephrology* and *The American Journal of Physiology and Renal Physiology*. Dr Schwartz has published over 170 papers, including articles, books, abstracts, and letters in nephrology. He is a member of the American Society for Clinical Investigation, American Society of Pediatric Nephrology, the International Pediatric Nephrology Association, the Society for Pediatric Research, and the American Society of Nephrology. He has received the AMA Physician's Recognition Award and has been recognized as a Specialist in Clinical Hypertension by the American Society of Hypertension.

PART 12. ACKNOWLEDGEMENTS

The work group thanks the National Kidney Foundation for support and guidance during this project. James Smith, Nadine Ferguson, Donna Fingerhut, and Kerry Willis, PhD, were instrumental in coordinating the project. The K/DOQI Chairs and Advisory Board provided constructive criticism that helped shape the project. The K/DOQI Support Group provided practical advice to facilitate implementation. Stefan Armstrong, consultant editor, provided invaluable assistance in preparing the report.

The Work Group is indebted to the Evidence Review Team, who worked tirelessly to assemble the evidence and creatively to synthesize the information.

The Work Group appreciates the careful review of the draft guidelines and suggestions for improvement by external reviewers. Each comment was carefully considered and, whenever possible, suggestions for change were incorporated into the final report. As a result, the CKD guidelines are the product of the Work Group, the Evidence Review Team, the NKF, and all those who contributed their effort to make the Guidelines better.

The following individuals provided written review of the draft guidelines: Hernan Aguirre, MD; Suhail Ahmad, MD; Pedro Aljama, MD; Jane Allen, FNPC; Sanford D. Altman, MD; Theresa M. Ambrose, PhD; Lawrence J. Appel, MD; Yoshinori Araki; Teri Arthur, MSW, CSW, LSW; Carolyn L. Atkins, RN, BS, CCTC; John Au; George R. Bailie, PharmD, PhD; George L. Bakris, MD; Vinod K. Bansal, MD; William Barrie, MD; Ruth Barry, RN; Bruce Becker, MD; Stengel Benedide, MD, PhD; Jeffrey S. Berns, MD; Richard K. Bernstein, MD, FACE, FACN, CWS; Charles W. Bishop, PhD; Roland C. Blantz, MD; Wendy T. Blouin, RN, BSN, CNN; Kline Bolton, MD, FACP; Jürgen Bommer, MD; Peggy Borum, PhD; James Brandes, MD; Delia Bravo, BSN, RN; Emmanuel Bravo, MD; Deborah I. Brommage, MS, RD, CSR; Eileen Brophy; Joanne Brown, BSN, RN, CNN, CPHQ; Wendy W. Brown, MD; Juan P. Bosch, MD; Sally Burrows-Hudson, MS, RN; Jerrilynn D. Burrowes, MS, RD, CDN; Carrie Butler; Bernard Canaud, MD; Claudia Campieri, MD; Anthony W. Cappa relli, MD; Fernando Carrera, MD; Judy Castagnola, RN, MSN; Gloria Chaigret, RN, CNN; Alice Chan, RD, CSR, LD; James C. M. Chan, MD; Alfred K. Cheung, MD; Michael P. Cinquegroni, MD; Nathaniel Clark, MS, RD, MD; Eric Cohen, MD; Aldo Colombi, MD; Ann D. Compton, MSN, RNC; Michael Conrad, MD; Rev. Ken Crossman; Gerry Curry, RN, BSN, CNN; Jeffrey A. Cutler, MD; Leslie Debaun, RN, MSN; James A. Delmez, MD; Mary Denno, MSN, RN, CNN; Maria DeVita, MD; Claudia Douglas, MA, CNN, APNC; Earl Dunnigan, MD, FACP; Catherine Dupre, MD; Kathy Edwards, RN; Sharon Ehlers, MA, RN, CNN, CCTC; Sameiro Faaria, MD; Mark D. Faber, MD; Steven Fishbane, MD; Michael J. Flanigan, MD; Edward Foote, PharmD; Harold A. Franch, MD; Blanca Ramos Frendo, MD; Eugene Freund, MD, MSPH; Tony Fuccello, MD, PhD; Wendy Funk Schrag, LMSW, ACSW; Suzanne Gagne, RN, CNN; Scott Garland; Richard S. Goldman, MD; Diane Goodwin, DCI; Frank A. Gotch, MD; John Graham, IV; Jane H. Greene, RD, CSR, LDN; Tomas L. Griebling, MD; Cheryl Grimes, PGDE, DPSN, RGN, ENB; Neil J. Groombridge, RN; Robert A. Gutman, MD; William E. Haley, MD; Morris Hamilton, MD; Tamara Harris, MD, MS; Georg Hasche, MD;

Carol M. Headley, RN, MSN; Lee A. Hebert, MD; Mary Jane Helenek, RPN, MS, MBA; Richard N. Hellman; Mary Henderson, RN; Sue High, RN, CNN; Karen Hill, RN, BSN; Lelia Holthus, RN, BS; Walter H. Hörl, MD; Thomas H. Hostetter, MD; Susanna S. Itty, RN, CNN; Bunea Jivanescu; Rosie Jones, RN; Kamyar Kalantar-Zadeh, MD, MPH; Mandip S. Kang, MD; Lynette Kartechner, RN; Bertram L. Kasiske, MD; Douglas Keith, MD; Carol A. Keller, MPA; Gwen A. Kendall, RD,LD; Rita-An Kiely, ACSW, CICSW; Michael J. Klag, MD, MPH; Janice Knouff, RN; Raymond Krediet, MD; Eduardo Lacson, Jr, MD; Craig B. Langman, MD; Sandra Lathrop, RD, CDN; Janez Lavre, MD; Claude Lenfant, MD; Jen Jar Lin, MD, PhD; Stan M. Lindenfield, MD; Francesco Locatelli, MD; Kathy Lueker, RN, CNN; Iain Macdougall, MD; Denise Mafra; Lionel U. Mailloux, MD, FACP; Donna Mapes, DNSc, MS; Gary R. Matzke; Hanna W. Mawad, MD, FACP; Linda M. McCann, RD, LD, CSR; Sally McCulloch, MSN, RN, CNN; Peter A. McCullough, MD, MPH; Patrick McGary, MD; Patrick Mc Kenna, MD; Maureen McKinley, MSW, LCSW, CNSW; Kim Meehl, CNN; C. Kenneth Mehr ling; Ira Meisels, MD; D. Mendelssohn, MD, FRCPC; Judy Mennig, RN, CNN; Maureen A. Michael, RN; Edgar R. Miller, III, MD, PhD; William E. Mitch, MD; Steve Montoya, Jr, MD; Gabriel Morduchowicz, MD; Bruce Z. Morgenstern, MD; Donna Mullen, RN, MSN, ARNP; Joseph V. Nally, Jr, MD; Jean M. Nardini, RN, MSN; Andrew S. Narva, MD; Pauline Nelson, RD; Ellen Newman, RN, CNN; Sheila Nulf; Paul M. Palevsky, MD; Thakor G. Patel, MD; Glenda M. Payne, RN; Tammy B. Pennington, MS, LDN, RD; Robert A. Phillips, MD, PhD, FACC; Delores J. Phipps, RN, CNN; Jean Pirozzi, BS, RN, CNN; Linda Plush, MSN, CNN, CNS/FNP; Geraldine Podgorski, BSN, RN, CNN; K.S. Prabhakar, MD; Debra Punch, RN, BS; Gopal K. Rangan, MD; Susan M. Reams, RD, CSR, LD; Carl Redding, MSW; Doris Redding; Sally I. Rice, LCSW, DCSW; Edward J. Roccella, MD; Noreen K. Rogers; Michele Root, CNS; Jerome Rossert, MD, PhD; Harry Rubenstein, MD; Mark P. Rutkowski, MD; Dori Schatell, MS; Seth Schulman, MD; Mary Ann Sevick, RN, PhD; Gaurang Shah, MD; Robert Shay, MD; Donald J. Sherrard, MD; James Shinaberger, MD; Jeffrey I. Silberzweig; Donald Silverberg MD, FRCP; Erik Skullerud; Donna Smolen, RN, BSM; Ann Snyder-Manson, MSW, CSW, BA; Edward Sondik, PhD; Leslie A. Spry, MD; Susan Stark; Theodore I. Steinman, MD; Pam Stephens, RN; D.G. Struggle, MD; Arlene Sukolsky; Timothy J. Swenson, AND, RN, CNN; Judy H. Taylor, MPH, BSN, RN, CNN; Brendan P. Teehan, MD; Carol A. Tindira, RN, MS, CNN; Vicente E. Torres, MD; Walter Tozzi, MSRPN, MBA; Ambrose Y. Tsang, MD; Shoji Tsujimoto, MD, DMCA; Jonah Ukiwe, MD; Abi Umra; Yoshie Uyeda, RD; Fernando Valderrábano, MD; L.J. Vleming, MD, PhD; Susan Vogel, MHA, RN, CNN; Mary Ann Webb; Burkhard Weimer, MD; Debra Wellman, RN; Nanette Wenger, MD; David C. Wheeler, MD, MRCP; Joseph D. White; Björn Wikström, MD; D. Winearls; Marion Winkler, MS, RD, LDN, CNSD; Nancy M. Wise, RD, MS; Sun Yang, MD; Mujdat Yenicesu, MD; Jeff Zavitz; Carmine Zoccali, MD; and Anthony W. Zydlewski, MD.

Organizations that took part in the review process include: AASK; American Association of Kidney Patients; American College of Physicians–American Society of Internal Medicine; American Diabetes Association; American Nephrology Nurses Association; American Regent Laboratories, Inc; American Society for Parenteral and Enteral Nutrition; American Society of Nephrology; Amgen Inc; Association for the Advancement of Medical

Instrumentation; AstraZeneca; Bone Care International; CNNT Executive Committee (NKF); CNSW Executive Committee (NKF); DaVita Dialysis Center; ESRD Network #3; ESRD Network #4; ESRD Network #6; ESRD Network of Florida, Inc, #7; ESRD Network #9/10; ESRD Network #11; Gambro Healthcare; Indian Health Service; Kaiser Permanente; Minority Outreach Committee (NKF); National Center for Health Statistics; National Heart, Lung, Blood Institute; National Institute for Health and Medical Research; National Institute of Diabetes and Digestive and Kidney Disorders; National Kidney Foundation Singapore; Ortho Biotech, Inc; Renal Care Group; Renal Physicians Association; Roche Diagnostics Corporation; Satellite Dialysis Centers, Inc; Scribner Kidney Center; Sigma-Tau Pharamaceuticals; Total Renal Care, Inc.

Participation in the review does not necessarily constitute endorsement of the content of the report by the individuals or the organization or institution they represent.

The National Kidney Foundation, as well as the Work Group, recognize the support of Amgen. The National Kidney Foundation is proud to partner with Amgen on this important initiative.

As Chair of the Work Group, I personally wish to thank the other members of the Work Group who volunteered their time, effort, wisdom, and humor to this project. Their willingness to think about the "big picture" while steadfastly adhering to accuracy about "small details" is responsible for the breadth and depth of these guidelines. I have learned a great deal from them. I would like to give special thanks to the following individuals: Josef Coresh, MD, PhD, Vice-Chair of the Work Group, for his expert analysis of the NHANES III database and wise counsel about the definition and classification of chronic kidney disease; Ronald J. Hogg, MD, Chair of the Pediatric Work Group, who insisted that we enlarge our viewpoint to include the problems of children; Adeera Levin, MD, who volunteered analysis of individual patient data from her study and coordinated presentations by the Work Group representatives; Ethan Balk, MD, MPH, who tirelessly worked with each member of the Work Group to develop forms, review articles, and synthesize data into tables; Ronald D. Perrone, MD, my close colleague of many years, who provided advice on the scope of the evidence review and supervised the nephrology fellows on the Evidence Review Team; and Joseph Lau, MD, whose creativity, practical approach, and humor helped us to overcome all obstacles. Finally, I would like to thank Garabed Eknoyan, MD, whose vision, leadership, and commitment guided me throughout the process.

Andrew S. Levey, MD

BIBLIOGRAPHY

1. Jones CA, McQuillan GM, Kusek JW, Eberhardt MS, Herman WH, Coresh J, Salive M, Jones CP, Agodoa LY: Serum creatinine levels in the US population: Third National Health and Nutrition Examination Survey. Am J Kidney Dis 32:992–999, 1998 (erratum 35:178, 2000)
2. US Renal Data System. USRDS 1998 Annual Data Report, National Institutes of Health, National Institute of Diabetes and Digestive and Kidney Diseases. Bethesda, MD, 1998
3. Sarnak MJ, Levey AS: Cardiovascular disease and chronic renal disease: A new paradigm. Am J Kidney Dis 35:S117-S131, 2000 (suppl 1)
4. US Renal Data System. USRDS 2000 Annual Data Report, National Institutes of Health, National Institute of Diabetes and Digestive and Kidney Diseases. Bethesda, MD, 2000
5. Coresh J, Wei GL, McQuillan G, Brancati FL, Levey AS, Jones C, Klag MJ: Prevalence of high blood pressure and elevated serum creatinine level in the United States: Findings from the third National Health and Nutrition Examination Survey (1988–1994). Arch Intern Med 161:1207–1216, 2001
6. Keane WF, Eknoyan G: Proteinuria, albuminuria, risk, assessment, detection, elimination (PARADE): A position paper of the National Kidney Foundation. Am J Kidney Dis 33:1004–1010, 1999
7. Hogg RJ, Portmann RJ, Milliner D, Lemley KV, Eddy A, Ingelfinger J: Evaluation and management of proteinuria and nephrotic syndrome in children: Recommendations from a pediatric nephrology panel established at the National Kidney Foundation conference on Proteinuria, Risk, Assessment, Detection, Elimination (PARADE). Pediatrics 105:1242–1249, 2000
8. American Diabetes Association: Clinical Practice Recommendations 2001. Diabetes Care 24:S69-S72, 2001 (suppl 1)
9. Levey AS, Beto JA, Coronado BE, Eknoyan G, Foley RN, Kasiske RL, Klag MJ, Mailloux LU, Manske CL, Meyer KB, Parfrey PS, Pfeffer MA, Wenger NK, Wilson PW, Wright JT Jr: Controlling the epidemic of cardiovascular disease in chronic renal disease: What do we know? What do we need to learn? Where do we go from here? Am J Kidney Disease 32:853–905, 1998
10. McClellan WM, Knight DF, Karp H, Brown WW: Early detection and treatment of renal disease in hospitalized diabetic and hypertensive patients: Important differences between practice and published guidelines. Am J Kidney Dis 29:368–375, 1997
11. Obrador GT, Ruthazer R, Arora P, Kausz AT, Pereira BJ: Prevalence of and factors associated with suboptimal care before initiation of dialysis in the United States. J Am Soc Nephrol 10:1793–1800, 1999
12. Kannel WB, Stampfer MJ, Castelli WP, Verter J: The prognostic significance of proteinuria: The Framingham study. Am Heart J 108:1347–1352, 1984
13. Iseki K, Iseki C, Ikemiya Y, Fukiyama K: Risk of developing end-stage renal disease in a cohort of mass screening. Kidney Int 49:800–805, 1996
14. Perneger TV, Brancati FL, Whelton PK, Klag MJ: Studying the causes of kidney disease in humans: A review of methodologic obstacles and possible solutions. Am J Kidney Dis 25:722–731, 1995
15. Pereira KI: Optimization of pre-ESRD care: The key to improved dialysis outcomes. Kidney Int 57: 351–365, 2000
16. NKF-K/DOQI Clinical Practice Guidelines for Peritoneal Dialysis Adequacy: Update 2000. Am J Kidney Dis 37:S65-S136, 2001 (suppl 1)
17. Levey AS, Bosch JP, Lewis JB, Greene T, Rogers N, Roth D: A more accurate method to estimate glomerular filtration rate from serum creatinine: A new prediction equation. Modification of Diet in Renal Disease Study Group. Ann Intern Med 130:461–470, 1999
18. Levey AS, Greene T, Kusek JW, Beck GJ: A simplified equation to predict glomerular filtration rate from serum creatinine. J Am Soc Nephrol 11:A0828, 2000 (abstr)
19. Warram JH, Gearin G, Laffel L, Krolewski AS: Effect of duration of type I diabetes on the prevalence of stages of diabetic nephropathy defined by urinary albumin/creatinine ratio. J Am Soc Nephrol 7:930–937, 1996
20. Barratt TM, McLaine PN, Soothill JF: Albumin excretion as a measure of glomerular dysfunction in children. Arch Dis Child 45:496–501, 1970
21. Davies AG, Postlethwaite RJ, Price DA, Burn JL, Houlton CA, Fielding BA: Urinary albumin excretion on school children. Arch Dis Child 59:625–630, 1984

22. Bangstad HJ, Dahl-Jorgensen K, Kjaersgaard P, Mevold K, Hanssen KF: Urinary albumin excretion rate and puberty in non-diabetic children and adolescents. Acta Paediatr 82:857–862, 1993

23. Cowell CT, Rogers S, Silink M: First morning urinary albumin concentration is a good predictor of 24-hour urinary albumin excretion in children with type 1 (insulin-dependent) diabetes. Diabetologia 29:97–99, 1986

24. Salardi S, Cacciari, Pascucci MG, Giambiasi E, Tacconi M, Tazzari R: Microalbuminuria in diabetic children and adolescents. Relationship with puberty and growth hormone. Acta Paediatr Scand 79: 437–433, 1990

25. Marshall SM, Hackett A, Court S, Parkin M, Alberti KG: Albumin excretion in children and adolescents with insulin-dependent diabetes. Diabetes Res 3:345–348, 1986

26. Ellis D, Buffone GJ: New approach to evaluation of proteinuric states. Clin Chem 23:666–670, 1977

27. Mathiesen ERS, Saurbrey N, Hommel E, Parving HH: Prevalence of microalbuminuria in children with type 1 (insulin-dependent) diabetes mellitus. Diabetologia 29:640–633, 1986

28. Brøchner-Mortensen J, Ditzel J, Mogensen CE, Rodbro P: Microvascular permeability to albumin and glomerular filtration rate in diabetic and normal children. Diabetologia 16:307–311, 1979

29. Mortensen HB, Marinelli K, Norgaard K, Main K, Kastrup KW, Ibsen KK, Villumsen J, Parving HH: A nation-wide cross-sectional study of urinary albumin excretion rate, arterial blood pressure and blood glucose control in Danish children with type 1 diabetes mellitus. Danish Study Group of Diabetes in Childhood. Diabet Med 10:887–977, 1990

30. Dahlquist G, Rudberg S: The prevalence of microalbuminuria in diabetic children and adolescents and its relation to puberty. Acta Paediatr Scand 76:795–8000, 1987

31. Erman A, van Dyk DJ, Rabinov M, Boner G, Rosenfeld JB: Urinary albumin excretion in the healthy population. Isr J Med Sci 26:389–392, 1990

32. Holl RW, Grabert M, Thon A, Heinze E: Urinary excretion of albumin in adolescents with type 1 diabetes: Persistent versus intermittent microalbuminuria and relationship to duration of diabetes, sex, and metabolic control. Diabetes Care 22:1555–1560, 1999

33. Huttunen NP, Kaar M, Puukka R, Akerblom HK: Exercise-induced proteinuria in children and adolescents with type 1 (insulin dependent) diabetes. Diabetologia 21:495–497, 1981

34. Chiumello G, Bognetti E, Meschi F, Carra M, Balzano E: Early diagnosis of subclinical complications in insulin dependent diabetic children and adolescents. J Endocrinol Invest 12:101–104, 1989 (suppl 3)

35. Laborde K, Levy-Marchal C, Kindermans C, Dechaux M, Czernichow P, Sachs C: Glomerular function and microalbuminuria in children with insulin-dependent diabetes. Pediatr Nephrol 4:39–433, 1990

36. Mullis P, Kochli HP, Zuppinger K, Schwarz HP: Intermittent microalbuminuria in children with type 1 diabetes mellitus without clinical evidence of nephropathy. Eur J Pediatr 147:385–388, 1988

37. Elises JS, Griffiths PD, Hocking MD, Taylor CM, White RH: Simplified quantification of urinary protein excretion in children. Clin Nephrol 30:225–229, 1988

38. Ginevri F, Piccotti E, Alinovi R, DeToni T, Biagini C, Chiggeri GM, Gusmano R: Reversible tubular proteinuria precedes microalbuminuria and correlates with the metabolic status of diabetic children. Pediatr Nephrol 7:23–26, 1993

39. Houser MT: Characterization of proteinuria using random urine samples. Int J Pediatr Nephrol 7: 197–202, 1986

40. Hjorth L, Helin I, Grubb A: Age-related reference limits for urine levels of albumin, orosomucoid, immunoglobulin G and protein HC in children. Scand J Clin Lab Invest 60:65–73, 2000

41. Schultz CJ, Konopelska-Bahu T, Dalton RN, Carroll TA, Stratton I, Gale EA, Neil A, Dunger DB: Microalbuminuria prevalence varies with age, sex, and puberty in children with type 1 diabetes followed from diagnosis in a longitudinal study. Oxford Regional Prospective Study Group. Diabetes Care 22:495–502, 1999

42. Gibb D, Shah V, Preece M, Barratt TM: Variability of urine albumin excretion in normal and diabetic children. Pediatr Nephrol 3:414–419, 1989

43. Schultz CJ, Dalton RN, Turner C, Neil HA, Dunger DB: Freezing method affects the concentration and variability of urine proteins and the interpretation of data on microalbuminuria. The Oxford Regional Prospective Study Group. Diabet Med 17:7–14, 2000

44. Yap C, Yap HK, Chio LF: Urine microalbumin/creatinine ratios in Singapore children. J Singapore Paediatr Soc 33:101–106, 1991

45. Jefferson IG, Greene SA, Smith MA, Smith RF, Griffin NKG, Baum JD: Urine albumin to creatinine ratio-response to exercise in diabetes. Arch Dis Child 60:305–310, 1985

46. Cesarini PR, Ferreira SR, Vivolo MA, Zanella MT: Different urinary albumin responses to submaximal exercise by normoalbuminuric diabetic children and controls. Brazilian J Med Biol Res 29: 1603–1610, 1996

47. Murakami M, Yamamoto H, Ueda Y, Murakami K, Yamauchi K: Urinary screening of elementary and junior high-school children over a 13-year period in Tokyo. Pediatr Nephrol 5:50–53, 1991

48. Lin CY, Sheng CC, Chen CH, Lin CC, Chou P: The prevalence of heavy proteinuria and progression risk factors in children undergoing urinary screening. Pediatr Nephrol 14:953–959, 2000

49. Vehaskari VM, Rapola J: Isolated proteinuria: Analysis of a school-age population. J Pediatr 101: 661–688, 1982

50. Wagner MG, Smith FG Jr, Tinglof BO Jr, Cornberg E: Epidemiology of proteinuria. A study of 4,807 schoolchildren. J Pediatr 73:825–832, 1968

51. Randolph MF, Greenfield M: Proteinuria. A six-year study of normal infants, preschool, and school-age populations previously screened for urinary tract disease. Am J Dis Child 114:631–638, 1967

52. Johnson A, Heap GJ, Hurley BP: A survey of bacteriuria, proteinuria and glycosuria in five-year-old schoolchildren in canberra. Med J Aust 2:122–124, 1974

53. Wolman IJ: The incidence, causes and intermittency of proteinuria in young men. Am J Med Sci 210:86–100, 1945

54. Kunin CM, Deutscher R, Paquin A Jr: Urinary tract infection in school children: An epidemiologic, clinical and laboratory study. Medicine (Baltimore) 43:91–130, 1964

55. Meadow SR, White RH, Johnston NM: Prevalence of symptomless urinary tract disease in Birmingham schoolchildren. I. Pyuria and bacteriuria. BMJ 3:81–84, 1969

56. Mitchell N, Stapleton FB: Routine admission urinalysis examination in pediatric patients: A poor value. Pediatrics 86:345–349, 1990

57. Hamill SM, Blackfan KD: Frequency and significance of albumin in the urines of normal children. Am J Dis Child 1:139–163, 1911

58. Dodge WF, West EF, Smith EH, Bruce H III: Proteinuria and hematuria in schoolchildren: Epidemiology and early natural history. J Pediatr 88:327–347, 1976

59. Hogg RJ, Harris S, Lawrence DM, Henning PH, Wigg N, Jureidini KF: Renal tract abnormalities detected in Australian preschool children. J Paediatr Child Health 34:420–424, 1998

60. Silverberg DS: City-wide screening for urinary abnormalities in schoolboys. Can Med Assoc J 7: 410–422, 1974

61. Silverberg DS, Allard MJ, Ulan RA, Beamish WE, Lentle BC, McPhee MS, Grace MG: City-wide screening for urinary abnormalities in schoolgirls. Can Med Assoc J 109:981–985, 1973

62. Bashford HH: Adolescent albuminuria: Incidence, significance, and after-history. Lancet 2: 1305–1307, 1926

63. Mueller PW, Caudill SP: Urinary albumin excretion in children: Factors related to elevated excretion in the United States population. Ren Fail 21:293–302, 1999

64. Pugia MJ, Lott JA, Kajima J, Saambe T, Sasaki M, Kuromoto K, Nakamura R, Fusegawa H, Ohta Y: Screening school children for albuminuria, proteinuria and occult blood with dipsticks. Clin Chem Lab Med 37:149–157, 1999

65. Hoy WE, Mathews JD, McCredie DA, Pugsley DJ, Hayhurst BG, Rees M, Kile E, Walker KA, Wang Z: The multidimensional nature of renal disease: Rates and associations of albuminuria in an Australian Aboriginal community. Kidney Int 54:1296–1304, 1998

66. Bernard A, Stolte H, De Broe ME, Mueller PW, Mason H, Lash LH, Fowler BA: Urinary biomarkers to detect significant effects of environmental and occupational exposure to nephrotoxins. IV. Current information on interpreting the health implications of tests. Ren Fail 19:553–566, 1997

67. Smith HW: Comparative physiology of the kidney, in Smith HW (ed): The Kidney: Structure and Function in Health and Disease. New York, NY, Oxford University Press, 1951, pp 520–574

68. Atiyeh BA, Dabbagh SS, Gruskin AB: Evaluation of renal function during childhood. Pediatr Rev 17:175–179, 1996

69. Heilbron DC, Holliday MA, Al-Dahwi A, Kogan BA: Expressing glomerular filtration rate in children. Pediatr Nephrol 5:5–11, 1991

70. Coultard MG: Maturation of glomerular filtratior in preterm and mature babies. Early Hum Dev 11: 281–292, 1985

71. Schwartz GJ, Feld LG, Langford DJ: A simple estimate of glomerular filtration rate in full-term infants during the first year of life. J Pediatr 104:849–854, 1984

72. Davies DF, Shock NW: Age changes in glomerular filtration rate, effective renal plasma flow, and tubular excretory capacity in adult males. J Clin Invest 29:496–507, 1950

73. Wesson LG: Physiology of the Human Kidney. New York, Grune and Stratton, 1969

74. Watkins DM, Shock NW: Age-wise standard value for C_{in}, C_{PAH}, and Tm_{PAH} in adult males. J Clin Invest 34:969, 1955

75. NKF-K/DOQI Clinical Practice Guidelines for Nutrition in Chronic Renal Failure. Am J Kidney Dis 35:S1-S140, 2000 (suppl 2)

76. Levey AS, Greene T, Burkart J: Comprehensive assessment of the level of renal function at the initiation of dialysis in the MDRD study. J Am Soc Nephrology 9:153A, 1998 (abstr)

77. Obrador GT, Arora P, Kausz AT, Ruthazer R, Pereira BJ, Levey AS: Level of renal function at the initiation of dialysis in the U.S. end-stage renal disease population. Kidney Int 56:2227–2235, 1999

78. Arora P, Obrador GT, Ruthazer R, Kausz AT, Meyer KB, Jenuleson CS, Pereira BJ: Prevalence, predictors, and consequences of late nephrology referral at a tertiary care center. J Am Soc Nephrol 10:1281–1286, 1999

79. Jungers P, Zingraff J, Albouze G, Chauveau P, Page B, Hannedouche T, Man NK: Late referral to maintenance dialysis: Detrimental consequences. Nephrol Dial Transplant 8:1089–1093, 1993

80. Sesso R, Yoshihiro MM: Time of diagnosis of chronic renal failure and assessment of quality of life in haemodialysis patients. Nephrol Dial Transplant 12:2111–2116, 1997

81. Fink JC, Burdick RA, Kurth SJ, Blahut SA, Armistead NC, Turner MS, Shickle LM, Light PD: Significance of serum creatinine values in new end-stage renal disease patients. Am J Kidney Dis 34:694–701, 1999

82. Iofel Y, Dawood M, Valcourt JS, Ifudu O: Initiation of dialysis is not delayed in whites with progressive renal failure. ASAIO J 44:M598-M600, 1998

83. Ifudu O, Dawood M, Homel P, Friedman EA: Excess morbidity in patients starting uremia therapy without prior care by a nephrologist. Am J Kidney Dis 28:841–845, 1996

84. Guidance for Industry Pharmacokinetics in Patients with Impaired Renal Function: Study Design, Data Analysis and Impact on Dosing and Labeling. Washington, DC, US Department of Health and Human Services, Food and Drug Administration, Center for Drug Evaluation and Research, Center for Biologics Evaluation and Research, 1998

85. German PS: Compliance with chronic disease. Hypertension 11:1156–1160, 1988

86. Frazier PA, Davis-Ali SH, Dahl KE: Correlates of noncompliance among renal transplant recipients. Clin Transplant 8:550–557, 1994

87. Kiley DJ, Lam CS, Pollack R: A study of treatment compliance following kidney transplantation. Transplantation 55:51–56, 1993

88. DiMatteo MR, Lepper HS, Croghan TW: Depression is a risk factor for noncompliance with medical treatment: Meta-analysis of the effects of anxiety and depression on patient adherence. Arch Intern Med :2101–2107, 2000

89. Schneider MS, Friend R, Whitaker P, Wadhwa NK: Fluid noncompliance and symptomatology in end-stage renal disease: Cognitive and emotional variables. Health Psychol 10:209–215, 1991

90. Shaw E, Anderson JG, Maloney M, Jay SJ, Fagan D: Factors associated with noncompliance of patients taking antihypertensive medications. Hospital Pharm 30:201–203, 1995

91. McLane CG, Zyzanski SJ, Flocke SA: Factors associated with medication noncompliance in rural elderly hypertensive patients. Am J Hypertens 8:206–209, 1995

92. Christensen AJ, Smith TW, Turner CW, Holman JM, Gregory MC, Rich MA: Family support, physical impairment, and adherence in hemodialysis: An investigation of main and buffering effects. J Behav Med 15:313–325, 1992

93. Billups SJ, Malone DC, Carter BL: The relationship between drug therapy noncompliance and patient characteristics, health-related quality of life, and health care costs. Pharmacotherapy 20:941–949, 2000

94. McGrath JM: Physicians' perspectives on communicating prescription drug information. Qual Health Res 9:731–745, 1999

95. Dusing R, Weisser B, Mengden T, Vetter H: Changes in antihypertensive therapy: The role of adverse effects and compliance. Blood Press 7:313–315, 1998

96. Johnson MJ, Williams M, Marshall ES: Adherent and nonadherent medication-taking in elderly antihypertensive patients. Clin Nurs Res 8:318–335, 1999

97. Sharkness CM, Snow DA: The patient's view of hypertension and compliance. Am J Prev Med 8: 141–146, 1992

98. Monane M, Bohn RL, Gurwitz JH, Glynn RJ, Levin R, Avorn J: Compliance with antihypertensive therapy among elderly Medicaid enrollees: The roles of age, gender, and race. Am J Public Health 86:1805–1808, 1996

99. Wright SJ: "Non-compliance": Meaningful construct or destructive, sticky, stigmatizing label? Edtna Erca J 24:35–38, 1998

100. 27th Bethesda Conference. Matching the Intensity of Risk Factor Management with the Hazard for Coronary Disease Events. September 14–15, 1995. J Am Coll Cardiol 27:957–1047, 1996

101. Harris MI, Flegal KM, Cowie CC, Eberhardt MS, Goldstein DE, Little RR, Wiedmeyet H-M, Byrd-Holt DD: Prevalence of diabetes, impaired fasting glucose, and impaired glucose tolerance in U.S. adults: The Third National Health and Nutrition Examination Survey, 1988–1994. Diabetes Care 21:518–524, 1998

102. Burt VL, Whelton P, Roccella EJ, Brown C, Cutler JA, Higgins M, Horan MJ, Labarthe D: Prevalence of hypertension in the US adult population. Hypertension 25:305–313, 1995

103. Lawrence RC, Helmick CG, Arnett FC, Deyo RA, Felson DT, Giannini EH, Heyse ST, Hirsch R, Hochberg MC, Hunder GG, Liang MH, Pillemer SR, Steen VD, Wolfe F: Estimates of the prevalence of arthritis and selected musculoskeletal disorders in the United States. Arthritis Rheum 41:778–799, 1998

104. US Renal Data System. Excerpts from the 2000 US Renal Data System Annual Data Report: Atlas of End Stage Renal Disease in the United States. Am J Kidney Dis 36:S1-S279, 2000 (suppl 2)

105. Profiles of General Demographic Characteristics: 2000 Census of Population and Housing, United States. Washington, DC, US Government Printing Office, 2001

106. Day JC: Population Projections of the United States by Age, Sex, Race, and Hispanic Origin: 1995 to 2050. Washington, DC, US Government Printing Office, 1996

107. Elixhauser A, Klemstine K, Steiner C, Bierman A: Procedures in U.S. Hospitals, 1997. Vol. HCUP Fact Book No. 2. Rockville, MD, Agency for Healthcare Resarch and Quality, 2001

108. HCUPnet: Healthcare Cost and Utilization Project. Website: www.ahrq.gov/data/hcup/hcup-net.htm, 7/4

109. McGoldrick MD, Bailie GR: Nonnarcotic analgesics: Prevalence and estimated economic impact of toxicities. Ann Pharmacother 31:221–227, 1997

110. Fries JE: NSAID gastropathy: The second most deadly rheumatic disease? Epidemiology and risk appraisal. J Rheumatol 18:6–10, 1991

111. Rose BD: Chapter 3: Renal Circulation and Glomerular Filtration Rate: Clinical Physiology of Acid-Base and Electrolyte Disorders. New York, NY, McGraw Hill, 1984

112. Lindeman RD, Tobin J, Shock NW: Longitudinal studies on the rate of decline in renal function with age. J Am Geriatr Soc 33:278–285, 1985

113. Perrone RD, Madias NE, Levey AS: Serum creatinine as an index of renal function: New insights into old concepts. Clin Chem 38:1933–1953, 1992

114. Perrone RD, Steinman TI, Beck GJ, Skibinski CI, Royal HD, Lawlor M, Hunsicker LG: Utility of radioscopic filtration markers in chronic renal insufficiency: Simultaneous comparison of 125I-iothalamate, 169Yb-DPTA, and inulin. The Modification of Diet in Renal Diseases Study. Am J Kidney Dis 16: 224–235, 1990

115. Wilson DM, Bergert JH, Larson TS, Liedtke RR: GFR determined by nonradiolabeled iothalamate using capillary electrophoresis. Am J Kidney Dis 30:646–652, 1997

116. Deinum J, Derkx FH: Cystatin for estimation of glomerular filtration rate? Lancet 356:1624–1625, 2000

117. Shemesh O, Golbetz H, Kriss JP, Myers BD: Limitations of creatinine as a filtration marker in glomerulopathic patients. Kidney Int 28:830–838, 1985

118. Levey AS, Perrone RD, Madias NE: Serum creatinine and renal function. Annu Rev Med 39: 465–490, 1988

119. Levey AS: Assessing the effectiveness of therapy to prevent progression of renal disease. Am J Kidney Dis 22:207–214, 1993

120. Gault MH, Longerich LL, Harnett JD, Wesolowski C: Predicting glomerular function from adjusted serum creatinine. Nephron 62:249–256, 1992

121. Cockcroft DW, Gault MH: Prediction of creatinine clearance from serum creatinine. Nephron 16: 31–41, 1976

122. Jelliffe RW: Estimation of creatinine clearance when urine cannot be collected. Lancet 1:975–976, 1971

123. Schwartz GJ, Gauthier B: A simple estimate of glomerular filtration rate in adolescent boys. J Pediatr 106:522–526, 1985

124. Schwartz GJ, Haycock GB, Edelmann CM Jr, Spitzer A: A simple estimate of glomerular filtration rate in children derived from body length and plasma creatinine. Pediatrics 58:259–263, 1976

125. Brion LP, Boeck MA, Gauthier B, Nussbaum MP, Schwartz GJ: Estimation of glomerular filtration rate in anorectic adolescents. Pediatr Nephrol 3:16–21, 1989

126. Brion LP, Fleischman AR, McCarton C, Schwartz GJ: A simple estimate of glomerular filtration rate in low birth weight infants during the first year of life: Noninvasive assessment of body composition and growth. J Pediatr 109:698–707, 1986

127. Counahan R, Chantler C, Ghazali S, Kirkwood B, Rose F, Barratt TM: Estimation of glomerular filtration rate from plasma creatinine concentration in children. Arch Dis Child 51:875–878, 1976

128. Barratt TM, Chantler C, Lederman S, Rigden SP: Assessment of renal function. Am J Kidney Dis 7: 347–349, 1986

129. Morris MC, Allanby CW, Toseland P, Haycock GB, Chantler C: Evaluation of a height/plasma creatinine formula in the measurement of glomerular filtration rate. Arch Dis Child 57:611–615, 1982

130. Jelliffe RW: Letter: Creatinine clearance: Bedside estimate. Ann Intern Med 79:604–605, 1973

131. Mawer GE, Lucas SB, Knowles BR, Stirland RM: Computer-assisted prescribing of kanamycin for patients with renal insufficiency. Lancet 1:12–15, 1972

132. Hull JH, Hak LJ, Koch GG, Wargin WA, Chi SL, Mattocks AM: Influence of range of renal function and liver disease on predictability of creatinine clearance. Clin Pharmacol Therapeutics 29: 516–521, 1981

133. Gates GF: Creatinine clearance estimation from serum creatinine values: An analysis of three mathematical models of glomerular function. Am J Kidney Dis 5:199–205, 1985

134. Bjornsson TD, Cocchetto DM, McGowan FX, Verghese CP, Sedor F: Nomogram for estimating creatinine clearance. Clin Pharmacokinet 8:365–369, 1983

135. Toto RD, Kirk KA, Coresh J, Jones C, Appel L, Wright J, Campese V, Olutade B, Agodoa L: Evaluation of serum creatinine for estimating glomerular filtration rate in African Americans with hypertensive nephrosclerosis: Results from the African-American Study of Kidney Disease and Hypertension (AASK) Pilot Study. J Am Soc Nephrol 8:279–287, 1997

136. Agarwal R, Nicar M: A comparative analysis of formulas used to predict creatinine clearance. J Am Soc Nephrol 5:386, 1994

137. Davis GA, Chandler MH: Comparison of creatinine clearance estimation methods in patients with trauma. Am J Health Syst Pharm 53:1028–1032, 1996

138. Edwards KDG, Whyte HM: Plasma creatinine level and creatinine clearance as a test of renal function. Aust Ann Med 8:218–224, 1959

139. Hallynck T, Soep HH, Thomis J, Boelaert J, Daneels R, Fillastre JP, De Rosa F, Rubinstein E, Hatala M, Spousta J, Dettli L: Prediction of creatinine clearance from serum creatinine concentration based on lean body mass. Clin Pharmacol Therapeutics 30:414–421, 1981

140. Mogensen CE, Heilskov NS: Prediction of GFR from serum creatinine. Acta Endocrinol (Copenh) Suppl 238:109, 1980

141. Nankivell BJ, Allen RDM, O'Connell PJ, Chapman JR: Erythrocytes after renal transplantation: Risk factors and relationship with GFR. Clin Transplant 9:375–382, 1995

142. Robinson BA, Frampton CM, Colls BM, Atkinson CH, Fitzharris BM: Comparison of methods of assessment of renal function in patients with cancer treated with cisplatin, carboplatin or methotrexate. Aust NZ J Med 20:657–662, 1990

143. Rowe JWA, Andres R, Tobin JD, Norris AH, Shock NW: The effect of age on creatinine clearance in men: A cross-sectional and longitudinal study. J Gerontol 31:155–163, 1976

144. Salazar DE, Corcoran GB: Predicting creatinine clearance and renal drug clearance in obese patients from estimated fat-free body mass. Am J Med 84:1053–1060, 1988

145. Sanaka M, Takano K, Shimakura K, Koike Y, Mineshita S: Serum albumin for estimating creatinine clearance in the elderly with muscle atrophy. Nephron 73:137–144, 1996

146. Siersbaek-Nielsen K, Hansen JM, Kampmann J, Kristensen M: Rapid evaluation of creatinine clearance. Lancet 1:1133–1134, 1971

147. Tougaard L, Brochner-Mortensen J: An individual nomogram for determination of glomerular filtration rate from plasma creatinine. Scand J Clin Lab Invest 36:395–397, 1976

148. Yukawa E, Hamachi Y, Higuchi S, Aoyama T: Predictive performance of equations to estimate creatinine clearance from serum creatinine in Japanese patients with congestive heart failure. Am J Ther 6:71–76, 1999

149. Shull BC, Haughley D, Koup JR, Baliah T, Li PK: A useful method for predicting creatinine clearance in children. Clin Chem 24:1167–1199, 1978

150. Traub SL, Johnson CE: Comparison of methods of estimating creatinine clearance in children. Am J Hosp Pharm 37:195–201, 1980

151. Ghazali S, Barratt TM: Urinary excretion of calcium and magnesium in children. Arch Dis Child 49:97–101, 1974

152. Evans GO, Griffiths PD: Limitations concerning the use in children of the relationship between plasma creatinine and body height to derive glomerular filtration rate. Ann Clin Biochem 18:295–298, 1981

153. Hernandez de Acevedo LH, Johnson CE: Estimation of creatinine clearance in children: Comparison of six methods. Clin Pharm 1:158–161, 1982

154. Jelliffe RW, Jelliffe SM: A computer program for estimation of creatinine clearance from unstable serum creatinine levels, age, sex, and weight. Math Biosci 14:17–24, 1972

155. Paap CM, Nahata MC: Prospective evaluation of ten methods for estimating creatinine clearance in children with varying degrees of renal dysfunction. J Clin Pharm Therapeutics 20:67–73, 1995

156. Parkin A, Smith HC, Brocklebank JT: Which routine test for kidney function? Arch Dis Child 64:1261–1263, 1989

157. Rudd GD, Hull JH, Morris CR, Bryan CK: Estimating creatinine clearance in children: Comparison of three methods. Am J Hosp Pharm 37:1514–1517, 1980

158. van den Anker JN, de Groot R, Broerse HM, Sauer PJ, van der Heijden BJ, Hop WC, Lindemans J: Assessment of glomerular filtration rate in preterm infants by serum creatinine: Comparison with inulin clearance. Pediatrics 96:1156–1158, 1995

159. Rolin HA III, Hall PM, Wei R: Inaccuracy of estimated creatinine clearance for prediction of iothalamate glomerular filtration rate. Am J Kidney Dis 4:48–54, 1984

160. Lemann J, Bidani AK, Bain RP, Lewis EJ, Rohde RD: Use of the serum creatinine to estimate glomerular filtration rate in health and early diabetic nephropathy. Collaborative Study Group of Angiotensin Converting Enzyme Inhibition in Diabetic Nephropathy. Am J Kidney Dis 16:236–243, 1990

161. Charleson HA, Bailey RR, Stewart A: Quick prediction of creatinine clearance without the necessity of urine collection. N Z Med J 92:425–426, 1980

162. Lewis J, Agodoa L, Cheek D, Greene T, Middleton J, O'Connor D, Ojo A, Phillips R, Sika M, Wright J Jr: African-American Study of Hypertension and Kidney Disease. Comparison of cross-sectional renal function measurements in African Americans with hypertensive nephrosclerosis and of primary formulas to estimate glomerular filtration rate. Am J Kidney Dis 38:744–753, 2001

163. Waller DG, Fleming JS, Ramsey B, Gray J: The accuracy of creatinine clearance with and without urine collection as a measure of glomerular filtration rate. Postgrad Med J 67:42–46, 1991

164. DeSanto NG, Coppola S, Anastasio P, Coscarella G, Capasso G, Bellini L, Santangelo R, Massimo L, Siciliano A: Predicted creatinine clearance to assess glomerular filtration rate in chronic renal disease in humans. Am J Nephrol 11:181–185, 1991

165. Bedros F, Kasiske B: Estimating GFR from creatinine clearance in renal transplant recipients. J Am Soc Nephrol 9:666A, 1998 (abstr)

166. Goerdt PJ, Heim-Duthoy KL, Macres M, Swan SK: Predictive performance of renal function estimate equations in renal allografts. Br J Clin Pharmacol 44:261–265, 1997

167. Filler G, Priem F, Vollmer I, Gellermann J, Jung K: Diagnostic sensitivity of serum cystatin for impaired glomerular filtration rate. Pediatr Nephrol 13:501–505, 1999

168. Seikaly MG, Browne R, Bajaj G, Arant BS Jr: Limitations to body length/serum creatinine ratio as an estimate of glomerular filtration in children. Pediatr Nephrol 10:709–711, 1996

169. Hellerstein S, Berenbom M, Alon US, Warady BA: Creatinine clearance following cimetidine for estimation of glomerular filtration rate. Pediatr Nephrol 12:49–54, 1998
170. Guignard JP, Torrado A, Feldman H, Gautier E: Assessment of glomerular filtration rate in children. Helv Paediatr Acta 35:437–447, 1980
171. Stake G: Estimation of the glomerular filtration rate in infants and children using iohexol and X-ray fluorescence technique, in Department of Radiology, Section of Paediatric Radiology. Oslo, Norway, University of Oslo, 1992
172. Seikaly MG, Browne R, Simonds N, Atkins C, Alexander SR: Glomerular filtration rate in children following renal transplantation. Pediatr Transplant 2:231–235, 1998
173. Springate JE, Christensen SL, Feld LG: Serum creatinine level and renal function in children. Am J Dis Child 146:1232–1235, 1992
174. Waz WR, Quattrin T, Feld LG: Serum creatinine, height, and weight do not predict glomerular filtration rate in children with IDDM. Diabetes Care 16:1067–1070, 1993
175. Bokenkamp A, Domanetzki M, Zinck R, Schumann G, Byrd D, Brodehl J: Cystatin C — A new marker of glomerular filtration rate in children independent of age and height. Pediatrics 101:875–881, 1998
176. Stake G, Monn E, Rootwelt K, Golman K, Monclair T: Influence of urography on renal function in children. A double blind study with metrizoate and iohexol. Acta Radiol 30:643–646, 1989
177. Stake G, Monn E, Rootwelt K, Monclair T: The clearance of iohexol as a measure of the glomerular filtration rate in children with chronic renal failure. Scand J Clin Lab Invest 51:729–734, 1991
178. Stake G, Monn E, Rootwelt K, Monclair T: A single plasma sample method for estimation of the glomerular filtration rate in infants and children using iohexol. II: Establishment of the optimal plasma sampling time and a comparison with the 99Tcm-DTPA method. Scand J Clin Lab Invest 51:343–348, 1991
179. Stake G, Monclair T: A single plasma sample method for estimation of the glomerular filtration rate in infants and children using iohexol. I: Establishment of a body weight-related formula for the distribution volume of iohexol. Scand J Clin Lab Invest 51:335–342, 1991
180. Stake G, Monn E, Rootwelt K, Gronberg T, Monclair T: Glomerular filtration rate estimated by X-ray fluorescence technique in children: Comparison between the plasma disappearance of 99Tcm-DTPA and iohexol after urography: Scand J Clin Lab Invest 50:161–167, 1990
181. Walser M: Assessing renal function from creatinine measurements in adults with chronic renal failure. Am J Kidney Dis 32:23–31, 1998
182. Arant BS Jr, Greifer I, Edelmann CM Jr, Spitzer A: Effect of chronic salt and water loading on the tubular defects of a child with Fanconi syndrome (cystinosis). Pediatrics 58:370–377, 1976
183. Randers E, Erlandsen E: Serum cystatin C as an endogenous marker of the renal function — A review. Clin Chem Lab Med 37:389–395, 1999
184. Holliday MA, Heilbron D, Al-Uzri A, Hidayat J, Uauy R, Conley SB, Reisch J, Hogg RJ: Serial measurements of GFR in infants using the continuous iothalamate infusion technique. Kidney Int 43:893–898, 1993
185. Hellerstein S, Alon US, Warady BA: Creatinine for estimation of glomerular filtration rate. Pediatr Nephrol 6:507–511, 1992
186. Winterborn MH, Beetham R, White RHR: Comparison of plasma disappearance and standard clearance techniques for measuring glomerular filtration rate in children with and without vesico-ureteric reflux. Clin Nephrol 7:262–270, 1977
187. Schwartz GJ, Brion LP, Spitzer A: The use of plasma creatinine concentration for estimating glomerular filtration rate in infants, children, and adolescents. Pediatr Clin North Am 34:571–590, 1987
188. Ross JW, Miller WG, Myers GL, Praestgaard J: The accuracy of laboratory measurements in clinical chemistry: A study of 11 routine chemistry analytes in the College of American Pathologists Chemistry Survey with fresh frozen serum, definitive methods, and reference methods. Arch Pathol Lab Med 122:587–608, 1998
189. Chiou WL, Hsu FH: A new simple and rapid methd to monitor the renal function based on pharmacokinetic consideration of endogenous creatinine. Res Commun Chem Pathol Pharmacol 10:315–330, 1975
190. Kwong MB, Tong TK, Mickell JJ, Chan JC: Lack of evidence that formula-derived creatinine clearance approximates glomerular filtration rate in pediatric intensive care population. Clin Nephrol 24: 285–288, 1985

191. Jacobson P, West N, Hutchinson RJ: Predictive ability of creatinine clearance estimate models in pediatric bone marrow transplant patients. Bone Marrow Transplant 19:481–485, 1997

192. Fong J, Johnston S, Valentino T, Notterman D: Length/serum creatinine ratio does not predict measured creatinine clearance in critically ill children. Clin Pharmacol Therapeutics 58:192–197, 1995

193. Gbadegesin RA, Adeyemo AA, Asinobi AO, Osinusi K: Inaccuracy of the Schwartz formula in estimating glomerular filtration rate in Nigerian children. Ann Trop Paediatr 17:179–185, 1997

194. Rocco MV, Buckalew VM Jr, Moore LC, Shihabi ZK: Capillary electrophoresis for the determination of glomerular filtration rate using nonradioactive iohexol. Am J Kidney Dis 28:173–177, 1996

195. Zelmanovitz T, Gross JL, Oliveira J, de Azevedo MJ: Proteinuria is still useful for the screening and diagnosis of overt diabetic nephropathy. Diabetes Care 21:1076–1079, 1998

196. Zelmanovitz T, Gross JL, Oliveira JR, Paggi A, Tatsch M, Azevedo MJ: The receiver operating characteristics curve in the evaluation of a random urine specimen as a screening test for diabetic nephropathy. Diabetes Care 20:516–519, 1997

197. Ahn CW, Song YD, Kim JH, Lim SK, Choi KH, Kim KR, Lee HC, Huh KB: The validity of random urine specimen albumin measurement as a screening test for diabetic nephropathy. Yonsei Med J 40:40–45, 1999

198. Schwab SJ, Dunn FL, Feinglos MN: Screening for microalbuminuria. A comparison of single sample methods of collection and techniques of albumin analysis. Diabetes Care 15:1581–1584, 1992

199. Ng WY, Lui KF, Thai AC: Evaluation of a rapid screening test for microalbuminuria with a spot measurement of urine albumin-creatinine ratio. Ann Acad Med Singapore 29:62–65, 2000

200. Ciavarella A, Silletti A, Forlani G, Morotti L, Borgnino LC, D'Apote M, Vannini P: A screening test for microalbuminuria in type 1 (insulin-dependent) diabetes. Diabetes Res Clin Practice 7:307–312, 1989

201. Webb DJ, Newman DJ, Chaturvedi N, Fuller JH: The use of the Micral-Test strip to identify the presence of microalbuminuria in people with insulin dependent diabetes mellitus (IDDM) participating in the EUCLID study. Diabetes Res Clin Practice 31:93–102, 1996

202. Poulsen PL, Hansen B, Amby T, Terkelsen TE, Mogensen C: Evaluation of a dipstick test for microalbuminuria in three different clinical settings, including the correlation with urinary albumin excretion rate. Diabetes Metab 18:395–400, 1992

203. Gerber LM, Johnston K, Alderman MH: Assessment of a new dipstick test in screening for microalbuminuria in patients with hypertension. Am J Hypertens 11:1321–1327, 1998

204. Schwab SJ, Christensen RL, Dougherty K, Klahr S: Quantitation of proteinuria by the use of protein-to-creatinine ratios in single urine samples. Arch Intern Med 147:943–944, 1987

205. Ginsberg JM, Chang BS, Matarese RA, Garella S: Use of single voided urine samples to estimate quantitative proteinuria. N Engl J Med 309:1543–1546, 1983

206. Rodby RA, Rohde RD, Sharon Z, Pohl MA, Bain RP, Lewis EJ: The urine protein to creatinine ratio as a predictor of 24-hour urine protein excretion in type 1 diabetic patients with nephropathy. The Collaborative Study Group. Am J Kidney Dis 26:904–909, 1995

207. Wilson DM, Anderson RL: Protein-osmolality ratio for the quantitative assessment of proteinuria from a random urinalysis sample. Am J Clin Pathol 100:419–424, 1993

208. Chu NF, Ferng SH, Shieh SD, Fan CD, Shyh TP, Chu PL: Assessment of proteinuria by using the protein/creatinine ratio of single-voided urine. J Formos Med Assoc 89:657–660, 1990

209. Steinhauslin F, Wauters JP: Quantitation of proteinuria in kidney transplant patients: Accuracy of the urinary protein/creatinine ratio. Clin Nephrol 43:110–115, 1995

210. Nathan DM, Rosenbaum C, Protasowicki VD: Single-void urine samples can be used to estimate quantitative microalbuminuria. Diabetes Care 10:414–418, 1987

211. Cottiero RA, Madaio MP, Levey AS: Glomerular filtration rate and urinary albumin excretion rate in systemic lupus erythematosus. Nephron 140:140–146, 1995

212. Yoshimoto M, Tsukahara H, Saito M, Hayashi S, Haruki S, Fujiswana S, Sudo M: Evaluation of variability of proteinuria indices. Pediatr Nephrol 4:136–139, 1990

213. Iyer RS, Shailaja SN, Bhaskaranand N, Baliga M, Venkatesh A: Quantitation of proteinuria using protein-creatinine ratio in random urine samples. Indian Pediatr 28:463–467, 1991

214. Chahar OP, Bundella B, Chahar CKJ, Purohit M: Quantitation of proteinuria by use of single random spot urine collection. J Indian Med Assoc 91:86–87, 1993

215. Mir S, Kutukcular N, Cura A: Use of single voided urine samples to estimate quantitative proteinuria in children. Turk J Pediatr 34:219–224, 1992

216. Houser MT: Assessment of proteinuria using random urine samples. J Pediatr 104:845–848, 1984
217. Abitbol C, Zilleruelo G, Freundlich M, Strauss J: Quantitation of proteinuria with urinary protein/ creatinine ratios and random testing with dipsticks in nephrotic children. J Pediatr 166:243–224, 1990
218. Sochett E, Daneman D: Screening tests to detect microalbuminuria in children with diabetes. J Pediatr 112:744–748, 1988
219. Fivush BA, Jabs K, Sullivan EK, Feld LG, Kohaut E, Fine RN: Chronic renal insufficiency in children and adolescents: the 1996 annual report of NAPRTCS. North American Pediatric Renal Transplant Cooperative Study (NAPRTCS). Pediatr Nephrol 12:328–377, 1998
220. Kitagawa T: Lessons learned from the Japanese nephritis screening study. Pediatr Nephrol 2:256–263, 1998
221. Committee on Practice and Ambulatory Medicine: Recommendations for preventive pediatric health care. Pediatrics 96:1–4, 1995
222. Kaplan RE, Springate JE, Feld LG: Screening dipstick analysis: A time to change. Pediatrics 100:919–921, 1997
223. American Diabetes Association: Diabetic nephropathy. Diabetes Care 21:S50-S53, 1998
224. The EUCLID Study Group: Randomised placebo-controlled trial of lisinopril in normotensive patients with insulin-dependent diabetes and normoalbuminuria or microalbuminuria. Lancet 349:1787–1792, 1997
225. Mathiesen ER, Hommel E, Hansen HP, Smidt UM, Parving H-H: Randomised controlled trial of long term efficacy of captopril on preservation of kidney function in normotensive patients with insulin dependent diabetes and microalbuminuria. BMJ 319:24–25, 1999
226. Ruggenenti P, Pagano E, Tammuzzo L, Benini R, Garattini L: Gruppo Italiano Di Studi Epidemilogici in Nefrologia (GISEN). Kidney Int 59:286–294, 2001
227. Wang PH: When should ACE inhibitors be given to normotensive patients with IDDM? Lancet 349:1782–1783, 1997
228. Grimm RH Jr, Svendsen KH, Kasiske B, Keane WF, Wahi MM: Proteinuria is a risk factor for mortality over 10 years of follow-up. MRFIT Research Group. Multiple Risk Factor Intervention Trial. Kidney Int 63:S10-S14, 1997 (suppl 63)
229. Couper JJ, Clarke CF, Byrne GC, Jones TW, Donaghue KC, Nairn J, Boyce D, Russell M, Stephens M, Raymond J, Bates DJ, McCaul K: Progression of borderline increases in albuminuria in adolescents with insulin-dependent diabetes mellitus. Diabet Med 14:766–771, 1997
230. Levey AS, Perrone RD, Madaio MP: Laboratory assessment of renal disease: Clearance, urinalysis and renal biopsy, in Brenner BM, Rector FR (eds): The Kidney. Philadelphia, PA, W.B. Saunders, 1991, pp 919–968
231. Norden AG, Scheinman SJ, Deschodt-Lanckman MM, Lapsley M, Nortier JL, Thakker RV, Unwin RJ, Wrong O: Tubular proteinuria defined by a study of Dent's (CLCN5 mutation) and other tubular diseases. Kidney Int 57:240-249, 2000
232. Tomlinson PA, Smellie JM, Prescod N, Dalton RN, Chantler C: Differential excretion of urinary proteins in children with vesicoureteric reflux and reflux nephropathy. Pediatr Nephrol 8:21–25, 1994
233. Weitgasser R, Schnoell F, Gappmayer B, Kartnig I: Prospective evaluation of urinary N-acetyl-beta-D-glucosaminidase with respect to macrovascular disease in elderly type 2 diabetic patients. Diabetes Care 22:1882–1886, 1999
234. Kordonouri O, Hartmann R, Mueller C, Danne T, Weber B: Predictive value of tubular markers for the development of microalbuminuria in adolescents with diabetes. From the Hormone Res 50:S23-S27, 1998 (suppl 1)
235. Reichert LJ, Koene RA, Wetzels JF: Urinary IgG excretion as a prognostic factor in idiopathic membranous nephropathy. Clin Nephrol 48:79–84, 1997
236. Bazzi C, Petrini C, Rizza V, Arrigo A, Beltrame A, D'Amico G: Characterization of proteinuria in primary glomerulonephritides. SDS-PAGE patterns: Clinical significance and prognostic value of low molecular weight ("tubular") proteins. Am J Kidney Dis 29:27–35, 1997
237. Woo KT, Lau YK, Lee GS, Wei SS, Lim CH: Pattern of proteinuria in IgA nephritis by SDS-PAGE: Clinical significance. Clin Nephrol 36:6–11, 1991
238. Reichert LJ, Koene RA, Wetzels JF: Urinary excretion of beta 2-microglobulin predicts renal outcome in patients with idiopathic membranous nephropathy. J Am Soc Nephrol 6:1666–1669, 1995

239. Hara M, Yanagihara T, Itoh M, Matsuno M, Kihara I: Immunohistochemical and urinary markers of podocyte injury. Pediatr Nephrol 12:43–48, 1998

240. Hara M, Yanagihara T, Takada T, Itoh M, Matsuno M, Yamamoto T, Kihara I: Urinary excretion of podocytes reflects disease activity in children with glomerulonephritis. Am J Nephrol 18:35–41, 1998

241. Hotta O, Taguma Y, Ooyama M, Yusa N, Nagura H: Analysis of CD14+ cells and CD56+ cells in urine using flow cytometry: A useful tool for monitoring disease activity of IgA nephropathy. Clin Nephrol 39:289–294, 1993

242. Nakamura T, Ushiyama C, Suzuki S, Hara M, Shimada N, Sekizuka K, Ebihara I, Koide H: Urinary podocytes for the assessment of disease activity in lupus nephritis. Am J Med Sci 320:112–116, 2000

243. Nakamura T, Ushiyama C, Suzuki S, Hara M: Urinary excretion of podocytes in patients with diabetic nephropathy. Nephrol Dial Transplant 15:1379–1383, 2000

244. Wilson PW, Culleton BF: Epidemiology of cardiovascular disease in the United States. Am J Kidney Dis 32:S56-S65, 1998 (suppl 3)

245. The Sixth Report of the Joint National Committee on Prevention, Detection, Evaluation, and Treatment of High Blood Pressure (JNC VI). Bethesda, MD, US Department of Health and Human Services, Public Health Service, National Institutes of Health, National Heart, Lung and Blood Institute, 1997

246. Burt VL, Cutler JA, Higgins M, Horan MJ, Labarthe D, Whelton P, Brown C, Roccella EJ: Trends in the prevalence, awareness, treatment, and control of hypertension in the adult US population. Data from the health examination surveys, 1960–1991. Hypertension 26:6069, 1995 (erratum 27:1192, 1996)

247. Wright JT Jr, Douglas JG, Rahman M: Prevention of cardiovascular disease in hypertensive patients with normal renal function. Am J Kidney Dis 32:S66-S79, 1998 (suppl 3)

248. Mailloux LU, Levey AS. Hypertension in chronic renal disease. Am J Kidney Dis 32:S120-S141, 1998 (suppl 3)

249. Bakris GL, Williams M, Dworkin L, Elliott WJ, Epstein M, Toto RDA, Tuttle K, Douglas J, Hsueh W, Sowers J: Preserving renal function in adults with hypertension and diabetes: A consensus approach. National Kidney Foundation Hypertension and Diabetes Executive Committees Working Group. Am J Kidney Dis 36:646–661, 2000

250. HCFA-1995: 1995 Annual Report. ESRD core indicator project. Opportunities to improve care for adult in-center hemodialysis patients. Baltimore, MD, Health Care Financing Administration, DHHS, 1996

251. Rocco MV, Flanagan MJ, Beaver S, Frederick P, Gentile DI, McClellan WM, Polder J, Prowant BF, Taylor L, Helgersson SD: Report from the 1995 core indicators for peritoneal dialysis study group. Am J Kidney Dis 30:165–173, 1997

252. National High Blood Pressure Education Program Working Group. 1995 Update of the working group reports on chronic renal failure and renovascular hypertension. Arch Intern Med 156: 1938–1947, 1995

253. Parving HH, Andersen AR, Smidt UM: Early aggressive antihypertensive treatment reduces rate of decline in kidney function in diabetic nephropathy. Lancet 1:1175–1179, 1983

255. Peterson JC, Adler S, Burkart JM, Greene T, Hebert LA, Hunsicker LG, King AJ, Klahr S, Massry SG, Seifter JL: Blood pressure control, proteinuria and the progression of renal disease: The Modification of Diet in Renal Disease Study. Ann Intern Med 123:754–762, 1995

256. Opelz G, Wujciak T, Ritz E: The Collaborative Transplant Study. Association of chronic kidney graft failure with recipient blood pressure. Kidney Int 53:217–222, 1998

257. Levin A, Singer J, Thompson CR: Prevalent left ventricular hypertrophy in the predialysis population: Identifying opportunities for intervention. Am J Kidney Dis 27:347–354, 1996

258. Lazarus JM, Bourgoignie JJ, Buckalew VM Jr, Milas NC, Paranandi L, Peterson JC, Porush JG, Rauch S, Soucie JM, Stollar C: Achievement and safety of a low blood pressure goal in chronic renal disease. Modification of Diet in Renal Disease Study Group. Hypertension 29:641–650, 1997

259. Jungers P, Massy ZA, Nguyen Khoa T, Fumeron C, Labrunie M, Lacour B, Descamps-Latscha B, Man NK: Incidence and risk factors of atherosclerotic cardiovascular accidents in predialysis chronic renal failure patients: A prospective study. Nephrol Dial Transplant 12:2597–2602, 1997

260. Foley RN, Parfrey PS, Harnett JD, Dent FM, Murray DC, Barre PC: Impact of hypertension on cardiomyopathy, morbidity and mortality in end-stage renal disease. Kidney Int 49:1379–1385, 1996

261. Foley RN, Parfrey PS, Sarnak MJ: Clinical epidemiology of cardiovascular disease in chronic renal disease. Am J Kidney Dis 32:112–119, 1998

262. Zagar PG, Nikolic J, Brown RH, Campbell MA, Hunt WC, Peterson D, Van Stone J, Levey A, Meyer KB, Klag MJ, Johnson HK, Clark E, Sadler JH, Teredesai P: ''U'' curve association of blood pressure and mortality in hemodialysis patients. Kidney Int 54:561–569, 1998

263. Buckalew VM Jr, Berg RL, Wang SR, Porush JG, Rauch S, Schulman G: Prevalence of hypertension in 1,795 subjects with chronic renal disease: The modification of diet in renal disease study baseline cohort. Modification of Diet in Renal Disease Study Group. Am J Kidney Dis 28:811–821, 1996

265. NKF-DOQI clinical practice guidelines for the treatment of anemia of chronic renal failure. National Kidney Foundation-Dialysis Outcomes Quality Initiative. Am J Kidney Dis 30:S192-S240, 1997 (suppl 3)

266. NKF-K/DOQI Clinical Practice Guidelines for Anemia of Chronic Kidney Disease: Update 2000. Am J Kidney Disease 77:S182-S288, 2001 (suppl 1)

267. McGonigle RJ, Wallin JD, Shadduck RK, Fisher JW: Erythropoietin deficiency and inhibition of erythropoiesis in renal insufficiency. Kidney Int 25:437–444, 1984

268. Radtke HW, Claussner A, Erbes PM, Scheuermann EH, Schoeppe W, Koch KM: Serum erythropoietin concentration in chronic renal failure: Relationship to degree of anemia and excretory renal function. Blood 54:877–884, 1979

269. Loge JP, Lange RD, Moore CV: Characterization of the anemia associated with chronic renal insufficiency. Am J Med 24, 1958

270. Ross RP, McCrea JB, Besarab A: Erythropoietin response to blood loss in hemodialysis patients is blunted but preserved. ASAIO J 40:M880-M885, 1994

271. Naets JP, Garcia JF, Tousaaint C, Buset M, Waks D: Radioimmunoassay of erythropoietin in chronic uraemia of anephric patients. Scand J Haematol 37:390–394, 1986

272. World Health Organization: Nutritional Anemia. Report of a WHO Scientific Group. Geneva, Switzerland, WHO, 1968

273. Working Party for European Best Practice Guidelines for the Management of Anaemia in Patients With Chronic Renal Failure: European best practice guidelines for the management of anaemia in patients with chronic renal failure. Nephrol Dial Transplant 14:1–50, 1999 (suppl 5)

274. Erslev AJ, Besarab A: The rate and control of baseline red cell production in hema-tologically stable uremic patients. J Lab Clin Med 126:283–286, 1995

275. Fisher JW: Mechanism of the anemia of chronic renal failure. Nephron 25:106–111, 1980

276. Besarab A, Levin A: Defining a renal anemia management period. Am J Kidney Dis 36:S13-S23, 2000

277. Chandra M, Miller ME, Garcia JF, Mossey RT, McVicar MI: Serum immunoreactive erythropoietin levels in patients with polycystic kidney disease as compared with other hemodialysis patients. Nephron 39:26–29, 1985

278. Eschbach JW Jr, Funk D, Adamson J, Kuhn I, Scribner BH, Finch CA: Erythropoiesis in patients with renal failure undergoing chronic dialysis. N Engl J Med 276:653–688, 1967

279. Collins AJ, Ma JZ, Xia A, Ebben J: Trends in anemia treatment with erythropoietin usage and patient outcomes. Am J Kidney Dis 32:S133-S141, 1998 (suppl 4)

280. Parfrey PS, Foley RN, Harnett JD, Kent GM, Murray DC, Barre PE: Outcome and risk factors for left ventricular disorders in chronic uraemia. Nephrol Dial Transplant 11:1277–1285, 1996

281. Levin A, Foley RN: Cardiovascular disease in chronic renal insufficiency. Am J Kidney Dis 36:S24-S30, 2000 (suppl 3)

282. Kausz AT, Obrador GT, Pereira BJ: Anemia management in patients with chronic renal insufficiency. Am J Kidney Dis 36:S39-S51, 2000 (suppl 3)

283. Locatelli F, Conte F, Marcelli D: The impact of hematocrit levels and Erythropoietin treatment on overall and cardiovascular mortality and morbidity: The experience of Lombardy Registry. NDT 13:1642–1644, 1998

284. Muirhead N, for the Canadian Erythropoietin Study Group: Association between recombinant human erythropoietin and quality of life and exercise capacity of patients receiving haemodialysis. BMJ 300:573–578, 1990

285. The US Recombinant Erythropoietin Predialysis Study Group: Double-blind, placebo controlled study of the therapeutic use of recombinant human erythropoietin for anemia associated with chronic renal failure in predialysis patients. Am J Kidney Dis 18:50–59, 1991

286. Austrian Multicenter Study Group of rHuEPO in predialysis patients: Effectiveness and safety of recombinant human erythropoietin in predialysis patients. Nephron 61:399–403, 1992

287. Winearls CG: Recombinant human erythropoietin: 10 years of clinical experience. Nephrol Dial Transplant 13:3–8, 1998

288. Levin A, Thompson CR, Ethier J, Carlisle EJ, Tobe S, Mendelssohn D, Burgess E, Jindal K, Barrett B, Singer J, Djurdjev O: Left ventricular mass index increase in early renal disease: Impact of decline in hemoglobin. Am J Kidney Dis 34:125–134, 1999

289. Taralov Z, Koumtchev E, Lyutakova Z: Erythrocyte ferritin levels in chronic renal failure patients. Folia Medica (Plovdiv) 40:65–70, 1998

290. Clyne N, Jogestrand T, Lins LE, Pehrsson SK: Progressive decline in renal function induces a gradual decrease in total hemoglobin and exercise capacity. Nephron 67:322–326, 1994

291. Ishimura E, Nishizawa Y, Okuno S, Matsumoto N, Emoto M, Inaba M, Kawagishi T, Kim CW, Morii H: Diabetes mellitus increases the severity of anemia in non-dialyzed patients with renal failure. J Nephrol 11:83–86, 1998

292. de Klerk G, Wilmink JM, Rosengarten PC, Vet RJ, Goudsmit R: Serum erythropoietin (ESF) titers in anemia of chronic renal failure. J Lab Clin Med 100:720–734, 1982

293. Urabe A, Saito T, Fukamachi H, Kubota M, Takaku F: Serum erythropoietin titers in the anemia of chronic renal failure and other hematological states. Int J Cell Cloning 5:202–208, 1987

294. Silverberg DS, Iaina A, Peer G, Kaplan E, Levi BA, Frank N, Steinbruch S, Blum M: Intravenous iron supplementation for the treatment of the anemia of moderate to severe chronic renal failure patients not receiving dialysis. Am J Kidney Dis 27:234–238, 1996

295. Lin JL, Kou MT, Leu ML: Effect of long-term low-dose aluminum-containing agents on hemoglobin synthesis in patients with chronic renal insufficiency. Nephron 74:33–38, 1996

296. Clyne N, Jogestrand T: Effect of erythropoietin treatment on physical exercise capacity and on renal function in predialytic uremic patients. Nephron 60:390–396, 1992

297. Portoles J, Torralbo A, Martin P, Rodrigo J, Herrero JA, Barrientos A: Cardiovascular effects of recombinant human erythropoietin in predialysis patients. Am J Kidney Dis 29:541–548, 1997

298. Dimitrakov D, Kumchev E, Tllkian E: Study of the effect of recombinant erythropoietin on renal anaemia in predialysis patients with chronic renal failure. Folia Medica (Plovdiv) 36:31–36, 1994

299. Klahr S, Breyer JA, Beck GJ, Dennis VW, Hartman JA, Roth D, Steinman TI, Wang SR, Yamamoto ME: Dietary protein restriction, blood pressure control, and the progression of polycystic kidney disease. Modification of Diet in Renal Disease Study Group. J Am Soc Nephrol 5:2037–2047, 1995 (erratum 6:1318, 1995)

300. Howard AD, Moore J Jr, Welch PG, Gouge SF: Analysis of the quantitative relationship between anemia and chronic renal failure. Am J Med Sci 297:309–313, 1989

301. Lim VS, Fangman J, Flanigan MJ, DeGowin RL, Abels RT: Effect of recombinant human erythropoietin on renal function in humans. Kidney Int 37:131–136, 1990

302. Besarab A, Caro J, Jarrell B, Burke J, Francos G, Mallon E, Karsch R: Effect of cyclosporine and delayed graft function on posttransplantation erythropoiesis. Transplantation 40:624–631, 1985

303. Brod J, Hornych A: Effect of correction of anemia on the glomerular filtration rate in chronic renal failure. Isr J Med Sci 3:53–59, 1967

304. Roth D, Smith RD, Schulman G, Steinman TI, Hatch FE, Rudnick MR, Sloand JA, Freedman BI, Williams WW Jr, Shadur CA: Effects of recombinant human erythropoietin on renal function in chronic renal failure predialysis patients. Am J Kidney Dis 24:777–784, 1994

305. Kuriyama S, Tomonari H, Yoshida H, Hashimoto T, Kawaguchi Y, Sakai O: Reversal of anemia by erythropoietin therapy retards the progression of chronic renal failure, especially in nondiabetic patients. Nephron 77:176–185, 1997

306. Hayashi T, Suzuki A, Shoji T, Togawa M, Okada N, Tsubakihara Y, Imai E, Hori M: Cardiovascular effect of normalizing the hematocrit level during erythropoietin therapy in predialysis patients with chronic renal failure. Am J Kidney Dis 35:250–256, 2000

307. Schwartz AB, Prior JE, Mintz GS, Kim KE, Kahn SB: Cardiovascular hemodynamic effects of correction of anemia of chronic renal failure with recombinant-human erythropoietin. Transplant Proc 23:1827–1830, 1991

308. Donnelley S, Shah BE: Erythropoietin deficiency in hyporeninemia. Am J Kidney Dis 33:947–953, 1999

309. Chaplin H, Mollison PL: Red cell life span in nephritis and in hepatic nephrosis. Clin Sci 12:351, 1953

310. Besarab A, Caro J, Jarrell BE, Francos G, Erslev AJ: Dynamics of erythropoiesis following renal transplantation. Kidney Int 32:526–536, 1987

311. Cavill I: Iron status as measured by serum ferritin: The marker and its limitations. Am J Kidney Dis 34:S12-S17, 1999 (suppl 2)

312. Sunder-Plassmann G, Horl W: Erythropoietin and iron. Clin Nephr 47:141–157, 1997

313. Eckard K-U, Möllmann M, Neumann R: Erythropoietin in polycystic kidney. J Clin Invest 84:1160–1166, 1989

314. Ikizler TA, Hakim RM: Nutrition in end-stage renal disease. Kidney Int 50:343–357, 1996

315. Klahr S, Levey AS, Beck GJ, Caggiula AW, Hunsicker L, Kusek JW, Striker G: The effects of dietary protein restriction and blood-pressure control on the progression of chronic renal disease. Modification of Diet in Renal Disease Study Group. N Engl J Med 330:877–884, 1994

316. Graham KA, Reaich D, Channon SM, Downie S, Goodship TH: Correction of acidosis in hemodialysis decreases whole-body protein degradation. J Am Soc Nephrol 8:632–637, 1997

317. Position of the American Dietetic Association: Cost-effectiveness of medical nutrition therapy. J Am Diet Assoc 95:88–91, 1995

318. Bergstrom J: Nutrition and mortality in hemodialysis. J Am Soc Nephrol 6:1329–1341, 1995

319. Lowrie EG, Huang WH, Lew NL, Liu Y: The relative contribution of measured variables to death risk among hemodialysis patients, in Friedman EA (ed): Death on Hemodialysis. Amsterdam, The Netherlands, Kluwer Academic, 1994, pp 121–141

320. Hakim RM, Lazarus JM: Initiation of dialysis. J Am Soc Nephrol 6:1319–1328, 1995

321. Holland D, Lam M: Predictors of hopitalization and death amongst pre-dialysis patients: A retrospective study. Nephrol Dial Transplant 15:650–658, 2000

322. Ikizler TA, Wingard RL, Harvell J, Shyr Y, Hakim RM: Association of morbidity with markers of nutrition and inflammation in chronic hemodialysis patients: A prospective study. Kidney Int 55:1945–1951, 1999

323. Stenvinkel P, Heimburger O, Paultre F, Diczfalusy U, Wang T, Berglund L, Jogestrand T: Strong association between malnutrition, inflammation, and atherosclerosis in chronic renal failure. Kidney Int 55:1899–1911, 1999

324. Kopple JD, Greene T, Chumlea WC, Hollinger D, Maroni BJ, Merrill D, Scherch LK, Schulman G, Wang SR, Zimmer GS: Relationship between nutritional status and the glomerular filtration rate: Results from the MDRD study. Kidney Int 57:1688–1703, 2000

325. Ikizler TA, Greene JH, Wingard RL, Parker RA, Hakim RM: Spontaneous dietary protein intake during progression of chronic renal failure. J Am Soc Nephrol 6:1386–1391, 1995

326. Mitch WE, Maroni BJ: Nutritional considerations in the treatment of patients with chronic uremia. Miner Electrolyte Metab 24:285–289, 1998

327. Mitch WE, Maroni BJ: Factors causing malnutrition in patients with chronic uremia. Am J Kidney Dis 33:176–179, 1999

328. Ballmer PE, Imberdorf R: Influence of acidosis on protein metabolism. Nutrition 11:462–468, 1995

329. Tonshoff B, Blum WF, Mehls O: Derangements of the somatotropic hormone axis in chronic renal failure. Kidney Int 58:S106-S113, 1997 (suppl 58)

330. Saborio P, Hahn S, Hisano S, Latta K, Scheinmann JI, Chan JC: Chronic renal failure: An overview from a pediatric perspective. Nephron 80:134–148, 1998

331. Boirie Y, Breyer M, Gagnadoux MF, Niaudet P, Bresson JL: Alterations of protein metabolism by metabaolic acidosis in children with chronic renal failure. Kidney Int 58:236–241, 2000

332. Panichi V, Migliori M, De Pietro S: C reactive protein in patients with chronic renal diseases. Ren Fail 23:551–562, 2001

333. Eustace JA, Astor B, Muntner PM, Ikizler TA, Coresh J: Inflammation and acidosis are important independent predictors of hypoalbuminuria in renal insufficiency. J Am Soc Nephrol 12:201A, 2001 (abstr)

334. Bistrian BR: Role of the systemic inflammatory response syndrome in the development of protein-calorie malnutrition in ESRD. Am J Kidney Dis 32:S113-S117, 1998 (suppl 4)

335. Bistrian BRK: The systemic inflammatory response and its impact on iron nutriture in end-stage renal disease. Am J Kidney Dis 34:S35-S39, 1999 (suppl 2)

336. Bergstrom J, Lindholm B: Malnutrition, cardiac disease, and mortality: An integrated point of view. Am J Kidney Dis 32:834–841, 1998

337. Tom K, Young VR, Chapman T, Masud T, Akpele L, Maroni BJ: Long-term adaptive responses to dietary protein restriction in chronic renal failure. Am J Physiol 268:E668-E677, 1995

338. Kopple JD, Berg R, Houser H, Steinman TI, Teschan P: Nutritional status of patients with different levels of chronic renal insufficiency. Modification of Diet in Renal Disease (MDRD) Study Group. Kidney Int 27:S184-S194, 1989 (suppl 27)

339. Coggins CH, Dwyer JT, Greene T, Petot G, Snetselaar LG, Van Lente F: Serum lipid changes associated with modified protein diets: Results from the feasibility phase of the Modification of Diet in Renal Disease Study. Am J Kidney Dis 23:514–523, 1994

340. Park JS, Jung HH, Yang WS, Kim HH, Kim SB, Park SK, Hong CD: Protein intake and the nutritional status in patients with pre-dialysis chronic renal failure on unrestricted diet. Korean J Intern Med 12:115-121, 1997

341. Pollock CA, Ibels LS, Zhu FY, Warnant M, Caterson RJ, Waugh DA, Mahony JF: Protein intake in renal disease. J Am Soc Nephrol 8:777-783, 1997

342. Walser M, Mitch WE, Maroni BJ, Kopple JD: Should protein intake be restricted in predialysis patients? Kidney Int 55:771–777, 1999

343. Chauveau P, Barthe N, Rigalleau V, Ozenne S, Castaing F, Delclaux C: Outcome of nutritional status and body composition of uremic patients on a very low protein diet. Am J Kidney Dis 34:500–507, 1999

344. Williams B, Hattersley J, Layward E, Walls J: Metabolic acidosis and skeletal muscle adaptation to low protein diets in chronic uremia. Kidney Int 40:779–786, 1991

345. Aparicio M, Chauveau P, De Precigout V, Bouchet JL, Lasseur C, Combe C: Nutrition and outcome on renal replacement therapy of patients with chronic renal failure treated by a supplemented very low protein diet. J Am Soc Nephrol 11:708–716, 2000

346. Walser M, Hill SB, Ward L, Magder L: A crossover comparison of progression of chronic renal failure: Ketoacids versus amino acids. Kidney Int 43:933–939, 1993

347. Mazouz H, Kacso I, Ghazali A, El Esper N, Moriniere P, Makdassi R, Hardy P, Westeel PF, Archard JM, Pruna A, Fournier A: Risk factors of renal failure progression two years prior to dialysis. Clin Nephrol 51:355-366, 1999

348. Monteon FJ, Laidlaw SA, Shaib JK, Kopple JD: Energy expenditure in patients with chronic renal failure. Kidney Int 30:741–747, 1986

349. Ando A, Orita Y, Nakata K, Tsubakihara Y, Takamitsu Y, Ueda N, Yanase M, Abe H: Effect of low protein diet and surplus of essential amino acids on the serum concentration and the urinary excretion of methylguanidine and guanidinosuccinic acid in chronic renal failure. Nephron 24:161–169, 1979

350. Stenvinkel P, Heimburger O, Tuck CH, Berglund L: Apo(a)-isoform size, nutritional status and inflammatory markers in chronic renal failure. Kidney Int 53:1336–1342, 1998

351. Walser M, Hill S: Can renal replacement be deferred by a supplemented very low protein diet? J Am Soc Nephrol 10:110–116, 1999

352. Cupisti A, Guidi A, Giovannetti S: Nutritional state of severe chronic renal failure patients on a low-protein supplemented diet. Contrib Nephrol 81:161–168, 1990

353. Sugimoto T, Kikkawa R, Haneda M, Shigeta Y: Effect of dietary protein restriction on proteinuria in non-insulin-dependent diabetic patients with nephropathy. J Nutr Sci Vitaminol 37:S87-S92, 1991 (suppl)

354. Guarnieri G, Toigo G, Situlin R, Crapesi L, Del Bianco MA, Zanettovich A, Faccini L, Lucchesi A, Oldrizzi L, Rugiu C: Nutritional assessment in patients with early renal insufficiency on long-term low protein diet. Contrib Nephrol 53:40–50, 1986

355. Di Landro D, Dattilo GA, Romagnoli GF: Comparative outcome of patients on a conventional low protein diet versus a supplemented diet in chronic renal failure. Contrib Nephrol 81:201–207, 1990

356. Vetter K, Kaschube I, Metzner C, Lindenau K, Frohling PT: Evaluation of nutritional status in the GDR trial. Contrib Nephrol 81:208–213, 1990

357. Barsotti G, Ciardella F, Morelli E, Cupisti A, Mantovanelli A, Giovannetti S: Nutritional treatment of renal failure in type 1 diabetic nephropathy. Clin Nephrol 29:280–287, 1988

358. Jenkins D, Burton PR, Bennett SE, Baker F, Walls J: The metabolic consequences of the correction of acidosis in uraemia. Nephrol Dial Transplant 4:92–95, 1989

359. Huang XH, Rantalaiho V, Wirta O, Pasternack A, Hiltunen TP, Koivula T, Malminiemi K, Nikkari T, Lehtimaki T: Angiotensin-converting enzyme insertion/deletion polymorphism and diabetic albuminuria in patients with NIDDM followed Up for 9 years. Nephron 80:17–24, 1998

360. Zeller K, Whittaker E, Sullivan L, Raskin P, Jacobson HR: Effect of restricting dietary protein on the progression of renal failure in patients with insulin-dependent diabetes mellitus. N Engl J Med 324: 78–84, 1991

361. D'Amico G, Gentile MG: Dietary control may influence several risk factors in patients with chronic renal failure. Contrib Nephrol 81:29–34, 1990

362. Parillo M, Riccardi G, Pacioni D, Iovine C, Contaldo F, Isernia C, De Marco F, Perrotti N, Rivellese A: Metabolic consequences of feeding a high-carbohydrate, high-fiber diet to diabetic patients with chronic kidney failure. Am J Clin Nutr 48:255–259, 1988

363. Goodship TH, Mitch WE, Hoerr RA, Wagner DA, Steinman TI, Young VR: Adaptation to low-protein diets in renal failure: Leucine turnover and nitrogen balance. J Am Soc Nephrol 1:66–75, 1990

364. Woodrow G, Oldroyd B, Smith MA, Turney JH: Measurement of body composition in chronic renal failure: Comparison of skinfold anthropometry and bioelectrical impedance with dual energy X-ray absorptiometry. Eur J Clin Nutr 50:295–301, 1996

365. Guarnieri GF, Toigo G, Situlin R, Carraro M, Tamaro G, Lucchesli A, Oldrizzi L, Rugiu C, Maschio G: Nutritional state in patients on long-term low-protein diet or with nephrotic syndrome. Kidney Int 27:S195-S200, 1989 (suppl 27)

366. Maroni BJ, Staffeld C, Young VR, Manatunga A, Tom K: Mechanisms permitting nephrotic patients to achieve nitrogen equilibrium with a protein-restricted diet. J Clin Invest 99:2479–2487, 1997

367. Mitch WE, Walser M, Steinman TI, Hill S, Zeger S, Tungsanga K: The effect of a keto acid-amino acid supplement to a restricted diet on the progression of chronic renal failure. N Engl J Med 311: 623–629, 1984

368. Milas NC, Nowack MP, Akpele L, Castaldo L, Coyne T, Doroshenko L, Kigawa L, Korzec-Ramirez D, Scherch LK, Snetselaar L: Factors associated with adherence to the dietary protein intervention in the Modification of Diet in Renal Disease Study. J Am Diet Assoc 95:1295–1300, 1995

369. Gillis BP, Caggiula AW, Chiavacci AT: Nutrition intervention program of the Modification of Diet in Renal Disease Study: A self-management approach. J Am Diet Assoc 95:1288–1294, 1995

370. Coyne T, Olson M, Bradham K, Garcon M, Gregory P, Scherch L: Dietary satisfaction correlated with adherence in the Modification of Diet in Renal Disease Study. J Am Diet Assoc 95:1301–1306, 1995

371. Dolecek T, Olsen MB, Caggiula AW, Dwyer JT, Milas C, Gillis BP, Hartmann JA, DiChiro JT: Registered dietitian time requirements in the Modification of Diet in Renal Disease Study. J Am Diet Assoc 95:1307–1312, 1995

372. Sherrard DJ, Hercz G, Pei Y, Maloney NA, Greenwood C, Manuel A, Saiphoo C, Fenton SS, Segre GV: The spectrum of bone disease in end-stage renal failure—An evolving disorder. Kidney Int 43: 436–442, 1993

373. Bushinsky DA: The contribution of acidosis to renal osteodystrophy. Kidney Int 47:1816–1832, 1995

374. Coen G, Manni M, Addari O, Ballanti P, Pasquali M, Chicca S, Mazzaferro S, Mapoletano I, Napoletano I, Sardella D, Bonucci E: Metabolic acidosis and osteodystrophic bone disease in predialysis chronic renal failure: Effect of calcitriol treatment. Miner Electrolyte Metab 21:375–382, 1995

375. Hsu CH: Are we mismanaging calcium and phosphate metabolism in renal failure? Am J Kidney Dis 29:641-649, 1997

376. Sherrard DJ: Control of renal bone disease. Semin Dial 7:284–287, 1994

377. Slatopolsky E, Bricker NS: The role of phosphorus restriction in the prevention of secondary hyperparathyroidism in chronic renal disease. Kidney Int 4:141–145, 1973

378. Kates DM, Sherrard DJ, Andress DL: Evidence that serum phosphate is independently associated with serum PTH in patients with chronic renal failure. Am J Kidney Dis 30:809–813, 1997

379. Llach F, Massry SG: On the mechanism of secondary hyperparathyroidism in moderate renal insufficiency. J Clin Endocrinol Metab 61:601–606, 1985

380. Budisavijevic M, Cheek D, Ploth D: Calciphylaxis in chronic renal failure. J Am Soc Nephrol 7: 978–982, 1996

381. Braun J, Oldendorf M, Moshage W, Heidler R, Zeitler E, Luft FC: Electron beam computed tomography in the evaluation of cardiac calcification in chronic dialysis patients. Am J Kidney Dis 27: 394–401, 1996

382. Andress DL, Maloney NA, Endres DB, Sherrard DJ: Aluminum-associated bone disease in chronic renal failure: High prevalence in a long-term dialysis population. J Bone Miner Res 1:391–398, 1986

383. Ferreira M: Diagnosis of renal osteodystrophy: When and how to use biochemical markers and non-invasive methods: When bone biopsy is needed. Nephrol Dial Transplant 15:S8-S14, 2000 (suppl)

384. Malluche HH, Langub MC, Monier-Faugere MC: The role of bone biopsy in clinical practice and research. Kidney Int 73:S20-S25, 1999 (suppl 73)

385. Slatopolsky E, Brown A, Dusso A: Pathogenesis of secondary hyperparathyroidism. Kidney Int 73: S14-S19, 1999 (suppl 73)

386. Wang M, Hercz G, Sherrard DJ, Maloney NA, Segre GV, Pei Y: Relationship between intact 1–84 parathyroid hormone and bone histomorphometric parameters in dialysis patients without aluminum toxicity. Am J Kidney Dis 26:836–844, 1995

387. Qi Q, Monier-Faugere MC, Geng Z, Malluche HH: Predictive value of serum parathyroid hormone levels for bone turnover in patients on chronic maintenance dialysis. Am J Kidney Dis 26:622–631, 1995

388. Eastwood JB, Bordier PJ, de Wardener HE: Some biochemical, histological, radiological and clinical features of renal osteodystrophy. Kidney Int 4:128–140, 1973

389. Torres A, Lorenzo V, Hernandez D, Rodriguez JC, Concepcion MT, Rodriguez AP, Hernandez A, de Bonis E, Darias E, Gonzalez-Posada JM: Bone disease in predialysis, hemodialysis, and CAPD patients: Evidence of a better bone response to PTH. Kidney Int 47:1434–1442, 1995

390. Slatopolsky E, Finch J, Denda M, Ritter C, Zhong M, Dusso A, MacDonald PN, Brown AJ: Phosphorus restriction prevents parathyroid gland growth. High phosphorus directly stimulates PTH secretion in vitro. J Clin Invest 97:2534–2540, 1996

391. Wilson L, Felsenfeld A, Drezner MK, Llach F: Altered divalent ion metabolism in early renal failure: Role of 1,25(OH)2D. Kidney Int 27:565–573, 1985

392. Hamdy NA, Kanis JA, Beneton MN, Brown CB, Juttmann JR, Jordans JG, Josse S, Meyrier A, Lins RL, Fairey IT: Effect of alfacalcidol on natural course of renal bone disease in mild to moderate renal failure. BMJ 310:358–363, 1995

393. Delmez JA, Slatopolsky E. Hyperphosphatemia: Its consequences and treatment in patients with chronic renal disease. Am J Kidney Dis 19:303–317, 1992

394. Llach F: Hyperphosphatemia in end-stage renal disease patients: Pathophysiological consequences. Kidney Int 73:S31-S37, 1999 (suppl 73)

395. Khosla S, Melton LJ III, Wermers RA, Crowson CS, O'Fallon W, Riggs B: Primary hyperparathyroidism and the risk of fracture: a population-based study. J Bone Miner Res 14:1700–1707, 1999

396. Bruce DG, St John A, Nicklason F, Goldswain PR: Secondary hyperparathyroidism in patients from Western Australia with hip fracture: Relationship to type of hip fracture, renal function, and vitamin D deficiency. J Am Geriatr Soc 47:354–359, 1999

397. Vestergaard P, Mollerup CL, Frokjaer VG, Christiansen P, Blichert-Toft M, Mosekilde L: Cohort study of risk of fracture before and after surgery for primary hyperparathyroidism. BMJ 321:598–602, 2000

398. Atsumi K, Kushida K, Yamazaki K, Shimizu S, Ohmura A, Inoue T: Risk factors for vertebral fractures in renal osteodystrophy. Am J Kidney Dis 33:287–293, 1999

399. Coco M, Rush H: Increased incidence of hip fractures in dialysis patients with low serum parathyroid hormone. Am J Kidney Dis 36:1115–1121, 2000

400. Block GA, Port FK: Re-evaluation of risks associated with hyperphosphatemia and hyperparathyroidism in dialysis patients: recommendations for a change in management. Am J Kidney Dis 35: 1226–1237, 2000

401. Block GA, Hulbert-Shearon TE, Levin NW, Port FK: Association of serum phosphorus and calcium x phosphate product with mortality risk in chronic hemodialysis patients: a national study. Am J Kidney Dis 31:607–617, 1998

402. Lau K: Phosphate excess and progressive renal failure: The precipitation-calcification hypothesis. Kidney Int 36:918–937, 1989

403. Avram MM, Fein PA, Bonomini L, Mittman N, Loutoby R, Avram DK, Chattopadhyay J: Predictors

of survival in continuous ambulatory peritoneal dialysis patients: A five-year prospective study. Perit Dial Int 16:S190-S194, 1996 (suppl 1)

404. Carlstedt F, Lind L, Wide L, Lindahl B, Hanni A, Rastad J, Ljunghall S: Serum levels of parathyroid hormone are related to the mortality and severity of illness in patients in the emergency department. Eur J Clin Invest 27:977–981, 1997

405. Martinez I, Saracho R, Montenegro J, Llach F: The importance of dietary calcium and phosphorous in the secondary hyperparathyroidism of patients with early renal failure. Am J Kidney Dis 29: 496–502, 1997

406. Pitts TO, Piraino BH, Mitro R, Chen TC, Segre GV, Greenberg A, Puschett JB: Hyperparathyroidism and 1,25-dihydroxyvitamin D deficiency in mild, moderate, and severe renal failure. J Clin Endocrin Metab 67:876-881, 1988

407. St John A, Thomas MB, Davies CP, Mullan B, Dick I, Hutchison B, van der SA, Prince RL: Determinants of intact parathyroid hormone and free 1,25-dihydroxyvitamin D levels in mild and moderate renal failure. Nephron 61:422–427, 1992

408. Reichel H, Deibert B, Schmidt-Gayk H, Ritz E: Calcium metabolism in early chronic renal failure: Implications for the pathogenesis of hyperparathyroidism. Nephrol Dial Transplant 6:162–169, 1991

409. von Lilienfeld-Toal H, Gerlach I, Klehr HU, Issa S, Keck E: Immunoreactive parathyroid hormone in early and advanced renal failure. Nephron 31:116–122, 1982

410. Cheung AK, Manolagas SC, Catherwood BD, Mosely CA Jr, Mitas JA, Blantz RC, Deftos LJ: Determinants of serum 1,25(OH)2D levels in renal disease. Kidney Int 24:104–109, 1983

411. Fajtova VT, Sayegh MH, Hickey N, Aliabadi P, Lazarus JM, LeBoff MS: Intact parathyroid hormone levels in renal insufficiency. Calcif Tissue Int 57:329–335, 1995

412. Rix M, Andreassen H, Eskildsen P, Langdahl B, Olgaard K: Bone mineral density and biochemical markers of bone turnover in patients with predialysis chronic renal failure. Kidney Int 56:1084–1093, 1999

413. Yumita S, Suzuki M, Akiba T, Akizawa T, Seino Y, Kurokawa K: Levels of serum 1,25(OH)2D in patients with pre-dialysis chronic renal failure. Tohoku J Exp Med 180:45–56, 1996

414. Christensen MS, Nielsen HE: Parathyroid function after renal transplantation: Interrelationships between renal function, serum calcium and serum parathyroid hormone in normocalcemic long-term survivors. Clin Nephrol 8:472–476, 1977

415. Malluche HH, Ritz E, Lange HP, Kutschera L, Hodgson M, Seiffert U, Schoeppe W: Bone histology in incipient and advanced renal failure. Kidney Int 9:355–362, 1976

416. McGonigle RJ, Wallin JD, Husserl F, Deftos LJ, Rice JC, O'Neill WJ Jr, Fisher JW: Potential role of parathyroid hormone as an inhibitor of erythropoiesis in the anemia of renal failure. J Lab Clin Med 104:1016-1026, 1984

417. Saha H: Calcium and vitamin D homeostasis in patients with heavy proteinuria. Clin Nephrol 41: 290–296, 1994

418. Messa P, Mioni G, Turrin D, Guerra UP: The calcitonin-calcium relation curve and calcitonin secretory parameters in renal patients with variable degrees of renal function. Nephrol Dial Transplant 10: 2259–2265, 1995

419. Tessitore N, Venturi A, Adami S, Roncari C, Rugiu C, Corgnati A, Bonucci E, Maschio G: Relationship between serum vitamin D metabolites and dietary intake of phosphate in patients with early renal failure. Miner Electrolyte Metab 13:38–44, 1987

420. Coen G, Mazzaferro S, Costantini S, Ballanti P, Carrieri MP, Giordano R, Smacchi A, Sardella D, Bonucci E, Taggi E: Bone aluminum content in predialysis chronic renal failure and its relation with secondary hyperparathyroidism and 1,25(OH)2D3 treatment. Miner Electrolyte Metab 15: 295–302, 1989

421. Tougaard L, Sorensen E, Christensen MS, Brochner-Mortensen J, Rodbro P, Sorensen AW: Bone composition and parathyroid function in chronic renal failure. Acta Med Scand 202:33–38, 1977

422. Madsen S, Olgaard K, Ladefoged J: Renal handling of phosphate in relation to serum parathyroid hormone levels. Acta Med Scand 200:7–10, 1976

423. Bedani PL, Tamarozzi R, Pinna L, Gilli P, Perini L, Farinelli A: Early skeletal changes of the hand phalanges in patients with chronic renal failure. Int J Artif Organs 8:325–330, 1985

424. Arata RO, Campos C, Mautalen CA: Effect of parathyroid hormone on bone resorption in uremic patients. Medicina (Mex) 36:113–120, 1976

425. Arnaud CD: Hyperparathyroidism and renal failure. Kidney Int 4:89–95, 1973
426. Reiss E, Canterbury JM, Egdahl RH: Experience with a radioimmunoassay of parathyroid hormone in human sera. Trans Assoc Am Physicians 81:104–115, 1968
427. Massry SG, Coburn JW, Lee DB, Jowsey J, Kleeman CR: Skeletal resistance to parathyroid hormone in renal failure. Studies in 105 human subjects. Ann Intern Med 78:357–364, 1973
428. Slatopolsky E, Robson AM, Elkan I, Bricker NS: Control of phosphate excretion in uremic man. J Clin Invest 47:1865–1874, 1968
429. Coburn JW, Koppel MH, Brickman AS, Massry SG: Study of intestinal absorption of calcium in patients with renal failure. Kidney Int 3:264–272, 1973
430. Coburn JW, Popovtzer MM, Massry SG, Kleeman CR: The physicochemical state and renal handling of divalent ions in chronic renal failure. Arch Intern Med 124:302–311, 1969
431. Ishimura E, Nishizawa Y, Inaba M, Matsumoto N, Emoto M, Kawagishi T, Shoji S, Okuno S, Kim M, Miki T, Morii H: Serum levels of 1,25-dihydroxyvitamin D, 24,25-dihydroxyvitamin D, and 25-hydroxyvitamin D in nondialyzed patients with chronic renal failure. Kidney Int 55:1019–1027, 1999
432. Nielsen SP, Sorensen OH, Lund B, Barenholdt O, Munck O, Pedersen K: Calcium metabolism in patients with chronic non-dialytic renal disease. Calcif Tissue Res 21:202–209, 1976 (suppl)
433. Hutchison AJ, Whitehouse RW, Boulton HF, Adams JE, Mawer EB, Freemont TJ, Gokal R: Correlation of bone histology with parathyroid hormone, vitamin D3, and radiology in end-stage renal disease. Kidney Int 44:1071-1077, 1993
434. Suzuki M, Hirasawa Y: Renal osteodystrophy in early chronic renal failure. Contrib Nephrol 22: 28–38, 1980
435. Coen G, Mazzaferro S, Ballanti P, Sardella D, Chicca S, Manni M, Bonucci E, Taggi F: Renal bone disease in 76 patients with varying degrees of predialysis chronic renal failure: A cross-sectional study. Nephrol Dial Transplant 11:813–819, 1996
436. Madsen S, Olgaard K, Ladefoged J: Degree and course of skeletal demineralization in patients with chronic renal insufficiency. Scand J Urol Nephrol 12:243–249, 1978
437. Local Medicare Review Policy Website. Website: www.lmrp.net, 6/26/01
438. Burn DJ, Bates D: Neurology and the kidney. J Neurol Neurosurg Psychiatry 65:810–821, 1998
439. Fraser C, Arieff A: Nervous system manifestations of renal failure, in Schrier RW, Gottschalk CW (ed): Diseases of the Kidney. Boston, MA, Little, Brown, 1993, pp 2804–2809
440. Bazzi C, Pagani C, Sorgato G, Albonico G, Fellin G, D'Amico G: Uremic polyneuropathy: A clinical and electrophysiological study in 135 short- and long-term hemodialyzed patients. Clin Nephrol 35: 176–181, 1991
441. Wetter TC, Stiasny K, Kohnen R, Oertel WH, Trenkwalder C: Polysomnographic sleep measures in patients with uremic and idiopathic restless legs syndrome. Mov Disord 13:820–824, 1998
442. Weinrauch LA, D'Elia JA, Gleason RE, Keough J, Mann D, Kennedy FP: Autonomic function in type I diabetes mellitus complicated by nephropathy. A cross-sectional analysis in the presymptomatic phase. Am J Hypertens 8:782–789, 1995
443. Campese VM, Romoff MS, Levitan D, Lane K, Massry SG: Mechanisms of autonomic nervous system dysfunction in uremia. Kidney Int 20:246–253, 1981
444. Sterner NG, Nilsson H, Rosen U, Lilja B, Sundkvist G: Relationships among glomerular filtration rate, albuminuria, and autonomic nerve function in insulin-dependent and non-insulin-dependent diabetes mellitus. J Diabetes Complications 11:188–193, 1997
445. Di Paolo B, Cappelli P, Spisni C, Albertazzi A, Rossini PM, Marchionno L, Gambi D: New electrophysiological assessments for the early diagnosis of encephalopathy and peripheral neuropathy in chronic uraemia. Int J Tissue React 4:301–307, 1982
446. Savazzi GM, Migone L, Cambi V: The influence of glomerular filtration rate on uremic polyneuropathy. Clin Nephrol 13:64–72, 1980
447. Goel MK, Gulati PD, Janki S, Ram SR, Raina V, Rizvi SN: Observations on peripheral neuropathy in chronic uraemics. J Assoc Physicians India 26:341–346, 1978
448. Nielsen VK: The peripheral nerve function in chronic renal failure. VI. The relationship betweeen sensory and motor nerve conduction and kidney function, azotemia, age, sex, and clinical neuropathy. Acta Med Scand 194:455–462, 1973
449. Knoll O, Dierker E: Detection of uremic neuropathy by reflex response latency. J Neurol Sci 47: 305–312, 1980

450. Teschan PE, Ginn HE, Bourne JR, Ward JW, Hamel B, Nunnally JC, Musso M, Vaughn WK: Quantitative indices of clinical uremia. Kidney Int 15:676–697, 1979

451. Savazzi GM: Nerve conduction times in uremia. Int J Artif Organs 4:211–212, 1981

452. Kutner NG: Assessing end-stage renal disease patients' functioning and well-being: measurement approaches and implications for clinical practice. Am J Kidney Dis 24:321–333, 1994

453. Tarlov AR, Ware JE Jr, Greenfield S, Nelson EC, Perrin E, Zubkoff M: The Medical Outcomes Study. An application of methods for monitoring the results of medical care. JAMA 262:925–930, 1989

454. Rettig RA, Sadler JH, Meyer KB, Wasson JH, Parkerson GR Jr, Kantz B, Hays RD, Patrick DL: Assessing health and quality of life outcomes in dialysis: A report on an Institute of Medicine workshop. Am J Kidney Dis 30:140–155, 1997

455. DeOreo PB: Hemodialysis patient-assessed functional health status predicts continued survival, hospitalization, and dialysis-attendance compliance. Am J Kidney Dis 30:204–212, 1997

456. Johansen KL: Physical functioning and exercise capacity in patients on dialysis. Adv Renal Repl Ther 6:141–148, 1999

457. Kutner NG, Cardenas DD, Bower JD: Rehabilitation, aging and chronic renal disease. Am J Phys Med Rehabil 71:97–101, 1992

458. Ifudu O, Mayers J, Matthew J, Tan CC, Cambridge A, Friedman EA: Dismal rehabilitation in geriatric inner-city hemodialysis patients. JAMA 271:29–33, 1994

459. Harris LE, Luft FC, Rudy DW, Tierney WM: Clinical correlates of functional status in patients with chronic renal insufficiency. Am J Kidney Dis 21:161–166, 1993

460. Bardage C, Isacson DG: Hypertension and health-related quality of life. An epidemiological study in Sweden. J Clin Epidemiol 54:172–181, 2001

461. Hall SE, Criddle RA, Comito TL, Prince RL: A case-control study of quality of life and functional impairment in women with long-standing vertebral osteoporotic fracture. Osteoporos Int 9:508–515, 1999

462. Schneider SM, Pouget I, Staccini P, Rampal P, Hebuterne X: Quality of life in long-term home enteral nutrition patients. Clin Nutr 19:23–28, 2000

463. Ahroni JH, Boyko EJ: Responsiveness of the SF-36 among veterans with diabetes mellitus. J Diabetes Complications 14:31–39, 2000

464. Beusterien KM, Nissenson AR, Port FK, Kelly M, Steinwald B, Ware JE: The effects of recombinant human erythropoietin on functional health and well-being in chronic dialysis patients. J Am Soc Nephrol 7:763–773, 1996

465. Revicki DA, Brown RE, Feeny DH, Henry DA, Teehan BP, Rudnick MR, Benz RL: Health-related quality of life associated with recombinant human erythropoietin therapy for predialysis chronic renal disease patients. Am J Kidney Dis 25:548–554, 1995

466. Eschbach JW, Abdulhadi MH, Browne JK, Delano BG, Downing MR, Egrie JC, Evans RW, Friedman EA, Graber SE, Haley NR: Recombinant human erythropoietin in anemic patients with end-stage renal disease. Results of a phase III multicenter clinical trial. Ann Intern Med 111:992–1000, 1989

467. Evans RW, Rader B, Manninen DL: The quality of life of hemodialysis recipients treated with recombinant human erythropoietin. Cooperative Multicenter EPO Clinical Trial Group. JAMA 263:825–330, 1990

468. Morena F, Aracil F, Perez R, Valderrabano F: Controlled study on the improvement of quality of life in elderly hemodialysis patients after correcting end-stage renal disease-related anemia. Am J Kidney Dis 27:548-556, 1996

469. Rocco MV, Gassman JJ, Wang SR, Kaplan RM: Cross-sectional study of quality of life and symptoms in chronic renal disease patients: The Modification of Diet in Renal Disease Study. Am J Kidney Dis 29:888–896, 1997

470. Korevaar JC, Jansen MA, Merkus MP, Dekker FW, Boeschoten EW, Krediet RT: Quality of life in predialysis end-stage renal disease patients at the initiation of dialysis therapy. The NECOSAD Study Group. Perit Dial Int 20:69–75, 2000

471. Shidler NR, Peterson RA, Kimmel PL: Quality of life and psychosocial relationships in patients with chronic renal insufficiency. Am J Kidney Dis 32:557–566, 1998

472. Klang B, Bjorvell H, Clyne N: Quality of life in predialytic uremic patients. Qual Life Res 5:109–116, 1996

473. Fujisawa M, Ichikawa Y, Yoshiya K, Isotani S, Higuchi A, Nagano S, Arakawa S, Hamami G,

Matsumoto O, Kamidono S: Assessment of health-related quality of life in renal transplant and hemo-dialysis patients using the SF-36 health survey. Urology 56:201–206, 2000

474. Griep MI, Van der Niepen P, Sennesael JJ, Mets TF, Massart DL, Verbeelen DL: Odour perception in chronic renal disease. Nephrol Dial Transplant 12:2093–2098, 1997

475. Sacks CR, Peterson RA, Kimmel PL: Perception of illness and depression in chronic renal disease. Am J Kidney Dis 15:31–39, 1990

476. Manninen DL, Evans RW, Dugan MK: Work disability, functional limitations, and the health status of kidney transplantation recipients posttransplant. Clin Transplant 5:193–203, 1991

477. Churchill DN, Torrance GW, Taylor DW, Barnes CC, Ludwin D, Shimizu A, Smith EKM: Measurement of quality of life in end-stage renal disease: the time trade-off approach. Clin Invest Med 10:14–20, 1987

478. Black SA, Goodwin JS, Markides KS: The association between chronic diseases and depressive symptomatology in older Mexican Americans. J Gerontol Series A Biol Sci Med Sci 53:M188-M194, 1998

479. Cagney KA, Wu AW, Fink NE, Jenckes MW, Meyer KB, Bass EB, Powe NR: Formal literature review of quality of llife instruments used in end stage renal disease. Am J Kidney Dis 36:327–336, 2000

480. Hunsicker LG, Adler S, Caggiula A, England BK, Greene T, Kusek JW, Rogers NL, Teschan PE: Predictors of the progression of renal disease in the Modification of Diet in Renal Disease Study. Kidney Int 51:1908–1919, 1997

481. Pei Y, Cattran D, Greenwood C: Predicting chronic renal insufficiency in idiopathic membranous glomerulonephritis. Kidney Int 42:960–966, 1992

482. Chitalia VC, Wells JE, Robson RA, Searle M, Lynn KL: Predicting renal survival in primary focal glomerulosclerosis from the time of presentation. Kidney Int 56:2236–2242, 1999

483. Levey AS: Nephrology Forum: Measurement of renal function in chronic renal disease. Kidney Int 38:167-184, 1990

484. Walser M: Progression of chronic renal failure in man. Kidney Int 37:1195–1210, 1990

485. Mitch WE, Walser M, Buffington GA, Lemann J: A simple method of estimating progression of chronic renal failure. Lancet 2:1326–1328, 1976

486. Rekola S, Bergstrand A, Bucht H: Deterioration of GFR in IgA nephropathy as measured by 51Cr-EDTA clearance. Kidney Int 40:1050–1054, 1991

487. Austin SM, Lieberman JS, Newton LD, Mejia M, Peters WA, Myers BD: Slope of serial glomerular filtration rate and the progression of diabetic glomerular disease. J Am Soc Nephrol 3:1358–1370, 1993

488. Dillon JJ: The quantitative relationship between treated blood pressure and progression of diabetic renal disease. Am J Kidney Dis 22:798–802, 1993

489. Gall MA, Nielsen FS, Smidt UM, Parving HH: The course of kidney function in type 2 (non-insulin-dependent) diabetic patients with diabetic nephropathy. Diabetologia 36:1071–1078, 1993

490. Hannedouche T, Albouze G, Chauveau P, Lacour B, Jungers P: Effects of blood pressure and antihy-pertensive treatment on progression of advanced chronic renal failure. Am J Kidney Dis 21:131–137, 1993

491. Biesenbach G, Janko O, Zazgornik J: Similar rate of progression in the predialysis phase in type I and type II diabetes mellitus. Nephrol Dial Transplant 9:1097–1102, 1994

492. Levey AS, Adler S, Caggiula A, England BK, Greene T, Hunsicker L, Kusek JW, Rogers NL, Teschan PE: Effects of dietary protein restriction on the progression of moderate renal disease in the MDRD Study. J Am Soc Nephrol 7:2626-2625, 1996

494. Yip JW, Jones SL, Wiseman MJ, Hill C, Viberti G: Glomerular hyperfiltration in the prediction of nephropathy in IDDM: A 10-year follow-up study. Diabetes 45:1729–1733, 1996

495. Ellis D, Lloyd C, Becker DJ, Forrest KY, Orchard TJ: The changing course of diabetic nephropathy: Low-density lipoprotein cholesterol and blood pressure correlate with regression of proteinuria. Am J Kidney Dis 27:809–818, 1996

496. Baboolal K, Evans C, Moore RH: Incidence of end-stage renal disease in medically treated patients with severe bilateral atherosclerotic renovascular disease. Am J Kidney Dis 31:971–977, 1998

497. Berrut G, Bouhanick B, Fabbri P, Guilloteau G, Bled F, Le Jeune JJ, Fressinaud P, Marre M: Microalbu-minuria as a predictor of a drop in glomerular filtration rate in subjects with non-insulin-dependent diabetes mellitus and hypertension. Clin Nephrol 48:92–97, 1997

498. Nielsen S, Schmitz A, Rehling M, Mogensen CE: The clinical course of renal function in NIDDM patients with normo- and microalbuminuria. J Intern Med 241:133–141, 1997

499. Massy ZA, Khoa TN, Lacour B, Descamps-Latscha B, Man NK, Jungers P: Dyslipidaemia and the progression of renal disease in chronic renal failure patients. Nephrol Dial Transplant 14: 2392–2397, 1999

500. Ruggenenti P, Perna A, Zoccali C, Gherardi G, Benini R, Testa A, Remuzzi G: Chronic proteinuric nephropathies. II. Outcomes and response to treatment in a prospective cohort of 352 patients: Differences between women and men in relation to the ACE gene polymorphism. Gruppo Italiano di Studi Epidemologici in Nefrologia (GISEN). J Am Soc Nephrol 11:88–96, 2000

501. Hannedouche T, Chauveau P, Kalou F, Albouze G, Lacour B, Jungers P: Factors affecting progression in advanced chronic renal failure. Clin Nephrol 39:312–320, 1993

502. Shah BV, Levey AS: Spontaneous changes in the rate of decline in reciprocal serum creatinine: Errors in predicting the progression of renal disease from extrapolation of the slope. J Am Soc Nephrol 2: 1186–1191, 1992

503. Levey AS, Greene T, Beck GJ, Caggiula AW, Kusek JW, Hunsicker LG, Klahr S: Dietary protein restriction and the progression of chronic renal disease: What have all the results of the MDRD Study shown? J Am Soc Nephrol 10:2426–2439, 1999

504. Mitch WE: Nephrology Forum: Dietary protein restriction in patients with chronic renal failure. Kidney Int 40:326–341, 1991

505. Biesenbach G, Zazgornik J: High mortality and poor quality of life during predialysis period in type II diabetic patients with diabetic nephropathy. Ren Fail 16:263–272, 1994

506. Bakris GL, Copley JB, Vicknair N, Sadler R, Leurgans S: Calcium channel blockers versus other antihypertensive therapies on progression of NIDDM associated nephropathy. Kidney Int 50: 1641–1650, 1996

507. Bakris GL, Mangrum A, Copley JB, Vicknair N, Sadler R: Effect of calcium channel or beta-blockade on the progression of diabetic nephropathy in African Americans. Hypertension 1997:744–750, 1997

508. Hovind P, Rossing P, Tarnow L, Smidt UM, Parving HH: Progression of diabetic nephropathy. Kidney Int 59:702–709, 2001

509. US Renal Data System. USRDS 1999 Annual Data Report. Bethesda, MD, National Institutes of Health, National Institute of Diabetes and Digestive and Kidney Diseases, 1999

510. Shulman NB, Ford CE, Hall WD, Blaufox MD, Simon D, Langford HG, Schneider KA: Prognostic value of serum creatinine and effect of treatment of hypertension on renal function. Results from the hypertension detection and follow-up program. The Hypertension Detection and Follow-up Program Cooperative Group. Hypertension 13:I80-I93, 1989

511. Walker WG: Hypertension-related renal injury: A major contributor to end-stage renal disease. Am J Kidney Dis 22:164–173, 1993 (erratum 22:626, 1993)

512. Krop JS, Coresh J, Chambless LE, Shahar E, Watson RL, Szklo M, Brancati FL: A community-based study of explanatory factors for the excess risk for early renal function decline in blacks vs whites with diabetes: The Atherosclerosis Risk in Communities study. Arch Intern Med 159:1777–1783, 1999

513. Breyer JA, Bain RP, Evans JK, Nahman NS Jr, Lewis EJ, Cooper M, McGill J, Berl T: Predictors of the progression of renal insufficiency in patients with insulin-dependent diabetes and overt diabetic nephropathy. The Collaborative Study Group. Kidney Int 50:1651–1658, 1996

514. Klein R, Klein BE, Moss SE, Cruickshanks KJ, Brazy PC: The 10-year incidence of renal insufficiency in people with type 1 diabetes. Diabetes Care 22:743–751, 1999

515. Samuelsson O, Attman PO, Knight-Gibson C, Larsson R, Mulec H, Wedel H, Weiss L, Alaupovic P: Plasma levels of lipoprotein (a) do not reflect progression of human chronic renal failure. Nephrol Dial Transplant 11:2237–2243, 1996

516. Nakano S, Ogihara M, Tamura C, Kitazawa M, Nishizawa M, Kigoshi T, Uchida K: Reversed circadian blood pressure rhythm independently predicts endstage renal failure in non-insulin-dependent diabetes mellitus subjects. J Diab Comp 13:224–231, 1999

517. Samuelsson O, Mulec H, Knight-Gibson C, Attman PO, Kron B, Larsson R, Weiss L, Wedel H, Alaupovic P: Lipoprotein abnormalities are associated with increased rate of progression of human chronic renal insufficiency. Nephrol Dial Transplant 12:1908–1915, 1997

518. Ruggenenti P, Gambara V, Perna A, Bertani T, Remuzzi G: The nephrology of non-insulin-dependent

diabetes: Predictors of outcome relative to diverse patterns of renal injury. J Am Soc Nephrol 9: 2336–2343, 1998

519. Tu WH, Petitti DB, Biava CG, Tulunay O, Hopper J Jr: Membranous nephropathy: Predictors of terminal renal failure. Nephron 36:118–124, 1984

520. Toth T, Takebayashi S: Factors contributing to the outcome in 100 adult patients with idiopathic membranous glomerulonephritis. Int Urol Nephrol 26:93–106, 1994

521. Jacobsen S, Starklint H, Petersen J, Ullman S, Junker P, Voss A, Rasmussen JM, Tarp U, Poulsen LH, van Overeem Hansen G, Skaarup B, Hansen TM: Prognostic value of renal biopsy and clinical variables in patients with lupus nephritis and normal serum creatinine. Scand J Rheumatol 28: 288–299, 1999

522. Ravid M, Brosh D, Ravid-Safran D, Levy Z, Rachmani R: Main risk factors for nephropathy in type 2 diabetes mellitus are plasma cholesterol levels, mean blood pressure, and hyperglycemia. Arch Intern Med 158:998–1004, 1998

523. Rosman JB, Langer K, Brandl M, Piers-Becht TP, van der Hem GK, ter Wee PM, Donker AJ: Protein-restricted diets in chronic renal failure: A four year follow-up shows limited indications. Kidney Int 27:S96-S102, 1989 (suppl 27)

524. Locatelli F, Alberti D, Graziani G, Buccianti G, Redaelli B, Giangrande A: Prospective, randomised, multicentre trial of effect of protein restriction on progression of chronic renal insufficiency. Northern Italian Cooperative Study Group. Lancet 337:1299–1304, 1991

525. Yokoyama H, Tomonaga O, Hirayama M, Ishii A, Takeda M, Babazono T, Ujihara U, Takahashi C, Omori V: Predictors of the progression of diabetic nephropathy and the beneficial effect of angiotensin-converting enzyme inhibitors in NIDDM patients. Diabetologia 40:405–411, 1997

526. Standards of Medical Care for Patients with Diabetes Mellitus, Position Statement. Clinical Practice Recommendations 2001. Diabetes Care 24:S33-S43, 2001 (suppl 1)

527. Diabetic Nephropathy, Position Statement. Clinical Practice Recommendations 2001, www.diabetes.org/clinicalrecommendations/Supplement101/S69.htm, 6/26/01

528. The Diabetes Control and Complications Trial Research Group: The effect of intensive treatment of diabetes on the development and progression of long-term complications in insulin-dependent diabetes mellitus. N Engl J Med 329:977–986, 1993

529. Microalbuminuria Collaborative Study Group, United Kingdom: Intensive therapy and progression to clinical albuminuria in patients with insulin dependent diabetes mellitus and microalbuminuria. BMJ 311:973–977, 1995

530. United Kingdom Prospective Diabetes Study Group: UK Prospective Diabetes Study 33: Intensive blood glucose control with sulphonylureas or insulin compared with conventional treatment and risk of complications in patients with type 2 diabetes. Lancet 352:837–853, 1998

531. Ohkubo Y, Kishikawa H, Araki E, Miyata T, Isami S, Motoyoshi S, Kojima Y, Furuyoshi N, Shichiri M: Intensive insulin therapy prevents the progression of diabetic microvascular complications in Japanese patients with non-insulin-dependent diabetes mellitus: A randomized prospective 6-year study. Diabetes Res Clin Pract 28:103–117, 1995

532. Gaede PV, Vedel P, Parving HH, Pedersen O: Intensified multifactorial intervention in patients with type 2 diabetes mellitus and microalbuminuria: The Steno type 2 randomised study. Lancet 353: 617–622, 1999

533. National High Blood Pressure Education Program Working Group on Hypertension Control in Children and Adolescents: Update on the 1987 Task Force Report on High Blood Pressure in Children and Adolescents: A working group report from the National High Blood Pressure Education Program. Pediatrics 98:649–658, 1996

534. Brown MJ, Palmer CR, Casaigne A, de Leeuw PW, Mancia G, Rosenthal T, Ruilope LM: Morbidity and mortality in patients randomised to double-blind treatment wit a long-acting calcium-channel blocker or diuretic the International Nifedipine GITS Study: Intervention as a Goal in Hypertension Treatment (INSIGHT). Lancet 356:366-372, 2000

535. Hansson L, Lindholm LH, Ekbom T, Dahlof B, Lanke J, Schersen B, Wester P-O, Hedner T, de Faire U: STOP-Hypertension-2 Study Group. Randomised trial of old and new antihypertensive drugs in elderly patients: Cardiovascular Mortality and Mrobidity in the Swedish Trial in Old Patients with Hypertension-2 Study. Lancet 354:1751–1756, 1999

536. Parving HH: Diabetic hypertensive patients. Is this a group in need of particular care and attention? Diabetes Care 22:B76-B79, 1999 (suppl 2)

537. UK Prospective Diabetes Study Group: Tight blood pressure control and risk of macrovascular and microvascular complications in type 2 diabetes. BMJ 317:703–713, 1998

538. Hansson L, Zanchetti A, Carruthers SG, Bahlof B, Elmsfeldt D, Julius S, Menard J, Rahn KH, Wedel H, Westerling S: Effects of intensive blood pressure lowering a low-dose aspirin in patients with hypertension: Principal results of the Hypertension Optimal Treatment (HOT) randomized trial. The HOT Study Group. Lancet 351:1755–1762, 1998

539. Ruggenenti P, Remuzzi G: Angiotensin-converting enzyme inhibitor therapy for nondiabetic progressive renal diseas. Curr Opin Nephrol Hypertens 6:489–495, 1997

540. Weir MR, Dworkin L: Antihypertensive drugs, dietary salt, and renal protection: How low should you go with which therapy? Am J Kidney Dis 32:1–22, 1998

541. Lewis EJ, Hunsicker LG, Clarke WR, Berl T, Pohl MA, Lewis JB, Ritz E, Atkins RC, et al: Renoprotective effect of the angiotensin-receptor antagonist irbesartan in patients with nephropathy due to type 2 diabetes. N Engl J Med 345:851–860, 2001

542. Brenner BM, Cooper ME, de Zeeuw D, Keane WF, Mitch WE, Parving H-H, Remuzzi G, Snappinn SM, Zhang Z, Shahinfav S: The RENAAL Study Investigators. Effects of losartan on renal and cardiovascular outcomes in patients with type 2 diabetes and nephropathy. N Engl J Med 345:861–869, 2001

543. Estacio ROM, Jeffers BW, Hiatt WR, Biggerstaff SL, Gifford N, Schrier RW: The effect of nisoldipine as compared with enalapril on cardiovascular outcomes in patients with non-insulin-dependent diabetes and hypertension. N Engl J Med 338:645–652, 1998

544. Hansson L, Lindholm LH, Niskanen L, Lanke J, Hedner T, Niklason A, Luomanmaki K, Dahlof B, de Faire U, Morlin C, Karlberg BE, Wester PO, Bjorck J: Effect of angiotensin-converting-enzyme inhibition compared with conventional therapy on cardiovascular morbidity and mortality in hypertension: The Captopril Prevention Project (CAPPP) randomised trial. Lancet 353:611–616, 1999

545. Yusuf S, Sleigh P, Pogue J, Bosch J, Davies R, Dagenais G: Effects of an angiotensin-converting-enzyme inhibitor, ramipril, on cardiovascular events in high-risk patients. The Heart Outcomes Prevention Evaluation Study Investigators. N Engl J Med 342:143–153, 2000

546. Jafar TH, Schmid CH, Landa M, Giatras I, Toto RDA, Remuzzi G, Maschio G, Brenner BM, et al, for the AIPRD Study Group: Angiotensin-converting enzyme inhibitors and the progression of nondiabetic renal disease: A meta-analysis of patient level data. Ann Intern Med 135:73–87, 2001

547. Agodoa LY, Appel L, Bakris GL, Beck GJ, Bourgoignie JJM, Briggs JP, Charleston J, Cheek D, Cleveland W, Douglas JG, Douglas M, Dowie D, Faulkner M, Gabriel A, Gassman J, Greene T, Hall Y, Hebert L, Hiremath L, Jamerson K, Johnson CJ, Kopple J, Kusek J, Lash J, Lea J, Lewis JB, Lipkowitz M, Massry S, Middleton J, Miller ER 3rd, Norris K, O'Connor D, Ojo A, Phillips RA, Pogue V, Rahman M, Randall OS, Rostand S, Schulman G, Smith W, Thornley-Brown D, Tisher CC, Toto RD, Wright JT Jr, Xu S: African American Study of Kidney Disease and Hypertension (AASK) Study Group. Effect of ramipril vs amlodipine on renal outcomes in hypertensive nephrosclerosis: A randomized controlled trial. JAMA 285:2719–2728, 2001

548. Teschan PE, Beck GJ, Dwyer JT, Greene T, Klahr S, Levey AS, Mitch WE, Snetselaar LG, et al: Effect of a ketoacid-aminoacid-supplemented very low protein diet on the progression of advanced renal disease: A reanalysis of the MDRD feasibility study. Clin Nephrol 50:273–283, 1998

549. Pedrini MT, Levey AS, Lau JY, Chalmers TC, Wang PH: The effect of dietary protein restriction on the progression of diabetic and nondiabetic renal diseases: A meta-analysis. Ann Intern Med 124:627–632, 1996

550. Kasiske BL, Lakatua JD, Ma JZ, Louis TA: A meta-analysis of the effects of dietary protein restriction on the rate of decline in renal function. Am J Kidney Dis 31:954–961, 1998

551. Krolewski AS, Warram JHG, Christlieb AR: Hypercholesterolemia — A determinant of renal function loss and deaths in IDDM patients with nephropathy. Kidney Int 45:S125-S131, 1994 (suppl 45)

552. Mäntäri M, Tiula E, Alikoski T, Manninen V: Effects of hypertension and dyslipidemia on the decline in renal function. Hypertension 26:670–675, 1995

553. Gall MA, Hougaard P, Borch-Johnsen K, Parving H-H: Risk factors for development of incipient and overt diabetic nephropathy in patients with non-insulin dependent diabetes mellitus: Prospective, observational study. BMJ 314:783–788, 1997

554. Muntner PM, Coresh J, Smith JC, Eckfeldt J, Klag MJ: Plasma lipids and risk of developing renal dysfunction: The atherosclerosis risk in communities study. Kidney Int 58:293–301, 2000

555. Scanferla F, Toffoletto PP, Roncali D, Bazzato G: Associated effect of hepatic hydroxymethylglutaryl

coenzyme A reductase + angiotensin converting enzyme inhibitors on the progression of renal failure in hypertensive subjects. Am J Hypertens 4:868, 1991

556. Hommel E, Andersen P, Gall M-A, Nielsen FSA, Jensen BSS, Rossing P: Plasma lipoproteins and renal function during simvastatin treatment in diabetic nephropathy. Diabetologia 35:447–451, 1992

557. Nielsen S, Schmitz O, Moller N, Porksen N, Klausen IC, Alberti KGMM: Renal function and insulin sensitivity during simvastatin treatment in type 2 (non-insulin-dependent) diabetic patients with micro-albuminuria. Diabetologia 36:1079–1086, 1993

558. Thomas ME, Harris KP, Ramaswamy C, Hattersley JM, Wheeler DC, Varghese Z, Williams JD, Walls J, Moorhead JF: Simvastatin therapy for hypercholesterolemic patients with nephrotic syndrome or significant proteinuria. Kidney Int 44:1124–1129, 1993

559. Aranda Arcas JL, Sanchez RAM, Guijarro C, Araque A, Pulido F, Praga M, Damiano A: [Effect of pravastatin on hypercholesterolemia associated with proteinuria]. Ann Med Interna 11:523–527, 1994

560. Lam KSL, Cheng IKP, Janus ED, Pang RWC: Cholesterol-lowering therapy may retard the progression of diabetic nephropathy. Diabetologia 38:604–609, 1995

561. Rayner BL, Byrne MJ, van Zyl Smit R: A prospective clinical trial comparing the treatment of idiopathic membranous nephropathy and nephrotic syndrome with simvastatin and diet, versus diet alone. Clin Nephrol 46:219-224, 1996

562. Smulders YMR, Van Eeden AE, Stehouwer CDA, Weijers RNM, Slaats EH, Silberbusch J: Can reduction in hypertriglyceridemia slow progression of microalbuminuria in patients with non-insulin-dependent diabetes mellitus? Eur J Clin Invest 27:997–1002, 1997

563. Tonolo G, Ciccarese M, Brizzi P, Puddu L, Secchi G, Calvia P: Reduction of albumin excretion rate in normotensive microalbumiuric type 2 diabetic pateints during long-term simvastatin treatment. Diabetes Care 20:1891–1895, 1997

564. Olbricht CJ, Wanner C, Thiery J, Basten A: Simvastatin in Nephrotic Syndrome Study Group. Simvastatin in nephrotic syndrome. Kidney Int 71:S113-S166, 1999

565. Nishimura M, Sasaki T, Oishi A, Oishi M, Kono S, Toya Y: Angiotensin converting enzyme inhibitor and probucol suppress time-dependent increase in urinary type IV collagen excretion of NIDDM with early nephropathy. J Am Soc Nephrol 10:131A, 1999 (abstr)

566. Buemi M, Allegra A, Corica F, Aloisi C, Giacobbe M, Pettinato G: Effect of fluvastatin on proteinuria in patients with immunoglobulin A nephropathy. Clin Pharmacol Ther 64:427–431, 2000

567. Fried LF, Orchard TJ, Kasiske BL: The effect of lipid reduction on renal disease progression: A meta-analysis. Kidney Int 59:260–269, 2001

568. Albertazzi A, Di Liberato L, Daniele F, Battistel V, Colombi L: Efficacy and tolerability of recombinant human erythropoietin treatment in pre-dialysis patients: Results of a multicenter study. Int J Artif Organs 21:12–18, 1998

569. Jungers P, Choukroun G, Oualim Z, Robino C, Nguyen AT, Man NK: Beneficial influence of recombinant human erythropoietin therapy on the rate of progression of chronic renal failure in predialysis patients. Nephrol Dial Transplant 16:307–312, 2001

570. Stoves J, Inglis H, Newstead CG: A randomized study of oral vs intravenous iron supplementation in patients with progressive renal insufficiency treated with erythropoietin. Nephrol Dial Transplant 18:967–974, 2001

571. Silverberg DS, Blum M, Agbaria Z, Deutsch V, Irony M, Schwartz D, Baruch R, Yachnin T, Steinbruch S, Iaina A: The effect of i.v. iron alone or in combination with low-dose erythropoietin in the rapid correction of anemia of chronic renal failure in the predialysis period. Clin Nephrol 55:212–219, 2001

572. Thadhani R, Pascual M, Bonventre JV: Acute renal failure. N Engl J Med 334:1448–1460, 1996

573. Adcox MJ, Collins B, Zager RA: The differential diagnosis of acute renal failure. Contemp Issues Nephrol 25:73–77, 1992

574. Perna A, Remuzzi G: Abnormal permeability to proteins and glomerular lesions: A meta-analysis of experimental and human studies. Am J Kidney Dis 27:34–41, 1996

575. Decker T, Kofoed-Enevoldsen A, Norgaard K, Borch-Johnsen K, Feldt-Rasmussen B, Jensen T: Microalbuminuria: Implications for micro and macrovascular disease. Diabetes Care 15:1181–1191, 1992

576. Nelson RG, Knowler WC, Pettitt DJ, Bennett PH: Kidney Disease in Diabetes: Diabetes in America

(ed 2). Washington, DC, National Diabetes Data Group, US Department of Health and Human Services, 1995, pp 349–400

577. Report and recommendations of the San Antonio Conference on Diabetic Neuropathy. Diabetes 37: 1000–1004, 1988

578. Mogensen CE: Microalbuminuria predicts clinical proteinuria and early mortality in maturity-onset diabetes. N Engl J Med 310:356–360, 1984

579. Jarrett RJ, Viberti GC, Argyropoulos A, Hill RD, Mahmud U, Murrells TJ: Microalbuminuria predicts mortality in non-insulin-dependent diabetes. Diabet Med 1:17–19, 1984

580. Jensen T, Borch-Johnsen K, Kofoed-Enevoldsen A, Deckert T: Coronary heart disease in young type 1 (insulin-dependent) diabetic patients with and without diabetic nephropathy: Incidence and risk factors. Diabetologia 144–148, 1987

581. Gall MA: Albuminuria in non-insulin-dependent diabetes mellitus. Prevalence, causes, and consequences. Dan Med Bull 44:465–485, 1997

582. Deckert T, Kofoed-Enevoldsen A, Norgaard K, Borch-Johnsen K, Feldt-Rasmussen B, Jensen T: Microalbuminuria: Implications for micro and macrovascular disease. Diabetes Care 15:1181–1191, 1992

583. Mogensen CE, Damsgaard EM, Froland A, Nielsen S, de Fine Olivarius N, Schmitz A: Microalbuminuria in non-insulin-dependent diabetes. Clin Nephrol 38:528–538, 1992

584. Gilbert RE, Cooper ME, McNally PC, O'Brien RC, Toft J, Jerums G: Microalbuminuria: Prognostic and therapeutic implications in diabetes mellitus. Diabetes Med 11:636–645, 1994

585. Alzaid AA: Microalbuminuria in patients with NIDDM: An overview. Diabetes Care 19:79–89, 1996

586. Dinneen SF, Gerstein HC: The association of microalbuminuria and mortality in non-insulin-dependent diabetes mellitus. A systematic overview of the literature. Arch Intern Med 157:1413–1418, 1997

587. Viberti GC, Yip-Messent J, Morocutti A: Diabetic nephropathy. Future avenue. Diabetes Care 15: 1216–1225, 1992

588. Orchard TJ, Stevens LK, Forrest KY-Z, Fuller JH: Cardiovascular disease in insulin-dependent diabetes mellitus: Similar rates but different risk factors in the US compared with Europe. Int J Epidemiol 27: 976–983, 1998

589. Epstein M, Parving HH, Ruilope LM: Surrogate endpoints and renal protection: Focus on microalbuminuria. Blood Press Suppl 2:52–57, 1997

590. Stehouwer CD, Donker AJ: Clinical usefulness of measurement of urinary albumin excretion in diabetes mellitus. Neth J Med 42:175–186, 1993

591. Panayiotou BN: Microalbuminuria: Pathogenesis, prognosis and management. J Int Med Res 22: 181–201, 1994

592. de Cotret PR: Relationships among diabetes, microalbuminuria, and ACE inhibition. J Cardiovasc Pharmacol 32:S9-S17, 1998 (suppl 2)

593. McKenna K, Thompson C: Microalbuminuria: A marker to increased renal and cardiovascular risk in diabetes mellitus. Scott Med J 42:99–104, 1997

594. Mogensen CE: Microalbuminuria, blood pressure and diabetic renal disease: Origin and development of ideas. Diabetologia 42:263–285, 1999

595. Poirier SJ: Preserving the diabetic kidney. J Fam Pract 46:21–27, 1998

596. Feldt-Rasmussen B, Borch-Johnsen K, Deckert T, Jensen G, Jensen JS: Microalbuminuria: An important diagnostic tool. J Diabetes Complications 8:137–145, 1994

597. Stephenson JM, Kenny S, Stevens LK, Fuller JH, Lee EJ: Proteinuria and mortality in diabetes: The WHO Multinational Study of Vascular Disease in Diabetes. Diabetes Med 12:149–155, 1994

598. Lee K-U, Park JY, Kim SW, Lee MII, Kim GS, Park S-K, Park J-S: Prevalence and associated features of albuminuria in Koreans with NIDDM. Diabetes Care 18:793–799, 1995

599. John L, Rao PSSS, Kanagasabapathy AS. Prevalence of diabetic nephropathy in non-insulin dependent diabetics. Indian J Med Res 94:24–29, 1991

600. Howard BV, Lee ET, Cowan LD, Fabsitz RR, Howard WJ, Oopik AJ, Robbins DC, Savage PJ, Yeh JL, Welty TK: Coronary heart disease prevalence and its relation to risk factors in American Indians. The Strong Heart Study. Am Epidemiol 142:254–268, 1995

601. Nelson RG, Sievers ML, Knowler WC, Swinburn BA, Pettitt DJ, Saad MF, Garrison RJ, Liebow IM, Howard BV, Bennett PH: Low incidence of fatal coronary heart disease in Pima Indians despite high prevalence of non-insulin-dependent diabetes. Circulation 81:987–995, 1990

---

602. Klein R, Klein BEK: Vision disorders in diabetes: Diabetes in America. Washington, DC, US Department of Health and Human Services, 1995, pp 293–338

603. Chavers BM, Mauer SM, Ramsay RC, Steffes MW: Relationship between retinal and glomerular lesions in IDDM patients. Diabetes 43:441–446, 1994

604. Parving H-H, Gall M-A, Skøtt P, Jørgensen HE, Løkkegaard H, Jørgensen F, Nielsen B, Larsen S: Prevalence and causes of albuminuria in non-insulin-dependent diabetic patients. Kidney Int 41: 758–762, 1992

605. Vigstrup J, Mogensen CE: Proliferative diabetic retinopathy: At risk patients identified by early detection of microalbuminuria. Acta Ophthalmol (Copenh) 63:530–534, 1985

606. Estacio RO, McFarling E, Biggerstaff S, Jeffers BW, Johnson D, Schrier RW: Overt albuminuria predicts diabetic retinopathy in Hispanics with NIDDM. Am J Kidney Dis 31:947–953, 1998

607. National High Blood Pressure Education Program Working Group Report on Hypertension in Diabetes. Bethesda, MD, National Institutes of Health, National Heart, Lung, and Blood Institute, 1995

608. Executive Summary of the Third Report of the National Cholesterol Education Program (NCEP) Expert Panel on Detection, Evaluation and Treatment of High Blood Cholesterol in Adults (Adult Treatment Panel III). JAMA 285:2486–2497, 2001

609. Management of dyslipidemia in adults with diabetes. Diabetes Care 24:S58-S61, 2001 (suppl 1)

610. Aspirin therapy in diabetes. Diabetes Care 24:S62-S63, 2001 (suppl 1)

611. Consensus development conference on the diagnosis of coronary heart disease in people with diabetes. Diabetes Care 21:1551–1559, 1998

612. Grundy SM, Benjamin IJ, Burke GL, Chait A, Eckel RH, Howard BV, Mitch WE, Smith SC Jr, Sowers JR: Diabetes and cardiovascular disease. A statement for healthcare professionals from the American Heart Association. Circulation 100:1134–1146, 1999

613. Diabetic retinopathy. Diabetes Care 24:S73-S76, 2001 (suppl 1)

614. Diabetic retinopathy. Preferred Practice Pattern. San Francisco, CA, American Academy of Ophthalmology (AAO), 1998

615. American Optometric Association Consensus Panel on Diabetes: Care of the Patient With Diabetes Mellitus (ed 2). St Louis, MO, American Optometric Association, 1998

616. Proceedings of a consensus development conference on standardized measures in diabetic neuropathy. Diabetes Care 15:1080–1107, 1992

617. Borch-Johnsen K, Andersen PK, Deckert T: The effect of proteinuria on relative mortality in type 1 (insulin-dependent) diabetes mellitus. Diabetologia 28:590–596, 1985

618. Nelson RG, Pettitt DJ, Carraher MJ, Baird HR, Knowler WC: Effect of proteinuria on mortality in NIDDM. Diabetes 37:1499–1504, 1988

619. Ritz E, Orth SR: Nephropathy in patients with type 2 diabetes mellitus. N Engl J Med 341: 1127–1133, 1999

620. Foley RN, Parfrey PS, Harnett JD: Clinical and echocardiographic disease in patients starting end-stage renal disease therapy. Kidney Int 47:186–192, 1995

621. Parfrey PS, Foley RN: The clinical epidemiology of cardiac disease in chronic renal failure. J Am Soc Nephrol 10:1606–1615, 1999

622. Culleton BF, Larson MG, Wilson PW, Evans JC, Parfrey PS, Levy D: Cardiovascular disease and mortality in a community-based cohort with mild renal insufficiency. Kidney Int 56:2214–2219, 1999

623. Levy D, Garrison RJ, Savage DD: Prognostic implications of echocardiographically determined left ventricular mass in the Framingham Heart Study. N Engl J Med 322:1561–1566, 1990

624. Morbidity and Mortality: 1998 Chartbook on Cardiovascular, Lung, and Blood Diseases. Bethesda, MD, US Dept of Health and Human Services, 1998

625. Wannamethee SG, Shaper AG, Perry IJ: Serum creatinine concentration and risk of cardiovascular disease: A possible marker for increased risk of stroke. Stroke 28:557–563, 1997

626. Beto JA, Bansal VK: Interventions for other risk factors: Tobacco use, physical inactivity, menopause, and homocysteine. Am J Kidney Dis 32:S112-S119, 1998 (suppl 3)

627. Kasiske BL: Hyperlipidemia in patients with chronic renal disease. Am J Kidney Dis 32:S142-S156, 1998 (suppl 3)

628. Bianchi S, Bigazzi R, Campese VM: Microalbuminuria in essential hypertension: Significance, pathophysiology, and therapeutic implications. Am J Kidney Dis 34:973–995, 1999

629. Sarnak MJ, Coronado BE, Greene T, Wang S-R, Kusek JW, Beck GJ, Levey AS: Cardiovascular disease risk factors in chronic renal insufficiency. Clin Nephrol 2002 (in press)

630. Keane WF: Proteinuria: Its clinical importance and role in progressive renal disease. Am J Kidney Dis 35:S97-S105, 2000 (suppl 1)

631. Culleton BF, Wilson PWF: Thrombogenic risk factors for cardiovascular disease in dialysis patients. Semin Dialysis 12:117–125, 1999

632. Massy ZA: Importance of homocysteine, lipoprotein (a) and non-classical cardiovascular risk factors (fibrinogen and advanced glycation end-products) for atherogenesis in uraemic patients. Nephrol Dial Transplant 15:81–91, 2000

633. Coresh J, Longenecker JC, Miller ER III: Epidemiology of cardiovascular risk factors in chronic renal disease. J Am Soc Nephrol 9:S24-S30, 1998 (suppl)

634. Ruilope LM, Salvetti A, Jamerson K, Hansson L, Warnold I, Wedel H, Zanchetti A: Renal function and intensive lowering of blood pressure in hypertensive participants of the hypertension optimal treatment (HOT) study. J Am Soc Nephrol 12:218–225, 2001

635. Schillaci G, Reboldi G, Verdecchia P: High-normal serum creatinine concentration is a predictor of cardiovascular risk in essential hypertension. Arch Intern Med 161:886–891, 2001

636. Pahor M, Shorr RI, Somes GW, Cushman WC, Ferrucci L, Bailey JE, Elam JT, Applegate WB: Diuretic-based treatment and cardiovascular events in patients with mild renal dysfunction enrolled in the systolic hypertension in the elderly program. Arch Intern Med 158:1340–1345, 1998

637. Mann JF, Gerstein HC, Pogue J, Bosch JP, Yusuf S: Renal insufficiency as a predictor of cardiovascular outcomes and the impact of ramipril: The HOPE randomized trial. Ann Intern Med 134:629–636, 2001

638. Sechi LA, Zingaro L, De Carli S, Sechi G, Catena C, Falleti E, Dell'Anna E, Bartoli E: Increased serum lipoprotein(a) levels in patients with early renal failure. Ann Intern Med 129:457–461, 1998

639. Sechi LA, Zingaro L, Catena C, Perin A, De Marchi S, Bartoli E: Lipoprotein(a) and apolipoprotein(a) isoforms and proteinuria in patients with moderate renal failure. Kidney Int 56:1049–1057, 1999

640. Fried LP, Kronmal RA, Newman AB, Bild DE, Mittelmark MB, Polak JF, Robbins JA, Gardin JM: Risk factors for 5-year mortality in older adults: The Cardiovascular Health Study. JAMA 279:585–592, 1998

641. Matts JP, Karnegis JN, Campos CT, Fitch LL, Johnson JW, Buchwald H: POSCH Group: Serum creatinine as an independent predictor of coronary heart disease mortality in normotensive survivors of myocardial infarction. J Fam Pract 36:497–503, 1993

642. Hemmelgarn BR, Ghali WA, Quan H, Brant R, Norris CM, Taub KJ, Knudtson ML: Poor long-term survival after coronary angiography in patients with renal insufficiency. Am J Kidney Dis 37:64–72, 2001

643. Damsgaard EM, Froland A, Jorgensen OD, Mogensen CE: Microalbuminuria as predictor of increased mortality in elderly people. BMJ 300:297–300, 1990

644. Beattie JN, Soman SS, Sandberg KR, Yee J, Borzak S, Garg M, McCullough PA: Determinants of mortality after myocardial infarction in patients with advanced renal dysfunction. Am J Kidney Dis 37:1191–1200, 2001

645. Friedman PJ: Serum creatinine: An independent predictor of survival after stroke. J Intern Med 229:175-179, 1991

646. Wagener DK, Harris T, Madans JH: Proteinuria as a biomarker: Risk of subsequent morbidity and mortality. Environ Res 66:160–172, 1994

647. Ljungman S, Wikstrand J, Hartford M, Berglund G: Urinary albumin excretion — A predictor of risk of cardiovascular disease. A prospective 10-year follow-up of middle-aged nondiabetic normal and hypertensive men. Am J Hypertens 9:770–778, 1996

648. Culleton BF, Larson MG, Parfrey PS, Kannel WB, Levy D: Proteinuria as a risk factor for cardiovascular disease and mortality in older people: A prospective study. Am J Med 109:1–8, 2000

649. Miettinen H, Haffner SM, Lehto S, Ronnemaa T, Pyorala K, Laakso M: Proteinuria predicts stroke and other atherosclerotic vascular disease events in nondiabetic and non-insulin-dependent diabetic subjects. Stroke 27:2033–2039, 1996

650. Agewall S, Wikstrand J, Ljungman S, Fagerberg B: Usefulness of microalbuminuria in predicting cardiovascular mortality in treated hypertensive men with and without diabetes mellitus. Risk Factor Intervention Study Group. Am J Cardiol 80:164–169, 1997

651. Jager A, Kostense PJ, Ruhe HG, Heine RJ, Nijpels G, Dekker JM, Bouter LM, Stehouwer CD: Microal-

buminuria and peripheral arterial disease are independent predictors of cardiovascular and all-cause mortality, especially among hypertensive subjects: Five-year follow-up of the Hoorn Study. Arterioscler Thromb Vasc Biol 19:617–624, 1999

652. Yudkin JS, Forrest RD, Jackson CA: Microalbuminuria as predictor of vascular disease in non-diabetic subjects. Islington Diabetes Survey. Lancet 2:530–533, 1988

653. Kliger AS: Clinical practice guidelines and performance measures in ESRD. Am J Kidney Dis 32: S173-S176, 1998 (suppl 4)

654. Kliger AS, Haley WE: Clinical practice guidelines in end-stage renal disease: A strategy for implementation. J Am Soc Nephrol 10:872–877, 1999

655. Jaeschke R, Guyatt GH, Sackett DL: Users' guides to the medical literature. III. How to use an article about a diagnostic test. B. What are the results and will they help me in caring for my patients? The Evidence-Based Medicine Working Group. JAMA 271:703–707, 1994

656. Laupacis A, Wells G, Richardson WS, Tugwell P: Users' guides to the medical literature. V. How to use an article about prognosis. Evidence-Based Medicine Working Group. JAMA 272:234–237, 1994

657. Plan and operation of the third national health and nutrition examination survey, 1988–1994. Vital and Health Statistics, Series 1. 407. Bethesda, MD, National Center for Health Statistics, 1994

658. Ezzati T, Wakesberg J, Chu A: Sample design: Third national health and nutrition examination survey, 1988–1994. Vital and Health Statistics, Series 2. Bethesda, MD, National Center for Health Statistics, 1992

659. Kasiske BL, Keane WF: Laboratory assessment of renal disease: Clearance, urinalysis, and renal biopsy, in Brenner BM, Rector FC Jr (eds): The Kidney. Philadelphia, PA, W.B. Saunders, 1996, pp 1137–1173

660. Coresh J, Toto RD, Kirk KA, Whelton PK, Massry SG, Jones C: Creatinine clearance as a measure of GFR in screenees for the African-American study of kidney disease and hypertension pilot study. Am J Kidney Dis 32:32–42, 1998

661. Coresh J, Astor B, McQuillan G: Calibration and random variation of the serum creatinine assay as critical elements of using equations to estimate glomerular filtration rate. Am J Kidney Dis 2002 (in press)

662. Chavers BM, Simonson J, Michael AF: A solid-phase fluorescent immunoassay for the measurement of human urinary albumin. Kidney Int 25:576–578, 1984

663. Report of the Expert Committee on the Diagnosis and Classification of Diabetes Mellitus. Diabetes Care 20:1183–1197, 1997

664. Stata Statistical Software: Release 6.0. College Station, TX, Stata Corp, 1999

665. Watson PE, Watson ID, Batt RD: Total body water volumes for adult males and females estimated from simple anthropometric measurements. Am J Clin Nutr 33:27–39, 1980

666. Maroni BJ, Steinman TI, Mitch WE: A method for estimating nitrogen intake of patients with chronic renal failure. Kidney Int 27:58–65, 1985

667. Gotch F, Keen ML: Care of the Patient on Dialysis: Introduction to Dialysis. New York, NY, Churchill Livingston, 1991, pp 101–179